AMERICA'S
SECRET JIHAD

the HIDDEN
HISTORY *of*
RELIGIOUS
TERRORISM *in the*
UNITED STATES

STUART WEXLER

COUNTERPOINT · BERKELEY, CALIFORNIA

Library of Congress Cataloging-in-Publication Data

Wexler, Stuart.
America's secret jihad : the hidden history of religious terrorism in the United States / Stuart Wexler.
pages cm
1. Terrorism—Religious aspects—United States. 2. Violence—Religious aspects—United States. I. Title.

BL65.T47W49 2015
363.3250973—dc23

2015009474

ISBN: 978-1-61902-741-1

Cover design by Kelly Winton
Interior design by Neuwirth & Associates

COUNTERPOINT
2560 Ninth Street, Suite 318
Berkeley, CA 94710
www.counterpointpress.com

Printed in the United States of America

To my parents.

Everything worthwhile I have ever accomplished should be credited to their love and support.

CONTENTS

15

PREFACE

America is waging a war against religious terrorism, but with an incomplete knowledge and understanding of its own history of domestic, religious terrorism.

But terrorism takes many forms, and is difficult, even for scholars, to define. The one-time radical revolutionary Thomas Jefferson thumbed his nose at the bloodthirsty mobs of France during the Reign of Terror (1793–1794), but he actively participated in a system of coercion in the southern states that relied upon violence and fear to run its economy; this went beyond the whippings that, daily, sustained the slave-plantation economy, but extended to the threat of torture and killing that maintained the white supremacist social order. If terrorism, as the FBI defines it, involves *"the unlawful use of force and violence against persons or property to intimidate or coerce a government, the civilian population, or any segment thereof, in furtherance of political or social objectives"* then the terror that motivated slaves to work, that deterred them from escaping and that cowed them from revolting, certainly meets the criteria (save, perhaps, for the unfortunate fact that it was "lawful" under state laws). One can easily see the parallels between ante-Bellum pro-slavery violence and the terrorism that the Islamic State of Iraq and Syria (ISIS) uses to impose its will on the Kurds and Yazidis in Northern Iraq.

A more conventional manifestation of terrorism emerged after the Civil War ended the practice of slavery. Many scholars now recognize that the Ku Klux Klan, first formed during Reconstruction as an insurgency against northern military occupation of the south, functioned as a terrorist group. Everything from their aesthetic—hooded men with torches on horseback—to their actions, from vigilante murders to random beatings, were designed to scare free slaves into reassuming their inferior position within southern society. That the Klan ultimately achieved this objective, with the acquiescence of northern elites, places the Reconstruction-era KKK among the few successful terrorist operations in the history of the modern world, so much so that they all but disappeared by the 1890s. The KKK reemerged in a second wave during World War I, becoming one of the largest fraternal organizations in the nation in the 1920s, reaching even into northern cities where southern blacks increasingly migrated to find work and escape routine violence. Increasingly, the organization directed its venomous hate against the large number of European immigrants who recently settled inside the United States, notably against Jews.

Here the KKK petered out, fragmenting with internal dissent and disputes between leaders, losing its force as Americans focused their attention on the economic calamity of the Great Depression. Never fully gone, the Klan reemerged as a major political force in response to the cultural revolution of the civil rights era (1954–1968), but failed, this time, to intimidate either African Americans, or the U.S. government, into preserving Jim Crow apartheid. But their failure did not come without a price for America, in the form of some of the most heinous acts of domestic violence in the nation's history.

These terrorist crimes, such as the bombing of the Sixteenth Street Baptist Church in Birmingham, Alabama in 1963, or the callous murder of three civil rights workers (popularly known as the Mississippi Burning killings) in 1964, have been well studied and documented by scholars. Less well-known is the development of a new ideological strain, built upon a foundation of Christian theology, that developed between the Klan revival of the 1920s and the reactionary violence that started in the 1950s. Until World War II, Christianity had provided an ad hoc veneer that helped legitimate the Ku Klux Klan in America. But while Christianity could and had been spun by racists to justify the southern caste system and segregation, its core message, of forgiveness and compassion, ran counter to the violence perpetrated by the Klan against blacks. At the same time, a growing number of bigots became attracted to Adolf Hitler's message against Jews; but Southern anti-Semitism, much less a variety of anti-Jewish hatred informed by a foreign enemy responsible for the death of hundreds of thousands of American soldiers, did not gain traction with rank-and-file racists. Christianity did not seem to accommodate a worldview that promoted open violence against Jews and blacks: at least not the kind of Christianity with which most Americans were familiar. But a small subset of scholars, with great care and only modest publicity, have identified and illuminated a strain of theology known as Christian Identity, that provided new justifications for terrorism after World War I.

Built on an idiosyncratic reading of the Book of Genesis that identifies Jews as the spawn of the devil, Christian Identity theologians, starting in the 1940s, spoke to a cosmic conspiracy, one where Jews manipulated sub-human minorities (notably blacks) in a covert war against the true chosen people: white Europeans. Having "otherized" Jews and blacks accordingly, killing them became not only morally acceptable, but a religious imperative. In fact, this book will demonstrate that the past 60 years of domestic terrorism in the United States is unintelligible outside of the context of Christian Identity theology.

In doing so, this book is revising the history of domestic terrorism in a fundamental way. Those scholars who assign Christian religious motives to acts of domestic terrorism have, to a person, started their narrative no earlier than 1983, with a cell of Identity-influenced terrorists known as The Order. In an otherwise excellent analysis of the types and styles of terrorism inside the United States since 1992, Dr. Arie Perliger, of West Point's Combatting Terrorism Center, asserted that the "fundamentalist movement" (of which Christian Identity was his main focus) was "relatively late" to develop its "violent nature"; that this was because, for decades, it "lacked an effective nation-wide organizational framework" and because it lacked a unifying "charismatic pastor." Hence a theology that was fully formed by the late 1950s did not motivate any acts of terrorism until the 1980s, other experts, such as RAND scholar Bruce Hoffman, assert.

These experts are not alone in this kind of assessment. Three scholars who wrote excellent treatments of Christian Identity theology, professors Chester Quarles, Michael Barkun, and Mark Juergensmeyer, offer similar narratives. They are all wrong. A network of religious terrorists did develop cross-affiliations and methods of communication that inspired horrible acts of violence, as early as 1957. This oversight is not a result of the scholars' lack of judgment, rather they have lacked access and exposure to sources that offer a very different perspective on major acts violence in American history. These sources, primarily law enforcement reports and documents, many of which are newly released or difficult to obtain, detail the internal thinking and operations of some of America's most notorious domestic terrorists and the groups that they managed. Law enforcement officers, conversely, failed to recognize the significance of this information in their own files, in part because they were unfamiliar with Christian Identity theology, and in part because they limited their own investigations for fear of exposing sources and methods. With the ability to data-mine these sources, to interview new witnesses, and to synthesize the documents with insights from religious scholars, a new picture emerges. A group of dedicated religious zealots, some well-known to historians, pursued a multi-decade strategy for a frightening goal: an apocalyptic race war inside the United States.

America's Secret Jihad presents this story for the first time. It begins by describing a forgotten yet unprecedented wave of anti-Semitic violence in the late 1950s, and revealing the man who orchestrated those crimes: racist Georgia attorney Jesse Benjamin "J.B" Stoner. Stoner is the archetypical Identity terrorist, a man who recognized great opportunities for foment racial polarization during the civil rights era, but who struggled to figure out how to leverage those opportunities. Chapter 2 connects Stoner, and the organization he co-founded, the National States Rights Party, to the milieu of Christian Identity theologians who develop their hateful ideology in the 1940s. These men synthesized separate theological threads and ideas which had been exported from England and germinated for decades. Chapter 3 introduces the pivotal figure in promoting this new synthesis, and the violence that follows from it, Reverend

Wesley Albert Swift. These chapters show how a series of events from 1961–1963 suggested to Swift, and to Stoner, a plan-of-action to realize their ultimate goal; from there, Identity terrorists become key figures in some of the most important domestic crimes of the 20th century. Chapter 4 connects Identity terrorism to the bombing of the 16th Street Baptist Church. Chapter 5 offers a new interpretation of the Mississippi Burning murders through the prism of religious terrorism; it also shows how the most cunning and violent of Klan leaders, Samuel Bowers, manipulated events in pursuit of a religious agenda. Chapters 6 through 9 show how developments during the Age of Social Upheaval inspired America's Identity terrorists to conspire to murder Martin Luther King Jr. Chapter 10 discusses the evolution of Identity thinking in the wake of King's murder, how it evolved in response to law enforcement tactics, how it came to influence other religiously-oriented racist ideologies, to the point that, as one former Klan member recently asserted, "Identity is embedded in the white supremacist movement." Chapters 11, 12, and 13 apply the insights from Chapter 10 to three additional acts of domestic terrorism: the Atlanta Child Murders starting in 1979, the assassination of radio host Alan Berg by The Order in 1984, and the Oklahoma City bombing in 1995. Chapter 14 shows how religious terrorism became synonymous with lone-wolf terrorism on through the new millennium, including a possible connection to a wave of church bombings from 1995–1999. Finally, in Chapter 15, we will consider how insights about six decades' worth of militant Christian Identity terrorism could help law enforcement, and the public, better appreciate modern, radical Islamic (militant Salafi) terrorism. The recent debate, over who the "enemy" is and how to define the enemy, will take center stage.

This book does not aspire to take sides in the culture war that has become part of the dialogue on terrorism, but in some ways this is unavoidable. There should no longer be any question that Christianity can and has accommodated domestic terrorism inside the United States, not as a veneer, but as at least one motivating force shaping the character and contours of the violence itself. In the 1960s, Swift's Church of Jesus Christ–Christian functioned in much the same way that Al Qaeda functioned from 1996 to the present:

as an ideological umbrella for a network of zealots, that facilitated interactions between otherwise decentralized "chapters" of terrorists, with key figures cross-affiliating among different groups. Neither Swift nor his successors plotted and executed these crimes on a case-by-case basis, any more than Osama Bin Laden and Ayman Zawahir micromanaged the terrorist attacks on the USS Cole, on American Embassies in Africa, on the Twin Towers and the Pentagon, on a passenger train in Madrid, or on the subway system in London. But if devout Christians fail to recognize their religion in the preaching of Wesley Swift or in the rants of J.B. Stoner, that too is understandable. The exegetical contortions necessary to change a religion that compels a follower to love his enemy, into a religion that condones genocide and ethnic cleansing, are enormous. But so too are the contortions necessary to change a religion that says that suicide is forbidden, that Muslims should never harm other Muslims, that respects Jesus Christ and Moses as high prophets, into a crusade that routinely uses suicide attacks to kill Jews, Christians, and primarily, other Muslims. Perhaps this book will lead non-Muslims to a measure of self-reflection and humility when a Muslim insists that Islam has been perverted or distorted by extremists.

1

TWISTED THEOLOGY

the SYNAGOGUE BOMBINGS

of 1957–1958

I n its forty-year history, the Jewish Telegraph Agency (JTA), formed in 1917 to collect and disseminate Jewish-centric news to journalism outlets worldwide, reported only two bombing attacks against Jewish targets inside the United States. So the following news story may have seemed an anomaly:

Attempt to Dynamite Charlotte Synagogue Fails;
Police Investigate

CHARLOTTE, N.C. (Nov. 26, 1957) Charlotte police today continued their investigation of an attempted dynamiting of Temple Beth El here which could have killed some 40 women who were attending a meeting.[1]

But by February 1958, when another dynamite bomb failed to detonate at Temple Emmanuel in Gaston, North Carolina, a sense of dread began to permeate America's Jewish community. Within another month it became clear that these concerns were well placed. The JTA reported:

F.B.I. Investigates Bombing of Jewish Centers in
Miami and Nashville

WASHINGTON (Mar. 17, 1958) The Department of Justice stepped in today to investigate the bombing yesterday of Jewish centers in Miami and Nashville with a view to determining whether a violation of Federal laws occurred.[2]

The two earlier attacks had failed because of issues related to the bombs' fuses. The first successful explosion occurred with the March 16 Miami bombing, producing a noise that local residents compared to a plane crash.[3] At eight o'clock that same evening, another bomb caused $6,000 worth of damage to the Jewish Community Center in Nashville, Tennessee, "smashing the front doors, ripping down the ceiling of the reception hall and smashing windows in the building."[4]

Like a double-tap gunshot execution, two more, almost simultaneous attacks occurred the following April in Birmingham, Alabama, and in Jacksonville, Florida. The former failed when the "25-foot fuse burned to within 18 inches" of fifty-four sticks of dynamite, enough, the JTA noted at the time, "to demolish the temple." The Jacksonville bomb did ignite, failing to kill or wound anyone but causing $3,000 in damages, almost $25,000 in today's money.[5]

Two additional bombings followed. The most notable occurred on October 12, 1958, when an estimated forty to fifty sticks of dynamite caused serious damage to Atlanta's oldest synagogue, the Hebrew Benevolent Congregation Temple, known to many simply as the Temple. A caller from a group referring to itself as the Confederate Underground—a then largely unknown organization that tied itself to several of the previous attacks—ominously warned that all Jewish and black-owned businesses were now potential targets. "We bombed a temple in Atlanta," the caller insisted. "This is the last empty building in Atlanta we will bomb."[6]

The bombings received national coverage and outraged the nation's political leaders. At a press conference on October 15, 1958, a reporter asked President Dwight Eisenhower:

Mr. President, over a period of months there have been bombings, explosions in the South . . . directed against Jewish churches and Jewish community centers. Some of these have been attributed to people who describe themselves as a Confederate Underground. Do you feel there is anything you can do to halt or discourage these incidents, and do you relate them in any way, sir, to the school integration issue?

President Eisenhower responded:

I went out of my way on Sunday afternoon when I heard about the bombing in Atlanta to speak extemporaneously about my

feeling about these bombings. Now you had certain phrases in
your question to which I want to advert. You said these people described themselves as part of the Confederate Underground. From
babyhood I was raised to respect the word "Confederate" very
highly, I might add, and for hoodlums such as these to describe
themselves as any part or any relation to the Confederacy of the
mid-19th Century is, to my mind, a complete insult to the word.
Indeed, they should be described as nothing but Al Capones and
Baby Face Nelsons and that kind of hoodlum.[7]

Having spent months resisting calls from Jewish groups and politicians to insert itself into local jurisdictions, the U.S. Justice Department finally formed a task force to coordinate the investigation
across state lines before the end of 1958.

The motivation for the wave of bombings on Jewish targets, unprecedented in American history, defied an easy explanation. Many
observers, then and now, simply placed the attacks in the general
context of anti-integrationist violence in America. Since the Supreme
Court, in its 1954 *Brown v. Board of Education* decision, had demanded desegregation of America's public schools and opened the
door to wider integration of the American South as a whole, white
supremacist violence had reached new levels of intensity. The simultaneous attacks on Jewish targets mirrored concurrent bombings
against black targets in Montgomery, Alabama, in 1957. Indeed,
the attack on the Jacksonville community center coincided with a
bombing of an all-black high school in the same city. Jewish leaders,
as part of a wider effort to stop both anti-Semitic and racist terrorism in the South, urged the government to investigate the attacks.

At first blush, the connection between anti-Jewish violence and
the wider effort by white supremacists to stop the push toward integration makes sense, and it indeed partially explains the wave of
attacks in 1957 and 1958. The leader of the Atlanta Temple, Rabbi
Jacob Rothschild, was an outspoken advocate in favor of the African
American civil rights struggle. The attack on his temple included
direct references to "nigger-lovers."[8] And on a wider scale, prominent racists, such as Tennessee Ku Klux Klan leader John Kasper,
openly blamed a Jewish conspiracy for the civil rights movement.[9]

But, as we will detail later, there was something at the bottom of Kasper's anti-Semitic rants that was even uglier and darker than a simple desire to protect the "southern way of life."

John Kasper's anti-Jewish extremism was somewhat rare, even in KKK groups. Anti-Semitism—as an idea—had a long pedigree in groups like the KKK, but it rarely translated into actual violence. The so-called second wave of KKK development—following the success of D.W. Griffith's pro-KKK movie *Birth of a Nation* and a famous 1915 cross-burning revival in Stone Mountain, Georgia—was in some ways driven by anti-Semitism, as part of a larger motif of nativism directed against the millions of first-generation immigrants (a sizable chunk of whom were Eastern European and Russian Jews) who arrived in the United States during the Progressive Era. Yet despite the KKK's wide popularity in the 1920s, when it included millions of members across several dozen states, this newly xenophobic fraternal organization never did much more than rant against Jewish influence. Historians can point to the ever-increasing number of lynchings of black Americans during the 1920s, but beyond the lynching of Georgian Leo Frank in 1915, there are no similar cases of vigilante hanging of southern Jews. Whites (presumably including KKK members) attacked enclaves of prosperous, middle-class blacks in places like Tulsa, Oklahoma. But there were no similar attacks on the small number of southern Jewish communities and institutions during the same time period. Reports from the JTA observed that the "mass of printed anti-Semitic propaganda" did not come from the ten Klans in the South but from "such places as Union, N.J., Los Angeles, St. Louis and Chicago." It added that White Citizens Councils, anti-integrationist groups formed from the South's upper crust, "repudiated anti-Semitism."[10] In fact, most of the bombings and attempted bombings in 1957–1958 did not involve targets with known ties to the civil rights movement.

This was in large part because Jews had largely assimilated into the fabric of the southern communities in which they lived. For the most part, that included passive acceptance of the racist policies of Jim Crow. Fearful for their own well-being, southern Jews "kept their heads down," even through the civil rights agitation of the 1960s. Some White Citizens Councils paradoxically included Jewish members. Melissa Fay Greene, whose excellent book on the Atlanta Temple bombing embraces the anti-integrationist rationale for that attack, acknowledged that southern Jews, including rabbis, only "occasionally, and from a distance, lent moral support but were little involved in the civil rights struggle."[11]

But preserving racial segregation does not serve as the sole explanation for the violence that plagued America's southern Jews at the time. Nor were such acts simply a warning against Jewish cooperation with civil rights activists. If the point was to send such a message, why did America's racists stop anti-Semitic bombings in the years that followed the 1958 attacks? Why, when northern Jews became an important constituency in the fight for civil rights in the early 1960s, did the KKK fail to strike at Jewish institutions with the same intensity for the same symbolic reasons? Why did the next major wave of orchestrated anti-Jewish bombings in American history occur several years after the passage of the Civil Rights Act of 1964 and the Voting Rights Act of 1965, when the KKK was in a state of rapid decline?

The riddle is not difficult to unravel: The men who planned these waves of violence embraced a broader agenda than simply defending the so-called southern way of life against the threats posed by integration. Fears of miscegenation only partially motivated the handful of men who planned many of the most egregious acts of domestic terrorism in American history, events like the Sixteenth Street Baptist Church bombing, which killed four preteen girls in 1963; the so-called Mississippi Burning murders of three civil rights activists in 1964; or the assassination of Martin Luther King Jr. in 1968. One need only examine the religious ideology of the man who planned the 1957–1958 synagogue bombings to understand the complete agenda and ultimate goals behind these acts of terrorism. Having formed multistate task forces and aligned their inquiries with the Federal Bureau of Investigation, law enforcement officers from across the nation quickly began to hone in on one suspect for this wave of bombings. The Confederate Underground, a newly formed group of about a dozen men in the Southeast, had executed the attacks, but the brains behind their operation was a white supremacist lawyer from Georgia named Jesse Benjamin (J.B.) Stoner.

On the surface, Stoner did not look the part of a domestic terrorist. Standing a portly five seven, with a deformed hand and a pronounced limp since childhood. Stoner often affected the persona of a country bumpkin at worst and a racist blowhard at best. But the image Stoner presented to the public obscured his strategic mind, one that earned him straight A's in law school. When skeptical law enforcement investigators interrogated one of their key informants inside the Confederate Underground, they suggested that Stoner was not the kind of person who knew his way around a bomb. "Oh yes he does," the informant insisted. "He has a good working knowledge of a lot of things." Those who participated in the plots on the ground level offered one consistent observation: Stoner would tell them how to build the bomb and when and where to plant it, but he made sure to be out of town on the day of the crime. He was too smart to get caught, they insisted. The outcome of the bombing investigation seemed to bear that out, as Stoner's legal colleagues ultimately represented many of the accused bombers and advised them to recant their accusations against J.B. In one case, an Alabama prosecutor refused to use informant reports against Stoner, because he knew Stoner would expose law enforcement's efforts as entrapment. Stoner never was convicted for his role in the crimes, even though every investigation pegged him as the ringleader.

However much his appearance belied his deviousness, J.B. Stoner was a dangerous man. Through his legal counsel, his incitements of mob violence in public speeches, his propaganda, and his involvement in several different acts of racial violence over three decades, J.B. Stoner was directly or indirectly connected to more acts of domestic terrorism than possibly any other American in history. The simplistic explanation for Stoner's activities points to his fondness for Nazism. As a teenager, Stoner openly supported the Nazis during World War II, going so far as to correspond with William Joyce, aka Lord Haw Haw, a pro-Nazi radio personality in Europe. If anything, Stoner famously asserted on many occasions that Hitler did not go far enough in exterminating the Jews. The FBI consistently referred to Stoner and his organizations as neo-Nazi in spirit, but this only captured part of Stoner's motivations, as Stoner never embraced national socialism and enjoyed only a lukewarm relationship with the American Nazi Party and its founder, George Lincoln Rockwell. As Stoner had grown up in segregated Georgia during the Great Depression, his racial animosity and anti-Jewish animosity blended together in a unique stew of hate. If anything, Stoner's anti-Jewish extremism alienated him from rank-and-file KKK members. When Stoner moved to Tennessee in the late 1940s and joined the Chattanooga Klavern (a subgroup of the statewide KKK organization), his anti-Semitism upset his fellow Klan members to the point that they expelled him from their group.[12] Undeterred, Stoner soon returned to Georgia and with local chiropractor Edward Fields cofounded the Christian Anti-Jewish Party in the early 1950s. Centered in Georgia, the group openly protested outside the Temple in Atlanta before the Confederate Underground bombed the institution. The name of the group that Stoner and Fields created points to an element of Stoner's motivation that has been missed by the FBI and by the few scholars who have focused their attention on Stoner's violence. Without question, Nazism informed Stoner's anti-Jewish agenda, just as racism informed his anti-black agenda. But at some point in Stoner's ever-more-radical shift to a life of domestic terrorism, a perverse understanding of Christianity became a dominant motif in motivating his violent crusade.

However much he dabbled in the occult, and however much he exploited centuries-old religious prejudices dating back to the times of Protestant reformer Martin Luther, Adolf Hitler's anti-Jewish rhetoric and actions were far more secular than religious in their spirit. Hitler's brand of anti-Semitism flowed from scientific racism: a belief in genetic contamination and degeneration popular among followers of the eugenics movement and a misguided understanding of anthropology that viewed white Europeans as a master race.

Little evidence of this kind of thinking can be found in Stoner's writings and speeches. Instead, one finds a devoutly religious motivation for Stoner's extremism. In 1994, reflecting upon his efforts to a meeting of the Aryan Nations, Stoner said:

> I've been fighting Jews and niggers all my life. Now I quote from the Bible, I believe in the Bible, I worship my Lord Jesus Christ, but I'm not a preacher. God didn't call me to be a preacher. God

called me to fight Jews and niggers. So I've engaged in that fight, against the Jews and the niggers, because that is the best way to serve and glorify God and to help the white race.[13]

This religious component to Stoner's hatred traces back fifty years. In 1947 Stoner wrote a treatise called "The Gospel of Jesus Christ vs. the Jews as Explained from the Holy Bible."[14] As early as 1944, Stoner had written to the U.S. Congress, requesting that it "pass a resolution recognizing that Jews are children of the devil and that consequently they pose a grave danger to the United States."[15]

The reference to Jews as "children of the devil" becomes important in connecting Stoner to a newly emerging, unorthodox strain of Christian theology that, by the early 1940s, was developing into a fully formed creed. Christian Identity (CI) theology, or simply Identity, has inspired generations of white supremacists, directly and indirectly, to acts of domestic terrorism.

Stoner in some ways was a member of an unholy trinity that also included the head of the Mississippi Ku Klux Klan, Samuel Holloway Bowers, and Wesley A. Swift, head of the Church of Jesus Christ–Christian (CJCC), a Christian Identity congregation based in southern California. In that metaphor, Swift, as will become clear, is the father, the inspiration and guiding force behind waves of violence, whom too few scholars recognize for his active role in domestic terrorism. Bowers, as we will see, is the son, the purist who commands a group of followers as they put the father's plan into earthly action. And Stoner, the Georgian lawyer who became the brains behind the Confederate Underground, is the unholy spirit, linking fellow travelers across time and distance, girding his clients against perceived persecution, and inspiring others to rash acts of mob violence.

Those who isolate Islam as a uniquely violent religion, one more suited to perversion by radicals than other religions, have missed a counter-narrative, one where Christian extremists distorted Jesus's message long before Muslim extremists hijacked Muhammad's teachings. In short, in failing to look deeply at people like Stoner, Bowers, and Swift and at the acts of terrorism they planned and inspired, we have missed an important piece of history that could provide an extremely useful frame of reference for contemporary America and for the world at large. An extensive look into the web of associations and organizations connected to J.B. Stoner will help bring this insight into sharper focus, revealing the twisted theology at the core of the white supremacy movement in the United States.

2

GENESIS

the CHRISTIAN
IDENTITY MOVEMENT

F or all the national outrage stemming from the 1957–1958 wave of anti-Jewish bombings, and despite several arrests, no one went to prison for any crimes. The Confederate Underground, and its informal leader J.B. Stoner, escaped justice.

But the attacks did spark a bout of national soul searching on the issue of anti-Semitic and racial violence in the 1950s. Some legislators openly condemned racial violence in the South, and President Dwight Eisenhower signed the Civil Rights Act of 1960, which among other things authorized federal agents to investigate the bombing of educational and religious institutions if authorities suspected that the perpetrators had fled across state lines. Congress also began to investigate the acts of violence. In a debate on the Senate floor, Senator Kenneth Keating listed eighty acts of domestic terrorism—many bombings and arson attacks on black targets—from 1955 to 1960. Of the eighty attacks, sixteen could be directly or indirectly traced to one group, the National States Rights Party (NSRP).[1] Formed in 1958 by Stoner and Fields, the NSRP became an important focus for law enforcement. In a report, the FBI noted:

> The National States Rights Party (NSRP) was created in July, 1958, from remnants of such segregationist and/or anti-Semitic organizations as the United White Party, the Christian Anti-Jewish Party, the Columbians, several Klan groups, and representatives of the States Rights Party. At the time the NSRP was organized, one of its founders, Jesse Stoner, observed: "The name of the National States Rights Party will sound so mild that a man belonging to it will not worry about his job."[2]

The NSRP's loci of operation logically paralleled the activities of its pro-integration rivals: the Southern Christian Leadership Conference (SCLC), the Congress of Racial Equality (CORE), and the Student Nonviolent Coordinating Committee (SNCC). Notably, by the early 1960s, Stoner and Fields had moved their base of operations to Birmingham, Alabama, at that time the site of America's most public civil rights battles.

With the shift in geographic focus, it appeared as if the NSRP had shifted its tactical focus from organized acts of terrorism to political activism. As the civil rights movement picked up nationwide momentum, Stoner and Fields directed their recently formed group toward counter-rallies, protests, and general agitation against groups that advocated for civil rights. But unlike most of its pro-integration rivals, the NSRP was far from Gandhian in its approach to civic participation.

Time and time again, NSRP members responded to nonviolence with violence. When volunteers from CORE launched a series of Freedom Rides to expose the lack of constitutionally mandated integration in America's public bus stations, a mob of racists met participants at their first stop in the Deep South: Anniston, Alabama. Led by local KKK leader Kenneth Adams, the mob surrounded one Freedom Rider bus and slashed its tires. Later the mob forced another bus off the road, firebombed it, and beat the escaping activists.[3] Many note Adams's KKK affiliations but fail to note that he was a leading member of the NSRP in a city, Anniston, that was in essence the weapons depot for the national organization. Racists from the NSRP joined other KKK rowdies and met that same group of Freedom Riders when the activists reached their next bus terminal, in Birmingham, Alabama. This mob assaulted and beat the Freedom Riders (some into unconsciousness) with wooden sticks and metal pipes.

As the civil rights movement began to make gains in Alabama through the collective efforts of leaders like the Reverend Fred Shuttlesworth and Martin Luther King Jr., the NSRP increased the intensity of its response. A notable example was the NSRP's reaction, in September 1963, to a court order and local mandates to desegregate Alabama's public schools. Police stopped one car of students

belonging to a caravan of some 150 teenagers on their way to an
NSRP-sponsored counter-protest at a Birmingham high school. From
this car, police confiscated a pistol, a straight razor, a bailing hook,
and a sawed-off shotgun.[4]

Stoner and Fields increasingly began to see how they could harness the toxic combination of youthful arrogance, neo-Confederate
racism, and male testosterone. More than anything, this concept was
obvious in Stoner's approach to counter-rallies and counter-protests.
Stoner, with his close colleague Charles "Connie" Lynch, toured
various cities that were home to civil rights struggles. There the
two men became what author Patsy Sims refers to in her book *The
Klan* as "a two-man riot squad." More than anyone, it was Lynch, a
southern California native who traveled in a pink Cadillac and wore
a jacket of stitched-together Confederate flags, who inflamed audiences, often to actual acts of violence. As Sims describes it:

> Lynch once told a Baltimore rally crowd: "I represent God, the
> white race and constitutional government, and everyone who
> doesn't like that can go straight to hell. I'm not inciting you to
> riot—I'm inciting you to victory!" His audience responded by
> chanting, "Kill the niggers! Kill! Kill!" After the rally, stirred-up
> white youths headed for the city's slums, attacking blacks with
> fists and bottles. At another rally in Berea, Kentucky, Lynch's di-
> atribe was followed by two fatal shootings. Again, in Anniston,
> Alabama, he goaded his audience: "If it takes killing to get the
> Negroes out of the white's man's streets and to protect our con-
> stitutional rights, I say, 'Yes, kill them!'" A carload of men left the
> rally and gunned down a black man on a stretch of highway.[5]

The most notable example of the rabble-rousing incited by Lynch
and Stoner came in St. Augustine, Florida, in 1964. Stoner and Lynch
joined regional NSRP leader Oren Potito as he fought efforts to desegregate a city that was on the edge of widespread civil disorder
and violence. Lynch especially pushed local segregationists over the
edge. Following one Lynch rant, young segregationists attacked a
protest march of nearly two hundred blacks. In one diatribe, Lynch
specifically called out a local civil rights leader Robert Hayling. "If

you were half the men you claimed to be," Lynch insisted, "you'd
kill him before sunup." Four men kidnapped Hayling and three colleagues, brought their victims to the rally, proceeded to beat them
to unconsciousness and nearly burned them to death. Lynch and
Stoner earned a reputation for demagoguery that alarmed even Klan
leaders. As Sims notes, during race rioting in Bogalusa, Louisiana,
the local Grand Dragon tried to run both men out of town.[6]

Often Stoner played a secondary role as an agitator but a primary
role as a lawyer, defending his friend Lynch against charges of incitement; Connie Lynch spent very little time in jail. Soon Stoner found
himself defending fellow racists and NSRP members across the nation.
He even extended the group's influence into Canada. While it rarely
had more than 150 active members, the NSRP established franchises
in more than a dozen states across the union, often run by very young
members trained under Fields and Stoner in Birmingham. These members included James P. Thornton, who helped grow the NSRP in California with the assistance of retired colonel William Potter Gale and
Neuman Britton, who ran the NSRP offshoot in Arkansas. Another
nexus of NSRP leaders came from Florida. They had fled the Sunshine
State for other places in the Southeast, in part to escape the scrutiny of local law enforcement after the violence in St. Augustine. One
example was Sidney Crockett Barnes, a painter and suspected bomb
maker, who fled to Mobile, Alabama, joining a preexisting contingent
of NSRP exiles from Florida, including a future member of Mobile's
White Citizens Council, Noah Jefferson Carden.[7]

But Stoner and Fields also parlayed the NSRP's growing membership and influence into more conventional expressions of political
dissent. In 1960 the group nominated two candidates for office in
the U.S. presidential election: Arkansas governor Orval Faubus at
the top of the ticket and Admiral John C. Crommelin, of Montgomery, Alabama, as the vice presidential candidate. Faubus had
virtually no connection to the NSRP but had earned a national profile among racists for his open resistance to federally imposed integration efforts. In the unusual role of a write-in nominee, Faubus
never agreed to his nomination; nor did he actively campaign for
office. But Crommelin was another story. A World War II naval hero
from an illustrious family line of naval officers, Crommelin arguably

became the most well-known public anti-Semite in America in the 1950s, meriting the label "most serious threat to Jewish security in the southern states."[8] By 1964 Crommelin had already failed to win the Democratic primary to represent Alabama in the U.S. Senate four times and had lost a 1958 bid to be governor of the Yellowhammer State. Referring constantly to a Jewish-led communist conspiracy to subvert the United States, he also echoed the literal party line of the NSRP: that the civil rights movement was part of that conspiracy. Together, Faubus and Crommelin received less than 0.1 percent of the national popular vote. Undeterred, Stoner himself joined a presidential ticket in 1964, as the vice presidential candidate, with his old friend from Tennessee, John Kasper, as the NSRP's presidential hopeful. It would be one among many unsuccessful political bids for Stoner, as the pair earned even fewer votes than the Faubus–Crommelin ticket.[9, 10, 11]

The NSRP's candidates focused most of their attention on their pro-segregation agenda, perhaps because they saw what impact overt and strident racism and anti-Semitism had on a campaign for national office. Crommelin's 1962 campaign for Alabama Senate had included "5 sound trucks all over the state blasting away the Christian message that Communism is Jewish from start to finish and that racial integration of . . . White people is a Jewish directed scheme to mongrelize the White Race, so that the almighty Jew can sit upon a throne to rule a world populated by a mass of mulatto like zombies."[12] Crommelin lost in landslides in each primary, never coming closer than third place.

In the 1964 race for the presidency, the Kasper–Stoner ticket tended to present its agenda in racist code, referencing states' rights, constitutional conservatism, anti-communism, and national sovereignty (meaning opposition to the United Nations). Many saw through this facade. A Florida state legislative committee, lamenting the agitation and violence that Stoner and Lynch had brought to St. Augustine, noted: "Today's hawkers of hate have made capital of hiding behind the facade of conservatism and waving the banner of anticommunism. With their bigotry thus cloaked, they have made converts who unwittingly serve to undermine the causes in which they believe."[13]

But the racism and anti-Semitism attributed to the NSRP by the committee only spoke to the by-products of what these men devoutly believed. A closer examination of the NSRP reveals a web of associations and group affiliations, and ultimately a commonly held and obscured agenda, that only a few understand. Virtually every senior leader of the NSRP just mentioned was also a devout follower of the Christian Identity religion. Lynch, Potito, Gale, Barnes, and Britton all became ordained ministers in the Reverend Wesley Swift's Church of Jesus Christ–Christian. Gale, in fact, was among Swift's closest aides and advisors and was frequently pictured wearing a priest's collar. When he waged his 1962 campaign for the Alabama U.S. Senate nomination, Crommelin invited five Identity ministers, including Swift himself, to openly campaign for him. Potito served as Crommelin's campaign manager. Others, including Kasper, Fields, Thornton, and Carden, were all on the mailing list to receive tapes of Swift's CI sermons. Stoner and Fields appointed Gordon Winrod as the NSRP's official pastor; Winrod, along with his father and son, belongs to three generations of Christian Identity ministers. Stoner was on an FBI list of Identity followers as late as 1974.

These individuals were not simply cogs in the NSRP machinery. In many cases they affiliated with, led, and founded concurrent white supremacist organizations that ranked among the most active purveyors of violence in America from 1960 through 1980; offshoots of those organizations promote and participate in violence to this day. A list of such groups, circa 1972, includes:

- ▶ The Minutemen (not to be confused with the present-day citizens' border patrol group), which openly advocated the violent overthrow of the U.S. government. Several Christian Identity devotees, including Lynch, Dennis Mower, and Kenneth Goff, assumed key roles in the group.
- ▶ The California Rangers, an early antecedent to modern-day militia groups, which was started, organized, and managed by Gale and Thornton.
- ▶ The Posse Comitatus, organized by Gale, a militant anti-tax and antigovernment group.

► Various Ku Klux Klan factions, most notably the White
Knights of the Ku Klux Klan of Mississippi, the most violent KKK subgroup, led by Sam Bowers, a Christian Identity
militant.

The violence these groups wrought on the United States is well
documented and extensive. In many ways, the plots they considered
but failed to execute are downright frightening. But scholars have
failed to see the interactions and connections between members of
these various groups—a protean social network of the most hard-
core white supremacists America has ever produced. In failing to see
the depth of these connections, scholars have also understated the
common bond of solidarity that united these men: a radical strain
of an offshoot Christian sect that predated the factious violence of
the 1960s by more than one hundred years and that did not even
originate in America.

The theological school now called Christian Identity traces its
roots back several hundred years, to when the "discovery" of the
Americas fueled speculation about biblical history, specifically the
destiny of the so-called ten lost tribes of Israel. Its most recogniz-
able incarnation developed in Victorian England as an idea known
as British Israelism. At the turn of the twentieth century, the idea
spread to North America. There, throughout the 1920s and 1930s, it
assumed an Ameri-centric hue and became more popular and more
widely known as Anglo-Israelism. In both the U.S. and Canadian
contexts, elements of Anglo-Israelism began to shift in a more racist
direction. The key moment in the intellectual development of Christian Identity theology emerged as World War II came to a close. It
centered around a major reinterpretation of the biblical creation
story, one that shaped the landscape of white supremacy and racist
violence in the decades that followed, thanks in large part to the
work of the Reverend Wesley Albert Swift.

But a new biblical genealogy lay at the heart of Christian Identity
teaching. For hundreds of years, scholars have speculated about the
"lost" tribes of Israel, who according to the Old Testament were deported by the Assyrians in the eighth century BCE. According to the
biblical narrative, following the prophet Abraham's covenant with

God, the descendants of the Hebrew patriarch became the genealogical foundation for the Jewish people. Specifically, God blessed
Abraham's grandson Jacob as the forefather of the nation of Israel.
Ten of Jacob's children and two of his grandchildren originated the
bloodlines of the migrants who settled Palestine after Moses led
the enslaved Hebrews out of Egypt during the Exodus. Ten tribes
became the demographic foundation of the northern half of Israel,
known as the Kingdom of Israel. (The southern half was known as
the Kingdom of Judah.) But King Shalmaneser V of Assyria, following his conquest of the northern kingdom, exiled the ten tribes
from the region. The Old Testament never discusses their ultimate
destiny, as the rest of the narrative focuses on the tribes that remained in Judah, the descendants of Judah and Benjamin.

The fate of the ten lost tribes (sometimes referred to as the House
of Israel) remained important to Jews and Christians alike because
of its association with biblical prophecy. Many theologians interpret
texts of the Bible to suggest that in the last days of the secular world,
on the eve of the so-called Final Judgment, the House of Israel and
the House of Judah will reunite in the Promised Land. Only then
will God send a Messiah to save his chosen people. Many Christians
believe this event will coincide with the second coming of Jesus.

In the 1500s various European scholars and adventurers claimed
to have discovered the lost tribes: in North America as Native Americans; in Afghanistan as the Pashtuns; in Ethiopia as the Falashas.
The foundational tenet of what is now called Christian Identity—
that some or all of these tribes mixed with early Europeans, especially Anglo-Saxons—can be found as early as the 1790s. In his book
A Revealed Knowledge of the Prophecies and the Times, Richard
Brothers, a British naval officer, claimed to have received a divine
revelation on this and related ideas. The book, and a very minor
movement started by Brothers, lost traction after his death in 1824.

A more meticulous and far less mystical articulation of the same
idea emerged in 1837, when Scottish linguist John Wilson published
research speculating that the British people (he specifically referenced
the bloodlines of the British monarchy) were connected to the lost tribe
of Ephraim. Publishers reprinted Wilson's book on the subject five
times during his lifetime. By the time of his death, another Englishman,

Edward Hine, had popularized a variation on the idea, arguing that white Europeans were the true chosen people of the Bible, that Jesus was an Aryan and not an ethnic Jew, and that European Jews were descendants of Mongolian-Turkish Khazars and had not originated in North Africa and the Middle East. In Victorian England, when the British Empire controlled more than one-quarter of the earth's land mass and the British Navy dominated the world's oceans, this kind of chauvinism gained wide currency. Hine's book became a best seller, selling 250,000 copies. In the 1880s Hine took himself and his ideas to another emerging world power with Anglo-Saxon roots: the United States of America. Hine gained a modest following in the Northeast and Canada, where he toured and gave presentations on his theory, which became known as British Israelism.[14]

But the religious ideas exported by Wilson and Hine were less anti-Jewish than they were pro-Anglo-Saxon. An unfortunate by-product of timing meant that the religious movement began its geographic spread inside the United States—mostly westward toward California—during the early twentieth century, when America was becoming increasingly xenophobic and hospitable to racism. The nation's second major wave of immigration, which brought millions of southern Italian Catholics and Eastern European Jews through places like Ellis Island, elicited a backlash against the new arrivals, which only intensified in the cauldron of ugly anti-ethnic feelings stirred up by World War I. Anti-Semitism and racism began to manifest themselves in both academic circles and popular culture as a whole.

At the turn of the twentieth century, a number of American community activists, biologists, and social scientists responded to the influx of European immigrants with alarm. Fearing that the newly arriving Americans could not assimilate into the wider culture, and worried that "inferior" races would contaminate America's gene pool or populate American society with generation after generation of imbeciles or criminals, these men and women became the foundation for the modern eugenics movement. Historian Ed Black asserts that the eugenicists hoped that by "identifying so-called 'defective' family trees and subjecting them to lifelong segregation and sterilization programs they could literally wipe away the reproductive capability of those deemed weak and inferior—the so-called 'unfit.'"[15]

Not surprisingly, eugenicists often counted Jews among the "unfit" given their sizable presence among the immigrant population.

In 1926 one of the leading eugenicists of his time, historian Lothrop Stoddard, described two races of Jews. He said that the "aristocratic" Sephardic Jews, who had entered the Mediterranean world, were the genuine Semites and that the Ashkenazic Jews (from Eastern Europe and Russia) were a mixture of diverse bloods, with features that reflected intermarriage with the Hittites. He said that these eastern Jews had migrated into southern Russia, where they had blended with the Khazars, whom Stoddard regarded as a combination of Turkish and Mongoloid peoples. Although Stoddard had no connection with British Israelism, the movement readily adopted the Khazar identity of the Jews as a further way to invalidate their claim to be descendants of the biblical Hebrews.[16]

According to religious scholar Michael Barkun, this secular strand of anti-Semitic genealogy developed from similar sources as British Israelism but evolved separately as an independent canon of pseudo-anthropological research. The scientific racism of people like Stoddard helped legitimize and reinforce racism against other minorities as well, blacks in particular.

In his highly influential work *The Rising Tide of Color*, Stoddard claimed that the black man's "most outstanding quality is his animal vitality." Blacks were "the quickest of the breeders," but they lacked "constructive originality," and had it not been for the intervention of other races, "the negro would have remained a savage." But while their "ineptitude" helped keep their populations in check, outside interventions by more cultivated races since the 1800s meant that blacks were "assured to multiply prodigiously" in the next few decades. The danger to white civilization came not from their growing numbers but because blacks could be easily manipulated by other (nonwhite) races and because of the potential for "crossbreeding." Stoddard asserted that "black blood, once entering human stock, seems never really bred out again."[17] These ideas would become a direct influence on the intellectual development of Christian Identity in the 1940s. By the 1960s, according to Nicholas Goodrick-Clarke, "the Khazar ancestry of the Jews was a firm article of faith" for white supremacists.[18]

In the meantime, eugenicists' ideas indirectly impacted the evolution of British Israelism in the United States by providing intellectual cover to deeply held prejudices with a long pedigree in certain
segments of American society. By the 1920s these prejudices were
becoming more and more widespread. During World War I, African
Americans began to migrate to northern cities in large numbers to
escape Jim Crow and to take readily available factory work. This
migration stoked latent racial antagonism in the North. World War I
also left a residue of xenophobia and jingoism directed at America's
immigrant population, including Jews. This combination of racism
and nativism found its outlet in what historians refer to as the first
Klan revival or the Second Klan, which began in 1915.

"The Klan looks forward to the day when the Negro problem will
have been solved on some much saner basis than miscegenation, and
when every State will enforce laws making any sex relations between
a white and a colored person a crime," said Hiram Evans, leader of
the national Ku Klux Klan from 1922 through 1939. Echoing the
work of Stoddard and others, he added:

> The Jew is a more complex problem. His abilities are great, he
> contributes much to any country where he lives. This is particu-
> larly true of the Western Jew, those of the stocks we have known
> so long. Their separation from us is more religious than racial.
> When freed from persecution these Jews have shown a tendency
> to disintegrate and amalgamate. We may hope that shortly, in the
> free atmosphere of America, Jews of this class will cease to be a
> problem. Quite different are the Eastern Jews of recent immigra-
> tion, the Jews known as the Askhenasim. It is interesting to note
> that anthropologists now tell us that these are not true Jews, but
> only Judaized Mongols-Chazars. These, unlike the true Hebrew,
> show a divergence from the American type so great that there
> seems little hope of their assimilation.[19]

That the evolution from British Israelism to Anglo-Israelism and
the acculturation of Hine's ideas into the North American context
coincided with the first major Klan revival carried important implications for what became known as Christian Identity. Many trace

the growing interest in the KKK to America's first major motion picture blockbuster, D.W. Griffith's film *Birth of a Nation*. The movie reinforced, in the nation's popular imagination, a nostalgic and positive image of the post–Civil War South, lionizing the Ku Klux Klan as noble guardians of domestic order and the dignity of white women. The movie focused its bias against blacks, but anti-Semitism played a crucial role in the Klan's reemergence as well. When, in 1915, the governor of Georgia commuted the death sentence of Leo Frank, a Jewish industrialist convicted for supposedly murdering Mary Phagan, one of his factory workers, a mob of twenty-five men forcibly removed Frank from prison and lynched him. This group, the Knights of Mary Phagan, became the foundation for the new Klan, which, under the leadership of former Confederate colonel William Simmons, held a symbolic cross-burning ceremony in 1915 that officially started the Klan revival in Stone Mountain, Georgia.

Thus began a surge in KKK activity that is almost unimaginable to modern sensibilities. At its peak, during the 1920s, the KKK enjoyed an estimated membership of up to 8 million, with franchises in most states, appealing to both urban and rural Americans concerned about the changing social and economic dynamics in the nation.

Becoming one of the largest fraternal organizations in the country, the Klan began to formalize its activities in ways reminiscent of groups like the Freemasons and the Knights of Pythias. It revamped the Reconstruction-era Klan hierarchy with a system of official ranks. The Imperial (or Grand) Wizard ran a multiregional Klan group, Grand Dragons ran state franchises, and Grand Giants ran county subgroups, or Klaverns. To these the Klan added the position of a Kleagle, or recruiter. It modeled its procedures and guidelines on established fraternal groups, making sure to use the letters *Kl* when appropriating such conventions. Its national rules and regulations could be found in a Klonstitution; its official meetings became Klonvocations; and each separate Klavern had its own Kloran, which set forth meeting procedures and rituals.

As they had during Reconstruction, many KKK members sought a veneer of biblical legitimacy to justify their ideas. Each Klavern had its own chaplain (called a Kludd), and each recruit was asked to confirm his religious bona fides as a (Protestant) Christian. But the KKK's preferred passage of scripture, Romans 12, put the lie to its pretense of piety. Romans 12, the "foundation of the Invisible Empire" according to luminaries such as William Simmons, implores Jews and gentiles alike to "live peaceably with all men" in a spirit of "brotherly love," to avoid revenge, and to feed one's enemies.[20] This is hardly a sincere foundation for a group associated with many of the 559 lynchings of African Americans that occurred from 1920 to 1929. The FBI rightfully called the KKK's pretense of religion a "false front" and "bait."[21] A genuine religious movement would not have lost members by the millions, in a precipitous fashion, as a result of the Great Depression. And while it directed violence at blacks, the Second Klan noticeably did not attack Jewish targets in large numbers after 1915.

At its core, the Klan remained a reactionary, ethno-chauvinist terrorist group, bent on preserving white supremacy. Over time, it became significant to any discussion of domestic, religious terrorism because elite members of the Ku Klux Klan often became the most zealous, if often covert, proponents of Christian Identity. The Second Klan's significance in the evolution of Anglo-Israelism is more representative than substantive: It shows how open 1920s and 1930s America was to anti-Semitism and racism. It was in that environment that two men popularized Anglo-Israelism and imbued it with concepts of anti-Semitism and racism that continue to resonate in Christian Identity theology. Howard Rand, a New England lawyer, coined the term *Christian Identity*. In Michael Barkun's excellent study of the origins of Christian Identity, *Religion and the Racist Right*, he describes Rand as the "the critical bridging figure between mainstream British Israelism and its subsequent American variant, Christian Identity." An "extraordinary organizer," Rand "single-mindedly . . . created a national movement," traveling, in one estimation, "eighteen thousand miles through the South; twelve thousand miles through the Middle West; and fifty thousand miles during eight months in the West" on behalf of his organization, the Anglo-Saxon Federation. Barkun also notes that while Rand "completed the consolidation" of Christian Identity in the United States, he also opened it to "right-wing and anti-Semitic influences that were to be amplified in postwar years."[22]

Just as if not more important to the development of those influences was William J. Cameron, a member of the Anglo-Saxon
Federation but more importantly a writer, editor, and publisher for
automobile tycoon Henry Ford's periodical the *Dearborn Independent*. Cameron used the pulpit of that paper, which boasted a circu-
lation, at its peak, of seven hundred thousand, to promote virulently
anti-Semitic messages. More than anything, Cameron focused his attention on an alleged international Jewish conspiracy to undermine
the common good. Cameron promoted the *Protocols of the Elders
of Zion*, a hoax supposedly documenting just such a Jewish cabal,
which has been read and believed by millions.[23] Cameron assembled his collective anti-Semitic works into a four-volume set, known
as *The International Jew*, and groups like the NSRP continued to
market it to white supremacists decades after Cameron began pro-
pagandizing in the 1920s.

Although KKK membership dissipated in the economic crisis of the
Great Depression, the idea that Jews were in some way responsible
for that calamity gained a noteworthy following inside the United
States, including among a circle of preachers taking advantage of the
growing popularity and availability of radio. These men shifted in
their stereotypes, at times playing on the age-old prejudices that Jews
ran the world's financial institutions and at other times conversely
claiming that Jews were active supporters of communism. Among the
most prominent was Catholic radio preacher Father Charles Edward
Coughlin, who once said, "By their failure to use the press, the radio
and the banking house, where they stand so prominently, to fight
communism as vigorously as they fight Nazism, the Jews invite the
charge of being supporters of communism."[24] Father Coughlin, it
should be noted, reached an audience so large that in some weeks
he received 1 million different pieces of fan mail. For all his anticommunism, Coughlin was an economic populist and supporter of Louisiana governor Huey P. Long's Share Our Wealth program.[25] It was
there that he influenced a young aide to Long, Gerald L.K. Smith, an
ordained minister since 1916 in the Disciples of Christ.[26]

Smith had already adapted many of the CI ideas espoused by the
likes of Rand and Cameron. In 1942 he parlayed the organizational
and communication talents he had honed working for Long into his

own movement, the Christian Nationalist Crusade. The group's stated purpose was to "preserve America as a Christian nation being conscious of a highly organized campaign to substitute Jewish tradition for Christian tradition."[27] Smith published a newsletter, *The Cross and the Flag,* which espoused these ideas to a national audience.

Smith's newsletters and literature became influential among an Atlanta-based white supremacist group known as the Columbians. Though no direct evidence exists, the group appears to have become an incubator for Christian Identity leaders in the Southeast. The group itself did not assume or aspire to any religious or spiritual identity. Instead, as World War II came to a close, the Columbians presented themselves as a pro-Nazi group that could "ethnically cleanse" Atlanta of its Jewish and black citizens. By 1949 it had recruited an estimated two hundred members with a simple pitch: "Do you hate Jews? Do you hate Negroes? Do you have 3 dollars?" Privately, the group hoped to lead what one author called a fascist "putsch" to take control of not only Atlanta but also the state of Georgia and the entire United States, if possible. It stockpiled weapons and encouraged ethnic violence to that end. It also nurtured two people who became important members of the NSRP: Emory Burke and Dr. Edward Fields. Burke, in fact, had cofounded the Columbians, and by the time Atlanta law enforcement completed its crackdown of his group, Burke had become an active member of Smith's Christian Nationalist Crusade.

The Columbians may have been influenced by Canadian fascist groups, which likely had connections to Anglo-Israelism factions in places like Quebec and Vancouver. The symbol the Columbians adopted, a thunderbolt, had for years belonged to the Union of Canadian Fascists, which in turn embraced the symbol in honor of the Nazi SS. It later became the symbol of the NSRP. Reports show that Canadian fascist material entered the United States in scores in the 1940s. Some of it became highly influential in helping students of Gerald Smith shape Christian Identity into a fully formed theological framework by 1949.

An Anglo-Israelism contingent emerged in Canada in the early 1900s and blossomed through the 1920s. But soon a schism divided the British-Israelite congregation in Vancouver, with some members shifting their ideology in the same racist, anti-Semitic direction as their American cousins. By the early 1940s, this Canadian offshoot, the British-Israelite Congregation of Greater Vancouver, appears to have anticipated several of the interpretative moves formalized by America's Identity theologians. The Canadians produced written works that heavily influenced many American white supremacists. Published anonymously in 1944, a small work of nonfiction called *When Gog Attacks* became especially important to CI thinking. Historian Robert Singerman characterized the book as follows:

> Drawing on Lothrop Stoddard, the writer dissolves away, much like the cube of sugar falling into a cup of tea, the Jews who are not Jews at all, beginning with the Ashkenazim who are the round-skulled (brachycephalic) descendants of a "mongrel breed of minor Asiatic races, with a strong admixture of Turko-Mongol blood . . . the Ashkenazim is [*sic*] therefore neither Jewish nor Semitic, and that therefore their claims to Palestine have no basis of fact whatsoever."[28]

Whereas Stoddard imagined two races of Jews, the author of *When Gog Attacks* applied the label of Ashkenazim to all self-proclaimed Jews. Those properly understood to be Jews by mainstream society were all imposters or "counterfeit." The Canadian racists extended this idea one step further in another influential 1944 work, *When? A Prophetic Novel of the Very Near Future*. Authored under the pseudonym H. Ben Judah, *When?* imagines an apocalyptic world through the experiences of a British intelligence agent who visits Palestine. There the agent discovers the secret behind history's darkest conspiracy, one that goes back to Cain, the murderer of his brother Abel, in the book of Genesis. In the Bible's telling, as punishment for the murder, God exiles Cain to the Land of Nod, fated to be "fugitive and a wanderer," his bloodline terminated by the Great Flood. But in his thriller, Ben Judah provides a different twist. The big reveal, according to Barkun, is as follows:

> Cain, it seems, founded a secret society to do the Devil's work on earth, and had been so successful that everyone on earth with the

exception of Noah and his family "appears to have come under the control of Satan." Unfortunately Noah's line was contaminated when Ham married a descendant of Cain's and thus "the contaminated blood was brought through the Flood." Cain's conspiracy continued on through history, controlled by certain of the Ashkenazim Jews."[29]

While there are only suggestions that the Canadian books found their way to the Columbians, there is no doubt that they became very important to a handful of Gerald Smith's mentees on the West Coast in the 1940s. Smith nurtured a generation of ministers who reinterpreted the book of Genesis, with Cain as the pivotal figure. They included among their ranks San Jacinto Capt, Bertrand Comparet, and Conrad Gaard. But the most influential and important apprentice to Smith was the Reverend Wesley Albert Swift.

Owing as much to his charisma as his biblical exegesis, Swift popularized a form of Christian Identity known as the two-seedline theory, rooted in a twist on the biblical creation story. Swift and others argued that Eve engaged in two conjugal relationships: one with Adam, creating the seedline for white Europeans, and a second with the serpent (representing Satan), creating the seedline for Jews. In arguing that Jews were literally Satan's spawn, Swift provided ideological justification for many acts of religious terrorism. This twisted theology continues to be believed and used as justification for violence to this day.

The son of a Methodist minister, Wesley Swift became an evangelical minister at age seventeen. He moved from New Jersey to Los Angeles to continue his studies at Kingdom Bible College. By the mid-1940s, he had established his own church in the nearby city of Lancaster. In California Swift became friendly with other sycophants of Gerald Smith, including San Jacinto Capt and Bertrand Comparet.

That southern California became the epicenter for Christian Identity thinking may not have been an accident. Readers of John Steinbeck's *The Grapes of Wrath* are well aware of the migration of Great Plains farmers to counties like San Bernardino and Orange. Among other things, the region's clime and soil allowed for the farming of cotton, a familiar crop to the disposed farmers. But those same farmers often came from states and regions with a history of Jim Crow segregation. Tom Joad, in other words, could well have been a racist. Connie Lynch, son of a cotton farmer from Texas, certainly was when he migrated to the Golden State in 1936.

Again, prior to the 1940s, Anglo-Israelism rooted its belief system in speculation on the genealogy of the lost tribes of Israel. For the most part, the religion followed the traditional interpretations of Christianity, at least in its fundamentalist, evangelical context. This belief system included a conventional interpretation of the book of Genesis and the human origin story. As has been told for centuries, the basic story has God creating the earth in seven days, forming Adam from dust on the sixth day, forming Eve from Adam's rib, and placing both in the Garden of Eden. Warned by God to avoid eating the fruit of the Tree of Knowledge, Eve succumbs to the temptations of the serpent, a manifestation of the devil, and both Adam and Eve are expelled from paradise. The children of Adam and Eve are Cain and Abel; the former kills the latter and then Eve gives birth to another son, Seth. Seth and Cain become the biblical basis for mankind's bloodlines. Generations hence, Abraham reaches a covenant with God; Abraham's descendants, the Hebrews, or tribes of Israel, are blessed by God. In the Christian tradition, centuries later the Jews are blessed with a savior, Jesus, who changes the covenant and extends God's grace to Jews and gentiles alike.

But Swift and others offered key revisionist interpretations to the original story of the Garden of Eden, with cascading effects for Christian Identity theology. In Swift's retelling, Eve engaged in an illicit sexual relation with the serpent. Cain is not the offspring of Adam and Eve; per Swift, he is the child of Eve and Satan. Cain's bloodline yields demonic offspring—and in Swift's genealogy, those descendants are the humanoids who in the modern world call themselves Jews. These Jews—referred to by Swift as Ashkenazic Jews—are imposters, engaged in a centuries-long cosmic conspiracy against the true chosen people, the descendants of Seth, white Europeans. The imposter Jews manipulate other races, who Swift insisted were not fully human either but instead were descendants of the "beasts of the field," animals that, per Genesis, roamed the world before and concurrently with Adam and Eve.

The introduction of another seedline, from Satan through Cain, closed the biblical circle for dedicated racists of a religious bent like Swift and his friends. They had already embraced the genealogical ideas proposed by men like Hine in the 1880s: The Hebrew patriarch Abraham still reaches a covenant with God; his grandchild Jacob still becomes the father of Israel; Jacob's son Joseph still becomes viceroy in Egypt; the prophet Moses still leads the Israelites out of Egypt and into Palestine. None of these events refers to the history of the people currently identified as Jews, however, for theologians like Swift. Rather, the descendants of Jacob, the twelve tribes (representing Jacob's children and grandchildren), are from a different bloodline. When ten of those tribes, occupying northern Israel, are deported by the Assyrians, they migrate to the European continent over a span of centuries. Two tribes in particular, descendants of Ephraim and Manasseh, migrate to and populate the United Kingdom. As descendants of Jacob's son Joseph, these two tribes are, according to biblical tradition, especially blessed by God to form the House of Israel.

It is here that the introduction of Cain as an agent of Satan and as a progenitor of the Jews becomes so important. A conventional interpretation of the Gospels of Jesus (and the letters of Paul) suggests the potential for all the world to embrace Jesus's message and in so doing find salvation. Presumably this could include Ashkenazic Jews, if they accepted Jesus as the Messiah. But if Ashkenazic Jews were not even human, if they were the spawn of Satan, then such grace could never be given. Taken out of context, passages in the New Testament where Jesus refers to Jews as "the Synagogue of Satan" or as a "brood of vipers" give support to this interpretation and become key parts of the Christian Identity message under Swift. The Pharisees and the Sanhedrin who Jesus confronts are not just the chosen people gone astray. They are servants of Lucifer.

According to Swift, Jesus is the savior for all *true* chosen people, including the lost tribes, but he condemned "false Jews" as serpents and devils. Over time, the descendants of Ephraim and Manasseh migrate to England and America, respectively; America becomes the new Holy Land.

From the end of World War II on through the 1950s, through the work of Swift, but also Gale, and many other Identity preachers, two-seedline theorists developed their own creed, with a set of biblical references that are important in distinguishing between religious zealots and conventional racists. One of the leading Identity churches today, Kingdom Identity ministries, offers the following doctrinal statement:

> WE BELIEVE the White, Anglo-Saxon, Germanic and kindred people to be God's true, literal Children of Israel. Only this race fulfills every detail of Biblical Prophecy and World History concerning Israel and continues in these latter days to be heirs and possessors of the Covenants, Prophecies, Promises and Blessings YHVH God made to Israel. This chosen seedline making up the "Christian Nations" (Gen. 35:11; Isa. 62:2; Acts 11:26) of the earth stands far superior to all other peoples in their call as God's servant race (Isa. 41:8, 44:21; Luke 1:54). Only these descendants of the 12 tribes of Israel scattered abroad (James 1:1; Deut. 4:27; Jer. 31:10; John 11:52) have carried God's Word, the Bible, throughout the world (Gen. 28:14; Isa. 43:10–12, 59:21), have used His Laws in the establishment of their civil governments and are the "Christians" opposed by the Satanic Anti-Christ forces of this world who do not recognize the true and living God (John 5:23, 8:19, 16:2–3).

> WE BELIEVE in an existing being known as the Devil or Satan and called the Serpent (Gen. 3:1; Rev. 12:9), who has a literal "seed" or posterity in the earth (Gen. 3:15) commonly called Jews today (Rev. 2:9; 3:9; Isa. 65:15). These children of Satan (John 8:44–47; Matt. 13:38; John 8:23) through Cain (I John 2:22, 4:3) who have throughout history always been a curse to true Israel, the Children of God, because of a natural enmity between the two races (Gen. 3:15), because they do the works of their father the Devil (John 8:38–44), and because they please not God, and are contrary to all men (I Thes. 2:14–15), though they often pose as ministers of righteousness (II Cor. 11:13–15).

Swift and his friends like Comparet and Capt were not the first people to interpret the Bible in a racist or anti-Semitic direction, but

they did so in a radical way. Most racist interpretations of Genesis—
the passages of the Bible used by some to justify slavery in the ante-
bellum South and segregation in the decades that followed—rely on
Chapters 9 through 11, which narrate the fate of mankind after the
Great Flood. Segregationists specifically rely on what author Stephen
Haynes calls Noah's curse or the curse of Ham and on the story of the
Tower of Babel. According to this racist interpretation, Ham, the son
of Noah, witnesses and gossips about his father's nakedness. Scholars
have debated what this means, but for our purposes, the punishment is
what mattered. Ham is cursed by Noah. In some treatments this curse
includes black skin and applies to Ham's descendants, the dreaded
Canaanites. Later, by Genesis 11, Ham's grandson Nimrod is king of
an area that includes the town of Babel, where men in their arrogance
build a mighty tower to make a name for themselves. God then "confused their language" and "scattered them abroad from there all over
the face of the Earth." While Nimrod is never directly mentioned as
the ringleader of the tower project, commentators have traditionally
associated him with it. Thus one can see, in a cohesive interpretation
of Genesis 9 through 11, a similar theme: the God-ordained differenti-
ation and separation of the races. Not surprisingly, this interpretation
served as justification for segregation and for the notion of the racial
inferiority (per Ham's curse) of blacks.[30]

These chapters do not leave much room for anti-Semitism, especially since the story of Abraham and Moses come later in the Bible.
Anti-Semitism, historically, has relied instead on an interpretation of
the books of the New Testament that show some Jews rejecting Jesus
as the Messiah and supposedly arranging for Jesus's Crucifixion. For
centuries, Jews were mistreated on the basis of these interpretations,
but their basic humanity, their original role as the chosen people,
and their potential for salvation have rarely been questioned. The
closest one comes to the type of exegesis one finds in Christian Identity theology would be Martin Luther's *The Jews and Their Lies*,
published in 1543. But even Luther reserved the term *devils* for Jews
who rejected Christ, not for all Jews; he did not assert that Jews were
literally the offspring of Satan.

A look at three different and highly influential ministers from the
1960s provides an interesting contrast to Swift. The Reverend Billy

Graham, who was a friend of Martin Luther King Jr.'s, rarely cited
any of the Christian Identity's favored biblical passages in his major
sermons. The Reverend Bob Jones, whose religious university embraced segregation well into the 1990s, referenced the Tower of
Babel in a sermon warning against segregation; he did not mention
the curse of Ham, and he was welcoming toward Jews. Segregationist
minister Ferrell Griswold quoted from Genesis 9 through 11, but
even though Griswold spoke to large gatherings of KKK members
throughout Alabama, he did not couch his anti-Semitism in the two-
seed theory of Genesis. What anti-Semitism appeared in Griswold's
sermons was similar to the charges voiced by Father Coughlin, who
associated Jews with international communism.

Swift's sermons and writings completely reoriented the narrative
and the justifications of racial and religious hatred. According to
Swift, Jews and nonwhite races were not even in Noah's bloodline,
much less Ham's. They were either satanic, in the case of Jews, or
subhuman, in the case of nonwhite minorities.

This shift has both substantive and evidentiary value as we proceed
through the study of America's hidden history of religious terrorism.
Substantively, the dehumanization of Jews and other minorities serves
the same function as dehumanization in many acts of human-on-
human violence: justifying and rationalizing horrible treatment of
"the Other." In 1968, for instance, Sam Bowers, Imperial Wizard of
the White Knights of the Ku Klux Klan of Mississippi, referenced this
very kind of religious rationale when publicly criticizing (in a letter)
a Mississippi law enforcement officer who had killed one of his operatives. In an event that will be described later in more depth, two
of Bowers's operatives targeted a local rabbi in his home but never
met their objective, as they were trapped in a law enforcement sting
operation. In his letter after the sting, Bowers praised the dead operative and harangued the law enforcement officer. His reasoning? The
operative was a good Christian. Though the rabbi's life may have been
spared by the officer, the rabbi was the spawn of Satan.[31] Likewise,
when Connie Lynch spoke at a St. Augustine, Florida, counter-rally
in 1963, in reference to the recent bombing murders of four young
black girls in Birmingham, Alabama, he commented, "The victims
weren't children. Children are little people. Little human beings, and

that means white people. . . . They're just little niggers, and if there's four less niggers tonight, then I say, 'Good for whoever planted the bomb!'"[32] Such hideous public rhetoric was almost unknown even to the most hardened bigots, but Lynch was simply echoing the thinking of a minister convinced of the two-seed theory.

From an evidentiary point of view, the unique nature of Swift's biblical analysis becomes an important tool in identifying actual acts of religious terrorism. In public, for reasons that will become clear, Identity adherents rarely spoke openly about their unique religious vision. But one can find reference to a handful of biblical verses favored by the CI movement in the literature (such as pamphlets) surrounding attacks and in references to the core concepts, however coded, in CI members' speeches.

The very fact that these biblical justifications were available to a small but influential group of the nation's most active white supremacists is also a testament to Wesley Swift. He not only shaped the theology of radical Christian Identity, he also became its chief evangelist. Swift, like Father Coughlin, became a major radio presence, delivering intense weekly sermons to over 1 million listeners.[33] Smith's reach and influence benefited from one innovation that Coughlin did not have access to: tape recordings. Christian Identity followers became their own distribution nodes for Swift's sermons, copying and playing the tapes for fellow travelers. As early as 1965, a mailing list of recipients of Swift's taped sermons included dozens of people in nearly every U.S. state, Canada, Europe, and parts of Asia.[34]

The appeal of these tapes to right-wing zealots cannot be overstated. More than one person claimed to have been personally indoctrinated into the Christian Identity faith from listening to Swift's taped sermons. Starting in the late 1960s, distributors in Jackson, Mississippi, held popular listening parties, where they played Swift's tapes. One Mississippi man, Burris Dunn, appears to have been brainwashed by Swift's message. Described by his ex-wife as a mild-mannered if dedicated segregationist, Dunn began listening to Swift's tapes, becoming more and more radicalized with each recording. Soon Dunn began forcing his wife and children to listen to the tapes, at the threat of violence. The wife was forced to flee with her children. For his part, Dunn became one of the key aides for Sam Bowers, whom he idolized.[35]

Just as importantly, Swift, a former rifle instructor for the California KKK, began to use his Church of Jesus Christ–Christian as a front for paramilitary activities connected to the Identity message. Together with his then-ally Colonel William Potter Gale, who had counterinsurgency expertise from his days in the military, Swift created the Christian Defense League (CDL) in the early 1960s. The group was a multilayered organization, aimed in part at hiding military-style hit squads behind seemingly benign fronts. Researcher David Boylan describes four such fronts:

> The "First Front" was the Church of Jesus Christ, Christian. Faithful members of the CJCC were recruited for the "Second Front" [known as] the AWAKE movement. The more militant members were then recruited in to the "Third Front" which was the Christian Knights of the Invisible Empire (CKIE) "which will have the outward impression of a political-religious group not interested in violence." It was from this group that the most militant members were recruited for the "Inner Den." These recruits were the ones that committed acts of violence. Gale stated that "leaders in our country might have to be eliminated to further the goals of the CKIE" and that "God will take care of those who must be eliminated."[36]

Gale and Swift experienced a rift in December 1963, but the CJCC and the CKIE persisted, and both men continued as influential members of the Christian Identity movement. But for all Swift's influence and publicity, few Americans, either during his lifetime or in the twenty-first century, understood the impact he had on racial violence in the United States.

Perhaps not surprisingly, one of the first (and only) people to catch on to the danger posed by groups like the NSRP and the CDL, and to recognize the web of connections between members of several right-wing organizations, was the attorney general of California, Thomas Lynch. In 1965 he wrote a report that singled out the NSRP as "more potentially dangerous than any of the American Nazi groups." The

report also covered the CDL, the California Rangers, and the Minutemen. Lynch even pointed out the connections between leaders of
these groups and the CJCC.[37] But the report failed to take the next
step: to argue that religion was one of the driving forces behind these
groups' terrorist actions.

There are at least two explanations for this oversight. First, as
noted in the previous chapter, the context for anti-Semitic violence
was shaped by the world community's experience during World War
II. Americans were not even a generation removed from the Holocaust, and Hitler's Final Solution was motivated primarily by scientific racism, not religious theology. The language of the report,
referring to these diverse right-wing organizations as "American Nazi
groups," suggests that that mind-set still dominated the thinking on
anti-Semitism.

But if the California attorney general was keen to the religious devotion of people like Stoner and Gale, why didn't he see these groups
as an exception to that rule? The obvious answer is that from 1959
through 1966, there were few attacks by these men or their organizations against Jewish targets such as synagogues (or rabbis). Many
people assume that the attacks on Jewish targets in the 1950s were
part and parcel of the wider resistance to integration that came later.
If this was Lynch's theory, the attacks on Jewish targets after racists lost their struggle against integration in the South raises serious
questions about that rationale. But the California attorney general
was writing before Sam Bowers targeted Jewish institutions in Mississippi from 1967 to 1968. Attorney General Lynch, and others,
could reasonably ask: If religion was such a motivating force, and
the men and groups in question hated Jews as much as if not more
than blacks, why did the attacks on Jewish targets stop from 1960 to
1965, when white supremacist groups were at their most powerful?

The answer lies in what at first seems to be a counterintuitive
observation: Because of their power and influence from 1960 to
1965, devotees of Christian Identity could not directly attack Jewish
targets during the peak of the civil rights movement. While it may
be accurate to refer to devotees such as Stoner as religious terrorists, it would not be accurate to refer to the rank-and-file members
as religious terrorists. For all its theological gymnastics, Christian

Identity theology, and two-seed theory in particular, is an outlier in the Christian world, and CI remains a very minor sect to this day. The typical KKK member, the typical subscriber to *The Thunderbolt* (the NSRP's periodical), if he was religious at all, had attended a Sunday school that had taught the conventional narrative of Adam and Eve. He had also grown up in an environment with few Jews— and Jews who "kept their heads down." To the average dues-paying Klansman, Jews did not pose a threat to the "southern way of life"— African American civil rights activists did.

Wallace Allen, one of the men tried (and acquitted) for bombing the Temple in Atlanta in 1958, wrote a letter to Emory Burke that same year, describing his frustration with the "no-goods" in right-wing organizations who "want to stop integration without fighting the Jews." Allen wanted a new set of leaders who would drive these "lukewarm" people out of the white supremacist cause. He longed for a "band of hard core, idealistic. fanatical leaders (who will tackle all, not part of the problem) to organize into a group of their own and set out, like the disciples to win over everyone in this fight to the death with the Jews. Anything less will never succeed." There is little doubt that Allen, like his colleague J.B. Stoner, embraced something like Christian Identity, as he closes the letter by calling for "a careful thought out mass movement as scientific as it is fanatical, idealistic, devoted, and determined to destroy the Asiatic Jewish Khazars, who are not only responsible for integration, but whose evil fangs are at the jugular vein of civilization itself—this I'll die for anytime."[38]

But Allen never got his wish. Even as the civil rights movement made gains in the early 1960s and white opposition became more intense, Christian Identity adherents could not sway the neo-Confederate southern nationalists to attack Jews.

Few mainstream KKK groups routinely interacted with the NSRP because of its extremism, especially on the Jewish question. Attempts were made, for instance by Sam Bowers in Mississippi, to convince the general membership of some KKK groups to shift their focus to Jewish violence—but that did not work, not even in 1964 when northern Jewish students flocked to Mississippi by the thousands to help blacks in the Delta register to vote.

Though speculative, it seems likely that the religiously motivated extremists were left with a choice between two options. They could align their goals to those of the wider segregationist movement and thus maximize their influence and financial backing, or they could commit to ideological purity and target Jews at all costs. Favoring the latter would mean sacrificing the former. Attacking Jewish targets would alienate many would-be foot soldiers who would otherwise be happy to burn down a black church or beat down civil rights protestors. Connie Lynch could inflame a crowd with a rant on race mixing, but similar rhetoric against Jews would probably baffle the same audiences.

As will become clear in the next several chapters, from 1959 to 1968, Christian Identity zealots like Bowers and Stoner chose the first option. They chose to hide their religious agenda from their rank-and-file followers. They engaged in Machiavellian manipulation, but they were not resigned to a life of "lukewarm" violence that ignored the core problem, as they saw it: the satanic Jewish conspiracy. America's early Christian Identity terrorists were playing the long game. To understand how men like Stoner and Bowers exploited vigilante racism and blue-collar KKK members, one must appreciate what that long game was. Once again, the answer lies in a radical reinterpretation of biblical texts. Only this time, the material in question is not about the beginning of time but the end of times.

3

THE DAYS OF NOAH

the 1962 OLE MISS
INTEGRATION RIOTS
and the 1963 MURDER *of*
MEDGAR EVERS

O
n September 30, 1962, the Reverend Wesley Swift delivered a sermon at the Church of Jesus Christ–Christian in Hollywood, California:

> As we turn tonight to survey the situation, you remember that we discussed quite thoroughly this afternoon as we talked about being surrounded by so great a cloud of witnesses—this continual invasion of state rights, and individual liberties by those who control the Federal Government. We only mention that there is nothing more abhorrent to every free American than increasing Federalism, guided by the enemies of Jesus Christ surrounding the President of the United States, whose mind they must hold captive. . . . I charge that the President of the United States has committed a felony. . . . And with his using of Federal troops which he used today in the state of Mississippi, he has become a felon whether there is courage enough in the Congress to charge him for impeachment and for the Senate to hear such a case.[1]

Swift referred his audience, including his many radio listeners and those who would hear his tapes, to the ongoing events at the University of Mississippi in Oxford. Before long, those events would become the basis for one of the most well-known riots in American history, one that would galvanize religious fanatics like Swift. But at the time of Swift's sermon, the situation at Ole Miss remained in flux. For several days prior, James Meredith, a twenty-nine-year-old African American air force veteran, was attempting to enroll at all-white Ole Miss, on a one-man mission for integration. Mississippi governor Ross Barnett personally blocked Meredith's court-ordered admission to the university on September 20, meeting Meredith on the steps of the locked registration office. The events received national attention, and Barnett's efforts became a cause célèbre for white supremacists from around the country, led by nationally known racial agitator and retired general Edwin Walker of Texas.[2]

Hundreds of racists not just from Mississippi but from across the Southeast flocked to join the protests. They included many armed men, among them a contingent of NSRP members from Florida led by the Reverend Oren Potito. In the same sermon, Swift noted that Colonel William Gale was also on his way to Mississippi.

The Kennedy administration, anxious to avoid the kind of public and international embarrassment that had followed racial violence in the 1961 Freedom Rides, worked behind the scenes to convince Governor Barnett to back down and admit Meredith. But Barnett waffled, and on September 28 a court found him guilty of civic contempt, with the possibility of arrest and an ongoing fine of $10,000 a day as long as the governor continued to use local law enforcement to stop the integration of Ole Miss. Soon after, Barnett reached a secret backroom deal with the Kennedy administration to admit Meredith. But Barnett, an unpopular politician before his stance against Meredith, changed his mind at the last minute, once again refusing to allow Meredith to register. This forced the hands of President John F. Kennedy and his brother, Attorney General Robert Kennedy, who reluctantly ordered five hundred federal marshals to protect Meredith and escort him onto campus.

The marshals surrounded Ole Miss's oldest building, the Lyceum, waiting for Meredith to arrive by plane. As the day turned into evening, tensions reached a boiling point and Ole Miss became a scene of mob violence. Wright Thompson, a Mississippi native, described the events vividly on the fiftieth anniversary:

> The violence increases, as if the dark offers absolution. First, it's a smashed camera. Then a tossed cigarette. The mob surrounds a Dallas television reporter, George Yoder, sitting in his station wagon with his wife in the passenger seat. Someone reaches in and grabs his camera, which is thrown at the marshals. Then the mob turns

on Yoder's wife, reaching for her like a scene from a zombie movie, screaming, "N————-loving Yankee bitch!" She is from Jackson, Miss.

Finally, after watching the scene with amusement, some state troopers lead the Yoders to safety. Later, their car will be flipped and burned. The mob closes on the marshals. Missiles come from every direction, starting adolescent, slowly becoming more adult, from rotten eggs to firebombs. A construction site not far away is discovered, and bricks rain down on the white-painted helmets of the marshals, too.

A group takes down the Stars and Stripes and runs up the Confederate flag. The chain snarls at half-staff, where the flag will remain throughout the night.[3]

That was only the beginning. Soon the marshals were attacked with pipes. The marshals responded with tear gas, only escalating the violence. Outside agitators joined the fray, firing gunshots. Per Thompson:

Later, the events of the night will seem impossible: an Associated Press reporter shot in the back with birdshot. A bulldozer and fire truck stolen and driven at the marshals. A French reporter shot dead. So is a local resident. Dozens of marshals are shot or injured. A sniper sets up on the Confederate statue, first shooting out the lights, then turning his weapon on the Lyceum, pushing the marshals inside, high-powered deer rounds shattering the door and window frames. The besieged marshals were running out of tear gas and desperately tried to enlist a member of the school's undefeated football team to calm down the crowd—the young man accepted the challenge, but was mocked for his efforts. It was as if the Civil War had begun anew, and the North was losing.[4]

President Kennedy then sent almost three thousand additional troops to calm the violence and enforce the court order. Through "a storm of bricks and Molotov cocktails . . . the newly arriving soldiers maintained tight discipline never breaking stride. The precision scares the rioters, as do the shining fixed bayonets. The sound of hundreds of rounds of live ammunition being jacked into hundreds of chambers echoes off the old white buildings, chilling the crowd."[5]

By October 1, the day after Swift's sermon, order had been restored in Mississippi. The riot had left 2 people dead and 375 people injured. But while a defeat for the cause of segregation, the events likely signaled a much more profound turn for the nation and the world. To religiously minded racial agitators like Swift and his followers, the incident may even have pointed a promising way forward in what was, to them, a cosmic struggle.

Certainly, white supremacists could not have been pleased about the immediate turn of events at Ole Miss. Stoner and others, in periodicals like the NSRP's *The Thunderbolt*, routinely warned about the prospect of race mixing and miscegenation, something symbolized by Meredith's admission to the all-white university. But from a long-term perspective, the riot at Oxford may have validated those in the white supremacist community who followed the radical strain of Christian Identity preached by Swift. To someone like Swift, the events of September 30, 1962, signaled, as other key events before it, that mankind was soon approaching God's Final Judgment.

Radical Christian Identity theology not only renarrates the origins of man as told in the book of Genesis, but it also proposes a radical new version for what modern Christians call the end-times or the End of Days—as described in the New Testament's book of Revelations. Many Christians, especially those of a fundamentalist bent, envision the final days of the secular world, when God will judge mankind for the last time and, vanquishing the forces of Satan, will usher in a spiritual paradise, the Kingdom of God, for righteous believers. The study of the end-times falls under a sub-branch of theology known as eschatology.

Key to Christian eschatology is a concept known as millennialism, referring to a period lasting one thousand years, when Jesus will reign on Earth upon his return, or second coming. The second coming of Jesus is described in the book of Revelations and has been given three mutually exclusive interpretations. Under the *amillennialist* interpretation, Jesus will not return for a literal thousand-year earthly reign. Rather, the millennium symbolically represents a spiritual return of Jesus. In contrast, *postmillennialists* believe that mankind and the world are being gradually perfected by God over time and that once all nations accept Jesus, mankind will enter into a one-thousand-year peace, after which Jesus will return in the flesh to lead his righteous followers (including those who have been resurrected) and the eternal Kingdom of God will commence. The most popular form of millennialism among fundamentalist Christians, however, is *premillennialism,* which holds that Jesus will return before his thousand-year reign.[6]

Key to premillennialism is the Great Tribulation, a seven-year period of plagues and other calamities visited upon mankind, when a false prophet (the so-called Antichrist) will promise a Trojan horse solution to humanity's crisis and assume the mantle of leadership in a one-government world, only to bend the world to Satan's will. Premillennialists typically believe that Jesus will come *before* the Great Tribulation and save the righteous from impending chaos by taking them into the Kingdom of God—a process known as the Rapture. Then, after destroying Satan once and for all, Jesus will return with those he saved and with the resurrected dead who followed his teachings to lead a thousand-year paradise on Earth, referred to as the millennium. Those who follow this version of premillennialism constitute the majority of fundamentalist, evangelical Christians and are known as pretribulation premillennialists. The idea is popular enough in America that Tim LaHaye's fictional series *Left Behind,* which dramatizes a pretribulation premillennial rendition of the book of Revelations in the modern world, has sold tens of millions of copies.

Conrad Gaard, who stands among the most influential, early Identity theologians, proposed an eschatology that rejected amillennialism outright but borrowed elements of premillennialism and postmillennialism. He concurred with the postmillenialists that Jesus "will return to rule and reign in a literal Kingdom on this earth" and in "restoration of the earth under God's law." But, in contrast to their optimism that men will help bring these circumstances forward, Gaard asserted, "Scripture teaches that sin and wickedness will grow unabated . . . until Jesus Christ returns to this earth." Here Gaard agreed with the premillennialists that "sin will proliferate to a state of great reprobation until we reach conditions much like those

of Noah's generation." He also believed, per the premillenialists, that
"Jesus Christ will return to this earth in advance of the millennium."
But importantly, Gaard and his fellow Identity theologians rejected
the idea of the Rapture. "There is nothing in the Bible about any
secret rapture of the Church. The Church will be saved in tribulation, not out of it," he emphasized. "The Church will remain on
earth during the great Tribulation and will be saved in this time of
trouble."[7] Identity adherents believe that the faithful will experience
the Great Tribulation and that Jesus will come to save them after
the chaos ends. This is why Christian Identity believers often embrace survivalist principles. The vast majority of them operate as
white separatists who detach themselves from a society that they
believe does not operate according to God's laws and that allows
the "abomination" of race mixing. They frequently form their own
separatist communities.

But an important subset of Christian Identity adherents—those
who hew most closely to the teachings of Wesley Swift—believe that
the faithful not only must experience the Great Tribulation but must
serve as soldiers in God's army in the fight against the Antichrist.
The Antichrist, in this scenario, has a very specific connotation—not
simply as a singular figure but as the entire collection of demonic
Jews. In this view, the Battle of Armageddon is a holy race war, with
Anglo-Saxon whites on one side and with Jews on the side of the
devil, and the Jews, predictably, manipulate minority groups, such
as blacks, into joining their army. But victory is guaranteed, and
the forces of God will prevail. In fact, under this radical Identity
eschatology, the Identity follower is expected to do his or her best to
accelerate or encourage a race war.[8]

For theologians like Swift, the cold war era, and the civil rights
movement in particular, illustrated all the hallmarks of an impending apocalypse. First, there was the institution of the United
Nations and its implications for one-world government. Time and
time again, Swift's sermons spoke to the nefarious plotting by the
"Jew-controlled" United Nations to dominate the world. Second,
there was the threat of communism, a system that did in fact aspire
to world subjugation. But in the rhetoric of someone like J.B. Stoner,
it became a satanic conspiracy to enslave white Christians by way

of the United Nations. In the NSRP publication *The Thunderbolt,*
Stoner and Fields never failed to remind their audience—twenty-five
thousand strong at its peak—that Karl Marx had been Jewish. That
Marx's parents had converted from Judaism to Protestantism, that
Marx himself embraced atheism, and that Marx wrote works that
were borderline anti-Semitic did not seem to bother these white supremacists. To these men, and to Swift and other Christian Identity ministers, the civil rights movement was nothing more than a
Jewish–communist plot to advance a satanic agenda—specifically
the "mongrelization," or mixing, of the races.[9] Jews were not as-
piring to control the United States, but as Swift's sermon on the
Ole Miss riot indicated, they already were controlling the levers of
power. The civil rights movement was the strongest sign yet of the
tribulation that would herald God's Armageddon.

Swift called his sermon of September 30, 1962, "As in the Days
of Noah," a reference to the world on the brink of God's previous
great judgment, when he had saved a select few (Noah's family and
the animal kingdom) but had brought his wrath, in the form of the
Great Flood, to destroy the remaining sinners in the world. Swift
may have bemoaned John F. Kennedy's "invasion" of Mississippi,
but he also hailed the prospects of God's saving judgment.

> It takes too much time to finish a subject like this. But I want you
> to know that you are in the latter days. "And as it was in the days
> of Noah" [refers to] a massive program of Satan's kingdom which
> is to mongrelize your race. They want to implement this program
> with troops. They want to back it by every conspiratorial measure
> that Satan can dream up. And some of these brainwashed people
> lifting up a standard of self-righteousness which is Satan's own
> lie—behind this shield they march to destroy. . . .
>
> I am going to tell you this. [The Lord] is coming in with a long
> sword and a sharp sickle. And He is coming in to reap the Grapes
> of Wrath. And to trample the Wine Press of Judgment. I want you
> to know tonight, that you are a part of this battle. So don't sur-
> render. Don't give in. If they are going to try to force your Race
> with violence, then we shall meet them in like token. Let me assure
> you of this. That in this occupation, have no fear. For He said: *"I*

shall be like a wall of fire about you." "No weapon formed against you shall prosper."

Again, I say that we are not alone. As I said this afternoon, He said—"I shall never leave nor forsake you even until the end of the age."[10]

In the passage above, Swift highlights a key difference between conventional millennialism and its variation in radical Christian Identity believers, who favor separatism and a wait-and-see approach to the end-times, and those who favor a more proactive approach to eschatology. For Swift and his followers, there is no time during the tribulation when God will remove the "elect" from the world. Instead, as he notes above, the Anglo-Saxons will "meet them"—the forces of Satan—"in like token." They would fight violence with violence. This is a major reason why so many followers of CI, then and now, stockpile weapons—to wage war during the end-times.[11] When Swift himself died, they found a virtual arsenal at his ranch in Lancaster, California.

Ideas like the Jewish–communist conspiracy, the threat of race mixing, the "real story of the book of Genesis," and the coming Battle of Armageddon were ubiquitous in Swift's sermons and teachings. They were motifs in his ministry years before the Ole Miss riot. What Oxford represented for the likes of Stoner and Potito and Gale, in both a spiritual and a practical sense, was the improving prospects for a holy race war. Swift's end-times theology does not draw any distinctions between members of his Church of Jesus Christ–Christian and the "everyday" Anglo-Saxon Christian. All are supposed to rise up and vanquish the forces of Satan (Jews, racial minorities, and so on). But until the riots at Oxford, there was very little evidence that the wider white race was ready to embrace this kind of fight. There were, without question, open efforts to resist and intimidate civil rights protestors. But almost all the actual violent opposition came from a limited set of individuals in KKK organizations. The Ole Miss riots were the first real instance of serious, widespread violence from rank-and-file whites in the face of integration. Such violence only intensified with the presence of federal marshals. The events suggested that a rabble-rouser such as General Walker could incite a mob, even composed of laypeople with no direct connection to the KKK. Over time, Identity leaders came to see instigation and provocation as the best hope for encouraging a racial holy war.

Tommy Tarrants, a former Swift follower who was intimately connected to several of the most important leaders in various white supremacist organizations, provided valuable insights into the mind-set and strategy of Christian Identity leaders in his autobiography, *The Conversion of a Klansman*.[12] The book documents Tarrant's evolution from an angst-ridden racist teenager in 1963 Alabama, to the chief terrorist for the White Knights of the Ku Klux Klan of Mississippi in 1968, to an ex-convict–turned–ordained minister working for a mainstream Christian organization, the C.S. Lewis Institute.

Angered as a high school senior about the shift toward integration in his hometown of Mobile, Thomas (Tommy) Albert Tarrants III joined the protests against integration in 1963. Soon he found himself inculcated into Christian Identity theology by Admiral John Crommelin and notorious white supremacist Sidney Crockett Barnes.

Tarrants helped spearhead a wave of anti-Jewish and racist bombings in Mississippi from 1967 to 1968, for which he was later arrested and sentenced to thirty years in the Mississippi State Penitentiary (Parchman Farm). But Tarrants had a major religious conversion while incarcerated, forsaking Identity theology to become a follower of mainline evangelical Christianity, and was released on good behavior in 1975. He became a pastor at an interdenominational church in Washington, D.C., and wrote books and gave speeches repenting for his past. Explaining his thought process while a follower of Identity teachings, Tarrants confessed:

> Part of the strategy was to create fear in the black community— but it was more important to produce racial polarization and eventual retaliation. This retaliation would then swell the ranks of whites who would be willing to condone or employ violence as a viable response to the racial problem. . . . *Our hope and dream was that a race war would come.*[13]

But if fomenting a race war was part of the CI vision, African Americans were not playing along. Time and time again, from the

mid-1950s and the Montgomery Bus Boycott through the Freedom
Rides in 1961, white racists attacked and harassed African Americans in the most blatant ways possible. But time and time again, the
violence and intimidation failed, not only at deterring the civil rights
movement but also at engendering a violent response. However easy
it was to inflame a white audience, these supremacists had yet to
inflame the black community.

If blacks continued to maintain disciplined nonviolence in the
face of ongoing attacks, the hopes of creating a cycle of violence that
would escalate into a holy race war would remain empty. Events in
the spring and summer of 1963, much like the events at Ole Miss in
1962, may have served as yet another cosmic sign that Armageddon
was soon approaching.

On May 5, 1963, Swift delivered another sermon, "Armageddon—
Local and Worldwide." Swift announced:

> I want you to know that the battle of Armageddon is a world-
> wide struggle by the powers to overthrow God's Kingdom. I want
> you to know that the battle of Armageddon has already been de-
> cided although the actual battle has not been launched in its full
> tempo.[14]

He echoed all his familiar motifs. For example, the Jewish-led
communist conspiracy had led President Kennedy to appease Russian leader Nikita Khrushchev several months before in the Cuban
Missile Crisis. What's more, according to Swift, the communists, far
from removing their missiles per a secret agreement, were only reinforcing them. Communists were also plotting to hijack America's
public education system. A Jewish attorney general in Swift's native
state of California, Stanley Mosk, was persecuting Swift's fellow extremists. And with an eye toward recent news, the "gyprocrat" (a
Swift term for a Jewish-controlled hypocrite) Martin Luther King Jr.
had "stirred up" the people of Alabama.

King probably would not have disputed this charge. Together with
other leaders, such as the Reverend Ralph Abernathy and Reverend
Fred Shuttlesworth, King had launched a major offensive to desegregate Birmingham, Alabama. Weeks of protests received national

attention, especially when King himself was jailed in Birmingham, where he penned his famous letter to sympathetic clergy who were nonetheless critical of the strategy of civil disobedience. He wrote, "I submit that an individual who breaks a law that conscience tells him is unjust, and who willingly accepts the penalty of imprisonment in order to arouse the conscience of the community over its injustice, is in reality expressing the highest respect for law."[15] Until then, local authorities had largely been successful in containing civil rights protests.

Upon King's release that April, his advisors suggested something bold: using middle and high school–aged children to protest discrimination. On May 2, 1963, just three days before Swift's sermon, more than one thousand students cut school and marched from the Sixteenth Street Baptist Church to the Birmingham Public Library, ostensibly to highlight the library's policies of discrimination. The young protestors were met by law enforcement under the direction of Birmingham's racist police commissioner Bull Connor, whose men proceeded to use hoses, German shepherds, and clubs on the nonviolent students. Local white supremacists were not happy when the negative publicity surrounding the event shamed Birmingham's white establishment into a tentative deal aimed at desegregation.

On May 11, 1963, one day after the deal was made, bombs went off at the A.G. Gaston Motel (where Martin Luther King stayed while organizing the Birmingham protests) and at the Birmingham home of the minister's younger brother, A.D. King (also a major player in civil rights activism). No one was injured, mostly because the targets happened to be late returning from a planning meeting. Still, the bombings triggered the first-ever race riot in the history of Birmingham. Newspapers described a city "under siege."[16] Nearly fifty police officers were injured in a riot that included some twenty-five hundred people. President Kennedy had to amass troops in the surrounding area, but luckily for the president, the situation calmed down in a few days.

No one was ever prosecuted and convicted for the bombing, although police reports seen by the author suggest that the attack was made by Birmingham KKK members with the possible support of the

NSRP. But who plotted the attacks may be less important than what they meant to figures like Wesley Swift, J.B. Stoner, or Sam Bowers. In a May 13, 1963, sermon, Swift directly referenced the riots (conveniently avoiding mention of the bombing that precipitated them). In a speech called "Evidence of Divine Assistance," Swift began, "As we open this service tonight, the federal government is moving. And on orders from the Kennedy Administration, they started flying in troops into McClelland field next to Montgomery, Alabama." He continued, "I consider that the President of these United States, at the present time, with his present advisors, and the Attorney General of these United States, are the greatest danger for the destruction of our society as anyone on Mr. Khrushchev's general staff." Calling the developments in Alabama a communist plot and Martin Luther King Jr. a "fat headed demagogue of the negroes," Swift also accused King of being a communist tool. Then he asserted,

> I am well aware that we are moving into the stages of Armageddon. . . . And I want you to know that being Christian Americans you have the right to defend yourself, your country and your faith. We are the majority, and we are going to keep it that way. . . . Do not ever think that you can save America without direct action. Someone said, "Yes, but Christians do not take direct action." Don't you believe this. For Christ is stepping into this situation with the Sword of Judgment in HIS hand, and with direct action. And it will continue until the blood flows to the horses' bits. And there may be the greatest deliverance that you ever saw. . . . I point this out to you tonight, that these signs of riots and distress, this racial upheaval, are all signs of the climax of an age. When you see these things come to pass, then look up. Remember the prophet Joel said: "When they call on ME, they shall be delivered."—Every last one whose name was written in the book, before the foundation of this world. Not taken out of the world, but empowered in it.
>
> Many people are praying to be taken out of the world. Sometimes I wish they would. I think the most dangerous people we have are those who do not want to stand up for victory with God.[17]

Those who wanted to "stand up for victory with God" presumably included Byron de la Beckwith. Born in California in 1920, Beckwith moved to the Mississippi Delta as a young boy. He grew into an outspoken critic of desegregation during the 1950s and eventually became an investigator for the Mississippi White Citizens Council. With groups in most states, these councils were supposedly white-collar manifestations of southern resistance to the civil rights movement, in contrast to the blue-collar Ku Klux Klan, with the former supposedly shunning violence in favor of legal obstruction. That being said, many scholars now recognize that White Citizens Councils worked behind the scenes with KKK groups to accomplish the same ends. It is difficult to say with whom Beckwith was working in June 1963, as the White Knights of the Ku Klux Klan of Mississippi, under Bowers's leadership, had yet to fully form.

On June 12, 1963, Medgar Evers, the Mississippi field organizer for the National Association for the Advancement of Colored People (NAACP), returned home late from his office in Jackson, Mississippi. Recently Evers had appeared on television to call for greater integration, something that certainly would have enraged white supremacists.

Evers, carrying T-shirts that read "End Jim Crow Now" from his car, moved toward his front door. His wife, Myrlie, was still awake with their young children. She had allowed them stay up to hear President John F. Kennedy deliver a landmark television address, publicly placing the administration squarely behind men like Evers in their push for civil rights. One chronicler, John C. Henegan, described the tragedy that unfolded:

> A single rifle shot hit Evers in the back. The sniper's bullet came out Evers' chest, shattered the living room window and venetian blinds, blasted through the living room wall, and ended its parabola of death in the Evers' kitchen, where the police later recovered the bullet. The full length of Evers' body fell along the concrete driveway, and he began hemorrhaging massively. His wife . . . hearing the rifle shot and shattering of glass . . . came rushing out of the house, kneeling down to comfort him as she cried to the gathering neighbors to call for an ambulance. Evers

died shortly after arriving at the University of Mississippi Medical Center. His last words were, "Turn me loose."[18]

As one might expect, major civil rights figures, including Martin Luther King Jr., came to mourn Evers. But even King's presence, following the funeral, could not contain the anger of black Mississippians. After the funeral and an organized protest march, rioting broke out in downtown Jackson, with throngs of angry black students gathering, throwing rocks at law enforcement, and demanding, "We want the murderer" and "Freedom! Freedom." Law enforcement gathered in a phalanx to put down the rioters. A courageous Justice Department lawyer, John Doar, moved to the front between both parties. Invoking the memory of Medgar Evers, he managed to get the crowd to disperse, preventing what likely would have been a major calamity.

It was thirty years before Byron de la Beckwith was convicted of murdering Medgar Evers. He avoided conviction from two all-white juries in the 1960s but did serve time in the early 1970s for a separate offense—an attempt to bomb the offices of a Jewish attorney in New Orleans. Before going to prison for that offense, Beckwith claimed that members of a satanic conspiracy framed him for the bombing attempt. Years later he would formally declare himself to be a member of the Phineas Priesthood, a Christian Identity offshoot movement.

No one knows what influence Christian Identity ideas had on Beckwith in 1963. But the Reverend Wesley Swift was clearly paying attention to the attack and the subsequent riots. On June 23, in a sermon entitled "The Strategy of the False Prophet," Swift asserted,

> A Negro by the name of Evers, was shot back in Mississippi and they are searching for the White man who shot him. They are calling for the blood of the White man who shot him. . . . I do not buy anything that would embrace the administration for it would be covered up. Today, you are faced with the fact that this racial crisis is hanging like a sword over the heads of our people. . . .
>
> The anti-Christ has captured the Negroes and are using them,

for the powers of World Jewry have enmeshed all of the forces of the world against the White race. But the great judgments of God are going to move against it. And remember that God has an appointment with your race. This, my friends, is one of the most important things that you can know and understand. God calls on you to resist. And I challenge every White Christian man to be prepared to defend White Christian womanhood and to resist the powers of darkness. If there is a riot on one end of town and a fire on the other, then White men better be looking for that block that they are moving on. And when these Negroes move on that block to kill and destroy, don't spare a one.[19]

Throughout 1963, Swift, who was known to reference astrology as well as the Bible, warned his audience that a major crisis was coming. He predicted that the growing domestic unrest would become so serious that the U.S. government, under the influence of "World Jewry," would use the disorder as a pretense to invite the United Nations into America as some kind of domestic peace-keeping force. Of course, this would really be a plot on behalf of the Antichrist. With the lessons of Oxford, Birmingham, and Jackson fresh in his mind and in the minds of his congregation, Swift was confident enough to offer his followers a clear time period for this upcoming conflagration: September 1963.

4

THE DESECRATED SANCTUARY

the 1963
SIXTEENTH STREET
BAPTIST CHURCH
BOMBING

On September 14, 1963, five very dangerous men met in Birmingham, Alabama.

Traveling farthest was Colonel William Potter Gale, former chief aide and consultant on guerrilla warfare to General Douglas MacArthur in the Philippines. By 1963 Gale was the paramilitary commander and cofounder of one of the most outspoken white supremacist organizations in his home state of California, the Christian Defense League.

Joining him was former admiral John Crommelin, a naval hero during World War II, who would soon plot a coup d'état against the American government with fellow senior military veterans. Crommelin, who came to Birmingham from his home near Montgomery, Alabama, by 1963 had already run repeatedly for public office, most recently as a 1962 candidate for the U.S. Senate in Alabama under the National States Rights Party.

Three men from Mobile also made the journey. Noah Jefferson (Jeff) Carden, described in military records as having "psychopathic tendencies" and suspected of bombings in his former home state of Florida, joined the two former military officers. So did fellow white supremacist Bob Smith, who was then mentoring a Mobile high school student, Tommy Tarrants, who in a few years would become the chief terrorist for the Ku Klux Klan in Mississippi. Tarrants did not make the trip, but another one of his mentors became the most important source on the mysterious gathering.

In interviews with Pulitzer Prize–winning journalist Jack Nelson in 1991, Tarrants described a common house painter and notorious white supremacist named Sidney Crockett Barnes as the most violent person he had ever known. Barnes, like Smith, was in the process of moving from Florida to Alabama, fearful that law enforcement would become aware of his connections to the wave of anti-integration terrorism then plaguing the Sunshine State.

All five men who met that day in Birmingham—Gale, Crommelin, Carden, Smith, and Barnes—were identified in FBI documents as loyal followers of the Reverend Wesley Swift. All were either on Swift's mailing list for tapes or were ordained ministers in the Church of Jesus Christ–Christian. During Crommelin's last Senate campaign, Swift himself had joined four other Christian Identity ministers, including Gordon Winrod, the official pastor for the NSRP, in campaigning for the former admiral.

It is through Barnes, though, that we know the details of the September meeting in Birmingham. In March 1964, Barnes described the gathering to a friend, Willie Somersett, who was secretly taping their conversation as a Miami police informant. Somersett described additional conversations, which were not taped, relating to the outcome of that meeting as well.

According to Barnes's taped conversation, Gale had met with segregationist Alabama governor George Wallace in the summer of 1963 with a plan to stymie the increasingly successful movement to integrate Alabama. But Wallace had rejected Gale's plan as too radical. Everything that had transpired in places like Birmingham since that time had convinced the five men that Wallace—the man who once defiantly proclaimed, "Segregation now, segregation tomorrow, segregation forever"—was becoming soft. Barnes told Somersett that in response, he and his associates decided to take measures that would both deal a blow to the civil rights movement *and* embarrass the populist governor. If the following day's events were connected with the September 14 meeting, the horrible atrocity did more than just deliver a blow to the psyche of Birmingham's black community; it shocked the conscience of the entire nation.[1]

United Press International described the dynamite blast that "ripped" through the Sixteenth Street Baptist Church on the Sunday morning of September 15, 1963, injuring "dozens of persons, and at least 20 were hurt badly enough to have hospital treatment." In the immediate aftermath, "the survivors, their faces dripping blood from the glass that flew out of the church's stained glass windows, staggered around the two-story brick and stone building in a cloud of white dust raised by the deafening explosion."[2] Four girls did not survive the attack. The coroner's report detailed the horror:

NAME: *Addie Mae Collins*

DEATH WAS CAUSED BY: *Multiple Fractures, Lacerations of Head and Back (Chest)*

AGE IN YEARS LAST BIRTHDAY: *14*

NAME: *Carol Robertson*

DEATH WAS CAUSED BY: *Fractured Skull and Concussion*

AGE IN YEARS LAST BIRTHDAY: *14*

NAME: *Cynthia Wesley*

DEATH WAS CAUSED BY: *Compound Fractures of the Head and Chest*

AGE IN YEARS LAST BIRTHDAY: *14*

NAME: *Denise McNair*

DEATH WAS CAUSED BY: *Fractured Skull and Concussion*

AGE IN YEARS LAST BIRTHDAY: *11*

DESCRIBE HOW INJURIES OCCURRED: *Dynamite Blast—Bomb*

The bombing of the Sixteenth Street Baptist Church remains a metaphor for the tragic sacrifice and principled persistence that marked the entire civil rights movement. That preceding May, children had left the middle-class church and marched onto the streets of Birmingham, eliciting a wave of violent police retaliation that shamed the Magic City into desegregating many of its public and private facilities. Just four months later, the martyrdom of four girls in that same but broken building shamed a lethargic Congress into a renewed focus on legislation that would, over time, desegregate the rest of the nation. But in the immediate wake of the bombing, it seemed at times as if the city itself could come undone.

UPI described the riots that followed the bombing as a "reign of violence and terror." It added:

> It took police two hours to disperse the crowd of 2,000 hysterical Negroes who poured out of their homes. . . . Shootings and stonings broke out spasmodically through the city, continuing through the afternoon and into the night. . . . At least five fires were reported. Police shot and killed a Negro boy stoning white persons' cars. A 13-year-old Negro riding a bicycle outside the city was ambushed and killed.[3]

Tensions remained high as President John F. Kennedy decided how to handle the trouble. On the one hand, the situation seemed too much for the Birmingham Police Department, the Alabama State Highway Patrol, and the Alabama National Guard to handle. On the other hand, Kennedy feared that federal intervention might inflame the situation further or give Alabama's racist, rabble-rouser governor, George Wallace, the kind of public attention he coveted. Kennedy sent two personal representatives to the city to negotiate a truce between civil rights leaders and Birmingham's white establishment.

Perhaps more than anything, the arrival of civil rights leaders from around the country, and the leadership of local activists, helped pacify the city. Notably, as he had after the murder of Medgar Evers, Martin Luther King Jr. came to Birmingham from his home in Atlanta to eulogize the four girls. This was not surprising, as Birmingham had been the major focus of King's operations for the previous two years. King told the gathering of mourners:

> These children—unoffending, innocent, and beautiful—were the victims of one of the most vicious and tragic crimes ever perpetrated against humanity.
>
> And yet they died nobly. They are the martyred heroines of a holy crusade for freedom and human dignity. . . . They say to us that we must be concerned not merely about who murdered them,

but about the system, the way of life, the philosophy which produced the murderers. . . .

The innocent blood of these little girls may well serve as a
redemptive force that will bring new light to this dark city. . . .
Indeed this tragic event may cause the white South to come to
terms with its conscience. . . .

And so I stand here to say this afternoon to all assembled here,
that in spite of the darkness of this hour, we must not despair. . . . We
must not become bitter nor must we harbor the desire to retaliate
with violence. No, we must not lose faith in our white brothers.
Somehow we must believe that the most misguided among them can
learn to respect the dignity and the worth of all human personality.[4]

The riots that initially plagued Birmingham following the bombing
could have metastasized into total chaos but for the appeals of lev-
el-headed leaders like King, who reminded residents of the city of
the power of nonviolence and compassion. These leaders were chan-
neling the spirit of the Sunday school lesson that was never delivered
that tragic Sunday morning, designed by a minister with the last
name of Cross, about a "A Love That Forgives."

For some, the bombing also validated the sentiment, frequently
cited by King, that the long "arc of the universe" ultimately "bends
toward justice." It took forty years, but three of the individuals responsible for the bombing went to prison for the crime. It required intense
media pressure and dogged Alabama prosecutors to pry incriminating
records from a reluctant FBI, but the system ultimately worked.

Such a sentiment, while reassuring, is misplaced. Records suggest
that the FBI is still concealing potentially important evidence in the
case. For reasons that are still unclear, the FBI may well have protected the mastermind of the attack, a man deeply steeped in Christian Identity theology until the day he died: Jesse Benjamin Stoner.
Such obstruction, however, as much sense as it made in 1963, can no
longer be justified.

The FBI routinely withheld material from local prosecutors in
the 1960s, believing that they would compromise Bureau sources
and methods for the sake of a state trial that was likely to be sab-
otaged by a racist police officer, a bigoted juror, or a segregationist

judge. The conventional understanding of the FBI's obstruction in the BAPBOMB case (the FBI's code name for the bombing) says that, as his men failed to develop a federal case, FBI director J. Edgar Hoover decided that it would be best to maintain these sources—including violent Alabama racists who were turned into informants during the course of the investigation—for other purposes, rather than waste them on a doomed state prosecution. As it turned out, even after the prosecution of one bomber, Robert Chambliss, fifteen years after the fact, the FBI continued to withhold vital informant and wiretap information from Alabama prosecutors. Only in the 1990s was this evidence released, resulting in the convictions, in 2001, of Tommy Blanton and Bobby Frank Cherry. Again, the FBI claimed that it was simply protecting living sources.[5]

But additional, new information raises a different and more alarming possibility, one that is rare but unfortunately familiar in FBI crime fighting. This new information, developed by historian Gary May, suggests that an FBI informant inside the Alabama KKK, Gary Rowe, a man whose service as a source predated the Sixteenth Street church attack, may have been involved in the actual bombing. Although this obviously would have occurred without the approval of the FBI, it would have placed the Bureau in a position of having to undermine its own informant and expose its own poor judgment for the sake of resolving the BAPBOMB case. Unfortunately, Hoover was known to look past even murders committed by his informants if it meant protecting the image of the FBI.

Yet another layer of obstruction may not only inhibit our understanding of the BAPBOMB case but also limit how we view the southern backlash against civil rights agitation as a whole. Most Americans are familiar with the types of individuals who were eventually convicted of the Birmingham church bombing—the racist vigilantes who wanted to protect "the southern way of life." They are the thugs memorialized in pictures and films, beating the Freedom Riders with iron pipes in an Alabama bus station and terrorizing nonviolent college and high school students sitting at the Woolworth lunch counter in Jackson, Mississippi. The violence in those cases seemed visceral, sudden, and reactionary. For that reason, the perpetrators were often easy to catch, even if they avoided conviction. The

FBI managed to identify these types of individuals and their roles in the church attack within months of the September 15 bombing—although the Bureau withheld that information from local investigators for almost fifteen years.

Less easy to identify, or certainly to prosecute, was a higher caste of racists, known to historians of "the southern counterrevolution" but less obvious to the layperson. These were the members of "respectable" segregationist groups like the White Citizens Councils, which outwardly sought legal remedies to resist integration. These individuals even avoided the coarse language of the "lower-class" rebels, couching their opposition to legal integration in the language of anticommunism. Yet some of these red-baiters openly associated with the rebels who blew up churches and burned crosses—always taking care to have plausible deniability in the event of a crime. Even with the late-coming FBI information, Attorney General Baxley was able only to cast aspersions on such people in the press. But the best histories of the case, such as Diane McWhorter's *Carry Me Home*,[6] routinely question whether these types of individuals knew about or instigated the Birmingham bombing or whether they served as accessories-after-the-fact. New information, developed here, suggests an even more nefarious connection between these individuals and the Birmingham bombing.

These red-baiters may have been a bridge between the racist rebels and the religious radicals discussed throughout this book. For the men and women in this latter category, the goal of violence went way beyond simply preserving Jim Crow. They were as dedicated in their religious zealotry as any member of Al Qaeda. As the 1960s proceeded, their radical interpretation of Christianity became very influential at the highest levels of a number of major racist organizations, blurring distinctions between the three castes of racists—southern nationalist foot soldiers, "respectable" anticommunist segregationists, and religious radicals—and obscuring the motivations behind some of the more well-known acts of terrorism during the era. The bombing of the Sixteenth Street Baptist Church may have been the first such fatal act of religious terrorism.

If a group of outside religious radicals or even elite Birmingham racists wanted to instigate or exploit an attack on a major center for civil rights activity, while keeping a safe legal distance between themselves and the bombing, they had their perfect outlet in the collection of rebels who eventually did the deed. The men of Eastview Klavern 13 were violent, reckless, and desperate, a collection of outcasts whose fondness for violence placed them on the fringes of even the United Klans of America (UKA), the nation's largest KKK organization. Known as the Cahaba River Group or the Cahaba Boys, because they met secretly underneath a bridge near Alabama's longest free-flowing river, they were still attempting to get an official charter from the UKA as of September 1963. One can easily imagine someone suggesting the Birmingham Baptist church bombing to these ruffians as a ticket to respectability, or a loose-lipped Cahaba Boy boasting of his plans for such an attack to the kind of men who would want to exploit the information. But if a renewed look at the records suggests that additional individuals expected or condoned the attack on September 15, it does nothing to exonerate the men who committed the actual crime. While overlooked leads point to the possibility that a handful of other individuals, some of whom are still living, may have assisted in the attack, what is astonishingly clear is that the FBI identified the men directly responsible for the bombing fourteen years before any of the conspirators went to prison.

The first man to eventually go to prison, Robert "Dynamite Bob" Chambliss, obtained the dynamite from Leon Negron's store in Blossburg, Alabama. Negron stocked dynamite and blasting caps for the surrounding mining community, but due to his political views, he was not averse to selling his dynamite for alternative purposes. On September 4, 1963, Chambliss and two fellow Cahaba Boys, Charles Cagle and John Wesley Hall (called Nigger Hall by Eastview Klan members because of his dark complexion), arranged to hide the cache for later purposes. A fifty-nine-year-old truck driver who licked his false teeth clean in public, Chambliss was not the kind of redneck that Blake Shelton celebrates in a country music song or that Jeff Foxworthy jokes about on a comedy record. Birmingham police connected Chambliss to several racial bombings as far back as 1947.[7] Days before the crime, Chambliss boasted about an impending attack to a family member, Mary Frances Cunningham, a threat she conveyed to a member of the sheriff's office. The deputy sheriff later claimed that he withheld the story from law enforcement because he did not want to expose the fact that he was having an affair with Cunningham.

By then, Levi "Quick Draw" Yarbrough, another Cahaba Boy, had recovered the dynamite stash and brought the explosives to fellow Klansman Troy Ingram. Yarbrough worked as an employee for the state of Alabama. His idea of fun, according to witnesses, included shooting near the feet of black prisoners who labored on state construction projects.

Questions remain as to whether Ingram or Chambliss constructed the actual dynamite bomb used to destroy the Birmingham Baptist church, supposedly a more sophisticated device than those normally used in similar attacks. Ingram, a forty-nine-year-old automobile mechanic, engaged in a perverse competition with Chambliss over who was the better bomb maker.[8]

The FBI considered the possibility that neither man was the bomb maker or that they had help from others with demolitions training. Levi Yarbrough's brother-in-law received such training in the military, and the FBI considered him a person of interest in several bombings, both before and after September 15. When questioned, the brother-in-law minimized his connections to members of Eastview Klavern 13, such as Charles Cagle, despite testimony suggesting a deeper association.[9] His name was listed among the original persons of interest in the BAPBOMB case files. Twenty-two years of age at the time, the brother-in-law was one of the few individuals with connections to the Cahaba Boys who comes close to the age profile of one of two white men, described by witnesses as approximately nineteen years old, seen walking away in the immediate aftermath of the church explosion. When shown photographs, witnesses identified Ingram as resembling the older of the two men. This older man also had a limp, and Ingram recently had been treated for an injured foot.

Witnesses also identified pictures of other Eastview members, including Chambliss, as resembling white men in suspicious cars with radio antennae flying Confederate flags in the early hours before the bombing. One witness described Chambliss in the backseat of a 1957 blue-on-white Chevy with two other men, parked by a funeral home near the church. This same witness, Kirthus Glenn, positively

identified a car in a picture as belonging to Cahaba Boy Tommy
Blanton. Here the FBI's decision to withhold wiretap material from
Attorney General Baxley risked becoming a public travesty of justice. Glenn, a major asset in helping prosecutors convict Chambliss
in 1977, had died by the time new prosecutors were able to bring
Blanton to trial, in 2001. Lucky for the FBI and its reputation, a jury
looked past the somewhat ambiguous but incriminating statements
recorded by a bug planted under Blanton's kitchen sink and convicted Blanton without Glenn's testimony.

Not all of the suspicious individuals reported by witnesses were
directly associated with Eastview Klavern 13. One man identified as
being near the scene was Howard Thurston Edwards, a KKK and
NSRP member from Irondale, Alabama. Edwards can be seen in photographs of the 1961 attack on Freedom Riders at the Birmingham
bus station brandishing a metal pipe, which he used to beat the civil
rights activists. In this case, the identification of Edwards is important
because the informant knew Edwards from years before and saw him
frequently agitating at rallies against integration. The FBI lost interest
in Edwards when it could not develop any additional evidence connecting him to the crime or to members of the Cahaba River Group.
But as author Diane McWhorter noted, the Birmingham police considered Edwards to be a prime suspect in the crime. In *Carry Me Home*,
McWhorter suggests that the Edwards lead distracted the police,
pushing them in the direction of another radical segregationist group,
the NSRP, and diverting them from the guilty party, the Cahaba Boys.
McWhorter referred to the NSRP lead as a wild goose chase.

But McWhorter documented a close relationship between key
members of Eastview Klavern 13 and the NSRP. Robert Chambliss and Tommy Blanton in particular consistently spent time with
NSRP members such as Ed Fields in the months leading up to the
September 15 attack. "The Klan wasn't violent enough for them,"
asserted Bob Eddy, Baxley's chief investigator, referring to the
Cahaba Boys. "They were responsible for fire-bombings, floggings,
dynamiting people's homes."[10] In fact, UKA leader Robert Shelton
expelled Blanton and Cherry from the group in part because "he
did not like them hanging out so much with the National States
Rights Party crowd."[11]

One NSRP member who enjoyed a particularly close relationship with Chambliss was Bob Gafford. Gafford owned a successful automotive repair shop that still exists today, and he later became an Alabama state legislator. Among the elite caste of segregationists in Alabama, Gafford and his wife, Florence, helped form the latest "respectable" pro-segregation group in Alabama, the United Americans for Conservative Government (UACG), in 1963. Couching their opposition to segregation in the language of anticommunism rather than blatant bigotry, the leaders of the UACG grew the organization to include an estimated sixty-three hundred members. But most historians recognize the group for what it was: a front for the KKK.

Gafford lived next to Chambliss and even employed the violent racist in his auto repair shop from time to time. In an event he never explained, Gafford called both Chambliss and Cherry in the early evening of September 14, 1963—the day before the bombing. Gafford then proceeded with his wife and two married friends, Bill and Mary Lou Holt, to a bowling alley. The Holts were no ordinary choice for a double date. Bill Holt, a second-generation pipe fitter, was viewed as an "elder statesmen" inside the KKK, according to McWhorter, and had served as a leading member of Eastview Klavern 13 until back problems had forced him to lessen his commitment. He also knew Chambliss, Blanton, and Cherry. His wife had the type of looks and engaging personality that drew the attention of many men. Because of her charms, the UACG sent Mary Lou to Washington, D.C., to lobby against integration. But she also enjoyed a darker reputation; "her name was often mentioned . . . as associated with the radical fringe of Birmingham vigilantism."[12]

More relevantly, evidence suggests that Bill Holt was among many members of the KKK who likely had foreknowledge of the church bombing. Historian Gary May notes that many of those with ties to Eastview Klavern 13 managed to have verifiable alibis on the evening of September 14, when, per the official narrative, a handful of Cahaba Boys finalized their plans for the following morning. Neglecting to mention Gafford, May notes how Bob Chambliss, "not a popular fellow with Eastview men . . . nonetheless received an unusual amount of phone calls" from key figures in the Klan, including Ross Keith, Hubert Page, Gene Reeves, Tommy Blanton, and Frank Cherry.

Subsequently, these callers "went out on the town, creating alibis for each other." A few "drank at a Birmingham bar," while others found their way to the bowling alley with the Gaffords and the Holts. Exalted Cyclops Robert Thomas and Eastview's Grand Titan Hubert Page (and his wife) joined the Gaffords and the Holts that night.[13]

According to McWhorter, Page (who eventually married Mary Lou Holt after she divorced Bill Holt) expected the bombing to occur between 10 PM and 2 AM that evening and became incensed when the bomb detonated in the morning, killing the four girls. Page later joined Gafford and the head of the UACG, Bill Morgan, at what McWhorter calls "the kiss of death meeting" at the Cahaba River bridge on the Thursday after the church bombing. There, according to an informant, the elder statesmen berated Chambliss and the others for the negative publicity surrounding the accidental murders of the four girls. "If any one of you ever talks, it will be the kiss of death for you," one of the attendees insisted.[14]

One person who talked a lot to authorities about the bombing was Gary Rowe, another member of the Eastview group. The FBI recruited Rowe, a "barroom brawler with a police record" to infiltrate the Alabama KKK in 1960. Rowe, May argues, considered himself to be a "redneck James Bond" and engaged in acts of violence to solidify his bona fides among his fellow KKK members. Rowe joined the attack on the Freedom Riders in 1961. Most famously, in March 1965, the FBI learned that Rowe had ridden in a car with three fellow Klansmen, some of whom had sprayed gunfire into the vehicle of Viola Liuzzo, a civil rights activist working on the Selma voting campaign, killing her. Although the FBI warned Rowe against participating in criminal activities, it nonetheless looked the other way at his transgressions, placing more value in the information he could provide than in holding him accountable for his wrongdoings.

But the information Rowe provided to the FBI about the Sixteenth Street Baptist Church bombing puzzles historians like May and McWhorter. Notably, Rowe implicated those with indirect associations to the crime—those like Holt, Page, and Thomas—early on in the investigation. But Rowe failed to finger those directly involved in the attack (Cherry, Blanton, and Chambliss) until December 1964, long after the FBI had established their culpability.

To May, this indicates that Rowe may have participated in the actual bombing. He clearly knew and associated with Chambliss and the other bombers, but he appeared to be protecting them for some reason. Rowe offered a confusing explanation about his own whereabouts on September 14 and 15 and could not provide a verifiable alibi. May believes that Rowe had already participated in a major bombing in May 1963, in part because he needed to pacify doubters like Bill Holt, who suspected Rowe of being a government informant. Perhaps, May speculates, Rowe needed to prove himself one more time. This would explain why the FBI remained reluctant to cooperate with Alabama investigators decades after the crime. The FBI lost a measure of public trust when Rowe exposed his history as an informant (and his history of crimes committed while on the FBI payroll) to Congress in 1975.[15]

Congress learned that the conflicts of interest obvious in the FBI's dealings with Rowe was not uncommon. It became clear that in the BAPBOMB case alone, the FBI had leveraged two of the conspirators, Ross Keith and John Hall, after the bombing, and it is not a coincidence that the FBI began cooperating with Attorney General Baxley only after these two men died. In fact, the decision to protect sources and methods, even at the expense of solving crimes, continues to be a problem for the FBI in the present day. Probably the most famous example, besides Rowe, is Whitey Bulger, the Massachusetts-based Irish mobster who helped the FBI's Boston field office in its operations against the Sicilian Mafia in New England. In using Bulger as a source to bring down the Sicilian Mafia, the FBI let Bulger and his criminal cohorts escape justice for everything from strong-arm robberies to murder. Each time the federal authorities allowed Bulger to escape scrutiny, they made it more likely they would do so in the future, so as not to expose the embarrassing lawlessness "overlooked" in the past. Bulger grew to have a form of pseudo-immunity; his prosecution eventually highlighted a retinue of scandalous FBI activity nearly as long as Bulger's criminal record. The FBI likely helped Bulger escape arrest by the Massachusetts State Police in 1994. Law enforcement finally arrested Bulger in 2011, but not before paying millions of dollars in lawsuit settlements to Bulger's victims.

Given the sheer number of informants the FBI uses to investigate criminal activity, and given the large number of waivers the
FBI grants each year to allow these informants to violate the law in
the name of ongoing investigations, there may be many more Gary
Rowes and Whitey Bulgers. In fact, the need to protect "sources and
methods" will emerge as a subtheme in our investigation of domestic
terrorist groups, and it may partially explain why law enforcement
agencies and students of American history have failed to notice the
influence of religious extremists in the early history of racial violence.

"Sources and methods" include not only human beings but also
wiretaps and electronic bugs—what the FBI refers to as TESUR, or
technical surveillance. To J. Edgar Hoover, a well-placed listening
device could be as if not more valuable than a human informant;
such bugs helped Hoover maintain power through blackmail of
American politicians. It now appears likely that the need to protect
one electronic surveillance source may have prevented Baxley and
his investigators, and later federal prosecutors, from identifying and
convicting the likely mastermind of the bombing of the Sixteenth
Street Baptist Church: J.B. Stoner. Stoner thus provides a key link between the southern nationalists who executed the actual crime and
the religious extremists who visited Birmingham on September 14.

When he reopened an investigation into the Birmingham bombing
in 1971, Baxley zeroed in on Stoner as his first suspect. Many people,
including Bob Eddy, suspect or have implied that Stoner masterminded the Birmingham bombing but admit that there is no strong
evidence to prove it. This is why a set of recent discoveries, which
show the FBI continuing to withhold potentially vital intelligence
on Stoner, is perhaps the most shocking story left to be uncovered
in the case.

Behind the scenes, law enforcement agencies, especially the FBI,
strongly suspected that Stoner had orchestrated more than one wave
of interstate, coordinated bombing campaigns against Jewish and
black institutions. These notably included the bombings of several
targets in Birmingham, which in 1963 became national headquarters for the NSRP, after moving from Stoner's home city of Atlanta.
There is little doubt that Stoner attempted to bomb the church of
indefatigable civil rights activist minister Fred Shuttlesworth, the

Bethel Street Baptist Church, in 1958. He telegraphed news of the
attack to an undercover informant before it happened and avoided
arrest only because the sting operation was too close to legal entrapment. Authorities also believed that Stoner planned the successful
bombing of that same church in 1962. (A jury convicted him for
that attack in 1983.) A car that closely resembled Stoner's was seen
at some Birmingham bombings earlier in 1963, including on May
11, when two bombs almost simultaneously destroyed the motel
room of Martin Luther King Jr. and the home of King's brother, A.D.
King. Neither man was present, but the bombings set off the first
major race riot in the history of Birmingham. On September 25, as
the race riots following the September 15 bombing began to settle
down, two shrapnel bombs blew up in the Titusville neighborhood
in Birmingham and broke the temporary calm. A secretary for the
Birmingham NSRP, Phillip Maybry, quoted Stoner as saying that the
shrapnel bombing was our "baby," referring to the NSRP.[16]

From the start, some of those who best knew Stoner accused him
of participating in the bombing of the Sixteenth Street Baptist Church.
An anonymous source provided a detailed account to national reporter
George McMillan, accusing Stoner of masterminding the attack using
members of an elite southeastern bombing group called NACIREMA
(American spelled backward). In the 1990s, Herbert Jenkins, a former
police chief of Atlanta, admitted that he was that anonymous source,
but no one knows how he obtained his information or if members of
NACIREMA may have helped in the crime.[17]

Reports indicated that Stoner may have offered bomb-making
training to the Cahaba Boys. Other, unconfirmed reports said that
Stoner, and two NSRP members he brought to Alabama from Atlanta, met with "Dynamite Bob" Chambliss immediately before and
not long after the church bombing. There is little doubt that Chambliss, Blanton, and other Cahaba Boys associated with the NSRP
and the likes of Fields and Stoner. In records the FBI provided to
Attorney General Baxley in the 1970s, entire sections are devoted
to investigating the Birmingham NSRP. Based on those files, Baxley
went public to the media about the strange circumstances of NSRP
member Bob Gafford's calls to Chambliss and Cherry on September
14. He also noted that Gafford met with Chambliss shortly after

the bombing. Even more suspiciously, when Baxley, in his 1970s in-
vestigation, went to reinterview Cherry about the church bombing,
Cherry asked to make a phone call in anticipation of the questioning.
When Baxley traced the phone call, it again led to Gafford.[18]

The FBI's investigation of the NSRP did not shed any additional
light on these matters, and as time went on, agents focused their
suspicions on the Cahaba Boys and their associates in the UACG
more than on the NSRP. But just as several members of the Eastview
Klavern 13 were rank-and-file members of the UACG, some leaders
of the UACG, such as Bob Gafford, were also affiliated with the
NSRP. Gafford and others had even attended a meeting with Stoner
earlier in September. The failure to fully examine the cross-affiliations
between members of the Cahaba River Group, the UACG, and the
NSRP appears to be one of the major oversights in the investigation.

But what seems like oversights may well be an artifact of se-
lectivity, as it is now rather obvious that the FBI did not provide
William Baxley and his investigators with the full story on its investigation of the NSRP, especially of Stoner. Baxley deposited his full
records, including records provided by the FBI, at the Birmingham
Public Library, where they can be viewed today. When one explores
the entire file, the dearth of material on Stoner sticks out like a sore
thumb. There is far less material on Stoner, for instance, than on his
NSRP cofounder, Edward Fields, even though Stoner had a much
more substantial résumé when it came to violence in general and
bombings in particular. Even more conspicuous is the fact that no-
where in the thousands of pages of material can one find a direct
interview with Stoner himself. The material is filled with dozens, if
not hundreds of interviews with possible suspects who provide alibis
and narratives relative to the crime, including first-person accounts
and sworn statements.

Less suspicious and less senior NSRP members provided their
alibis directly to the FBI, but not Stoner. Yes, there are instances
when suspects refuse to cooperate with the FBI, but at least their
records document an attempt to interview the suspect and often-re-
peated efforts to get the suspect to change his mind. The FBI files
provided to Baxley do not even contain a record of Stoner rejecting
an interview.

Even when pressure from national news organizations forced the FBI to finally relent and give Baxley the files, in 1976, the FBI was far from forthcoming with information. Bob Eddy says that the original stash of documents was much less extensive than what is now available to the public in the Birmingham library. The Bureau told Eddy that he would have to develop additional leads on his own from the initial, limited material it provided to him. Then, if Eddy requested material based on those leads, the Bureau would provide him with additional records from its BAPBOMB file. It is important to note here that if Eddy was not given enough information to suspect that additional files might exist, he obviously would never have the impetus to request them. Eddy says he still suspects that Stoner may have been a key player in the church bombing. But he also said that the available evidence to support an indictment was lacking. Nor did any additional evidence emerge during the later prosecutions of Blanton and Cherry (although attorneys for Blanton suggested Stoner as an alternative suspect in the crime). Eddy's experiences in the latter two cases, when the FBI provided a new Alabama attorney general with wiretap records that helped cinch the case against both men, did nothing to disabuse him of his frustrations with the FBI. But he had no reason to think that the FBI continued to withhold vital information after that point.[19] That good faith now appears to be misplaced. It may well be that Eddy could not build a case against Stoner in 1977 or in the decades that followed because he was never given or told about potentially vital material that the Bureau developed on Stoner.

In contrast to the material disclosed to Eddy that is now available at the Birmingham Public Library, the BAPBOMB file the FBI provides to the public on its online vault is extensive in volume, but it is heavily redacted. Many pages are deleted or removed from the file set, and the material that is exposed to the public is often so covered in black ink that the narrative is barely comprehensible. But the online vault does provide one unique advantage relative to the Birmingham library files: One can search the digital text through the FBI's internal search engine and through Google. In contrast, the hard copy original of the FBI's BAPBOMB file is available in Birmingham without missing pages and without any redactions. This material, together with records from local investigations, makes it clear that the FBI did not provide its entire file to Attorney General Baxley. This is not particularly surprising given the scandal associated with the FBI's decision to withhold the wiretap tapes on Blanton and Cherry until 2001. What is surprising is that the complete files contain evidence that the FBI never revealed to Alabama prosecutors and investigators: That it also had wiretaps planted in Stoner's Atlanta law office.

The records are very clear on this. An October 9, 1963, document shows J. Edgar Hoover asking U.S. attorney general Robert Kennedy for wiretaps on Stoner. The document reads:

MEMORANDUM FOR THE ATTORNEY GENERAL

In view of the tense racial situation in Birmingham, further inflamed by the bombings, it is believed that additional activity on the part of those who are responsible for the bombings could easily lead to more rioting, bloodshed and loss of life, materially affecting the security of the United States.

It is requested that you authorize the installation of a technical surveillance at the office of Jesse Benjamin Stoner in Atlanta, or at any address to which he may move.

Respectfully,
JOHN EDGAR HOOVER
Director[20]

Former FBI agent Wesley Swearingen says that when Hoover wanted a wiretap, even if an attorney general turned down his request, Hoover would plant the bug anyway. But Bobby Kennedy even approved Hoover's requests for bugs on Martin Luther King Jr., so it is unlikely that he refused a request on a noted white supremacist like Stoner, especially at a time when his brother, the president, was stationing federal troops outside Birmingham to prevent the kind of "rioting, bloodshed and loss of life" Hoover was describing in his request. Any doubt that RFK approved the Stoner wiretap was resolved two pages later in the same file. Following the aforementioned request by Hoover is a page referencing the same date, October 9, but which has been deleted. Anyone familiar with FBI records would recognize this kind of form, which indicates that a record has been removed for classification purposes "and placed in the Special File Room of Records Branch." Just two pages later, we find the following:

Subject UNKNOWN SUBJECTS; BOMBING OF SIXTEENTH STREET BAPTIST CHURCH, BIRMINGHAM, ALABAMA, 9/15/63

BOMBING MATTERS

This serial, the original memorandum from the FBI to the Attorney General dated 10/9/1963, which was returned to the Bureau signed by the Attorney General authorizing FBI to conduct electronic surveillance, has been permanently removed for retention in the National Security Electronic Surveillance File, per memorandum XXXXXXXX to Mr. XXXXXXXXX dated 7-13-73. See 62-115687-1 for details and where maintained.[21]

Stoner is not referenced by name (nor is anyone else), but the date of the relevant Stoner technical surveillance (TESUR) request is referenced, and the account appears two pages later in the overall file section. The FBI consistently keeps records in a logical order by subject matter. But if there is any further doubt that such surveillance was not only approved but took place, further records make it obvious. Additional files show the FBI doing a "survey" of an office in Atlanta, albeit for someone with a redacted name. Such surveys were simply surreptitious visits (possibly even break-ins) to a designated area for technical surveillance, to see if planting a bug was feasible and, if so, how exactly to accomplish that. The record makes it clear that the FBI determined that the surveillance of the Atlanta office was viable, and for an indefinite period of time rather than a fixed length of days. Furthermore, additional documents, from weeks later, show the FBI asking for more recording devices to continue the technical surveillance of the Atlanta office. In other words, the surveillance, as one would expect, succeeded, and routine adjustments needed to be made to continue it.

Because the names on the other documents are redacted, one could conceivably argue that they refer to another person, not Stoner. A recent Freedom of Information Act (FOIA) request, however, puts that suspicion to rest. The FBI transferred a number (but not all) of its files on Stoner to the National Archives. The author's FOIA request for that material resulted in the release of twenty-five hundred pages—but four hundred pages were withheld in full because they were wiretap records. This may not even represent the full amount. Other files have not been released to the author, and the FBI refused to release or even acknowledge the existence of anything relating to Stoner from its National Security Electronic Surveillance File.

When told about this development, Bob Eddy was surprised. He never saw any records of any transcripts or recordings on J.B. Stoner. Moreover, he never had any reason to think they existed because the original Hoover memo, requesting the TESUR, was never given to him. Bill Fleming, an FBI agent who reviewed FBI files in connection with the later prosecutions of Blanton and Cherry, was also contacted by the author. Fleming said that he never saw any records on a Stoner wiretap; nor did he have any reason to suspect they existed.[22] Attorney General Bill Baxley was also surprised to learn about the Stoner wiretaps. Stoner was the first person Baxley investigated for masterminding the church bombing.[23] Although Baxley is still less convinced of Stoner's guilt than Eddy, both men believe the transcripts should be released.

There is reason to be concerned that some material, at least on Stoner, could have been destroyed. Researcher Ernie Lazar claims that the FBI destroyed its Birmingham field office file on Stoner. Obviously, this would be the most likely file to hold any new information on Stoner's connection to the Birmingham bombing. The destroyed file might augment information, reported in Birmingham police files, that Admiral John Crommelin stayed with Stoner in Birmingham the weekend of the church bombing.

All five Christian Identity zealots who met in Birmingham on September 14, 1963, were, in fact, also members of the NSRP. Gafford's friends Mary Lou and Bill Holt were also on the mailing list for Wesley Swift's sermons. If Stoner was not an official minister in the church, he acted like one. Stoner used the official NSRP newsletter,

The Thunderbolt, to promote ideas that could have served as sermons for Wesley Swift. Regarding Jews, the publication said that "Jew-devils have no place in a White Christian nation."[24] Of blacks it said, "The Negro is actually a higher form of gorilla. God did not wish for the white race to mix with these animals. Tell your friends and children these scientific truths so that communist teachers and preachers will not be able to brain wash them with 'the Big Lie' that all men are equal."[25]

Stoner, of course, also traveled the country with Identity minister Connie Lynch, riling up southerners into fits of violence. On the surface, this work appears to be counterproductive. By inciting violence, the rabble-rousers increased the chances that a riot would elicit federal intervention, a development that few southerners, raised from childhood to resent military occupation under post–Civil War Reconstruction, would welcome. This would be particularly true for a provocative attack like the shrapnel bomb that struck the Birmingham neighborhood of Titusville on September 25, 1963.

No right-thinking person who experienced the riots that followed the murders of little Denise McNair, Addie Mae Collins, and the other children could expect such an attack to do anything other than incite further violence. Klan terrorists often used conventional dynamite bombs to cause property damage and to scare targeted groups rather than to kill victims. This appears to have been the intended purpose of the bomb that exploded on September 15; an apparent problem with the triggering mechanism delayed the detonation, and thus the four girls died.[26]

But the shrapnel bombs used on September 25 had only one purpose: to maim and kill. The perpetrators had actually designed one of the two bombs for a delayed explosion. It appears that the bomb makers intended the first device to lure out spectators and law enforcement; the second explosion could then have killed dozens of police officers and citizens. It was a sheer stroke of luck that no one got injured in the Titusville bombing. If, as Phillip Maybry quoted Stoner as saying, the shrapnel bomb was our "baby," what motive could explain such a brazen act of attempted terrorism?

The issue here again involves the differences between rank-and-file segregationists, even violent KKK members, and the men who believed in radical, Christian Identity theology. To the former, federal intervention was anathema to their customs and traditions going back to the era of Reconstruction. To the radical religious zealots, that same deep-rooted resentment among the general white population was exactly what stoked a violent response from bystanders at the University of Mississippi in 1962. The provocative riots that triggered the federal intervention in the first place—in Alabama and in Mississippi—developed only when the black community boiled over after major, provocative acts of violence. Thus, for the religious zealot, who as Tommy Tarrants revealed wanted to "polarize the races" in hopes of fomenting a race war, the shrapnel bomb, and the bombing of the Sixteenth Street Baptist Church itself, represented the best hope for accelerating the end-times. Wesley Swift pointed to this idea in his sermon "Armageddon: Local and Worldwide" in May 1963, saying:

> I tell you that here in America we are on the edge of an unusual chain of events, and it may be that the sudden movement of your enemy may be your salvation. Someone said: "there may not be another election but there is going to be deliverance." You are in one of the most unusual periods in the history of our nation. You are going to see brush fire wars which can break into the big ones and could start anytime.[27]

Any Identity believer observing the tinderbox that was Birmingham in 1963 could have guessed what would happen if someone attacked a target as honored in the black community as the Sixteenth Street Baptist Church. After several months of bombings and bombing attempts, the city became known as Bombingham and the neighborhood that included the church was known as Dynamite Hill. The bombing of Martin Luther King Jr.'s hotel room, which coincided with the attack on his brother's home, on May 11, ignited the first major race riot in the history of the city. In early September, after several months of bombings and other acts of racial violence, President John F. Kennedy prepared for an armed intervention in the city. In just the period from September 1 to September 14, there were three bombings in Birmingham. All the ingredients were present for racial violence on a scale that would impress even Wesley Swift.

Yet the weight of the evidence suggests that the bomb that went off on September 15 was not intended to kill anyone. The reaction of the suspects after the fact certainly point to that. Hubert Page was furious that the four girls were killed. Robert Shelton wanted nothing to do with those associated with the bombing and may have used a source, Don Luna, to implicate the men to the FBI. But even if the five Swift followers could not have anticipated the killing of the four girls, they still could have known, through someone like Stoner, about the impending attack on the church. Their hope for racial violence and federal intervention on a grand scale would be in the local reaction to the bombing. In the perverted worldview of religious radicals like Swift, the unintended death of four girls presented a unique opportunity.

The riots that followed the bombing of the church on September 15 could actually have been much worse, with far more violence and casualties. The Reverend Ed King, a white minister who became a leading member of the Mississippi Freedom Democratic Party, described the tension in an interview with the author.

He went to Birmingham to help mourn the girls' deaths and to lead protest marches against the violence. The activist became concerned when he went outside and noticed "whites with machine gun emplacements a block away from the church. . . . I realized some of them thought there would be a march or a demonstration." No such event was planned. Then again, no marches had been planned following the funeral for Ed King's close friend Medgar Evers, but chaos followed in Jackson when local police overreacted to peaceful protests by black Mississippians. In Birmingham, a few months later, thousands of mourners joined the family to pounce. In the marches that followed, Ed King saw moments when misunderstandings could have led to another disaster. In Jackson, "the police panicked . . . in Birmingham I realized the same thing could happen." Only in Birmingham the police had "machine guns ready, and we could have a massacre. . . . All it would have taken was a bottle breaking that sounded like a gun."[28] He approached Diane Nash Bevel, a major civil rights activist, then married to one of Martin Luther King's top lieutenants, James Bevel, with his fears. She patiently convinced the thousands of mourners to go home.

But if the five Swift followers who had visited Birmingham on the eve of the church bombing had had their way, a bloodbath would have been unavoidable. In his secretly taped conversations with Somersett, Sidney Barnes told the informant that the five men stayed in Birmingham to try to assassinate Martin Luther King Jr. after he arrived to deliver the eulogy for the four girls. They followed King in Birmingham—with Noah Carden waiting to shoot the minister with a rifle—but they could not get close enough to take a clear shot.

One can imagine the impact that killing King would have had on a black population already stirring with anger over the murders of September 15. The attitude among America's black community, according to Ed King, "was 'there is nothing the white racist will not do.' There is nothing Washington will do to protect us. They [the white supremacists] have killed these little girls. This wasn't voter registration." "If white police had killed more blacks at a funeral" following an uprising over the assassination of Martin Luther King, "I think there would have been riots in Jackson, in Atlanta, in New Orleans."[28]

The most obvious interpretation of Barnes's account is that the Swift followers came to Birmingham with foreknowledge of the church bombing and took advantage of an opportunity to piggyback on the bombing when the unanticipated carnage created horrible riots, bringing Martin Luther King Jr. from his home in Georgia back to Alabama. But it is also the case, as Ed King makes clear, that anyone who followed Martin Luther King's activities in Birmingham would have anticipated that a bombing of the Sixteenth Street Baptist Church would draw him to the city. Either way, whether such an attack resulted in unexpected killings or not, the state of Alabama is very lucky that Barnes's efforts to kill King failed. Even still, Barnes told Somersett that the assassination plot on King remained active for several more months, but the group never had an opportunity to strike again.

In fact, according to historian Neil Hamilton, killing Martin Luther King had been a major goal of Swift and Gale since they had founded the Christian Defense League in 1960. Multiple attempts on King's life can be traced to followers of the Church of Jesus Christ–Christian. Stoner, for instance, offered a bounty on King's life as early as 1958.

None were more determined to kill King than a new arrival to the white supremacist scene in Mississippi, Samuel Holloway Bowers. Bowers's tenure as head of the White Knights of the Ku Klux Klan of Mississippi, from 1964 to 1968, places him among the most violent sponsors of domestic terrorism the nation has ever known. Many are familiar with the most public act of violence—the murder of three civil rights workers in June 1964, known to some as the Neshoba County murders and to others as the Mississippi Burning killings. Few, however, have looked deeply enough at the crime, or more particularly at Bowers, to see that that terrorist act was even darker in its objective than anyone had imagined.

5

THE BLOOD OF MARTYRS

the 1964
(NESHOBA COUNTY)
MISSISSIPPI BURNING
MURDERS

June 21, 1964. The three civil rights workers traveling the dirt roads in Neshoba County knew the dangers of driving at night—two whites, one black driver—in Sam Bowers's Mississippi. Just two weeks earlier, at 9 PM on June 8, white vigilantes had forced three New York graduate school students over to the side of the road in nearby McComb County. When the students refused to exit the vehicle at gunpoint, the vigilantes beat the men with brass knuckles after breaking the windows of their car. Many believe the only thing that saved the graduate students' lives was the likelihood that passing motorists would witness the crime.

When they left the Meridian, Mississippi, office of the Congress of Racial Equality (CORE) on June 20, Michael "Mickey" Schwerner and Andrew Goodman, white New Yorkers of Jewish descent, and James Chaney, black and Mississippi-born, told Sue Brown, the CORE chapter secretary, to start making calls if the three men did not return by 4 PM. The three men then began their dangerous mission: to investigate the burning of the Mount Zion Baptist Church, which had occurred five days earlier in Neshoba County, Mississippi.

The men reached and inspected the remains of the church. They interviewed three black parishioners who told them a harrowing story. According to the interviewees, on the evening of July 16, as many as thirty men surrounded and confronted several church members leaving Mount Zion. The mob beat several congregants and then set fire to the church. But the parishioners added something that must have greatly disturbed the trio: The mob demanded that the members of Mount Zion provide them with information on "the goatee" or "Jewboy." The reference would have been clear: The attackers wanted Mickey Schwerner.[1]

Schwerner had established himself as a man of action since arriving with his wife, Rita, in February 1964. "The first white civil rights worker based outside of the capitol of Jackson," he had "earned the enmity of the Klan by organizing a black boycott of a white-owned business and aggressively trying to register blacks in and around Meridian to vote," according to law professor Douglas O. Linder.[2] If he did not know earlier, Schwerner knew for certain on June 21, from the congregants at Mount Zion, that he now was a major target for local racists. No one knows if Schwerner realized what many historians now suspect: that the burning of Mount Zion was a trap, set by members and associates of the White Knights of the Ku Klux Klan of Mississippi with the hopes of luring Schwerner to his death.

What is clear is that the men took the less direct path back to Meridian, bypassing Highway 491, by which they had come to Mount Zion, instead choosing Highway 19, through the county seat of Philadelphia, Mississippi. Linder believes that this was the less dangerous route to the CORE chapter in Meridian, one less open to an ambush. They left at approximately 3 PM.

But the Klan's plan of attack was unfortunately more elaborate than simply running a few men off the road in the off chance that they happened to pass a posse of Klan members. It is true that the unfortunate events that ended the three men's lives may well have started as a case of mistaken identity. While passing the trio on the highway, Neshoba County deputy sheriff Cecil Price noticed a black man (Chaney) driving the prototypical CORE vehicle, a blue Ford station wagon. Price thought that Chaney was another target of interest, activist George Raymond, and radioed this into his headquarters. Price then gave chase and arrested the men just as they were about to pass Philadelphia's city limits. Arrested on the trumped-up suspicion of having set the Mount Zion Church fire, the three civil rights workers were taken to the jail in Neshoba County, under the direction of Sheriff Lawrence Rainey, a member of the White Knights. But once it became clear that Schwerner was among the men in custody, the operation to kill him (and the others) went into effect. The accidental arrest by Price likely triggered what many experts believe was a general plan hatched weeks in advance to kill Schwerner.

The sheriff consulted with White Knight Kleagle Edgar Ray Killen and finalized the particulars of a murder conspiracy. According to Horace Doyle Barnett, a racist from Louisiana and an associate of Mississippi KKK members, calls were placed for those in the local area willing to help on "a job." Barnett claims that he first discovered the particulars when he and his friend Jimmy Arledge visited a trailer park in Meridian. Edgar Ray Killen—known as Preacher Killen because he pastored at a number of small rural churches—told a crew of several men that "these three civil rights workers were going to be released from jail and that we were going to catch them and give them a whipping."[3] Foreshadowing something much more sinister, Killen then made sure that all the men present wore gloves. The men drove to Philadelphia in separate vehicles, arriving at approximately 9:30 PM.

At 10:30 PM Sheriff Rainey released the three civil rights workers. The trio again took Highway 19, but this time Deputy Sheriff Price tracked their movements in his patrol car. Price relayed their bearings to other patrolmen, who in turn told the convoys of Klansmen, two cars' worth, to hustle after the civil rights workers. Once the bigots caught up in their vehicles, Price forced the blue station wagon to the side of Rock Cut Road. Striking the driver, Chaney, with a blackjack, he then stepped aside as the KKK members finished their operation. While six men, including law enforcement officers like Price, were involved in the ambush, Barnett's description of the killing focuses on two individuals: Wayne Roberts, a twenty-six-year-old ex-marine and Meridian window salesman with a reputation for being "as mean as a junkyard dog," and James Jordan, a motel clerk and illegal speakeasy operator.

Before I could get out of the car Wayne ran past my car to Price's car, opened the left rear door, pulled Schwerner out of the car, spun him around so that Schwerner was standing on the left side of the road, with his back to the ditch and said "Are you that nigger lover" and Schwerner said "Sir, I know just how you feel." Wayne had a pistol in his right hand, then shot Schwerner. Wayne then went back to Price's car and got Goodman, took him to the left side of the road with Goodman facing the road, and shot Goodman.

When Wayne shot Schwerner, Wayne had his hand on Schwerner's shoulder. When Wayne shot Goodman, Wayne was standing within reach of him. Schwerner fell to the left so that he was laying alongside the road. Goodman spun around and fell back toward the bank in back.

At this time Jim Jordan said "save one for me." He then got out of Price's car and got Chaney out. I remember Chaney backing up, facing the road, and standing on the bank on the other side of the ditch and Jordan stood in the middle of the road and shot him. I do not remember how many times Jordan shot. Jordan then said, "You didn't leave me anything but a nigger, but at least I killed me a nigger." The three civil rights workers were then put into the back of their 1963 Ford wagon.[4]

The perpetrators left the workers' vehicle in the woods, singed from blue to black by fire, for other authorities to find. They buried the bodies of the three men in an earthen dam at the estate of Olan Burrage, known as Old Jolly Farm. The disappearance of two northern whites scandalized the nation and resulted in one of the largest federal investigations in history. The FBI would call the crime the Mississippi Burning murders (abbreviated as MIBURN), the name for which it has become famous thanks to a 1988 Hollywood movie of the same name. (We will alternately refer to them as the Neshoba murders.) In the forty-four days it took to finally find the bodies, Mississippi governor Paul B. Johnson Jr. joined a chorus of segregationists in insisting that the three activists had staged the whole affair for the sake of publicity. But in Oxford, Ohio, where civil rights veterans were training hundreds of volunteers for the Mississippi Freedom Summer, where Schwerner, Goodman, and Chaney had in fact been residing in the days before reports of the Mount Zion Church arson drew them back to Mississippi, long-time activists knew the score right away. "People have been killed," SNCC leader Bob Moses told the young idealists. "You can decide to go back home, and no one will look down on you for doing it."[5]

If, as many believe, the goal of the Mississippi Burning murders was to halt the approach of Freedom Summer, set to begin in a matter of days, it did not work. Many of the volunteers bravely ventured forward to proceed with the plan, conceptualized in October 1963 by leaders of the Council of Federated Organizations (COFO), an umbrella civil rights group that included organizations such as CORE, SNCC, and the SCLC. The thrust of Freedom Summer was to publicize the need for voting rights protections in the South and also to educate the people of Mississippi about the power that could come with such rights.

The passage of the Civil Rights Act of 1964 by the U.S. Senate on June 19 promised the end of legal discrimination in the South. But President Lyndon Johnson removed voting rights provisions from the bill to guarantee its eventual passage. Although blacks enjoyed the franchise under the Fifteenth Amendment to the U.S. Constitution, southern states still determined voting qualifications under the principle of federalism. They enacted a host of measures, from poll taxes to literacy tests, that effectively denied African Americans their constitutionally guaranteed right to vote.

Even if the Civil Rights Act of 1964 and various Supreme Court decisions, such as *Brown v. Board of Education*, guaranteed some form of equality in theory, the lack of voting power made such prospects hollow. Blacks could not choose local officials to fund mostly black schools or to monitor efforts to integrate schools, hotels, or hospitals; they could not hold officials accountable. A major thrust of Freedom Summer was to make black citizens of Mississippi aware of the potential their votes could have in combination with the protections afforded by the Civil Rights Act of 1964. Veterans of the civil rights movement in COFO enlisted hundreds of volunteers from across the nation, including many middle-class whites like Goodman and Schwerner. If the activists could publicize to the nation that there was widespread demand for the right to vote, even in a state as poor as Mississippi, it would become a major impetus for a voting rights act to join the Civil Rights Act.

But the white power structure of the South recognized that black voting rights posed an even greater threat than civil rights to the system of white supremacy. The very officials who benefited from white-only voting in parts of the South that included high concentrations of blacks stood to lose their offices in a fair election. This group included mayors, state legislators, local sheriffs, prosecutors, and judges. The law enforcement officers had a powerful arrow in their quivers, however: absent access to voter registration, blacks could not serve on juries. Potential jurors are selected from voter rolls. It may not be surprising, then, that in places like Jackson, Mississippi, or Selma, Alabama, the most hostile and violent opposition to voting rights often came not only from the KKK but from law enforcement—people like Sheriff Lawrence Rainey. If the law enforcement officers themselves were not members of the KKK (a phenomenon pervasive in many southern towns), they offered tacit approval for the KKK to victimize anyone of color hoping to vote. Part of Freedom Summer, in fact, would include the Freedom Vote—a voter registration campaign to bypass racist registrars and to create provisional ballots for blacks to cast in upcoming statewide elections. This parallel apparatus attempted to allow Mississippi's black population to vote with less risk of violence and intimidation.

Basic opposition to voting rights for blacks and to what southern nationalists referred to as "outside agitation" by northerners likely motivated the men who arrested, followed, and ambushed the three civil rights workers. Nothing in the public record suggests that men like Rainey, Price, Roberts, or Jordan had any connections to, much less awareness of, Christian Identity theology. Yet nothing suggests that the men who bombed the Sixteenth Street Baptist Church the year before were anything other than southern nationalists and bigots either. But the men who killed Schwerner, Goodman, and Chaney did not do so impulsively. They were under orders. And to understand just how insidious the ideology of Christian Identity is, to see how it likely tainted some of the worst acts of domestic terrorism in American history, one must go beyond the men who follow orders to those who instigate and exploit these events. One must look at people like Samuel Holloway Bowers.

Bowers, the first Imperial Wizard of the White Knights of the Ku Klux Klan of Mississippi (WKKKKOM) and the mastermind behind the murder of the three civil rights workers in Neshoba County, Mississippi, fifty years ago, did not fit the caricature of a backward racist. Educated as an engineer at the University of Southern California and at Tulane University (he did not complete the degree), he was described by associates as an ideologically driven strategist.

"He is very intelligent. I have no question about that," Thomas Tarrants, once the self-described chief terrorist for Bowers, told journalist Patsy Sims for her book *The Klan*. "And I believe he was like I was, indoctrinated, brainwashed. . . . Absorbed into an ideology that took on the awe of a holy cause and blinded his mind to everything else. I think Sam believes what he is doing is right and has the sanction of God."[6]

Tarrants later renounced racism and is currently an ordained evangelical minister. But at one time he saw himself as occupying the same unique space as Bowers in the counterrevolution against integration and desegregation: that of a holy warrior. As Bowers described it to theologian Charles Marsh in 1994:

> There are two really powerful figures in the world: the priest and the preacher. I think I came here as a priest, though not a preacher. A priest is interested in visible, public power relations; this is what makes him powerful as a warrior. A preacher is an evangelist; he will tell people what to do. But the priest will arrange the means and operations to implement this into concrete action. When the priest sees the heretic, he can do only one thing: he eliminates him.[7]

Scholars have been confused by Bowers's protestations that religion drove his activities. Religion, to many historians, was simply a cover for white supremacists of all stripes to retroactively justify their racial animus—epitomized by the ritual burning of the cross. Despite this mind-set, Marsh chose to view Bowers through the prism of mainstream Christianity. Marsh recognized religion as a motivating force behind Bowers's activities. For Bowers, anyone who accepted communism—which for him included almost anyone in the civil rights movement—had embraced a godless ideology and relinquished God's grace. Consequently, Bowers used creative interpretations and rationalizations of the Bible to justify his militant actions. In this rendering, Bowers is still a reactionary, vigilante racist, but one who attempts to sincerely reconcile his actions with his conventional Christian faith.

But new research suggests that religion not only drove Bowers's violent activities but also influenced his tactics in ways that were opaque not simply to outside observers but even to rank-and-file members within the WKKKKOM, the group Bowers led from 1964 through 1968. Bowers made a point of hiding his true motivations, according to Delmar Dennis, a high-ranking WKKKKOM member who became the FBI's most important informant inside the group. "The typical Mississippi redneck doesn't have sense enough to know what he is doing," Dennis described Bowers as saying to him privately. "I have to use him for my own cause and direct his every action to fit my plan."[8]

The historical record now makes it clear that Bowers's goal was to incite a holy race war. Marsh and other experts on Bowers recognize that as of 1967, Bowers had embraced the radical interpretation of Christianity espoused by the Christian Identity movement, which devalued people of color as subhuman and saw Jews as satanic conspirators against Anglo-Saxon whites. What many have failed to see was that, in the hands of a militant like Bowers, this theology became the driving force behind his violent strategy and tactics. The record indicates that Bowers likely embraced this theology early in his tenure as the head of the WKKKKOM, possibly before he became its leader. Evidence suggests that Bowers likely planned the Neshoba County murders with this religious worldview as his guide. Viewed through the lens of religious terrorism, the murders on the night of June 21, 1964, of Mickey Schwerner, Andrew Goodman, and James Chaney become even more dark and twisted than they appeared at the time. Rather than simply trying to thwart the Freedom Summer set to begin shortly after the three civil rights activists disappeared, Bowers's plans appear to have been more ominous and far reaching.

There is little doubt that the religious dimensions to Bowers's racism began before he became a Grand Wizard. Born in New Orleans in 1924, Samuel Holloway Bowers Jr. told Marsh that he developed his interest in religion during World War II. But it was in 1955, when he was disillusioned to the point of near suicide, that Bowers experienced a life-changing spiritual event. According to Marsh:

On a drive along a two-lane highway on a late summer afternoon in south Mississippi, contemplating suicide and equipped for the task, Bowers felt suddenly transported by a power greater than he had ever before experienced. In a moment of mystical intensity,

God spoke to him. . . . "The living God made himself real to me even when I did not deserve it."[9]

This religious impulse would manifest itself in the way Bowers ran the WKKKKOM. He opened every meeting with a prayer and was always seen with a Bible. Even as the group he commanded engaged in a bonanza of violence—including, per Marsh, "nine murders, seventy-five bombings of black churches, and three hundred assaults, bombings, and beatings"—Bowers believed that "a *Solemn, determined Spirit* of Christian Reverence must be stimulated in all members" of the WKKKKOM. When he was finally convicted, three decades late, for the murder of Mississippi NAACP leader Vernon Dahmer, Bowers's defense lawyers relied on witnesses who pointed to Bowers's service as a Sunday school teacher in the 1990s in hopes of bolstering Bowers's character in the opinion of the jury. And there were a lot of "character flaws" to overcome. In 1966 Bowers arranged for Dahmer's home to be firebombed, almost killing Dahmer's wife and children; the voting rights activist died from smoke inhalation and burns he incurred while laying down cover fire as his family escaped the residence.

But what seems like a fundamental contradiction to anyone familiar with the nonviolent teachings of Jesus in the New Testament was, to Bowers, something consistent with the worldview of a rapidly growing and militant Christian sect: the Christian Identity movement. It now appears likely that this radical offshoot of Christianity may have gained purchase with Bowers by 1964, the year he took command of the newly formed WKKKKOM, and that it likely played a key role in motivating and shaping the contours of the Mississippi Burning killings.

Specifically, Bowers likely planned the Mississippi Burning killings with the same theological motivation described by Tommy Tarrants. It was the same mind-set that likely motivated Noah Carden and his fellow Identity followers to attempt to kill Martin Luther King Jr. in Birmingham: to further provoke already boiling racial tensions in hopes that such killings would trigger a holy race war.

Mississippi, a state with the most serious history of racial violence in the nation, would be a perfect place to start such a conflagration.

Mississippi had one of the largest concentrations of people of color in the entire South. This not only included African Americans but Chinese Americans (present since the construction of railroads) and Native Americans. Together, these groups represented a near majority of the state's population, and in certain areas of Mississippi a clear majority. The civil rights movement threatened the social and political fabric of Mississippi, undergirded by white supremacy, like no other state in the South. Something as simple as a lunch counter sit-in, which in states like Tennessee broke segregated dining places with little or no retaliation, elicited horrific violence in a city like Jackson, Mississippi. Such hostility, much like the 1962 Ole Miss race riots, came from people with no obvious KKK affiliations; it was spontaneous mob violence. If he looked to the black community, Bowers saw civil rights groups committed to a policy of nonviolence but that, as in Birmingham in May and September of 1963, could tip into violence under the right circumstances. The murder of Medgar Evers broke a period of relative calm in June 1963 and nearly caused a major race riot in Jackson. Mississippi held the promise, to someone immersed in Christian Identity eschatology, of white-versus-black violence.

With the newly formed White Knights of the Ku Klux Klan of Mississippi, five thousand strong according to some estimates, Bowers had the vehicle to initiate this strategy. No state had more racial lynchings in its history than the Magnolia State, yet violence before 1963 did not stop the Civil Rights Act. By the end of 1963, hard-core racists in Mississippi believed that their local White Citizens Councils, more actively pro-segregation than most similar groups throughout the nation, were too passive. Even other active Ku Klux Klan groups, such as the United Klans of America, appeared too weak to a sizable subset of Mississippi racists. Bowers and others formed the White Knights of the Ku Klux Klan of Mississippi from the Original Knights of the Ku Klux Klan, a reactionary group with membership in northern Louisiana and southern Mississippi. The WKKKKOM quickly grew its membership to an estimated five thousand people. But these were southern nationalists, not Christian Identity radicals. Bowers told Delmar Dennis that he had to manipulate these "rednecks" to fit his plan. He also described that plan to Dennis:

Bowers outlined on a blackboard the overall strategy of which
the White Knights were merely a part. He said he was trying to
create a race war, and open violence on the part of white Mississippians against native Negro citizens and civil rights agitators. He
predicted that Secretary of Defense Robert McNamara would be
required to send troops into Mississippi to restore order. Martial
law would be declared and the state would be under full dictato-
rial control from Washington. The excuse for the control would
be the race war he was helping to create by engendering hatred
among whites in the same manner as it was being fomented by
leftist radicals among blacks.[10]

Unfortunately, Dennis is not clear on the timing of this revelation,
although the context suggests it was in 1964. That Bowers shared
the same vision as Tarrants and his Identity mentors is likely not
an accident. Bowers could have been influenced by the same kind
of ideology at roughly the same impressionable age Tarrants was
when he became enthralled by Swift. In 1947, sixteen years before
Tarrants had dropped out of high school to become a true believer
in the white supremacist cause, Bowers was an engineering student
at the University of Southern California. This was the same time that
people like Bertrand Comparet, San Jacinto Capt, and Wesley Swift
were formulating and propagating two-seedline Christian Identity.
There is no direct evidence that Bowers was exposed to Swift's message when Swift was beginning his ministry. But, according to Marsh,
in the late 1940s, after his stay in California, Bowers returned home
to Mississippi and began studying religion alongside Nazi ideology.

What is without question is that within twenty years, Bowers,
like a number of bigots in Mississippi, was undoubtedly under the
sway of Wesley Swift and the Christian Identity movement. FBI documents show that in 1967, when Bowers set up a covert hit team
led by Tarrants, WKKKKOM leaders referred to it as the Swift Underground. Investigative reporter Jerry Mitchell describes Bowers
and Tarrants enthusiastically discussing Swift's latest taped sermons.
Even experts on Christian Identity, such as the late Ole Miss professor Chester Quarles, believed that Bowers joined the Christian
Identity movement no later than 1967. The key question, when it

comes to the motive for the Mississippi Burning murders, is whether or not Bowers fell under the influence of Swift as early as the summer of 1964. Some might argue that his lack of attention to targeting Jewish institutions and individuals in 1964 (in contrast to the wave of anti-Jewish attacks he ordered in 1967) suggests that Bowers was not yet under Swift's influence.

But it appears as though Bowers tried to get the WKKKKOM to target Jews but failed. FBI informant reports show Bowers attempting to convince the WKKKKOM to move in an anti-Jewish direction as early as 1965. According to informants, Bowers told the group that there are two kinds of KKK groups: those that target "niggers" and those that target Jews. He hoped the WKKKKOM would focus on the latter, as Jews, in Bowers's estimation, were the root of the racial problems in the South. But Bowers could not convince his rank-and-file members to target Jews. To the average racist, blacks, outside agitators, and the federal government were the obvious threats to white supremacy, not southern Jews. It was only after the success of the Civil Rights Act of 1964 and the Voting Rights Act of 1965, when his membership had diminished to a few hundred hard-core followers, that Bowers could redirect his efforts against Jews, and then only with a closely controlled group of Swift followers who, like Tarrants, shared Bowers's anti-Semitic sensibilities.

For Bowers to target Jews in 1964, he had to align his anti-Semitic worldview within the broader framework of violent resistance to integration. Just as he had told Delmar Dennis, Bowers had to manipulate his rank-and-file members without their knowledge. He could not explicitly attack Jews unless Jews were directly involved in promoting civil rights. The evidence suggests that the murders of Schwerner, Goodman, and Chaney provided Bowers with just such an opportunity.

To say that the murder of the three civil rights workers in the Mississippi Burning murders was an act of religious terrorism is not the same thing as saying that anti-Semitic animus played a role in the murder of the two Jewish men. Anti-Semitism had a long history within the Ku Klux Klan going back to the 1920s, when a wave of anti-immigrant sentiment, directed in large part at Jews and Catholics, helped fuel a resurgence of the KKK, with membership growing into the millions. When the KKK revived from its post–Great Depression dormancy in the 1950s in response to the civil rights movement, anti-Jewish rhetoric was still a feature of Klan literature. What distinguished ideological (Christian Identity) terrorist groups like the NSRP from conventional racist organizations like the United Klans of America was their willingness to both violently attack Jewish targets and use extreme, provocative violence even when it was certain to invite a federal response. The goal for the religious terrorist is to create a new world order, and for the Swift follower in the 1960s, this meant eliciting a holy race war. Three lines of evidence suggest that, while the actual perpetrators of the awful crimes of June 21, 1964, were not religious terrorists, the attack itself was shaped by Sam Bowers's religious worldview (likely without the actual perpetrators' knowledge).

One line of evidence relates to Sam Bowers's own rhetoric, which is both cryptic and suggestive. Many scholars have pointed to the comment by Bowers that the attack on the three civil rights workers was "the first time that Christians had planned and carried out the execution of a Jew."[11] This is in keeping with the prevailing view of the crime, that its chief target was Schwerner, who had worked in the WKKKKOM stronghold of Meridian on behalf of CORE for weeks before Freedom Summer. The more telling rhetoric, however, comes from the earliest pieces of propaganda produced by the White Knights in the wake of Freedom Summer. In the fall of 1964, several weeks after law enforcement found the bodies of the three men in an earthen dam at Olan Burrage's property, Bowers produced a new edition of the *Klan Ledger*, a periodical, much like the NSRP's *The Thunderbolt*, that spread racist propaganda. "The 'long, hot summer,' has passed," the periodical read. Referring to the civil rights activists who worked to register black voters during Freedom Summer, Bowers claimed they had "no laurels to their credit, and the general public of Mississippi has had a fill of their very existence. . . . For the success of our struggle against this scum, we offer our thanks to Almighty God, our Creator and Saviour."[12] What followed was an extended rant, theological and political, directed at civil rights sympathizers and the federal government, but primarily at Jews. It is here that the early Identity influence on Bowers becomes evident.

The rant begins by referencing two sections of the book of Revelations: 2:9–10 and 3:9. These passages reference the "Synagogue of Satan" and those who "lie" and "say they are Jews." As Chester Quarles has noted, these specific New Testament passages are foundational texts for two-seedline CI adherents. Under two-seed theology, Jews have conspired to convince the world that they are the chosen people, when in fact they are the offspring of Satan. If there is any doubt that this is the thinking of Bowers, the *Klan Ledger* continues, "Today's so-called Jews persecute Christians, seeking to deceive, claiming Judea as their homeland and they are God's Chosen. . . . They 'do Lie,' for they are not Judeans, but Are the Synagogue of Satan!" It adds, "If a Jew is not capable of functioning as an individual, and must take part in Conspiracies to exist on this earth, that is his problem." Passages also reference "Jew consulting anti-Christs" and assert that "Satan and the Anti-Christ stalk the land."[13]

Again, anti-Semitism was common to KKK groups in the 1960s. But it was often in the same form as anti-Semitism the world over—the claim that Jews were responsible for the death of Jesus. The refusal of Jews, the chosen people of the Old Testament, to accept Jesus as their Messiah is the other long-standing grievance leveled against Jews by hostile gentiles. What distinguishes Christian Identity from other forms of anti-Semitism is the blatant rejection that Jews were ever the chosen people, that they were ever in a position to accept Jesus as their savior in the first place. Swift and his followers frequently referred to what he called Ashkenazi Jews as imposters. That this line of thinking is evident in a periodical so close to the MIBURN murders suggests that Bowers had accepted this idea before 1967. Was this theological worldview a motivation for the actual MIBURN crime?

Bowers's rhetoric on the eve of the murders strongly suggests it may have been. In a speech on June 7, 1964, two weeks prior to the Neshoba murders, Bowers predicted a groundbreaking event to his followers—most of whom had no idea that the attack in Neshoba was in the works. Many have assumed that Bowers was simply foreshadowing the upcoming conflict over Freedom Summer. But the proximity of the speech to the murder of the three activists, and Bowers's certainty that there would be violence and federal intervention within days, suggests the likelihood that Bowers had the upcoming killings on his mind when he spoke to the rank and file. Many experts believe that planning for the crime had begun as early as May, after Mickey Schwerner began his work in Meridian, Mississippi, on behalf of CORE. Two elements of this speech are worth highlighting, and they point to the likelihood that Bowers saw the Neshoba murders as a potential entrée into the cycle of violence that Swift followers believed would escalate into an end-times race war. Taken together with other facts, they represent two additional lines of evidence suggesting the crime was an act of religious terrorism.

In his June 7 speech, Bowers begins with a prayer and then tells his audience, "This summer . . . the enemy will launch his final push for victory here in Mississippi." Bowers then speaks in military terms, saying that the enemy will have "two basic salients." The first would be "massive street demonstrations and agitation by blacks in many areas at once, designed to provoke white militants into counterdemonstration and open, pitched street battles," which would then lead to a "decree from the communist authorities in charge of the national government . . . declaring martial law."[14] Bowers then outlines the WKKKKOM's plan of response—a combination of outwardly "legal" resistance alongside local authorities and a "secondary group" who use guerrilla tactics as part of a "swift and extremely violent hit-and-run" strategy. To the rank and file to whom he was speaking, Bowers presented this as an unfortunate but necessary (and imminent) future. But again, he was addressing people who had never heard anything like Christian Identity theology in their churches on Sundays. More to the point, Bowers surely knew that federal intervention of any kind in the South, especially in Mississippi, was bound to be offensive to his audience. These were many of the same people who had violently attacked National Guardsmen sent by President Kennedy to protect James Meredith when he integrated the University of Mississippi in 1962. To welcome such intervention would be anathema to a group of people schooled in the idea that the northern military occupation of the South during Reconstruction was a travesty of the first order.

. . . If anything, Bowers's actions after the Neshoba murders only would have courted the federal intervention that most of his followers abhorred. Bowers escalated the violence in Mississippi—as many as sixty-five bombings occurred during Freedom Summer[15]— at a time when polls showed that the general public favored massive federal intervention in Mississippi if the violence in that state persisted. When he outwardly placed a moratorium on violence in response to the growing presence of federal law enforcement, Bowers stopped bombings only in counties that were subject to intense law enforcement scrutiny. In fact, he actually asked for violence to increase in outlying counties to divert the FBI's resources. It seems likely that at least part of the violence that marked Freedom Summer was intended to provoke further federal intervention. To say otherwise is to impute a level of ignorance to Bowers that none of his contemporaries describe.

But one aspect of the Neshoba murder plot certainly suggests that Bowers was creating the very conditions likely to generate federal intervention and thus his envisioned racial holy war. This was the decision to bury the three men deep beneath the earthen dam at Old Jolly Farm. Many scholars believe the decision to use the dam was conceived as far back as May, a level of planning that itself was remarkable. Certainly, disposing of bodies was not unknown in Klan violence. But it was almost always ad hoc—as evidenced by the other bodies discovered in Mississippi swamps and marshes during the search for the three missing activists. To make arrangements to carefully bury bodies weeks in advance of a crime is largely unknown in the annals of racial violence. For someone hoping that federal intervention would antagonize white southerners, such an action was a stroke of genius. It would all but guarantee that federal law enforcement would spend days, if not weeks, searching through Mississippi to find the three men, especially if the activists' burned car was left out in the open for law enforcement to find first. And recall that during the mounting federal intervention to find the men, the WKKKKOM expanded its reign of terror. Other records show that if Bowers had had his way, things likely would have gotten much worse in Mississippi.

In the same June 7 speech where he foreshadowed "pitched battles" between whites and blacks in Mississippi, Bowers insisted that the primary targets for "any personal attacks" be "the leaders and the prime white collaborators of the enemy." FBI evidence revealed in my coauthored book *The Awful Grace of God* suggests that Bowers had reached out to a criminal network, including a professional hit man, with the goal of assassinating Martin Luther King Jr. if he came to Mississippi in 1964. Other FBI documents show that the WKK-KKOM openly discussed the possibility of "eliminating" King at its meetings.[16] But this goal presented a problem for the WKKKKOM: King rarely visited Mississippi before the summer of 1964, and he did so unexpectedly. What was clear, from the Birmingham bombing and the assassination of Medgar Evers the previous year, was that an outrageous act of violence would provoke King to visit the scene of the crime and to lead protests and services against such violence. It is speculative, but if Bowers wanted to lure King into an ambush, an act of violence like the Neshoba murders may well have been planned to trigger just such an opportunity.

This is not simply a case of imputing a level of cunning and tactical sophistication to Bowers after the fact. Many believe that the burning of the Mount Zion Church in Meridian, Mississippi, on June 20, 1964, was part of a similar plan: to lure Schwerner (and Goodman and Chaney) back to Mississippi. If so, it worked; the three men abandoned their Freedom Summer volunteer training sessions in Oxford, Ohio, and came to Mississippi on June 20 to investigate the Mount Zion Church burning.

In further support of this theory, evidence presented at the 1999 trial of one of the murderers of African American farmer Ben Chester White in Natchez, Mississippi, in 1966 showed that Bowers plotted White's murder with a similar strategy in mind: to lure King to Natchez for an ambush. If King came to protest White's seemingly wanton and senseless murder (White had no known connection to civil rights activity), King could be more easily and sensationally assassinated. Both the 1964 and the 1966 plots against King failed, as the terrorist acts did not result in King changing his itinerary—possibly because FBI informant Dennis had warned law enforcement about an assassination attempt in advance.

As with the CI/NSRP plots against King in the wake of the Birmingham bombing the previous September, any effort to kill King would have exacerbated racial tensions emanating from the Neshoba murders. The murder of NAACP leader Medgar Evers the previous summer had provoked race riots in Mississippi. Any reasonable person would have expected that killing King, the spokesperson for the civil rights movement, would have a similar impact, one that would have the added bonus to an Identity enthusiast of being national in scope. The murder of Martin Luther King Jr. had been a goal of Identity followers as far back as 1958.

It seems likely that Bowers was motivated by religious ideology when he planned the Mississippi Burning murders. On the other hand, there is no direct evidence that this ideology motivated the men who lured Schwerner, Goodman, and Chaney to Mississippi, jailed them under false pretenses, shadowed them by car, and kidnapped and ultimately shot them in cold blood fifty years ago. These men, including law enforcement officers, were likely motivated by the bigotry and irrational fear that informed so many acts of violence in the South. But Bowers's case shows how the leaders who planned and plotted these acts of violence could share an agenda that coincided and went beyond the goals of protecting the so-called southern way of life. The leaders of some of America's most radical groups wanted to create their own version of Armageddon. They believed, alongside the Reverend Wesley Swift, that the secular world was in its final days and that soon the day would come when the forces of God would do battle with the forces of Satan.

Within two months of the Neshoba killings, America officially entered a conflict against the communist-backed North Vietnamese. By the end of 1964, growing frustration with the pace of political change had created a major schism within the civil rights movement, between those who continued to favor nonviolence and those who favored militancy and black nationalism. Together, these two developments would escalate social upheaval in the United States and around the world, forcing law enforcement to resort to unprecedented tactics in its fight against extremists on both sides, left and right. To those listening to the sermons of Wesley Swift, his message of impending crisis and spiritual renewal was becoming more appealing.

6

THE GRAPES OF WRATH

BLACK MILITANT
REACTION *and the*
URBAN RIOTS *of*
1964–1965

The White Knights of the Ku Klux Klan of Mississippi failed to meet their immediate goals with the Neshoba murders. Among other things, they failed to intimidate the thousands of volunteers coming to Mississippi for Freedom Summer—the campaign to register black voters and to educate black children. They even failed to intimidate the large numbers of local black Mississippians who participated in Freedom Summer, housing activists from the COFO, registering to vote, and sending their children to Freedom Schools (organized by activists to teach a civics-heavy, Afrocentric curriculum to black Mississippi students). The public outcry over the Neshoba murders spurred the FBI to launch a massive investigation into the crime, resulting in the creation of an FBI field office in Jackson, Mississippi. Despite the KKK's efforts, President Lyndon B. Johnson signed the Civil Rights Act of 1964 on July 2, effectively ending legal discrimination in America. And the murders breathed new life into Johnson's other initiative: to pass comprehensive voting rights legislation.

At first blush, the outcome seemed to undermine the hidden agenda of Sam Bowers as well. After all, Bowers had predicted, to Delmar Dennis, a massive federal intervention creating a cycle of violence between blacks and whites. Neither happened—certainly not to the degree that Bowers wanted. But Sam Bowers and his fellow devotees of radical Christian Identity theology were playing the long game. And in the years that followed the Mississippi Burning murders, Bowers and his fellow religious extremists could only have been pleased with social developments, not only in Mississippi but in America as a whole.

In September 1964, with the help of informant Delmar Dennis, authorities uncovered the bodies of the three slain civil rights activists at Olan Burrage's farm. By December, a U.S. commissioner

from Mississippi had voided the indictments of all nineteen men responsible for the killings. Fed up, thirty-seven teenage activists from
the Student Nonviolent Coordinating Committee (SNCC) met with
Mississippi Freedom Democratic Party leader Fannie Lou Hamer at
Hotel Theresa in New York City to listen to famed Muslim minister
and human rights activist Malcolm X. Urging his young audience to
"see for yourself and listen for yourself and think for yourself," the
former spokesman for the militant black separatist group the Nation
of Islam (NOI) continued:

> If the leaders of the nonviolent movement can go into the white
> community and teach nonviolence, good. I'd go along with that.
> But as long as I see them teaching nonviolence only in the black
> community, we can't go along with that. We believe in equality,
> and equality means that you have to put the same thing over here
> that you put over there. And if black people alone are going to
> be the ones who are nonviolent, then it's not fair. We throw our-
> selves off guard. In fact, we disarm ourselves and make ourselves
> defenseless.[1]

Malcolm X had befriended members of SNCC in a chance encounter with SNCC leaders on a tour of Africa. Highlighting the need
to link the African American civil rights struggle to similar liberation
movements in Africa, the activist asserted, "Whenever anything happens to you in Mississippi, it's not just a case of somebody in Alabama
getting indignant, or somebody in New York getting indignant. The
same repercussions that you see all over the world when an imperialist or foreign power interferes in some section of Africa—you see
repercussions, you see the embassies being bombed and burned and
overturned—nowadays, when something happens to black people in
Mississippi, you'll see the same repercussions all over the world."[2]
Malcolm X and the group he once served, the NOI, had long
argued that violence, especially in retaliation for harassment, was
not only acceptable but was politically and morally necessary.
Though he had split from the NOI and softened his antagonism
toward whites as a race, he still favored fighting fire with fire. He
closed his exhortation to his New York City audience by adding,

"You'll get freedom by letting your enemy know that you'll do anything to get your freedom; then you'll get it. It's the only way you'll
get it. When you get that kind of attitude, they'll label you as a 'crazy
Negro,' or they'll call you a 'crazy nigger'—they don't say Negro. Or
they'll call you an extremist or a subversive, or seditious, or a red or
a radical. But when you stay radical long enough, and get enough
people to be like you, you'll get your freedom."[3]

According to Stokely Carmichael, an SNCC leader in Mississippi
at the time, the young activists returned to the Magnolia State very
impressed with what Malcolm X had to say. For years, Malcolm X
had been the most outspoken voice for armed self-defense in the
civil rights struggle. Now, after the killing of Medgar Evers, after
the Neshoba murders and the multiple bombings that followed, his
message began to have much more resonance.

The debate over armed resistance in nonviolent organizations,
such as SNCC and CORE, predated the Neshoba murders. As far
back as 1963, members had proposed softening or eliminating
written policy banning the use or brandishing of firearms. On the
eve of Freedom Summer, in June 1964, the debate reemerged in anticipation of massive violence from Bowers's Klan. The proposals
failed, but the reality was that many civil rights activists either quietly
flouted the mandate against armed resistance (for example, Medgar
Evers had carried a weapon for protection) or relied on others, including the local black farmers who welcomed activists into their
homes and communities, to provide armed protection. Many civil
rights activists, including Stokely Carmichael, regarded nonviolence
simply as a tactic to win public support, not as a philosophy and
moral code (à la Martin Luther King Jr.). Others had abandoned the
pretense of nonviolence years before; as far back as 1956, Robert
Williams, president of the Monroe, North Carolina, chapter of the
NAACP, had gathered armed men to confront the KKK. King and
others had shown the political value of nonviolence in Alabama and
elsewhere, but the Neshoba murders and the wave of bombings that
immediately followed went a long way to changing attitudes about
armed self-defense. Famously, at the funeral for the three murdered
activists, SNCC activist Dave Dennis asserted:

I'm sick and tired of going to the funerals of black men who have been murdered by white men. . . . I've got vengeance in my heart, and I ask you to feel angry with me. . . . If you go back home and sit down and take what these white men in Mississippi are doing to us . . . if you take it and don't do something about it . . . then God damn your souls![4]

Just one month before the thirty-seven students heard Malcolm X speak in New York City, a seemingly minor event in Waveland, Mississippi, foreshadowed this shift in approach. In his book *We Will Shoot Back: Armed Resistance in the Mississippi Freedom Movement,* Professor Akinyele Omowale Umoja describes an attack on an SNCC staff retreat that November 1964:

Retreat participants were alerted when they heard a low-flying plane soaring near the facilities. Later that evening, a vehicle drove near the meeting place and threw a Molotov cocktail on a nearby pier. Suddenly, several male members of SNCC ran from the meeting carrying arms, and the nightriders were abducted and released after a warning from the young freedom fighters. Lorne Cress, a Chicago native and SNCC staffer in McComb, was surprised by the armed response from her comrades. Up until that day, she had believed she was a member of a non-violent organization. She turned to Howard Zinn—a college professor, historian, and advisor to SNCC—and stated, "You have just witnessed the end of the non-violent movement."[5]

But the nonviolent movement was not quite dead. King and others would score another moral victory with their voting rights protests in Selma, Alabama, the following year. The widely publicized scenes of armed police officers on horseback beating unarmed protestors with batons shocked the nation, giving President Johnson's Voting Rights Act the public support it needed to pass. With its passage, almost every state-level obstacle to constitutionally guaranteed voting rights—notably literacy tests—was removed. But for many in the African American community, the legislation—and the civil rights act that had preceded it—were not enough to pacify their increasingly growing frustration with the status quo.

More and more, economic concerns joined political concerns for African Americans. In the 1960s, America entered into a period of rapid economic dislocation as countless numbers of factories closed, reopening in cheaper labor markets outside the nation. This foreign outsourcing profoundly affected the African American community in many cities. The types of factory jobs that had lured waves of African American migrants to abandon the life of southern sharecropping and that could, in the post–World War II economic boom, sustain a nuclear family on one income, were disappearing. Even when such jobs were available, discriminatory lending practices and prejudicial housing schemes (called redlining) forced even middle-class blacks into ghettos. These were injustices not addressed in either of the two major pieces of legislation in 1964 and 1965.

In fact, the two laws changed little for black Americans outside the South. Northern and western cities already permitted blacks to vote (and had done so for decades), and blacks there faced little in the way of overt legal discrimination. One rarely saw formally segregated bathrooms, swimming pools, or dining facilities in these regions. But what African Americans there did face was de facto discrimination, which was just as pernicious. One found all-black and all-white schools, not because of the legacy of *Plessy v. Ferguson* but because of historical patterns of housing discrimination and economic prejudice—the kind that allowed blacks to work in factory jobs but refused them entry into many labor unions. And while the attacks on nonviolent protestors in the land of Jim Crow scandalized the rest of the country, the nation all but ignored similar problems elsewhere. America's police departments were among the most racially homogenous labor sectors in the nation—not just in the South but in almost every major city in the country. And urban blacks were all too familiar with the kind of discrimination and harassment that generally accompanied an all-white police force. In northern and western cities, this harassment was among the most serious forms of overt racism they faced. But by 1964, many were no longer prepared to turn the other cheek.

The first major crack in the national nonviolent facade came one month after the Neshoba murders. The Associated Press described events in New York that began on July 19:

Missiles rained from roofs, crowds knocked down barricades, fists and knives flashed in the steady heat, and police guns barked. Harlem was rioting. . . . The initial outburst followed protest rallies over the fatal shooting of a Negro boy by a white policeman. The violence left one man shot to death, 108 arrested and more than 100 injured, including a dozen patrolmen.[6]

Soon the unrest spread to nearby Bedford-Stuyvesant and then to Brooklyn, continuing for six days and leading to more than 450 arrests. More riots began soon afterward in upstate New York in response to perceived police abuses in Rochester. United Press International described "three successive nights" (July 24 to 27) of "violence and pillage," including "hurled rocks, bottles and firebombs." At one point, "three persons were killed when a Civil Defense helicopter . . . crashed into a rooming house turning it into an inferno." In response to the chaos, the UPI noted, "New York Governor Nelson Rockefeller committed 1,200 to 1,300 National Guardsmen to the riot-torn city." By the end of the three days, 555 people had been arrested; the "burned buildings and looted stores" resulted in "over one million dollars worth of damages."[7]

The rage continued to spread as quickly as a virus. That August, urban race riots flared in Jersey City, Paterson, and Elizabeth, New Jersey, again in response to perceived police abuses. Soon the rioting reached Philadelphia, where just the rumor that an African American woman had been killed by police sparked unrest in the area near Temple University. According to Dr. Ellesia Ann Blaque, over two days the area "was battered and looted by thousands of people. When the riot ended, more than 300 people were injured, close to 800 had been arrested, and over 220 stores and businesses were damaged or permanently devastated."[3] Later in August, another riot broke out in Dixmoor, Illinois, just south of Chicago.

All in all, there were eleven urban riots in 1964, with two killed, 996 injured, almost three thousand arrests, and more than 230 acts of arson. It was the most widespread race-related rioting since the Red Summer of 1919, which saw twenty-six racially motivated riots between April and October. In 1965 matters got notably more intense. For a second year there were eleven riots in the United States, but this time there were thirty-five killed, more than one thousand injured, more than four thousand arrested, and, stunningly, more than three thousand acts of arson.[9]

The bulk of this staggering increase (thirty-four of the thirty-five killed and more than nine hundred of the one thousand injured) came from a single event: the August 1965 riots in the Watts section of Los Angeles. Following the arrest of a black driver by a white police officer on suspicion of drunk driving, a crowd of blacks pelted the police with rocks and bottles. The tension escalated, and the riot—the most destructive in U.S. history to that point—raged for six days. *Time* magazine called the rioting an "Arson and Street War" on one cover, and *Life* magazine printed the cover headline "Out of a Cauldron of Hate." The latter featured a "menacing image of an angry black youth. The underlying caption read, 'Get Whitey!'"[10]

Martin Luther King Jr., a recent winner of the Nobel Peace Prize, visited Watts in an attempt to promote calm. At one point he addressed a crowd:

> However much we don't like to hear it, and I must tell the truth. I'm known to tell the truth. While we have legitimate gripes, while we have legitimate discontent, we must not hate all white people, because I know white people now. . . . Don't forget that when we marched from Selma to Montgomery, it was a white woman who died on that highway 80, Viola Liuzzo. We want to know what we can do to create right here in Los Angeles a better city, and a beloved community. So speak out of your hearts and speak frankly.[11]

The response Dr. King received symbolized what would become a growing schism within the civil rights movement. An unidentified attendee from the crowd insisted:

> The only way we can ever get anybody to listen to us is to start a riot. We got sense enough to know that this is not the final answer,

but it's a beginning. We know it has to stop, we know it's going to stop. We don't want any more of our people killed, but how many have been killed for nothing? At least those who died died doing something. No, I'm not for a riot. But who wants to lay down while somebody kicks em to death? As long as we lay down we know we're gonna get kicked. It's a beginning; it may be the wrong beginning but at least we got em listening. And they know that if they start killing us off, it's not gonna be a riot it's gonna be a war.[12]

Dr. King did not see this warning as hyperbole. Having received a less-than-warm response in his Watts visit, and having failed to negotiate a truce between local black leaders and the white political establishment in Los Angeles, King briefed his political ally President Lyndon B. Johnson about the situation on the ground. In a private conversation, the Reverend King worried, "Now what is frightening is to hear all of these tones of violence from people in the Watts area and the minute that happens, there will be retaliation from the white community." He added, ominously, "People have bought up guns so that I am fearful that if something isn't done to give a new sense of hope to people in that area, that a full-scale race war can develop."[13]

Another minister, whose base of operations near Hollywood was not far from the riots, welcomed the prospects of just such a war. The Reverend Wesley Swift, in a sermon titled "Power for You Today," directly referenced the recent violence.

Don't let Watts suppress your souls, it's just, my friends, a demonstration of the animal nature of A SATANIC CONTROLLED SOCIETY IN UPROAR AGAINST GOD, AGAINST LAW, AGAINST RIGHTEOUSNESS, IT'S A PART OF A DESIGN TO INTIMIDATE YOU WITH THE FEAR OF THE BEAST, but I want you to know that with all these patterns, we are prepared to do the work of the Kingdom, to defend ourselves against any area of catastrophe, to defend ourselves against the Beast invasion, to participate in all the events that relate to the status of this day and TO FULFILL IT AS SONS AND DAUGHTERS OF GOD IN ACCORDANCE WITH THE KNOWLEDGE AND THE PURPOSE OF GOD'S PLAN.

This doesn't mean acquiescence to evil, it doesn't mean that we buy off evil, it doesn't mean we bribe people not to do the things which the enemy or the Kingdom would like to do. The way to handle some of these situations today is to meet them with power. The way, my friends, to put down an uprising is to march in the Police Force and the troops and then let it sit there afterwards and don't, my friends, reward people for their evil. Don't make people think by violence and uproar against the Kingdom of God that they are going to gain greater power and more expansive ends. Just remember that you are in a day WHEN IT'S THE SONS AND DAUGHTERS OF GOD WHO SHALL WAKE UP AND SHALL DETERMINE THE COURSE AND THE DESTINY OF AMERICA AND EVERY OTHER CHRISTIAN NATION AND EVENTUALLY THE WHOLE WORLD SHALL COME UNDER THE ADMINISTRATION OF GOD'S KINGDOM [emphasis in original].[14]

He returned to the subject of the riots shortly afterward:

You know why this is an important week? Because by its measures since they always start with the following cycles of the moon that three and a half years from that time was going to start THE JUDGMENTS IN THE HOUSE OF GOD UPON THE ENEMIES OF GOD'S KINGDOM AND THOSE THAT RISE UP TO DESTROY. Do you realize that would make the beginning of that period by its farthest perimeters this September which we're almost in and, of course, if you go back to the measure of when it happened, why, these riots were going on right in the beginning of that judgment time and I'm going to tell you something. It wasn't 35 that were killed, there were hundreds of them killed and hundreds of them that brought it on themselves. There are over a thousand bodies in those ruins right now. You say, how do you know? Because Guardsmen reported what happened when they were fired on, some of them had to kill 20 or 30 of them themselves for protection. Bodies were dumped back into burning stores because they were moving down the way. I know at this moment that there are a thousand dead minimum in that crisis.[15]

One cannot know if the Reverend Swift was deliberately exaggerating the casualties from the riots to manipulate his audience or if he, for some reason, believed his own propaganda. But he clearly saw the riots as a major sign that "we are in a climactic time." The minister continued:

> Someone said, oh, if we could only push these things off. I don't want to push it off, if I could bring it all in the next 24 hours, I'd precipitate it because I know GOD WOULD BE HERE BEFORE THE 24 HOURS WAS OVER. . . . WE ARE IN THE DAY, WE ARE IN THE CLIMAX, WE ARE IN THE EXPERIENCE OF WATCHING ONE AGE FOLD UP AND A NEW ONE COME IN, ONLY IT'S GOD'S DAY THIS TIME.[16]

Events of the next year only reinforced Swift's enthusiasm for an approaching Armageddon. The eleven riots in 1965 grew to fifty-three by the end of 1966. While there were fewer people killed and injured than in 1965, more rioters were arrested than in the previous year, because the nation had experienced 109 total days of urban rioting compared to just 20 in 1965. After occurring again in Los Angeles, riots broke out in Washington, D.C., Cleveland, Baltimore, and Atlanta. They even spread to unexpected cities such as Omaha, Nebraska, and Des Moines, Iowa.[17]

As Martin Luther King Jr. shifted his focus to de facto racism and economic issues in northern cities, he became increasingly frustrated by the growing tendency toward violence by both blacks and working-class whites. This trend became abundantly clear in Chicago, where King moved his movement and his family, famously living in a public housing tenement to highlight the poverty inherent in the city's racially tinged housing policies. Even after King managed to negotiate a ten-point deal with the city's political leadership, skeptical members of CORE launched a protest march in violation of King's agreement. Marching in all-white Cicero, Illinois—the site of a racial conflagration in 1951—250 protestors "were met by several hundred hecklers who hurled, rocks, eggs, and small explosives."[18] But this was an extremist group of CORE activists. Rather than turn the other cheek, they picked up the bottles and bricks and threw them back at the hecklers. In the end, the National Guard was needed to bring order to the city.

By 1966, to the dismay of Gandhian leaders like the Reverend Ed King and Martin Luther King, groups like CORE and SNCC openly embraced armed resistance in their charters. Borrowing from the late Malcolm X's famous phrase, they contended that liberation should be obtained by "any means necessary." But SNCC and CORE were relatively tame compared to other groups that rose to prominence in the mid-1960s. Most notable among these was the Black Panther Party, which formed in Oakland, California, in October 1966. As a sign of the growing shift in the disposition of civil rights activists toward violent resistance, the Panthers got the inspiration for their name from outspoken SNCC activist Stokely Carmichael, who in 1966 told an audience:

> In Lowndes County, we developed something called the Lowndes County Freedom Organization. It is a political party. The Alabama law says that if you have a Party you must have an emblem. We chose for the emblem a black panther, a beautiful black animal which symbolizes the strength and dignity of black people, an animal that never strikes back until he's back so far into the wall, he's got nothing to do but spring out. Yeah. And when he springs he does not stop.[19]

The Panthers also borrowed from Carmichael the much-misunderstood phrase that came to symbolize the growing schism between integrationists and black nationalists: "Black Power." Ostensibly a slogan of racial pride, self-determination, and equality, "Black Power" represented a "menace to peace and prosperity" to more conservative civil rights groups like the NAACP. Martin Luther King Jr., who valued the concept of black self-empowerment even as he demanded legal and socioeconomic recognition from the American government, argued that the concept was "unfortunate because it tends to give the impression of black nationalism . . . black supremacy would be as evil as white supremacy."[20] In the perception of the white political establishment, which was manifested in the media, "Black Power" became associated with separatism, violence, and militancy due its association with the Black Panther Party.

Making no effort to hide their revolutionary Marxism, the Panthers favored the violent overthrow of what they saw as America's imperialist and capitalist society, as a means to racial and economic liberation. While providing social services in the communities where they resided, the Panthers also responded to allegations of police brutality by brandishing shotguns, dressing in "radical chic" black clothing, and at times ambushing or engaging in pitched street battles with law enforcement officers.

The rise of the Panthers, the radicalization of once nonviolent groups like SNCC and CORE, the growing number of urban race riots—all of these affirmed the aspirations of those Swift devotees, like Sam Bowers, who hoped that conflicts between leftists in the black community and conservative whites would invite federal military intervention and escalate into a holy race war. Bowers privately told Delmar Dennis that he wanted to instigate such a conflict. And he continued to do his part, leading a group that from 1964 to 1968 would commit 300 of the estimated 538 acts of anti-black violence occurring since the *Brown v. Board of Education* decision in 1954. Joining Bowers in his effort to stoke the flames of white resentment were fellow CI devotees like the Reverend Connie Lynch, who in 1966 visited scenes of racial tension and urban riots, inciting white-on-black violence with his bombastic and virulently racist speeches. In Baltimore Lynch delivered what the UPI called the "To Hell with Niggers" rally, where Lynch "called for war against the city's Negroes. . . . After the rally broke up, gangs of white youths charged into a predominantly Negro area, throwing bottles at Negroes and attacking those they could lay their hands on with their fists."[21]

Clearly, as in the past, the CI radicals were not content to passively wait for Armageddon. Swift had insisted that they were already in the end-times and that his followers must actively participate in the events. Foreign affairs, notably the rapidly escalating war in Vietnam, which was exacerbating social divisions within the United States, reinforced Swift's notion that the world was "on the edge of terrific events."

But for all of the racial unrest in America after 1964, the prospects for white supremacist groups to actively accelerate Armageddon seemed dim—at least on the surface. While the Civil Rights Act of 1964 and the Voting Rights Act of 1965 did little to address the immediate socioeconomic concerns of the wider African American community, the two laws represented a double-fisted blow to overt white supremacist groups. Membership in racist groups across the country declined dramatically, and outside support fell as well. Congress and law enforcement began to openly turn against the KKK. Once southern nationalists lost the fight to save segregation and Jim Crow, the costs of staying in the organization greatly outweighed the benefits. The remaining members and leaders, who included several hard-core CI followers, appear to have faced a conundrum. Before 1965, when their organizations' memberships were at their highest, CI followers like Bowers had to work toward their hidden religious objectives by manipulating their fellow members. Now, in 1966, when conditions in the country finally seemed to conform to their religious worldview, these organizations seemingly lacked the membership to wage the prophesied race war.

But a deeper analysis suggests that the CI terrorists were far more dangerous in the late 1960s than people realize. The Minutemen, who were radical anti-communists, hid their white supremacist bona fides behind a veneer of pro-American militancy and were positioned to take advantage of the situation on the ground during the 1960s era of social upheaval. J. Edgar Hoover viewed the Minutemen as mildly dangerous due to their fondness for violence and their disregard for federal firearms regulations. But the FBI director did not consider the group nearly as threatening as the communist Black Panther Party, which he dubbed public enemy number one. As with other segregationist groups, CI leaders were found in the highest ranks of the Minutemen—a group perhaps better situated than any organization before or since to become foot soldiers in a national race war. But for the activity of an increasingly engaged law enforcement community in its cities and states (and eventually the federal government), America may have experienced the worst wave of terrorism in its history.

Swift had groups like the Minutemen in mind when, early in 1966, he delivered a sermon titled "Coming Liberation of America." He told his congregation and army of listeners:

> There is a strategy to destroy these United States forever, and to crush Christian Civilization and destroy the ability of HIS church to stand out and proclaim the truth. This is something that stirs the people to search for truth. This stirs some men to stand and denounce this evil strategy. It causes some men to respond with patriotic fury. It causes some men to band together and arm themselves for the show-down day. This design of Treason to destroy these United States has caused many men to react in many ways. There are men who are standing to dedicate their lives and their future in their fight to save these United States. They are ready to fight in the streets in all the cities of our nation, if that be necessary. There are those who are doing their utmost to awaken the people to this danger, and others who realize that it is very late but they are still looking for a solution to the best way to meet this situation and to save America.[22]

For years Swift and his fellow travelers, notably Colonel William Potter Gale, had nurtured militant, antigovernment patriot groups—those who saw in the growing power and scope of the federal government a fundamental threat to the American way of life. Anticipating the modern-day militia movements, these groups, such as Gale's California Rangers, acquired weapons and received paramilitary training to oppose what they believed would be a tyrannical government takeover of white society, not simply by the U.S. government but by the United Nations. Just as white supremacist groups aligned (often unknowingly) with Identity leaders on the issue of anti-black racism, antigovernment patriot groups aligned with CI ideology most clearly on the dangers posed by communism and one-world government.

As far back as at least 1963, religious terrorists like Gale and Swift envisioned these armed radicals as guerrilla-style strike teams that would go into action when the inevitable world-government

takeover took place, per their Biblical interpretations. George
Harding, who was a member of Swift's church, told the FBI in May
1963 that he was recruited to be part of one of several eight-person
military teams, with each group assigned to kill public officials and
business leaders when the time came.[23]

This information is consistent with Miami police informant reports from April 1963 regarding a meeting of the Congress of
Freedom, a white supremacist group with many Swift devotees in
its leadership. At the April 1963 meeting, attendees also spoke about
strike teams set to attack many leading (and mostly Jewish) officials
in the event of a United Nations takeover. It is worth noting that in
1964, Sam Bowers also spoke about elite strike teams that would
assassinate leading civil rights figures once federal troops had over-
whelmed Mississippi. Obviously, neither event—a UN takeover or a
federal usurpation of Mississippi—took place by 1964. But, in the
minds of CI followers, developments since that time pointed to an
even greater conflagration. More to the point, they were prepared to
make it happen if necessary.[24]

The Christian Identity movement found the perfect partner for
the revolutionary, guerrilla warfare it predicted in the Minutemen.
The group's membership and financial support appeared to increase
after 1965. It was also an organization with national reach and a
legacy of paramilitary training, Formed in 1960, supposedly by a
group of duck hunters who wanted to prepare an insurgency against
a future communist takeover, the group believed that *"any further
effort, time or money spent in trying to save our country by political means would be wasted. . . . Therefore the objectives of the
Minutemen are to abandon useless efforts and begin immediately
to prepare for the day when Americans will once again fight in the
streets for their lives and their liberty. We feel there is overwhelming
evidence to prove that this day must come."*[25]

Led by Robert Bolivar DePugh, a middle-aged businessman and
biochemist from Missouri with strong organizational skills, the
group did not at first embrace the strategy of provoking or instigating that day when, as Swift predicted in his sermon, "Americans
will once again fight in the streets for their lives and liberty." Known
to students of terrorism as the propaganda of the deed, this strategy

has been traced to anarcho-terrorists who attacked Western targets, including those in the United States, from the 1870s through the 1930s. "One deed is worth more than 10,000 pamphlets," one anarchist famously insisted. The idea was not only that actions speak louder than words but that those actions could elicit the kind of retribution from a target that would illustrate the ultimate goal of an ideological terrorist group.

For the anarcho-terrorists, this meant encouraging the state to crack down oppressively on its population in its hunt for subversive terrorists, proving the capacity for tyranny and violence that anarchists insisted was endemic to any government. For modern-day Islamic terrorists, it means baiting the West into invading Muslim nations to reveal to potential recruits and the Muslim world at large that the United States and its allies are enemies of Islam. For the Christian Identity terrorists, this meant polarizing the races into a would-be race war.

At first, the Minutemen resisted provocative acts of violence. DePugh personally stopped his Minutemen from assassinating Senator William Fulbright and Neiman Marcus business tycoon Stanley Marcus. In addition, after conceiving the plot himself, DePugh decided against an attack on the United Nations that would have dispersed cyanide through the ventilation system of the much-hated institution.

DePugh referred to his approach as the "principle of deliberate delay . . . which means all the emphasis is on recruiting and propaganda and stockpiling arms, so you don't zap anybody till the outfit's ready to function fully underground."[26] And stockpile they did. In 1965 law enforcement raided the residence of Minuteman Richard Lauchli. There officers seized "1,000 submachine guns" as well as "eight M-2 carbines, 43 rifles, shotguns and pistols, 36,000 rounds of ammunition, 58 antitank grenades, 17 60-millimeter mortar shells, 11 antipersonnel mines, four Army hand grenades, 21 pounds of black powder and two military rockets." That same year law enforcement found "gun caches in at least six other states," belonging to groups connected with the Minutemen, with weapons that included "rifles, bazookas, anti-tank guns and bayonets." An investigative report from journalists in Denver found that in Colorado, the Minutemen kept stashes of weapons hidden at several key locations in the mountains. In California law enforcement "confiscated 800,000 rounds of ammunition, 400 machine guns, 10 anti-tank guns, and other warfare items" from Minutemen sympathizers. Most alarmingly, when the Minutemen allowed investigative reporter Eric Norden into one of their secret compounds, they showed him thirty four-foot-long rockets, which senior Minuteman leader Roy Frankhouser said could reach a target over several miles away.[27]

While on "deliberate delay," DePugh and his group gathered intelligence on potential targets. In the Minutemen periodical, DePugh urged,

> We must know our enemies by name, address and phone number. Their leaders must be subject to special scrutiny. We must know their habits, their likes, their strong and weak points. We must have a complete physical description of them. We must know the license number of their cars and where they are apt to hide in time of danger. . . . We must show the left-wing professor and the pro-communist minister that liberalism is not always a bed of roses. There are penalties which they too must pay for selling their country out.[28]

Former FBI agent and journalist William Turner, who in 1966 was given considerable access to Minutemen headquarters at Norborne, Missouri, described filing cabinets full of this kind of information, with as many as sixty-five thousand names of those who "manifested an ultra-liberal philosophy" according to DePugh. Turner noted that "new members spend three tedious months as part of their First Phase of Training poring over some 600 'left wing' periodicals culling names." Among those selected were the noted television news anchors Chet Huntley and David Brinkley. The "First Phase of Training" referenced by Turner was one of "five rigorous phases of training" that culled would-be Minutemen down to a "fanatical hard-core who dangle Crusader's Crosses inscribed 'We Will Never Surrender' around their necks and who fully understand that to defect automatically brings the mark of death."[29]

In 1966, as race riots continued to rage inside the United States, the Minutemen became more proactive. They formed a separate political party, the Patriot Party, which ultimately endorsed George Wallace for president, and they began to engage in more overt acts of terrorism. But for the efforts of law enforcement, several major attacks could have caused serious damage and untold casualties.

One of the most publicized would-be attacks is also one of the most revealing when it comes to understanding the danger posed by the Minutemen. In 1966 multiple law enforcement agencies, in a joint sting operation, raided a Minuteman compound in upstate New York. The goal: stop an impending siege by the Minutemen on three leftist retreats. If the arsenal of weapons recovered by law enforcement was any indication, the Minutemen planned on a very bloody affair. The cache included "1,000,000 rounds of rifle and small-arms ammunition, chemicals for preparing bomb detonators, considerable radio equipment—including 30 walkie-talkies and shortwave sets tuned to police bands, 125 single-shot and automatic rifles, 10 dynamite bombs, 5 mortars. 12 .30-caliber machine guns, 25 pistols, 240 knives (hunting, throwing, cleaver and machete), 1 bazooka, 3 grenade launchers, 6 hand grenades and 50 80-millimeter mortar shells. For good measure, there was even a crossbow replete with curare-tipped arrows."[30]

The dozen or so men arrested in the plot, which included a wealthy upstate businessman and senior Minuteman official, were described by Norden as "a cabdriver, a gardener, a subway conductor, a fireman, a mechanic, a plasterer, a truck driver, a heavy-equipment operator, a draftsman, several small businessman, a horse groom and two milkmen. Most were respectable family men in their late 20s or early 30s, known to their neighbors as solid, church-going pillars of the community." Unbeknownst to their neighbors, these men were also stockpiling weapons. A copywriter cached "machine guns . . . bazookas . . . mortars" and an "anti-tank missile launcher." A businessman stored "hyperdermic needles . . . rifles . . . shotguns . . . and 5000 rounds of ammunition."

Just as disturbing to law enforcement was the discovery that three members of the New York State Police had secretly acquired the weapons for the Minutemen. For years, many members of law enforcement saw the group as toy soldiers and did not believe their boasts of having members hidden among all walks of American life, including in the business community and law enforcement agencies. By 1966, however, state law enforcement agencies had begun to take the Minutemen much more seriously. Speaking of the entire milieu of right-wing radicals, one New York investigator insisted, "Kooks they are, harmless they are not. . . . It's only due to their incompetence, and not any lack of motivation, that they haven't left a trail of corpses in their wake."[31]

Another discovery by law enforcement confirmed what investigative reporters Eric Norden and William Turner unearthed: Machiavellian efforts by the Minutemen to provoke racial conflict by inflaming the black community. The reporters found fake pamphlets, designed to look like Black nationalist propaganda, urging blacks to riot. "Kill the white devils and have the women for your pleasure" the pamphlets read. At one point, Minutemen sped through black neighborhoods tossing these pamphlets out the window.

In FBI files, more alarming evidence emerged. Several independent informants spoke to plans by the Minutemen to provoke a racial civil war by assassinating key black civil rights figures such as James Farmer and Martin Luther King Jr. If this sounds familiar, it should be noted that the shift away from a strategy of "deliberate delay" toward a more proactive stance that included alarming levels of weapons hoarding and efforts to antagonize the black community came as followers of the Christian Identity movement assumed highly influential roles inside the Minutemen. Indeed, almost every single leader—save perhaps for DePugh—had direct ties or exposure to Swift's church. This group included Wally Peyson, DePugh's "right-hand man"; the Reverend Kenneth Goff, head of the largest subunit of the Minutemen; Frankhouser, one of the leading Minutemen organizers on the East Coast; and Dennis Mower, another West Coast organizer. Peyson was a minister in Swift's church; Goff was also a CI minister, and Frankhouser would soon become one; Mower was one of Swift's chief aides. It is no wonder that, in their strategy, the Minutemen increasingly began to see their inevitable revolution inside the United States as a civil war *and* as a race war. They also increasingly became openly anti-Semitic in their rhetoric. Norden describes the following exchange with Frankhouser:

"Have Minutemen been involved in inciting the race riots?" I asked.

"You mean shooting at both sides to heat things up?" He smiled. "Not yet. Right now we can afford to just stand back on the side lines and pick up the pieces; we're the inheritors of social bankruptcy, you might say. And the same holds true for the black nationalists; after each bloody riot they get a lot of uncommitted niggers going over to their side. It's sort of a symbiotic situation. Let them shoot the Jews on their list, we'll shoot the Jews on ours, and then we can shoot each other!"

Most of the group's following—between five thousand and ten thousand direct members and thirty thousand to forty thousand supporters, according to the best estimates—likely had no connection to Christian Identity. They were simply antigovernment activists who saw, in the growth of the militant American left and black nationalism, evidence that America was heading toward communist subversion and widespread disorder—and they prepared accordingly. But those same fears could be harnessed by those who wanted to polarize the races to foment the race war.

What stood in their way was an equally cunning and Machiavellian response by the national government, one that at times created problems as surely as it solved them. Law enforcement agencies and the military feared extremists on both ends of the political spectrum and targeted them accordingly.

In the late 1960s, the radical right and militant left shared a deep hatred for the American political establishment. The militant left saw the consensus between New Deal liberals and moderate Republicans on America's makeshift social safety net as a tonic that dulled the public from pursuing much more radical reforms of capitalism. The radical right saw that same consensus as evidence of a growing shift toward communism, especially with the advent of Lyndon Johnson's Great Society program. For the militant left, the broad foreign policy consensus behind cold war containment was an excuse to send working-class whites and urban blacks to die to expand the influence of capitalism around the world. For the radical right, the failure to go above and beyond in that fight showed weakness in the face of the alarming spread of world communism. Of course, for the religious radicals who followed Wesley Swift, all of this was part of the "beast system"—the beast being the Antichrist (aka Jews) working on Satan's behalf in the time before God's final judgment.

The establishment all but ignored the religious dimensions of the violence and disorder that marked the 1960s. Yet, as the decade proceeded, more and more of those in power began to fear what the radical religious extremists coveted: another American civil war, even some kind of race war. Rightly or wrongly, the establishment realized something had to be done. Those in charge of America's domestic security—the FBI, the National Guard, local law enforcement—acted accordingly.

The central military planners at the Department of Defense adjusted America's entire national security posture. While keeping foreign policy focused on preventing the spread of communism, military leaders also concerned themselves with domestic security. They feared what one historian called a "made-in-America Tet Offensive"[32] on domestic soil—a sudden, possibly coordinated series of urban uprisings that would spread like a wildfire and push America toward civil war. The growing violence associated with protests against the Vietnam War only reinforced this fear. In 1966, having found themselves forced into a supporting role during the Watts riots in 1965, the Joint Chiefs of Staff created an ongoing, formal operation, first known as Operation Steep Hill and ultimately as Operation Garden Plot. The operation parlayed the recently created U.S. Army Intelligence Command, a collection of military intelligence groups with a focus on domestic security, into an intelligence-gathering operation aimed at watching America's political and urban hotspots and spying on antiwar and radical-left groups. The focus increasingly became geared toward preemption or rapid response in the event of civil disorder.[33]

The FBI, for its part, created the Counterintelligence Program, or COINTELPRO. The Bureau divided the program into two major components. COINTELPRO White focused on right-wing and white supremacist groups, and COINTELPRO Black focused on civil rights and black nationalist groups. Like Garden Plot, COINTELRPO also included extensive surveillance operations. But it differed from other programs in its willingness to rely on provocation and dirty tricks. The FBI would play upon the natural tendency of many of these groups toward paranoia by pitting members against each other and instigating schisms and rivalries within the groups.

This work included spreading false rumors, sending inflammatory mailings, and sabotaging operations. In each case, the Bureau blamed members of the groups for actions taken by FBI agents or operatives. One humorous example, described to me by a former FBI official, referred to the not uncommon phenomenon of KKK members sleeping around with each other's spouses. At times, in places like Mississippi, the FBI actually observed these relationships as they developed. Late FBI special agent Jim Ingram, a senior member of the Jackson, Mississippi, field office, said that the FBI successfully took advantage of this phenomenon by placing notes in the mailboxes of KKK members, hinting that someone "knew where your wife was last evening," eliciting predictable resentments and infighting after the pranks.[34]

At other times the dirty tricks were more serious. The FBI, to its historical shame, lumped nonviolent civil rights organizations such as the SCLC together with groups like the Black Panthers under COINTELPRO Black. A major target of the program was Martin Luther King Jr., whom J. Edgar Hoover suspected, incorrectly, of being a tool of the Communist Party, and whom Hoover resented for publicly criticizing the Bureau's handling of racial crimes. In what has to be one of the ugliest episodes in the history of the FBI, the Bureau sent a purported tape recording of Dr. King engaged in extramarital relations to the minister's family while sending a note to the civil rights leader himself, urging him to commit suicide. The FBI never relented in its effort to gather illicit information on King, through surveillance that included wiretaps and feeding scurrilous material in anonymous leaks to Hoover's many assets in the media.

With respect to the less sympathetic white supremacist groups, the "fun and games" involving pitting one white supremacist cad against another gave way to much more serious countermeasures—even what would amount to an FBI conspiracy to murder white supremacists. Controversy also continues to persist over whether or not federal law enforcement looked the other way regarding, or perhaps even instigated, murders of Black Panther leaders.

As much as anything else, FBI operations against both white supremacist and black nationalist groups focused on developing informants and infiltrators within radical organizations and undermining the groups from within. In particular, by leveraging potential prison sentences against radicals arrested for various crimes, the FBI turned dedicated KKK members, including senior leaders, into ongoing sources of information and potential players in FBI dirty tricks campaigns. Supporting this thesis, internal reports on groups like the White Knights of the Ku Klux Klan of Mississippi start with huge lists of redacted names—sometimes dozens for each report—of informants inside the group. At times the FBI would also use code names for human informants to disguise information obtained from wiretaps and mail intercepts. To this day, the FBI jealously protects the identities of these informants.

Some of that reticence may go beyond simply protecting these individuals against danger. As noted in the chapter on the Birmingham bombing, some suspects in that case were or became FBI informants. The problem for the FBI is that many of those informants were still dedicated racists; they did not change their stripes overnight simply because they began working for the FBI. And informants often found themselves at the scene of, or even participants in, major acts of domestic terrorism. The FBI must frequently decide whether or not to prosecute crimes committed by informants in the furtherance of, or in conjunction with, ongoing FBI investigations. For instance, thousands of secret waivers against prosecution were granted in 2013. But this process can come at a great price to the FBI if the nature of the forgiven crimes is publicized.

The effort to protect the Bureau against embarrassment becomes an important point to consider when one tries to assess what the FBI knew about the religious dimensions of white supremacist violence in the 1960s. Why has it taken so long for the theological foundations of white supremacist violence to be revealed to the American people? J.B. Stoner was clearly motivated by the theology of Christian Identity. But the connection of J.B. Stoner to the Birmingham bombing may well be concealed by the FBI's ongoing decision to withhold surveillance data obtained from wiretaps in his law office. The same protectionist mind-set may also be in play in additional crimes described in this book that Stoner might have been involved in.

In any event, public statements and testimony from the 1960s show that the FBI greatly underestimated the potential danger of white supremacist groups in comparison to black nationalists. Perhaps owing to his obsession with fighting communism, or perhaps because of implicit racism (or both), J. Edgar Hoover called the Black Panthers the number-one threat to American domestic order. In contrast, as William Turner noted, Hoover minimized the danger posed by the Minutemen, placing their total membership at only five hundred. He insisted that the FBI had thoroughly penetrated the group with informants (something that was at least partly true) and that he had them under control. The growing number of federal prosecutions against white supremacists by early 1967 provided some evidence that the FBI did have this problem under control. The FBI prosecuted Sam Bowers and his senior WKKKKOM members in connection with the Neshoba murders. Charges against Robert DePugh and Wally Peyson for bank robbery had forced both men underground by 1968. (They were caught in 1969.)

But Bowers and fellow travelers like J.B. Stoner would not be deterred. Those with the best access to white supremacists groups, such as investigative reporters Norden and Turner, described an interesting development from 1966 to 1968. Seemingly disparate white supremacist groups—organizations like the National States Rights Party, the National Knights of the Ku Klux Klan (the second largest KKK group in the country, headquartered in Georgia but with a national reach), the White Knights of the Ku Klux Klan, and the Minutemen—increasingly tightened their relationships with each other. FBI documents confirm such developments. This went beyond simple cross-affiliations by various members to actual cooperation. Turner and Norden also began to note the religious impulse inspiring several of these groups. Progressively, Swift's taped sermons and Bible studies gained a wider audience among the cadre of radicals who remained dedicated to the white supremacist cause despite their failures in 1964 and 1965.

Those listening to the Reverend Wesley Swift's words in February 1967 would hear some familiar themes. "Now, we have had the sign of the 'son of man' in the heavens February 4, 1962," he began. Swift was echoing a landmark sermon he had given several years before, in February 1962. In the earlier sermon, Swift referred to a recent solar eclipse in 1962, a sign of the beginning of the end-time, when God will "awaken" his followers and they will fulfill their destiny by "chalneng[ing] the power and forces of darkness. And from this time forward, expanding and moving and working to this destiny, Christian civilizations and the white nations of the western world shall move forward, against the enemy." Swift called this 1962 sermon "Zero Hour," a reference to the beginning of the countdown to the End of Days.[35]

But in February of 1967, with riots and civil unrest seemingly having confirmed his prophecy, Swift combined the reference to zero hour with a reference to Chapter 14 of the book of Revelations: "We have passed the time of the beginning of tare time. And we have come to the time of the abomination of the desolator who stands in the Holy place. This shows us that we are in the end time or in the last days."[36] For many evangelical fundamentalists, Chapter 14 of the book of Revelations describes the Great Tribulation, when God imposes a series of plagues on mankind.

One of the signs of these end-times is the "reaping of tares." Tares are weeds that are difficult to distinguish from wheat and that absorb needed nutrients from wheat. In the Great Tribulation, God directs his flock to harvest both the wheat and tares but to burn the tares. For Swift, the identity of the tares was obvious: "The Jews are the tares and the tares are the enemies of God's Kingdom." "Tare time," as Swift called it, had already begun by early 1967. In February he predicted that the rest of the year would be marked by

> increasing catastrophes, Negro riots. And anything Communism has its hands on will increase as they try to destroy Christian America and Western Civilization . . . the White man will stand— shoulder to shoulder against the Negro and the anti-Christ.[37]

What remained to be begun was yet another prophecy in the book of Revelations, one also deeply rooted in symbolism: the winepress of fermented grapes. Chapter 14 of the book of Revelations prophecies that

> Another angel, the one who has power over fire, came out from the altar; and he called with a loud voice to him who had the sharp sickle, saying, "Put in your sharp sickle and gather the clusters from the vine of the earth, because her grapes are ripe." So the angel swung his sickle to the earth and gathered the clusters from the vine of the earth, and threw them into the great wine press of the wrath of God. And the wine press was trodden outside the city, and blood came out from the wine press, up to the horses' bridles, for a distance of two hundred miles.

As one commentator describes the metaphor: "Satan and his angels will gather all the enemies of the God of heaven" and "Jesus alone will crush them and their blood will mingle with water that makes up their bodies and run like streams."[38] In February 1967, Swift did not mention what biblical scholars refer to as the grapes of wrath. But as will become clear, Swift's followers were determined to see his prophecy come to pass. And to do it, they likely perpetrated one of the most consequential acts of terrorism in American history.

7

THE ALPHA

the FAILED ATTEMPTS
to ASSASSINATE
MARTIN LUTHER KING JR.,
1958–1967

On March 31, 1968, the Reverend Martin Luther King Jr. and the Reverend Wesley Albert Swift each delivered a sermon about the future of America, but rooted in very different ideas about God's design for humanity.

Dr. King spoke to an audience at the National Cathedral in Washington, D.C., in an oration entitled "Remaining Awake through a Great Revolution." King had delivered the speech before, at a commencement at Oberlin College, in Ohio, in 1965. But the civil rights movement and King's mission had undergone many changes in the intervening three years. At Oberlin, King spoke mainly to the socioeconomic challenges still facing the black underclass. "Remaining awake" in 1965 meant recognizing the need to expand one's conception of social justice in a world that demanded more compassion with greater urgency. "To rise to our full moral maturity as a nation, we must get rid of segregation whether it is in housing, whether it is a de facto segregation in the public schools, whether it is segregation in public accommodations, or whether it is segregation in the church," King urged the Oberlin graduates.[1]

But by 1968, King's speech had evolved to fit the changing dynamics of a nation in upheaval over economic and racial inequality, a country bitterly divided over the Vietnam War (that King hinted at in 1965 but did not mention by name). In the nation's capital, King assumed the role of an Old Testament prophet, warning America about God's judgment if it maintained its current course. "One day we will have to stand before the God of history and we will talk in terms of things we've done," King told the crowd at the National Cathedral. "It seems that I can hear the God of history saying, 'That was not enough . . . you cannot enter the kingdom of greatness.'" King remained convinced that the world would change, quoting, at the beginning of his sermon, from the book of Revelations, Chapter 16: "Behold I make all things new; former things are passed away." But now he saw "the Great Revolution" as three interlocking revolutions—economic, moral, and military—happening at once. The dangers posed by automation to the working poor, the moral decay stemming from racism, the threat of nuclear conflict as a result of the cold war: They could destroy a nation that, in a metaphor King used to great effect, chose to sleep through these times like Rip Van Winkle. But, King argued, if a courageous people managed the situation correctly, these seemingly intractable developments would finally convince a slumbering society of the promise of a "new day of justice and brotherhood and peace." King, as was his custom, struck an optimistic note: "We're going to win our freedom because both the sacred heritage of our nation and the eternal will of the almighty God are embodied in our echoing demands."[2]

But for all his faith in God's benevolence, King nonetheless ended his sermon with an explication for divine guidance and with a conditional assertion about the future, in lines not found in the 1965 commencement address: "God grant that we will be participants in this newness and this magnificent development. If we will but do it, we will bring about a new day of justice and brotherhood and peace."[3]

If the Reverend King lacked a degree of certainty in the future in 1968, it was not simply because he recognized, like a good student of the book of Genesis, the problems that human free will and temptation presented even to God's grand designs. As far back as 1965, the growing schism inside the United States and within the civil rights movement had worried King. The nation's continued unraveling from 1967 through 1968 chastened his expectations for the country even further.

Urban and racial rioting continued to plague the nation in the summer of 1967, a level of domestic disorder not seen since post–Civil War Reconstruction. In Newark, New Jersey, false rumors that a black cab driver had died in police custody sparked four days of rioting from July 12 to July 17, requiring massive intervention by local and state police as well as by the National Guard. The urban combat that commenced resulted in twenty-three dead and 750 injured. Follow-up studies indicated that law enforcement, including the National Guard, had expended 13,319 rounds of ammunition in pursuit of snipers who may not have actually existed.[4] A week later, Detroit, Michigan, experienced the single worst urban riot in the history of the nation: After five days of rioting, 43 people were dead, 1,189 were injured, and over 7,000 were arrested. Sandra West, a UPI reporter who had lived her whole life in Detroit, described the chaos:

> Sunday I saw sights I never dreamed possible. . . . Raging fires burned out of control for blocks and blocks. Thick black smoke and cinders rained down at times so heavily they blocked out homes as close as 20 feet away.
>   Looters drove pickup trucks loaded with everything from floor mops to new furniture. Price tags still dangled from the merchandise.[5]

Riots also struck Birmingham, Chicago, and Milwaukee, among other major cities. In sum, during the "long hot summer" of 1967, the United States experienced 158 different riots, resulting in eighty-three deaths, 2,801 injuries, and 4,627 incidents of arson.[6]

With national press reports that "guns—hand guns, rifles, shot-guns—are selling as though they were about to close down the gun factories,"[7] King continued to insist on nonviolence. But in August of 1967, he told a crowd of frustrated young civil rights activists that blacks "still live in the basement of the Great Society." He observed some months later that a "riot is the language of the unheard. And what is it America has failed to hear? It has failed to hear that the plight of the Negro poor has worsened over the last twelve or fifteen years. It has failed to hear that the promises of freedom and justice have not been met. And it has failed to hear that large segments of white society are more concerned about tranquility and the status quo than about justice and humanity."[8]

In December 1967, with a renewed sense of purpose, King launched what would be his final mission, the Poor People's Cam-paign (PPC): a proposed march of several thousand members of America's underclass from America's poorest state (Mississippi) to the nation's capital. The protestors would camp out on the National

Mall. King hoped that if they were arrested, waves of new people would take their place, as they had in Birmingham in the spring of 1963. The goal of this campaign was to scandalize President Lyndon Johnson and the American government into a massive investment in social services, way beyond anything implemented in LBJ's War on Poverty. King had already burned his bridges with his onetime White House ally, and with the liberal political establishment in general, by openly opposing the Vietnam War, calling America the world's "greatest purveyor of violence" in 1967.

King's public opposition to the Vietnam War and his focus on economic justice also alienated him from a large swath of the general public that had openly supported his fight for legal equality in the South prior to 1966. In 1965, when he spoke at Oberlin, King found himself in fourth place on Gallup's poll of America's most admired people. But as soon as he began to focus on socioeconomic conditions in northern cities, starting in 1966, public opinion began to shift against him. By the time he gave the sermon at the National Cathedral in March 1968, a majority of white Americans—more than 70 percent—held an unfavorable opinion of Dr. King. More alarming, perhaps to King, was the fact that 57 percent of black Americans considered him to be irrelevant.[9] Groups like the Black Panthers and the more radicalized version of SNCC increasingly captured the imagination of a frustrated African American community.

Even King's longtime nemesis J. Edgar Hoover began to question the civil rights leader's prominence given the growing influence of black nationalism. Hoover continued to leak negative rumors and innuendo about Dr. King in 1968, but internal documents show that Hoover's concerns increasingly began to focus on militant black nationalist groups and leaders. A memo dated March 4, 1968, from the director to every FBI field office, raised alarm at the growing civil disorder in America and spoke to the need to "neutralize" a potential black "Messiah" who could trigger "a true black revolution" inside the nation. The document offered three potential candidates: Martin Luther King, Nation of Islam leader Elijah Muhammad, and Stokely Carmichael. But King was not seen as a threat as long as he retained his "'obedience' to 'white liberal doctrines' (non-violence)." The FBI instead focused its attention on Carmichael as the real danger.[10]

King spoke to his predicament, a result of taking bold but unpopular stances, in his sermon at the National Cathedral.

On some positions, cowardice asks the question, is it expedient? And then expedience comes along and asks the question, is it politic? Vanity asks the question, is it popular? Conscience asks the question, is it right?

There comes a time when one must take the position that is neither safe nor politic nor popular, but he must do it because conscience tells him it is right.[11]

Like his reference to God's judgment, these words had been absent from the 1965 Oberlin commencement speech. In 1968 King knew the price he had paid for challenging "white liberal doctrines." Indeed, when he preached at the National Cathedral, the potential efficacy of the Poor People's Campaign looked very much in doubt even as it was set to begin later in April. Financial support remained low, and skepticism persisted about whether or not the march would have the manpower it needed. Dr. King had just visited Mississippi to enlist leaders of the Mississippi Freedom Democratic Party, the political group that had emerged as a result of Mississippi Freedom Summer's 1964 voting drive, for help with grassroots mobilization. Some questioned whether or not the Reverend King, with his waning influence, could hold marchers to a standard of disciplined nonviolence. Would the émigrés to the Mall, they wondered, respond to police coercion in the same way that residents of Detroit and Newark had responded?

In the last week of March 1968, concerns of nonviolence occupied Martin Luther King's attention above all other matters. At the urging of his friend, the Reverend James Lawson, Dr. King agreed to lend support to the Memphis sanitation workers strike, a labor protest that had been gaining momentum since February. The predominantly black sanitation force in Memphis worked under terrible conditions for low wages. They were expected to dispose of trash in any and all weather conditions. Matters came to a head when two sanitation workers, seeking shelter from the severe weather in their truck, were crushed by its compactor.

King agreed to lead a protest march in support of the laborers, but snow delayed the demonstration until March 28. Events did not go according to plan. Violence erupted, and shops were looted. Police shot and killed a sixteen-year-old protester. Tennessee governor Buford Ellington ordered National Guardsmen to pacify Memphis, and at the urging of his advisors, the Reverend King was forced to leave Memphis unceremoniously. On his own initiative, Dr. King insisted that he had to return to Memphis to lead a peaceful strike, to calm the nation (and supporters) about the prospects of the forthcoming Poor People's Campaign, and to convince campaign participants that nonviolence was still feasible and desirable. Not long after speaking at the National Cathedral, King returned to Atlanta. He announced on April 1 his plans to return to Memphis. King made his way by plane to Memphis on April 3, but not before a bomb threat delayed his departure.[12]

No one listening in California to the Reverend Wesley Swift's sermon on March 31 would have detected that he too had plans for Memphis. In his speech "Power in the Word," Swift simply echoed themes familiar to his Christian Identity flock. The focus was on the sustenance provided by faith. The end-times, as always, became a major motif. Swift asserted:

We find that in our intelligence and purpose, we have accepted a plan that is in the word of God and we are participating in it. You are not only participating in it, but you accept it and you are working to bring in the kingdom, and these prophecies of God.[13]

Cycling through several books of the Bible, Swift ended where King began his March 31 oration, with the book of Revelations:

This word of God is for your protection in the hour of emergency. The word of God shall see America thru. And not only is this true, but the children of America have the Faith to believe every word that comes out of the mouth of God. And they believe that it will be fulfilled. This does not eliminate you from defending your home and battling the enemy. But it gives you the capacity to know that those of your household with you will come thru this battle. . . . And we thus understand that the world was made by the Word of God. And we also understand that the new world will also be made by the Words of your mouth. And the children—you and I—shall participate. And we shall have absolute victory.[14]

The evidence strongly suggests that when the Reverend Wesley Swift assured his followers that the word of God promised them victory in the upcoming battle with the enemy, he knew about and likely endorsed a conspiracy to assassinate Martin Luther King Jr. on April 4, 1968, in Memphis. In many ways, such a plot was only the final iteration of a much broader effort to murder the civil rights leader, one that persisted, through many failures, for more than a decade.

From 1958 to 1967, individuals and groups within the Christian Identity social network had plotted and made as many as seven serious attempts on Martin Luther King Jr.'s life. Scholars and congressional investigators have documented most of these attempts on a case-by-case basis, but ignorance about the influence of Christian Identity extremism has blinded them to the common ideological thread connecting each effort: eliminating the most important voice advocating for nonviolence and harmonious relations between the races and in so doing setting the stage for a holy race war. It is very likely that one of the plots, from 1964, evolved into a conspiracy that finally succeeded in killing King on April 4, 1968, in Memphis. Indeed, with each successive attempt, the plotters appeared to have built on tactical elements in earlier plots. This is not surprising, inasmuch as two men, J.B. Stoner and Sam Bowers, likely spearheaded no fewer than six of them. Hence it is valuable to quickly review these seven attempts, with the goal of illuminating the murder on April 4.[15]

1958: The Stoner Birmingham Bounty

As noted in earlier chapters, the first major effort by a Christian Identity zealot to murder Martin Luther King occurred in 1958. J.B. Stoner offered to have his "boys from Atlanta" come to Birmingham and kill King for a "special bargain price"—per Stoner—of $1,500. Stoner proffered this to undercover police informants as part of a wider effort to kill a number of civil rights figures. Lest there be any doubt as to how serious he was, two of Stoner's Atlanta associates nearly demolished Birmingham's Bethel Baptist Church on June 29, 1958, one week after meeting with the informants. A security guard discovered a smoking five-gallon paint can full of explosives and placed it in the middle of the street; "the ensuing explosion broke windows and shook homes for several blocks." Already the site of a 1956 bombing, the Bethel Baptist Church, referred to by some as the mother of the civil rights movement in Alabama, included the parsonage for the Reverend Fred Shuttlesworth, a major civil rights leader who, with his friend Martin Luther King Jr., was among the list of bounty targets. Stoner soon realized that he had been the victim of a police sting operation, established in part because local authorities hoped to understand, and stop, the recent spate of bombings against Jewish targets (also plotted by Stoner). But authorities never charged Stoner, because they believed that in requesting that Stoner help them eliminate civil rights officials, even if the goal was to develop charges against the violent bigot, a judge would see the effort as entrapment and throw out the charges.

1963: The Twin Birmingham Attempts

The next two attempts on King's life also likely involved Stoner. Both plots developed in Birmingham in 1963. The first, discussed earlier, involved the bombing of Dr. King's room at the Gaston Motel on May 11, 1963, which coincided with the bombing of the home of the civil rights leader's brother, A.D. King. Both men were fortunate to have stayed late at a meeting, or they could have been killed or injured. Although no one was ever arrested for the attack on the King brothers, internal records from the FBI and from the Birmingham police, as well as histories by people like Diane McWhorter and Gary May, suggest that individuals associated with Eastview Klavern 13 implemented the attacks. As noted in Chapter 4, members of the Eastview Klavern (aka the Cahaba Boys) were closely associated with the National States Rights Party in 1963. Anyone hoping for a racial conflagration, such as Stoner and Ed Fields, would have been impressed with the aftermath of the May attempts on Dr. King's life. The May bombing, on the heels of a successful effort led by King and Shuttlesworth to force greater racial integration in Birmingham, caused the first major riot in the history of the Steel City.

The second major riot occurred in Birmingham after the September 15 bombing of the Sixteenth Street Baptist Church, which killed four girls. As noted earlier, several Christian Identity radicals had met in Birmingham the day before the bombing. These same men, including retired colonel William Potter Gale, Sidney Crockett Barnes, retired admiral John Crommelin, and Noah Carden, planned to assassinate Martin Luther King with rifle fire when he came to eulogize the four girls. The chosen sniper, Noah Carden, could not get a clear shot on King, according to Barnes. The Reverend Ed King, a civil rights activist from Mississippi who came to lead protests against the bombing, asserts that any additional violence on the part of rioting blacks would have triggered massive retaliation by Alabama law en-forcement. While there is no direct evidence that Stoner took part in the King murder plot, all the Christian Identity figures who came to Birmingham were members of Stoner's National States Rights Party. Informant reports say that Crommelin even stayed with Stoner on September 14. Barnes insisted that the sniper project to murder Dr. King was ongoing through 1964 and that another attempt failed when King did not visit Barnes's (and Carden's) hometown of Mobile, as the minister had originally planned and publicized.

1964: The Alpha Plot in Mississippi

If scholars hope to understand the civil rights leader's murder in 1968, investigating the failed 1964 plot against King is key. We will refer to this plot as the alpha plot, as it becomes the basis for the conspiracy that, evidence suggests, ended with King's assassination on April 4, 1968. For the sake of clarity, and with a nod to Christian eschatology (the alpha and omega are important symbols for those who believe in an end-times apocalypse), let us refer to the ultimate, successful conspiracy, beginning in 1967, as the omega plot. The alpha plot, described briefly in an earlier chapter, involved an effort by Sam Bowers and the White Knights of the Ku Klux Klan of Mississippi to offer another bounty to assassinate King, this time to a professional hit man by the name of Donald Sparks. Due to its significance in the successful assassination of King in 1968 (the omega plot), it is worth exploring in considerable depth.

A 1970 investigation by the attorney general of Kansas[16] (supported by FBI documents) established that Sparks belonged to a subgroup of a wider collection of loosely connected criminals, known to historians of crime and known in popular literature (and movies) as the Dixie Mafia. More of a phenomenon than an organization, the so-called Dixie Mafia was known by law enforcement in its early years as the Crossroaders or the traveling criminals. They formed bonds with other criminals, often across state lines, in America's federal prisons. With the development of the interstate highway system in the 1950s, and with the growing availability of home phones, it became much easier for criminals with various and complementary skill sets to plot and execute major crimes across state lines. If the prospective monetary haul was sufficiently high, a safecracker, a getaway driver, and a "strong-arm man" who was handy with firearms could help each other score a major robbery. Over time, these men formed loosely knit gangs, concentrated in the Midwest and Southeast. The Dixie Mafia earned a reputation for greed-fueled ruthlessness that surpassed even that of the Sicilian Mafia. By the late 1960s, Mafia dons were outsourcing contract killings to Dixie Mafia hit men like Sparks. According to KKK historian Michael Newton, the "Ku Klux Klan collaborated with the Dixie Mafia on strong-arm work."[17]

No scholar detailed the 1964 bounty offer until 2012, when I (with coauthor Larry Hancock) described it with great detail in *The Awful Grace of God,* a book on the King murder. The details of the alpha plot emerge in a 1965 FBI memo. In it, a man named Herman Wing informs agents in the FBI's Oklahoma City field office of a $13,000 bounty offer on MLK's life. The money was fronted by the White Knights to Donald Sparks in 1964.[18]

Sparks told Wing about this bounty after the two completed a robbery spree in Alabama in 1965. Purportedly, Sparks even visited

Mississippi and stayed at a hotel in Jackson, waiting for his money before committing the murder. The murder never occurred, Sparks told Wing, because the White Knights failed to raise the contract money in time. The FBI followed Wing's lead to Mississippi, where they found important pieces of corroboration. The FBI's Jackson field office found a local law enforcement officer who confirmed having heard of a similar plot in 1964. Agents also discovered that Sparks (a native of Oklahoma who primarily worked with a Tulsa-based gang in the Great Plains) was known to KKK members in Mississippi. A local KKK member knew his nickname, Two Jumps, a reference to Sparks's dalliance with competitive rodeo. But the FBI dismissed Wing's claim because Wing also connected Sparks to the murder of the FBI's most wanted fugitive, John Dillon. The FBI was convinced that Dillon had been killed in Oklahoma, where his body was found.

Several additional factors cement the 1964 alpha plot as fact. For one thing, a second colleague of Sparks, Kenneth Knight, confirmed the plot independently in 1968. Internal documents from the Oklahoma Bureau of Investigation confirm that close associates of Sparks likely did kill Dillon. In fact, one of the last people seen in the company of Dillon was a known associate of Sparks, Leroy McManaman, a native of Kansas. McManaman's criminal record included arrests and convictions for a multimillion-dollar interstate bootlegging operation, a series of home robberies, and the interstate transportation of stolen cars. McManaman's activities in the spring of 1964 provide one of the most important sources of corroboration for the alpha plot and, as we shall see, reveal the bridge between the alpha plot and the omega plot.

Like Sparks, McManaman also suddenly showed up in Jackson, Mississippi, in 1964. Like Sparks, McManaman was a member of a Dixie Mafia gang based out of Tulsa. Like Sparks, his criminal record shows little or no association with Mississippi. In fact, McManaman violated a federal appeal bond in traveling to Mississippi in 1964. In 1963 a federal jury in Kansas had convicted McManaman for leading an interstate stolen car ring conspiracy with Rubie Charles Jenkins, Sparks's closest friend. Out on bond, McManaman risked additional prison time if caught on his jaunt to Mississippi.

Yet he stayed there for several weeks at the home of Sybil Eure, a real estate broker who ran her own company from her home in Jackson. Eure would later claim to the FBI that friends (whom she never identified) had introduced her to McManaman, that McManaman (a "big time criminal operator" according to FBI reports) was a real estate guru, and that she had hoped to work with him in real estate in the future. It is very likely, as we shall see, that McManaman was in Jackson to help his friend Sparks in any 1964 attempt on King's life and that Eure, who admitted to being in financial straits in 1964, had some (perhaps unwitting) connection to the plot. But McManaman lost his appeal and returned to Leavenworth Prison in April 1964. The records show that he maintained an ongoing correspondence with Eure, something that will become significant when we discuss the omega plot from 1967 to 1968.

1965: Attempts in Ohio, Mississippi, and California

Christian Identity fanatics, including Bowers and Stoner, did not give up on their efforts to kill King. A 1965 FBI report cites informants describing a plot by Stoner and National Knights of the Ku Klux Klan leader James Venable to kill King in 1965. Stoner enjoyed a long relationship with Venable going back several years. Among other things, Stoner had shared a law office with Venable in Atlanta for a spell, and Venable represented members of Stoner's Confederate Underground when they were indicted for bombing the Temple in Atlanta in 1958.

The informants did not discuss details of the Stoner–Venable plot in 1965. But other sources, notably a letter and testimony of a young Ohio racist named Daniel Wagner, suggest the outlines of a conspiracy. Ohio police arrested Wagner in 1965 for carrying explosives across state lines. In custody, and later in testimony to the House Un-American Activities Committee (which from 1965 through 1967 led more than three investigations into KKK terrorism), Wagner described an offer made by Ohio KKK Grand Empress Eloise Witte, who wanted him to kill King. Witte connected her offer to a $25,000 bounty on King offered by James Venable.

Witte's Ohio Klan group fell under the umbrella of Venable's NKKKK, the second largest KKK group in the nation. According to Wagner, the money was supposed to be used to buy the services of some sort of rifle team, who would open fire on King and his entourage when King came to Ohio in the summer of 1965 to offer the commencement address at Antioch College, the alma mater of his wife, Coretta. The plot fell through when Wagner could not assemble a team in time. In testimony to Congress, an Ohio NSRP member and independent witness, Richard Hannah, confirmed overhearing Witte discuss the plot. It is worth noting that the explosives found in Wagner's car came from a group of men in Georgia with close ties to Venable. The explosives were meant to blow up police barracks and to destroy buildings belonging to the Nation of Islam, the radical black nationalist group led by Elijah Muhammad. The goal of these explosions, according to Wagner, was to ignite a race war.

The race war agenda suggests the possibility that Venable, like Stoner, had religious allegiances to the Reverend Wesley Swift and the Church of Jesus Christ–Christian. This association is far more difficult to pin down for Venable than it is for Stoner. Unlike Stoner, whose close associations with Swift's ministers stretched for more than a decade and whose rants against Jews included Christian Identity–type exegeses of the book of Genesis and the genealogy of Jesus, Venable was far less open about his anti-Jewish agenda. Yes, he represented the accused in the bombing of the Atlanta Temple, but other, non-Identity Klansmen harbored resentment toward Jews. Without question, internal documents show that Venable had been talking about killing Martin Luther King as far back as 1961, but that by no means puts someone in the Christian Identity camp. Evidence to be discussed shortly shows that by 1967 Venable and close allies within the National Knights had developed strong ties to Swift and had embraced Swift's thinking on Jews. But even if Venable did not attempt to kill King out of religious animus in 1965, his coconspirator, Stoner, certainly would have been motivated by religious ideology. Hence it is likely that the 1965 Stoner–Venable Ohio attempt against King fits the pattern of Christian Identity violence since 1958.

Two other attempts on King's life in 1965 fit that pattern. In one instance, documented in newspapers as well as in FBI documents, a member of the Minutemen, Keith Gilbert, stole hundreds of pounds of dynamite as part of a plot to blow up the Hollywood Palladium. The city of Los Angeles had invited King to speak in February 1965 in honor of his 1964 Nobel Peace Prize. An anonymous tip allowed the police to apprehend Gilbert and prevent the attack, a disaster that likely would have killed or injured hundreds of people. Though Gilbert went to prison for his offense, Swift ordained him as a minister in the Church of Jesus Christ–Christian shortly thereafter.

A tip from another informant, Delmar Dennis, stopped yet another effort by the White Knights of the Ku Klux Klan of Mississippi to assassinate King in 1965. The WKKKKOM plot involved a team of shooters, who would open fire on the Reverend King's entourage as he passed through Mississippi on his way to lead voting rights protests in Selma, Alabama. If the shooting team failed, the backup plan involved using explosives to destroy a bridge as King's vehicle crossed it. Dennis's information, along with pressure on federal authorities from President Johnson, combined to thwart the plan. But Sam Bowers was not through yet.

1966: The Ben Chester White Murder

As described in Chapter 5, Sam Bowers arranged with three prospective White Knights, Ernest Avants, James Lloyd Jones, and Claude Fuller, to lure Martin Luther King Jr. into a death trap in Natchez, Mississippi. The first phase of the plan succeeded with the murder of black farmer Ben Chester White on June 10, 1966. The men selected White mostly as a target of opportunity, but also because he had no substantive connection to the civil rights movement, so his death would seem more senseless than reactionary. Having convinced White to help them find their lost dog, the men lured the farmer into a pickup truck and brought him to a bridge, where they abruptly stopped. Using FBI records and court transcripts (the three men were convicted of murder in 1998), *Clarion-Ledger* (Jackson, Mississippi) investigative reporter Jerry Mitchell described the scene four decades later:

Claude Fuller got out of the Chevy, grabbed his rifle and loaded it before going around the car and opening the door where White was. Avants stood beside him.

"All right, Pop," Fuller told him. "Get out."

Spotting the rifle, White withered in his seat, bowing his head to pray.

"Get out!" Fuller barked.

"Oh, Lord," White said, "what have I done to deserve this?"

Fuller answered with his automatic rifle, firing two quick bursts that emptied the gun of all 18 shots.

Fuller then turned to Avants and told him to fire, too.[19]

The men heaved White's dead body into the waterway below, and in the days that followed, Sam Bowers waited for the second phase of his plan. White's body was found on June 12. In previous assassination attempts on the civil rights icon, King's movements and decisions had confounded the efforts to kill him. If the murderers could dictate King's movements (rather than the other way around), an ambush would be much more likely to succeed. Anyone studying King's past behavior would be safe in assuming that a murder like White's would elicit some appearance by the SCLC leader. King had attended the funeral of Medgar Evers in Jackson in June 1963; he had visited Birmingham to eulogize the four young murder victims three months later; he had visited Mississippi, more than once, to mourn the Neshoba victims and to raise public awareness about the lack of justice in that case. The gruesome nature of White's death was expected to capture the attention of someone like Dr. King. According to Mitchell:

There were so many injuries that almost any of the bullets could have killed him. Bullets had pulverized his liver and ripped his diaphragm. At least one had carved a gaping hole in the left side of his heart. The aorta, which carried vital blood to the rest of the body, had been torn in many places. There was no question that he bled to death.[20]

But Bowers had miscalculated in believing that White's murder would bring King to Natchez. For one thing, another white man had attempted (but failed) to murder James Meredith on June 6. Meredith, famous for integrating Ole Miss, had begun a one-man 220-mile March Against Fear from Memphis to Jackson, Mississippi, early that morning to inspire African Americans to register to vote. But thirty miles into the march, Meredith had sustained serious injuries when Aubrey Norvell, an unemployed hardware store worker, had struck him with three rifle bullets. King joined several others in taking up Meredith's mantle, a three-week trek that did not include a detour to protest White's homicide in Natchez.

The failure to impose some level of external control on King's movements, itself a tactical evolution designed to aid in the murder of a man whose itinerary changed on a day-to-day, hour-by-hour basis, likely shaped the contours of the omega plan in 1967 and 1968. It should have been clear that any conspiracy to murder King had to be ongoing and flexible. Independently of each other, the men in Swift's informal network of radical Identity terrorists tried to kill King on a situational basis, if King happened to come to their local region, and then only if he exposed himself to potential harm. It became obvious that the civil rights leader was a moving target, not a fixed one. Thus a better approach was to maintain an ongoing murder conspiracy that could strike at King regardless of which state or region he visited; if an attempt failed in one city, the conspiracy could adjust and try again in another place. But that required a greater level of cooperation between various segments of the Identity movement, something that became more and more evident as 1967 approached.

The attempts on King highlight that Swift's Identity network included regional hubs: J.B. Stoner and Ed Fields dominated Georgia and Alabama, via the National States Rights Party. Stoner, in turn, could leverage his close association with James Venable to influence events in other states, such as Ohio, through the various state chapters and Klaverns of the National Knights of the Ku Klux Klan. Sam Bowers controlled the Mississippi hub by manipulating and exploiting the activities of the White Knights of the Ku Klux Klan. And the most influential hub was in California under the direction of the Reverend Swift and Colonel Gale, through the umbrella of the Christian Defense League. Evidence indicates that beginning in

1967, these hubs increasingly began to tighten their relationships to each other, to strengthen the network.

Prior to 1967, Stoner rarely visited Mississippi; he did not even have NSRP chapters in cities like Meridian and Jackson, two places with relatively high concentrations of violent bigots. But starting in 1967, ostensibly as a legal advisor to the men accused of the Neshoba murders, Stoner made frequent visits to Meridian and Jackson. Senior leaders of the WKKKKOM attempted to form NSRP chapters in both cities and distributed hundreds of copies of *The Thunderbolt*. That same year, James Venable made several visits to California. Notably, he absorbed the California Knights of the Ku Klux Klan under the umbrella of the NKKKK; the California Knights were directly run by the Reverend William V. Fowler of the Church of Jesus Christ–Christian and were indirectly managed by Swift himself. Venable spoke at the Hollywood Women's Club, a major meeting place for Swift and the CJCC. By 1967 the mouthpiece of the NKKKK, the *Nighthawk*, increasingly printed articles with an anti-Semitic focus, indicating that the vector of the Swift–Venable relationship ran both ways.[21] The January 1968 edition of the periodical, for instance, announced its purpose to "expose the anti-Christ and their satanical plans for the destruction of the White Race" and "to expose and destroy the careers of all politicians who willfully or through ignorance of brainwashing, support the Atheistic-Jewish-Communist Conspiracy."[22] Another man in Stoner's southeastern orbit, Identity minister Sidney Barnes, established strong ties with members of the WKKKKOM, eventually moving to Jackson in 1968. When members of the White Knights were not listening to Barnes and his wife, Pauline, as they held court in home Bible studies highlighting the Jewish–communist conspiracy, Mississippi's bigots could hear the same message on tapes of Swift's sermons. These recordings became a phenomenon in southern Mississippi, played at so-called Swift parties.

Such sermons, in 1967, increasingly spoke to an imminent racial apocalypse at a time when America experienced its worst episodes of urban rioting. If simply blowing up King's hotel room in May of 1963 triggered the first riot in the history of Birmingham, killing the minister in 1968 could be expected to ignite a nationwide powder

keg of racial tension during an age of social upheaval. In 1963, when
King's push for nonviolence had dominated the ethos of the civil
rights movement, America had experienced only eleven riots. After
1965, when the civil rights movement was animated by a spirit of
anger and frustration more consistent with the bold defiance of the
late Malcolm X, racial violence spiked. Just as the Reverend Swift
had predicted, the summer of 1967 exposed a nation that was tearing
along the seams of race and class. The urban violence thawed, as
it always did, in the cool and cold weather of fall and winter. But
nothing changed the underlying dynamics of the country's racial climate as 1968 approached. In 1963 it had taken the assassination of
Medgar Evers to spark a riot in Jackson; by 1967 mere rumors of
police brutality could turn Newark, New Jersey, into a virtual war
zone. In such an environment, killing King held the promise of creating utter chaos.

It also, more than ever before, offered the possibility that such
chaos would trigger the cycle of violent outrage and retaliation predicted by Sam Bowers. When Bowers told Delmar Dennis about his
plans to foment racial conflict by instigating a cycle of recrimina-
tion and violence between militant blacks and rank-and-file whites,
nonviolence permeated the push for black liberation. King was the
most outspoken and well-known of a group of leaders who placed
their faith in Gandhi's philosophy and tactics. The group he led, the
SCLC, was just one of several grassroots organizations that held
training sessions to teach activists how to participate in nonviolent
protests. But the situation had changed after the Mississippi Burning
murders.

While the prospect of violent resistance had always appealed to
pockets of civil rights activists, by 1965 it had moved from the background to the foreground. Militant leaders such as Stokely Carmichael and groups such as the Black Panthers became increasingly
popular among liberation activists. Bowers's vision, which he fore-
told to his audience on the heels of the Neshoba killings, may not
have come to pass in the summer of 1964 in Mississippi. Militant,
leftist blacks did not attack white "civilians"; whites did not respond
with violent retaliation against blacks; the federal government did
not declare martial law in Mississippi or anywhere else. But in 1967,

in places like Detroit and cities across the nation, that vision was increasingly becoming a reality.

In that context, King became an even more attractive target to Identity radicals. Of the three men whom the FBI identified as potential "black messiahs," two—Stokely Carmichael and Elijah Muhammad—openly called for violent resistance to racial and economic oppression, for separation rather than integration. Only one of those listed, Martin Luther King Jr., continued to push for nonviolence; only he held out hope for racial harmony, even though, as he realized, the facts on the ground demanded a much bolder approach to socioeconomic justice.

His commitment to nonviolence may have lost him a measure of influence, but King remained a revered figure for much of the African American community, respected even by those who disagreed with nonviolence as a tactic. Anyone who continued to invest in the prospects of "propaganda of the deed" and who wanted to provoke a race war would have seen the potential in King's assassination. In the calculus of men like Swift, eliminating King would not only ignite a race war, but it would also remove the only person capable of pacifying the nation once the race war started.

The idea of an impending Armageddon permeated Swift's sermons, homilies that reached the ears of ardent listeners at Swift parties in Mississippi. Among Swift's most enthusiastic Mississippi listeners was WKKKKOM member Burris Dunn. Dunn forced his wife and children to listen to Swift's tapes. According to his ex-wife, Dunn (one of the most active promoters of Stoner's NSRP outreach in Mississippi) frequently invited his hero, fellow White Knight Sam Bowers, over for dinner, where they discussed Swift's sermons. She recounted that the conversations often developed into hate-filled tirades against Martin Luther King Jr.[23]

No one had tried to kill King more often than Bowers. For Bowers, one historian noted, King became "the ultimate prize." Perhaps the most tactically sophisticated of America's leading racists, Bowers would be the logical choice to spearhead the final plan to murder King.

Bowers also was famously paranoid about informants—what he and Stoner would call pimps—and with good cause. By 1967 infiltrators and informants were decimating the ranks of the WKK-KKOM. If the members of Swift's network compared notes on King assassination plots, it would become obvious that several attempts had been thwarted by insiders like Delmar Dennis. By the summer of 1967, Bowers began turning to outsiders to perpetrate violence through a newly formed clique known as the Swift Underground. But this group, like many who came before it, focused its attention on arson and demolitions. Shootings took the form of drive-bys at relatively close range. The 1963 Birmingham attempt highlighted the difficulty of such a close-range shooting of King, as the minister was frequently surrounded by an entourage.

A truly flexible plan to kill King would need people willing and able to kill at longer range, professional hit men. Bowers had already developed ties to a group with that kind of skill set: the Dixie Mafia. Someone in the White Knights had approached Donald Sparks as part of the 1964 alpha plot to kill King, but the WKKKKOM could not raise the $13,000 bounty money in time. In 1967, with apparent access to money from James Venable, and with help from many of the Identity radicals involved in previous attempts to kill King, Bowers reached out to criminals with a bounty on King's life. Thus began the omega plot.

THE OMEGA

the FINAL PLOT
to ASSASSINATE
MARTIN LUTHER KING JR.,
1967–1968

It would be inaccurate to say that the omega plot began in the spring of 1967. Rather, evidence shows that the omega plot refined and expanded upon the alpha plot from 1964. It would be more accurate to say that in executing the omega plot, Identity terrorists revived a dormant plan, developed by the White Knights, to use a contract killer to murder King, a plan that didn't succeed because the White Knights could not raise the bounty money in time. If the earlier concerns over money had given Dixie Mafia members pause when it came time to accept another contract offer on King's life, in 1967–1968, the new dollar amount likely overrode any qualms: From $13,000 in 1964, the offer had ballooned to $100,000.[1]

But by 1967 the original constituents of the 1964 alpha plot both were in prison. The FBI had finally arrested Donald Sparks in early 1967, after a spree of home and bank robberies that had landed the Tulsa-based criminal on the FBI's Most Wanted list. Convicted not long after, Sparks was sent to federal prison in Alabama. Sparks's fellow gang member Leroy McManaman was serving his sentence in Leavenworth Federal Penitentiary, a result of a 1963 conviction for the interstate transportation of stolen cars. McMamanan joined Sparks in Jackson, Mississippi, in 1964 while out on appeal bond. (He lost the appeal in April 1964.) While in Jackson, McManaman stayed with a local businesswoman, real estate agent Sybil Eure. The record shows that Eure had maintained contact with McManaman since he had lost his federal appeal, visiting him more than any of McManaman's family members did and engaging in ongoing correspondence with the felon through the prison mail. It is possible that Eure provided McManaman with the update on the growing bounty offer. Or McManaman could have received the information through criminal contacts in Leavenworth. Increasingly, by 1967 not only did the Dixie Mafia have a network of gangs inside prisons, but gang members also helped plan crimes while still serving time.

Such was the case when McManaman approached fellow prisoner Donald Nissen with an offer to kill King in the spring of 1967. Nissen did not belong to any Dixie Mafia gang, but he had enjoyed a successful criminal career in home robberies and similar crimes. Convicted in 1963 for forgery, Nissen kept to himself in Leavenworth. He did not associate with McManaman, although the two worked together in Leavenworth's shoe factory. But McManaman likely knew something about Nissen that made Nissen an attractive candidate for use in a King murder conspiracy. In a matter of weeks, Nissen would be released from Leavenworth with a prearranged job as a book salesman. As a traveling salesman, Nissen could travel across the country without raising alarms. Similarly, he could justify such travels to investigators if he became a suspect. To a criminal conspiracy that stretched across state lines, such mobility could be valuable. But however much he could travel without scrutiny, it was Nissen's ultimate base of operations that likely enhanced his résumé as a potential conspirator. Nissen's future residence would be in Atlanta, Georgia, Martin Luther King Jr.'s hometown.

With that likely in mind, McManaman offered Nissen two possible roles in the omega plot. Nissen could be a scout who tracked King's movements and reported the information to go-betweens, who could relay it to other contract killers. Or, if Nissen wanted to obtain a larger share of the $100,000 bounty, the soon-to-be-released con could also directly participate in King's murder. In addition, McManaman hoped that Nissen would approach his cell mate, John May, about taking a role in the plot. May was an expert machinist, and McManaman hoped Nissen could convince his friend to help design a rifle specifically suited to kill the civil rights leader.

Donald Nissen wanted no part of any murder plot against King—or against anyone else for that matter. In his previous crimes, he had used violence only once, reluctantly, to pacify an aggressive homeowner during a robbery. He had never even fired a gun. But McManaman's offer placed Nissen in a compromising position. Nissen knew that by saying no to McManaman, he risked retaliation; McManaman might kill Nissen in fear that he would talk.

On the other hand, saying yes would implicate Nissen in a criminal conspiracy. Nissen told his story to his cell mate, John May, more to talk through the dilemma than to recruit the machinist to design a special gun with which to kill King. Nissen ultimately decided to say nothing either way. He thought, incorrectly, that by waiting out Mc-Manaman, he could avoid violence and extricate himself from the plot. On the first account, Nissen was correct: He left Leavenworth prison in May 1967 without any attack from McManaman. But as it will become clear, McManaman took Nissen's silence as tacit consent to a conspiracy. Nissen would come to understand that— but only later, after events had trapped him inside a conspiracy he wanted nothing to do with.[2]

Nissen did not know that other bounty offers, similar to the one offered by the White Knights and fronted by McManaman, were circulating throughout America's prison system. Records suggest, for instance, that also in 1967, a group of unidentified, wealthy Georgia businessmen bribed guards in a federal prison in Atlanta to approach prisoners with a bounty offer on King. The son of one of the prison guards (his sister confirmed the story to the author) reported the offer to the FBI in the mid-1970s, after his father had died under suspicious circumstances; the father apparently had taken affidavits from prisoners and used them to blackmail the businessmen.[3] Following the father's death, the mother hid or destroyed those records. But it is in another prison where offers of a bounty on King likely contributed to the leader's ultimate death.

At Missouri State Penitentiary (MSP) in Jefferson City, several prisoners reported either hearing about or being approached with a proposal to murder King for money. Some details are vague and difficult to make sense of, so it is hard to tell if the prisoners were describing the same bounty or more than one offer. That said, the general outlines suggest that some group, located in the South, offered a considerable amount of money to any MSP inmate who could help assassinate King. Some doubt the veracity of these claims, arguing that the prisoners fabricated reports of MSP bounty offers based on the promise of a large reward from law enforcement or reduced prison sentences for their help in apprehending King's assassin. Some of the reports lack credibility. But several of the prisoners who spoke of a bounty had already been released from Leavenworth; some openly rejected a monetary reward. More importantly, in one instance, corroboration for a bounty came from an unpaid law enforcement source who had served time in the Jefferson City prison and had gone on to work for the police for three years.

The specific plot, confirmed by two prisoners, traced back to two St. Louis businessmen with close ties to the National States Rights Party. The dollar amount was high: one prisoner said he was offered $50,000 to participate in a murder conspiracy against King.[4]

This bounty offer, or something like it, likely captured the attention of the most significant figure in any discussion of the King assassination: James Earl Ray, the man who, according to official accounts, assassinated Martin Luther King Jr. in Memphis on April 4, 1968. A St. Louis native with a history of arrests for armed robbery and similar offenses, Ray was motivated by the pursuit of money far more than anything else, according to his brothers and others. Several prisoners, some of whom were close to Ray, say that Ray spoke glowingly about the prospect of a King bounty. Some prisoners attributed this enthusiasm as latent racial animus on Ray's part, but while the evidence suggests that Ray shared the kind of prejudice common to those raised in Jim Crow Missouri, he had never participated in any racial violence. On the other hand, a bounty prize of $50,000 or $100,000 represented far more cash than Ray had ever stolen in any robbery.

Still, in 1967 Ray faced another twelve years of prison time at MSP, the result of a conviction for robbing a Kroger convenience store in 1959; participating in any conspiracy against Martin Luther King Jr. would be impossible—unless he escaped. To that end, Ray finagled his way into work detail at the prison bakery that "made the bread for the institution and its outlying farms and honor dorms. Every day, a truck laden with bread would head out of the prison away from the city toward the remote farms." Ray, who had failed at escaping twice before, succeeded on April 23, 1967, when, with "the assistance of another prisoner," he climbed "into a large 4-by-4 bread box, covering himself with a false bottom and having the accomplice cover the crate with loaves of bread. The box was pushed onto the truck with the other boxes and after a cursory search by guards."[5]

Ray's decisions and actions in the first several months following his escape suggest that any bounty offer was of secondary importance to him. Ray assumed false identities and aliases, worked odd jobs, and raised money through criminal activity, first in St. Louis and then Chicago, with one goal in mind: reaching Canada. There he could obtain a fake passport and travel documents to escape North America. As will become clear, Ray's failure to execute this plan likely made a King bounty more attractive to the fugitive. It would be several months before he became part of the omega plot.

From the time of his conviction in 1969 to the day he died of liver disease in 1997, James Earl Ray insisted that he never knew of any bounty on King's life. He claimed that he had never agreed to join any murder plot. He asserted that others, notably a mysterious criminal mastermind whom he knew only as Raul, had manipulated him into incriminating behavior, such as buying a sniper rifle. As the remaining narrative will make clear, the Raul story allowed Ray to deflect blame away from himself and the actual conspirators onto others, such as the U.S. government. It was a ploy to get him out of prison and possibly to help him collect a share of the bounty money he had failed to obtain prior to his 1969 conviction.

The omega plot likely did involve a patsy—just not Ray. This individual came to the attention of the White Knights of the Ku Klux Klan of Mississippi at the same time that Leroy McManaman proposed the bounty to Donald Nissen, which was the same time that Ray escaped MSP in a breadbox. Thomas Albert Tarrants, then a twenty-year-old Christian Identity radical from Mobile, Alabama, had migrated to Laurel, Mississippi, in April 1967. He wanted to offer his services to the most actively violent white supremacist in the nation: Samuel Holloway Bowers. Despite his young age, Tarrants could point to a host of influential Christian Identity radicals to vouch for him, including Admiral John Crommelin, Noah Carden, and Sidney Barnes (all partners in the 1963 Birmingham assassination attempt on King). These men had mentored Tarrants and nourished his rage since the young man had quit high school in 1963 out of disgust with racial integration. Tarrants convinced the always-skeptical Bowers that they were like-minded in their opposition to racial equality, to communism, and most importantly to Jews.

It is unclear whether Bowers identified Tarrants as a future scapegoat in a King murder plot during their first months of contact in 1967. For a while at least, Tarrants served another important purpose for Bowers, as leader of a team of outsiders who could perpetrate violence while eluding law enforcement. By 1967, with an ever-dwindling pool of native Mississippians to use in terrorist operations, someone like this became more and more necessary.

Bowers already feared the kind of infiltration and surveillance employed by the FBI in its COINTELPRO operations. But in Mississippi the level of harassment from the Jackson FBI field office went far beyond the disruptive dirty tricks associated with COINTELPRO; it reached a level of intensity that stretched the bounds of legal propriety. The record now shows that during its investigation of the murder of civil rights activist Vernon Dahmer in 1966, the FBI used out-of-state mobsters to bully and threaten KKK members, pressuring them to reveal details of their crimes.[6] Jackson's FBI agents looked the other way as the local police fired warning shots into the homes of KKK members and physically accosted them in front of their families.[7]

The White Knights countered the FBI with a level of bravado not seen in other Klan–FBI rivalries throughout the nation. The White Knights even placed FBI agents on hit lists. In 1967 a caravan of KKK members forced a team of FBI agents, who had been following other KKK members as part of a surveillance operation, off the road. The Klan members held the FBI agents at gunpoint while the target of their surveillance mission, Joe Daniel (Danny Joe) Hawkins, exited his vehicle and confronted the agents. A young precocious racist whose entire family, including his father and mother, dedicated their lives to the White Knights, Hawkins proceeded to smack one of the FBI agents. He and the others knew that they could escape criminal liability because the White Knights had infiltrated and compromised Mississippi juries and local and state law enforcement agencies. That level of hubris infuriated the FBI even more.[8]

But in 1967 the scales of official justice finally began to turn against the White Knights. Increasingly, the Justice Department began to use early civil rights laws, some dating back to the Reconstruction era, to charge KKK members with crimes in federal, rather

than local, courts. Such cases were far less apt to be corrupted by
tainted juries or racist law enforcement officers. In February 1967
the Justice Department leveled federal charges against several of
the conspirators in the Neshoba murders, including Sheriff Lawrence Rainey, Deputy Sheriff Cecil Price, Wayne Roberts, and Sam
Bowers himself. With the Imperial Wizard and his longtime followers under constant harassment and scrutiny, Bowers decided
on his most brilliant move yet: assembling a team of dedicated terrorists, unknown to the FBI, to perpetrate one of the worst waves
of arson and bombing ever seen in Mississippi. As part of Bowers's
plan, Tarrants, the outsider from Alabama, became, in his own
words, "the chief terrorist for the White Knights of the Ku Klux
Klan of Mississippi."

Bowers took this devious plan to another level when he teamed
Tarrants with a female, Kathy Ainsworth. Historically, women
served an auxiliary role for the Klan. At rare times, some women
assumed positions of leadership. But women were never used to perpetrate acts of violence—that is, before Kathy Ainsworth.

A pretty young married elementary schoolteacher, Ainsworth
defied all profiles of a KKK operative. But she was a true believer,
raised on hate in Florida by her single mother, Margaret Capomacchia, a woman whose bigotry made George Wallace look like a
Freedom Rider. Capomacchia took her daughter on trips to Mobile
to visit Sidney Barnes, where Kathy became indoctrinated into the
teachings of Wesley Swift. She roomed with Barnes's daughter at college in Mississippi, and Barnes gave Kathy away at her wedding to
Peter Ainsworth. Privately, Barnes did not approve of the marriage,
as Peter Ainsworth did not belong to any radical white supremacist
groups. Barnes had wanted Kathy to marry Tommy Tarrants; the
two young Identity believers had met at Barnes's home in Alabama
sometime before Tarrants had moved to Mississippi, before Kathy
Ainsworth had met her future husband.

Unbeknownst to her husband, Kathy Ainsworth began training
in firearms and explosives in 1967. Along with Hawkins and another young KKK member, Benny Waldrup, Tarrants and Ainsworth
became part of what another KKK leader Laude E. (L.E.) Matthews
called the Swift Underground.

As summer approached, the always-paranoid Sam Bowers insisted that he and Tarrants meet in the woods of Laurel to elude surveillance. Even then, the Imperial Wizard demanded that they communicate by exchanging notes on paper, for fear that the FBI might be listening. They burned the correspondence after each meeting. Tarrants later said that the get-togethers often involved exchanging ideas about Swift's latest sermons and planning future violent operations in Mississippi. Today, having long abandoned Christian Identity theology and racial violence, Tarrants asserts that he never heard of any plot to kill King. Bowers may have been compartmentalizing his operations to limit exposure to infiltration and disruption. His choosing to outsource the omega plot to contract killers suggests exactly that. In betting on the Dixie Mafia's cooperation and silence, Bowers was placing his faith in a group whose members rarely cooperated with law enforcement as informants and who routinely murdered their own on account of disloyalty.

But Donald Nissen was not part of the Dixie Mafia. While Tarrants and Bowers discussed Christian Identity theology in the forests of Laurel, Nissen, just released from Leavenworth Penitentiary, encountered a roadblock on his trip to Atlanta. Having gone to Texas to pick up a company car to travel to Georgia, Nissen was arrested by officers in Sherman, Texas, on charges of check fraud that predated his stay at Leavenworth. Privately, Nissen knew he was guilty of the crime, but he also knew that the case was too weak to be successfully prosecuted. Apparently, so did the local sheriff, who detained Nissen in jail while refusing to arraign him in court. In essence, Nissen found himself detained without charge, with nothing to suggest that the situation would change. He knew that if he could get word to federal authorities, the situation would likely be resolved. But he also saw this as an opportunity to fully divorce himself from any murder conspiracy hatched by Leroy McManaman. Nissen managed to sneak a note out to the Bureau of Prisons, making sure to say that he had information about a murder conspiracy.[9]

On June 2, 1967, two FBI agents from the Dallas field office visited Nissen in the Sherman, Texas, jail. According to their report, the agents told Nissen that they would not promise to help him with his current dilemma. Nissen chose to provide them with information on the King plot anyway. He relayed McManaman's offer to the FBI: the $100,000 bounty fronted by the White Knights to kill King; the two available roles in the conspiracy (as a scout or as a direct participant in the murder). He told them about John May, his cell mate, whom McManaman hoped would design a gun to kill King. He even gave them details on the go-betweens, the people Nissen would use to maintain indirect connection to McManaman. One of these cutouts was a federal law enforcement officer out of Mississippi, but Nissen could not remember either his first or last name. Nissen did know the first name, but only the first name, of the second go-between: someone named Floyd. Nissen knew the full name and location of the third go-between: Sybil Eure of Jackson, Mississippi. The Dallas FBI passed that information on to FBI headquarters in Washington, D.C.[10] Either the FBI or officials in the Bureau of Prisons soon told a judge about Nissen's legal predicament, and as Nissen had predicted, the Sherman, Texas, prosecutors could not develop a case against him. Within days, Nissen was released from the Sherman jail and had found his way to Atlanta. He thought, wrongly, that he had exculpated himself from the omega plot by revealing the details to the FBI.

Indeed, in early June 1967, not long after Nissen arrived in Atlanta, someone named Floyd approached him to ask a favor. Floyd Ayers, a fellow salesman, asked Nissen to drop off a package at a real estate office in Jackson, Mississippi. Such requests were routine among salesmen, and Nissen agreed, thinking nothing of it. When he next visited Mississippi, sometime in late June or early July by his reckoning, Nissen visited the address provided by Ayers. Nissen was surprised to see that the real estate office was not an office but someone's home; he was also surprised that the manager of the office was a relatively tall, modestly attractive middle-aged woman. He gave her the package, and they barely exchanged words.

Nissen did not know that the woman was Sybil Eure, the same woman whom McManaman had named in Leavenworth as the third go-between in the King operation, the same woman who had provided shelter to McManaman during the alpha plot in 1964. Nissen knew nothing about any alpha plot to begin with. (Larry Hancock and I established the particulars of the 1964 Sparks/McManaman assassination attempt only after 2006.) Nissen did not realize that Floyd Ayers was likely the Floyd whom McManaman had named as the second go-between in the omega plot. In several interviews with the author since 2009, Nissen asserted that he always assumed the go-between Floyd was a Mississippian, as was the case with other two cutouts (Eure and the unknown federal law enforcement officer). Moreover, Nissen, understandably, did not realize, after their interaction in prison, that McManaman viewed his nonanswer as some sort of affirmation that Nissen wanted to help murder Martin Luther King Jr.

Some of these revelations came into focus only recently, but others became clear within weeks of Nissen's trip to Mississippi in the summer of 1967. Nissen cannot recall if it was weeks or months later, but Floyd Ayers eventually revealed to Nissen the contents of the package that the ex-con had delivered to the real estate office in Mississippi: money for a bounty offer on Martin Luther King Jr. As it turns out, Floyd Ayers had worked closely with James Venable, the Grand Wizard of the NKKKK, who had fronted $25,000 for a bounty on King in 1965.

An eccentric individual, Ayers was a perfect conduit to move money from white supremacists in the Southeast to Bowers's group in Mississippi. Accounts of Ayers's behavior, from magazine articles to interviews with his brother, point to a Walter Mitty–type personality: someone who wanted to be a mover and shaker in the world of crime or espionage. Atlanta-based civil rights activist Julian Bond described an illustrative incident with Ayers to *Jet* magazine. Ayers recognized Bond waiting on a long line to enter a popular restaurant, and Ayers told the future leader of the NAACP that he could arrange for Bond to move to the top of the queue. Ayers attributed this ability to his background in the CIA and the Secret Service—both fabrications that Bond found laughable. But for all his zaniness, Ayers did manage to get Bond into the restaurant ahead of everyone else, just as he had promised.[11]

The incident underscores what Ayers's brother told the author: Despite his connection to Venable, Floyd Ayers was not a violent racist;[12] no hard-core member of the KKK would have given Julian Bond the time of day, much less helped him to an early dinner. But

Ayers worked with Venable and did what Venable wanted because Ayers saw that connection as a way to burnish his fabulist résumé. It is not hard to imagine him agreeing to take part in a cloak-and-dagger operation against Martin Luther King Jr. At the same time, Ayers's reputation for telling tall tales and exaggerating his background could help Venable in another way. No one would take Ayers seriously if he reported on the omega plot either before King's murder or afterward. This is not idle speculation; witnesses reported that Ayers talked about the King assassination in the weeks before April 4, and he appears to have tried to clear his conscience about the crime afterward. In both cases, authorities dismissed him as a crank.

As it stands, recent disclosures by historical researcher Lamar Waldron corroborate the idea that the Southeast hub of the Identity network was the source for the omega plot bounty money. A source told Waldron that a group of racist Georgians had for years been secretly diverting union dues from factory workers at the Lakeland auto plant in Atlanta and directing them toward a King assassination bounty. This group included Hugh Spake, who worked at the plant. By 1967 the diverted dues had grown into a sizable nest egg, coming from hundreds of workers earning what was then a solid middle-class salary. Some union members were aware that their dues were being used to fund fights against integration, but very few knew about the more sinister reason for collecting the money.

A key figure in the latter effort was Joseph Milteer, an independently wealthy traveling salesman with close ties to the NSRP, to Venable's top aides, and to Swift.[13] (Milteer had obtained dozens of Swift's taped sermons.) Milteer is well-known in the study of another assassination, the John F. Kennedy murder, for having predicted elements of the president's assassination weeks in advance of November 22, 1963. As he had with Sidney Barnes in 1964 while gathering information on the Birmingham church bombing, Miami police and FBI informant Willie Somersett surreptitiously recorded Milteer saying that John F. Kennedy would be killed "from an office building with a high-powered rifle." Less known is the fact that Milteer also spoke about an ongoing effort to assassinate Martin Luther King Jr. in 1963. That plot had involved a leader of the Tennessee-based Dixie Klans named Jack Brown. Brown enjoyed a close relationship with

J.B. Stoner, and reports from a source inside Eastview Klavern 13 suggest that Brown helped train the Cahaba Boys to develop the explosive device for the Sixteenth Street Baptist Church bombing.[14] If that's true, Brown was yet another Identity follower (he was on Swift's mailing list) connected to the Birmingham murders. Those same Identity followers, as noted earlier, had tried to murder Martin Luther King Jr. when he came to eulogize the four young victims of the September 15, 1963, blast.

The insider information provided to Somersett by Milteer suggests that Milteer was part of the Identity network trying to murder Dr. King as far back as 1963. That the well-connected Georgian would work to secretly hoard cash for a King bounty and provide it to someone like Venable is thus not surprising. Nor is it surprising that Venable would, in turn, move that money through intermediaries like Ayers to Sam Bowers. Bowers's White Knights more than earned their reputation as the most violent KKK organization in the nation. Unfortunately, Waldron's source would cooperate only if his identity was protected. The source remains anonymous, and it is thus impossible to fully evaluate his credibility.

However Venable raised the money, the fact that a significant amount of cash transferred from Atlanta to Jackson becomes important in legitimizing the omega plot. It suggests that the operation was well past the planning stage and that the objective, King's murder, was a top priority. In 1967 most white supremacist organizations were strapped for cash, devoid of dues-paying members and on the hook for legal fees, none more so than the White Knights in Mississippi. Yet nothing in the available record shows that Bowers ever attempted to use cash from the $100,000 pot for legal fees, assuming that he could even access the money or that he would even dare if the money was promised to a group as ruthless as the Dixie Mafia.

The narrative suggests that Sybil Eure, given her role as a conduit for the bounty money, somehow found herself in a critical position inside the omega plot, at the junction between the Dixie Mafia and the White Knights. If the money remained in her hands, Eure would be the person to pay Dixie Mafia hit men once King had been killed. Her relationship with McManaman establishes her connection to the criminal element. Her family ties may provide the connection to the White Knights. One of Eure's associates was Robert C. Thomas, a clerk for the federal district courts in Mississippi. Before assuming that position, Thomas worked as a lead investigator for the Mississippi Sovereignty Commission, a group formed by the Mississippi State Legislature to help public officials oppose integration. The commission spied upon and developed informants inside civil rights groups and collected dossiers on activists. If his work with the commission suggests that Thomas was a southern nationalist, his malfeasance as a federal court clerk reinforces that impression. The records show that Thomas secretly helped Sam Bowers rig juries to win court cases, a criminal offense in its own right.

Thomas also fits the description that Donald Nissen gave for the first cutout mentioned by Leroy McManaman. Nissen told the FBI that the first go-between, per McManaman, was a federal law enforcement official from Mississippi, but he could not remember his name. In interviews with the author after 2009, Nissen recalled another important detail: The official worked for the marshal's office. In fact, McManaman had said that this man was the last person to assume the role of deputy marshal in Mississippi.

On the surface, this information would suggest that the individual was Charlie Sutherland, who by coincidence was also a cousin of Sybil Eure. But this seems very unlikely, based on interviews with Sutherland and with several people who knew him. Photographs show that in 1964, Robert C. Thomas was temporarily deputized as a federal marshal to help stop civil rights protests at the Jackson courthouse steps. Everything, including the fact that Thomas helped rig juries to benefit Dixie Mafia members in Mississippi, points to Thomas as the federal law enforcement officer who participated in the omega plot. As a federal court clerk, Thomas would have been in a convenient position to help McManaman in 1964, when he was violating his federal appeal bond as part of the alpha plot with Donald Sparks. But one is forced to speculate, in large part because the FBI failed to adequately follow up on leads provided by Nissen.

The FBI did interview Nissen's friend and Leavenworth cell mate, John May, who confirmed that Nissen had once discussed the $100,000 bounty from McManaman. But if agents placed any stock in May's report, their confidence in Nissen's story evaporated in a fog of male chauvinism once they found and interviewed Sybil Eure.

Agents from the Jackson FBI field office visited Eure in August 1967—not long after Donald Nissen left the package of bounty money as a favor to Floyd Ayers. By all accounts, the real estate woman maintained her composure. She denied ever hearing about any bounty offer on Martin Luther King Jr. She admitted knowing Leroy McManaman; in the spring of 1964, friends had introduced the two, and McManaman had stayed at Eure's home for several weeks. The married woman insisted that her relationship with Mc-Manaman was strictly professional and that McManaman, whose only previous experience with property management consisted of running an illegal gambling operation out of a motel in Colorado, was some sort of authority on real estate.

The Jackson FBI agents did not ask any follow-up questions. They did not inquire as to why Eure shared mutual acquaintances with a lifelong criminal or why her friends would suggest that she allow a dangerous felon to stay with her. They did not challenge her characterization of McManaman as a real estate expert. They did not ask Eure about the contents and context of her ongoing correspondence and visits with McManaman. Instead, convinced that the White Knights would never use a woman in any operational capacity, especially a respectable businesswoman like Eure, the FBI closed the book on the Nissen investigation. Agents did not even interview Leroy McManaman until several months after King's assassination.[15]

Of course, the record now shows that at the very moment the FBI dismissed Eure as a suspect because of her gender and social status, Sam Bowers intended to use a woman to help bomb Jewish and black targets in Mississippi. The FBI can be forgiven for its oversight, as it would not discover Kathy Ainsworth's role in Bowers's hit squad until late June 1968, when police officers shot her dead in a sting operation that also nearly killed Tommy Tarrants. Bowers chose Ainsworth and Tarrants for his terrorist operations precisely because neither party was known to or scrutinized by the local FBI. The wave of violence would begin in earnest one month after the FBI interviewed Eure.

One might expect that the FBI's visit to Eure would deter the Dixie Mafia from pursuing the King contract. But members of the Dixie Mafia were no ordinary criminals. They took enormous risks for money. Donald Sparks, for instance, once robbed the home of the mayor of Payne, Alabama, and then escaped in a police car when he was arrested at the scene. (It turned out that the local sheriff and an officer were in on the robbery scheme.)[16] Some suspect that Sparks participated in the murder attempt on Sheriff Buford Pusser, whose one-man war against the Dixie Mafia was immortalized in the movie *Walking Tall*. A long-range shot missed Pusser but killed his wife. The very fact that a Dixie Mafia gang even tried to kill a law enforcement officer placed them outside of the informal code of ethics honored by other violent groups, such as the Sicilian Mafia. Many believe that a Dixie Mafia gang assassinated Attorney General Albert Patterson in Phenix City, Alabama, in 1954, after the prosecutor tried to bring law and order to a town beset by vice and violence. Decades later, in 1987, Dixie Mafia members with connections to Oklahoma and Mississippi assassinated a federal judge, Vincent Sherry, and his wife, Margaret. Pusser, Patterson, and Sherry had all put themselves between the Dixie Mafia and its money, and the Dixie Mafia criminals remained undaunted.

August 1967 could have represented a turning point for the omega plot had the FBI done more to prod Sybil Eure. In one key respect, the path of the operation did change, in a way that ultimately contributed to Martin Luther King's murder. In Canada James Earl Ray failed in his mission to obtain false travel documentation that would allow him to flee North America. In reality, Ray simply misunderstood the process involved in acquiring a fake passport. Living under the alias Eric Galt, Ray mistakenly assumed that a Canadian citizen would have to vouch for his credentials before he could acquire the papers to leave. To that end, he began dating an attractive Canadian woman, in hopes of convincing her to help him. The woman grew very fond of Ray, but Ray soon learned that she worked for the Canadian government. Fearing that she might soon discover who he was and turn him into Canadian authorities for extradition to the United States, Ray abruptly abandoned the relationship. For reasons that are still unclear, Ray decided to risk recapture and return to the United States. More perplexingly, he decided to visit a city completely unfamiliar to him: Birmingham, Alabama.[17]

In 1969, after he agreed to plead guilty to avoid a death sentence for the King murder, Ray retracted his confession and insisted that he had met the Machiavellian figure Raul in Montreal and that Raul had convinced him to participate in a drug-smuggling scheme based in Birmingham. In Ray's telling, Raul spent the fall of 1967 through the spring of 1968 involving Ray in various drug-running and arms-trafficking schemes, stringing Ray along with the promise that he would soon provide Ray with the false documentation that he needed to flee North America. In reality, according to Ray and to those who favor Ray's total innocence, Raul simply manipulated Ray like a puppet, in ways that implicated the fugitive in the King murder several months later.

But there are many problems with the Raul story. For one thing, Ray's physical description of Raul changed with almost every retelling. In various narratives, Raul appears as a "blonde Latin," as a "red-haired French Canadian," as an "auburn-haired Latin," and as a "sandy-haired Latin."[18] In the early 1970s, Ray said that Raul bore a "striking resemblance" to one of the suspicious-looking hobos seen in pictures of Dealey Plaza on November 22, 1963. New Orleans district attorney Jim Garrison, who reopened an investigation into President Kennedy's assassination from 1966 to 1969, showed images of these tramps on *The Tonight Show Starring Johnny Carson*, highlighting the vagrants' uncharacteristically fashionable attire and insisting that the hobos were really presidential assassins in disguise. In making the comparison, Ray was thus connecting the King assassination to the JFK assassination at a time when Americans became increasingly convinced that the latter was a conspiracy.[19]

Yet two decades later, Ray positively identified Raul as a Portuguese immigrant to America, selecting his picture from a poorly constructed photo array.[20] The problem is that the hobo in Dealey Plaza looks nothing like the Portuguese native in the photo array; in both cases, Ray simply told sympathetic investigators what they wanted to hear and then watched as these individuals worked tirelessly to clear him of involvement in MLK's murder. Inventing fake individuals to deflect blame away from himself was nothing new to Ray.

When under arrest for an earlier crime, Ray had invented a figure named Walter McBride, whom he had blamed for masterminding the crime in question.

For the most part, one must rely on Ray himself to piece together his movements and associations after his escape from MSP, and Ray's tendency to dissemble and prevaricate for his own self-interest clouds any hope of fully understanding what—and who—motivated his decisions. Some researchers, such as Dartmouth professor Philip Melanson, argue that Ray fabricated the Raul character as a composite of individuals who really did assist or guide him into a conspiracy. One of the main investigators on Ray's early defense team, Harold Weisberg, became convinced that the convicted assassin had offered false leads (or withheld legitimate leads) to protect actual conspirators. Weisberg postulated that Ray did this for fear of retaliation in prison and that he did not play a major role in the King murder. Whatever his motives, and whatever conspirators may have influenced those motives, one is forced to speculate on Ray's choices.[21]

Ray's choice to return to the United States from Montreal, risking recapture, lends itself to much speculation, especially when one considers that the risk is amplified if a criminal goes to a city with which he is unfamiliar and where he lacks any support network, as Ray did when he visited Birmingham. The money-obsessed Ray may have frequented bars in Montreal, just as he said he did, hoping to find more information about the King bounty referenced at MSP. Canada was not short on white supremacists who could have pointed Ray in the right direction. Some evidence suggests that that's what happened.

One woman in Quebec told investigators that her boyfriend, whom she knew as Rollie and whose real name was Jules Ricco Kimble, had associated with Ray in Canada. She said that Kimble carried guns and monitored police radio broadcasts in Montreal. Records show that Kimble frequently went back and forth from his native United States to Canada, including during the relevant time period in the summer of 1967. Moreover, Kimble enjoyed close working relationships with the Ku Klux Klan in his home state of Louisiana and had engaged in various acts of Klan-inspired violence. Kimble himself claimed to be involved in the King murder, but his stories of intrigue worthy of a Robert Ludlum novel are difficult to believe or corroborate.[22]

Records of the congressional reinvestigation of the King murder in the late 1970s show that the House Select Committee on Assassinations (HSCA) developed two other possible contacts for Ray in Canada. House investigators asked the Royal Canadian Mounted Police to provide information on two Americans, both connected to the NSRP, who had moved to Canada sometime after 1963. Unfortunately, records that explain why the committee became suspicious of these two men, and more importantly what it learned about the two individuals, are still sealed. What is known is that both of these men once worked closely with Stoner and Fields in Birmingham.[23]

Perhaps this is why Ray, when he moved to Birmingham in September 1967, chose to stay (under the alias Galt) at a rooming house not far from NSRP headquarters on Bessemer Road. None of the other boarders saw Ray interact with anyone at the rooming house (or with anyone resembling Raul, for that matter). And we know only some of what Ray did when he was outside of the rooming house.

He purchased a white Ford Mustang, the vehicle that would become famous as the getaway car after the King murder. We also know that he took dance classes and purchased photographic equipment, the latter almost definitely with the intent of producing amateur pornography. He rented a safety deposit box at the Birmingham branch of Trust National Bank, the first and only time he is known to have done so.

The safety deposit box may be more significant than previously thought. Researcher Charles Faulkner discovered that in 1966, government investigators identified the Trust banks as the primary banks for the United Klans of America.[24] Information obtained from the investigation of the bombing of the Sixteenth Street Baptist Church indicates that several notable NSRP members, including J.B. Stoner, used the Birmingham branch. When, decades later, researcher Gerald Posner asked Edward Fields if he had any direct contact with Ray— if Ray had ever visited NSRP headquarters on Bessemer Road— Fields said no. But the longtime Identity radical qualified his answer, saying that while he personally never interacted with Ray, he could not discount the possibility that other NSRP members had engaged with the fugitive that September.[25]

It seems clear that if Ray pursued a King bounty in Birmingham, he failed to immediately introduce himself into such a conspiracy. Within weeks he would be in Mexico, where he stayed for almost two months, possibly engaging in low-level drug dealing but most definitely pursuing a career as a pornographic film producer, even enticing two Mexican women into salacious photo sessions. Ray's Mexican jaunt and his initial efforts to produce pornographic films ended in the middle of October 1967, with little to show for them. There is no sign of any direct connection of Ray to a King plot during his time in Mexico. Restless, Ray moved to Los Angeles in November. There, in the spiritual capital of the Christian Identity world, Ray appears to have continued exploring a possible bounty on Martin Luther King Jr. As will become clear, the evidence suggests that in December, Ray finally began to make progress in entering the omega plot.

While Ray moved from Birmingham to Mexico to Los Angeles, Sam Bowers's activities in Mississippi suggest that the omega plot may have been on hold. One could expect this if word of the FBI's visit to Sybil Eure had reached the paranoid Imperial Wizard. Always cautious, Bowers may have waited to see if Eure was under surveillance or if the FBI continued to investigate the bounty. Of course, Bowers also listened to the sermons of Wesley Swift and discussed them with his newest acolyte, Tommy Tarrants. Back in February of 1967, Swift had spoken about the reaping of tares, the weeds that resemble wheat but that rob genuine wheat of its nourishment. During the end-times, God has these tares harvested for destruction. But in Swift's rendition, the metaphorical weeds are satanic Jews. If Bowers paused the omega plot, he still initiated his plan to target Jewish Mississippians and their subhuman minions (blacks) at a never-before-seen rate.

Tommy Tarrants and his colleagues in the Swift Underground began their reign of terror on September 18, 1967. The target: the Temple Beth Israel in Jackson. Two dynamite bombs caused $25,000 worth of damage to the Mississippi capital's only synagogue. Within a few weeks, the same crew bombed the home of Rabbi Perry Nussbaum, who had for years associated himself with the cause of civil rights, creating much controversy even within Mississippi's small Jewish community. The next target on the list was William T. Bush, dean of the all-black Tougaloo College. The attacks continued: the rectory of black minister Allen Johnson in Laurel, Mississippi, on November 15; the home of civil rights activist Robert Kochitzky on November 19.

The bombings shocked southern Mississippi and deflated some of the hope that law enforcement entertained in light of recent federal prosecutions of key violent racists. In October 1967, seven men, including Grand Wizard Sam Bowers, were convicted of civil rights violations in the murders of Michael Schwerner, Andrew Goodman, and James Chaney (the MIBURN killings) and were sentenced to three to ten years in prison. In November trials began for thirteen men, again including Bowers, accused of killing activist Vernon Dahmer. The White Knights began to make arrangements for a transfer of power from Bowers to L.E. Matthews, a bomb maker from Forrest County, Mississippi. Yet the plan Bowers hatched for using outsiders like Tarrants and Ainsworth worked to perfection, baffling Mississippi police and special agents of the FBI's Jackson field office even as law enforcement maintained constant surveillance of Bowers and his remaining loyalists.

For Tarrants, soon to be known by the FBI as simply The Man, times were good. He reached out directly to Swift, impressing the racist theologian so much that Swift invited Tarrants to California to serve as his understudy.

In December 1967, life was also going fine for Donald Nissen. He was making a good living selling books. He had remarried, and his new wife was pregnant. He dutifully maintained his parole requirements and avoided criminal activity. The concern he had over the McManaman offer and the package delivery for Floyd Ayers was a distant memory—or so it seemed. Everything changed when Nissen visited his probation officer. Nissen cannot recall if it was the first or second of December, but when he left his parole officer at the Atlanta Federal Building, a man accosted him outside. "Are you Donald Nissen?" he asked. When Nissen answered in the affirmative, the man made a vague reference to Leroy McManaman and then issued a veiled threat to Nissen about "talking too much." At that moment, the man who had driven Nissen to the building called for him, and the mysterious figure quickly left.

Nissen was convinced that the incident involved his decision to tell the FBI about the White Knight bounty offer on King. As he has related in a series of interviews since 2009, his fears intensified when the windows of his car were shot out in the days that followed. Equally scary was something he remembered from McManaman's initial offer: A federal marshal was one of the cutouts in the plot. To Nissen, this opened the possibility that his own probation officer, or someone connected to him, might be involved in the King plot. Paranoid, Nissen resolved that he could not go to federal law enforcement again. Even with a new marriage, a pregnant wife, and a well-paying job, Nissen jumped parole—a crime that would send him back to federal prison if he were to be caught.[26] Luckily for Nissen, officials did not discover his absence until April 2, 1968, two days before King's assassination.

The threat to Nissen suggests that conspirators had resumed the omega plot by December of 1967. Perhaps not coincidentally, that December marks the first instance when James Earl Ray's behavior became indicative of someone making serious inroads into a King murder conspiracy.

Ray used money, most likely from minor drug dealing in Mexico, to settle in a residential Los Angeles neighborhood. He stayed there for several weeks and would later claim that he wanted to find a job with the merchant marine, more or less giving up on Raul as a source for immigration papers. He continued to pursue dance lessons, in efforts to meet potential performers for his films, and he began to see a hypnotist, purportedly to overcome his problem with shyness.

He also continued to frequent bars, where he met Marie Martin, who eventually introduced him to her two cousins, Charles Stein and his sister, Rita. The family originated in New Orleans and had relatives in the area, notably Rita Stein's children. Charles Stein asked Ray to drive him to New Orleans to pick up Rita's children. Ray agreed, although Stein was convinced that Ray had a separate agenda. If so, Ray's next act offers a hint at what he might have been up to.

In a very strange series of events, Ray insisted that as a condition of the trip, Marie Martin and her cousins register for onetime Alabama governor and arch-segregationist George Wallace's American Independent Party (AIP). He took them to campaign headquarters, where they completed the forms. Ray was never known to be motivated by politics; money was his inspiration.

Ray's own explanation for the visit contradicts the account of Martin and the Stein siblings. Unlike Ray, who for a number of reasons wanted to avoid associating himself with racists like those in the AIP after his arrest for King's murder, Marie Martin, Rita Stein, and Charles Stein had no reason to lie. Ray may have seen the AIP as the safest avenue to ingratiate him with would-be plotters without attracting the attention of law enforcement.

But Ray himself did not register for the AIP, suggesting that he either did not think it was safe enough or that he had another purpose in visiting that building; one possibility is that Ray was looking for a particular individual who worked for the Wallace campaign. While the AIP avoided the violence associated with more radical groups, it was still known to attract radical supporters. One such individual was James P. Thornton, a California native nurtured in his racism by Stoner and Fields in Alabama in the early 1960s; Thornton also belonged to the Church of Jesus Christ–Christian. Thornton's life as a white supremacist had been interrupted by a brief stint in the military. Following his service, Thornton returned to California to start the state's chapter of the NSRP. When Ray visited Birmingham in 1967, Thornton had already left the city. Perhaps members of the Birmingham NSRP suggested that Ray find Thornton in Los Angeles at AIP headquarters. If so, Ray was late again, as Thornton had moved to Atlanta a few months earlier, after being fired by the AIP for his radicalism. Whatever Ray's interest was in the AIP, he and Charles Stein began their road trip to New Orleans on December 15, 1967.

If Ray wanted to find a gateway to a King bounty plot, New Orleans was a hub for both racist and criminal activity. Indeed, according to a senior WKKKOM official, New Orleans was where his group obtained guns and weapons for its criminal activities. The Dixie Mafia had connections to New Orleans through several former

members of Sicilian Mafia kingpin Carlos Marcello's criminal enter-
prise—some of whom shifted their allegiance to the less formal Dixie
Mafia after Marcello faced federal prosecution in 1967. Dixie Mafia
members also used New Orleans to sell weapons to the Klan. But
no direct evidence confirms any contacts between criminals, be they
members of the Dixie Mafia or the Sicilian Mafia, and Ray. Again,
Ray's own dissembling renders any definitive understanding of his
preassassination connections and associations all but inscrutable.

It does appear likely, however, that Ray met someone in New
Orleans who provided him with access to additional money—either
in the form of a cash advance or, more likely, drugs to sell in Los
Angeles. An analysis by government investigators showed a clear
and unusual spike in Ray's spending habits immediately after he returned to Los Angeles. Ray's actions became increasingly suspicious
as the weeks proceeded, suggesting his recruitment into a very real
conspiracy. Ray ultimately claimed that he was framed for the King
killing, an assertion that does not stand up to scrutiny. But concurrent events in Mississippi in December suggest the possibility that
Sam Bowers may have been testing Tommy Tarrants, with an eye
toward setting up the young terrorist as a patsy.

On December 22, 1967, Sam Bowers did something highly unusual: He convinced Tommy Tarrants to join him on a trip to Collins, Mississippi. The purpose was to machine-gun the home of Ancie
McLaurin, a black man accused of shooting a white police officer.
This represented a major departure from Bowers's usual cautious
behavior. Bowers ordered crimes but rarely participated in them in
any direct way. What's more, federal prosecutors had already convicted Bowers for his role in ordering the Mississippi Burning killings that October, although Bowers had escaped with a relatively
minor sentence. Out on appeal, Bowers was now risking a capital
sentence by going on this mission. Indeed, he was risking not only
himself but also his secret operative, Tarrants, to potential exposure.

Bowers may have been testing Tarrants's willingness to participate
in a crime. For Bowers to have accepted Tarrants into his fold without
suspicion is odd to begin with, as Bowers came to suspect even his
closest allies of snitching to federal law enforcement. The fact that no
one died in any of Tarrants's many bombings may have raised alarms

with Bowers, and now he had the opportunity to see firsthand if Tarrants would kill for the cause. Bowers never got the chance to imple-
ment this test, however, as Collins police officers, suspicious of the
Alabama license plates on Tarrants's car, approached the men when
they pulled into a gas station. The car was stolen, and the men were
arrested; police found an unlicensed machine gun in the vehicle.

Whether Bowers was testing Tarrants or not, the arrest had the
effect of suspending the recent wave of violence in Mississippi. If the
pause was due to caution, the charges did little to raise alarms about
Tarrants among law enforcement figures. Bowers escaped conviction
for the gun charges that following January, and Tarrants's arraign-
ment was set for later in 1968. Yet the subsequent lull in activity in
Mississippi suggested that Bowers was exercising caution. If events
on the ground had delayed the plot against King in the fall, then this
most recent brush with the law likely had the same impact. James
Earl Ray's activity after his suspicious trip to New Orleans suggests
just that.

Not long after Tarrants and Bowers encountered law enforcement
in Collins, Ray returned to Los Angeles after his sojourn to New
Orleans. His activities in the weeks immediately following his return
hint that he was more entwined in a King murder conspiracy, but he
was far from operational. It is as if Ray expected that he might be
used in the crime but was ignorant of when and how. On December
28, 1967, Ray wrote to several groups connected with countries such
as Rhodesia and South Africa for information about immigrating
to those nations. Both were English-speaking countries that lacked
extradition treaties with the United States; they were also highly segregated countries with a well-publicized record of apartheid against
native blacks. To burnish his résumé, Ray specifically referenced the
John Birch Society, a right-wing, antigovernment organization but
one that distanced itself from racist violence. Of course, Ray had
been trying to flee North America for months. But his financial ex-
penditures suggest that he was delaying that escape, something with
no innocent explanation. Something like the high-money bounty
offer on King's life was probably keeping him stateside.

By the end of January, whatever extra money he had obtained in
New Orleans seemed to have vanished for Ray. Sticking with the

Galt alias, he moved from more comfortable surroundings on North Serrano Street to a room at the St. Francis Hotel in downtown Los Angeles. One person described Ray's new community as a "den of iniquity, teeming with prostitution and drug trafficking." Ray had prepaid for a number of side activities, such as dance lessons and bartending classes, so for a while money issues weren't pressing. Now they were. Through February at least, Ray still looked like someone on the periphery of the omega plot. He continued his mundane life, posing as Eric Galt. This lull coincided with a similar break in activity from the people we believe were organizing the plot in Mississippi. Both with the White Knights and Ray, this appears to have been the calm before the storm

As Ray continued to elude federal authorities in California, Tarrants found himself in law enforcement's crosshairs for the first time since 1965, when he was arrested, as a teenager, for carrying an illegal firearm. Two years later, no one knew of his terrorist bombings and shootings in Mississippi, but his arrest with Sam Bowers meant that for the second time he was facing federal firearms charges.

On his attorney's advice, Tarrants returned to his family in Mobile and registered for classes at a community college, ostensibly to clean up his image in anticipation of a court date. But records show that Tarrants was not much of a student. His mind was still dedicated to fighting the "Jewish–communist conspiracy" against white America.

For his part, Bowers escaped conviction for the firearms charges in mid-January. While the Justice Department convicted other White Knights for their roles in the 1966 Dahmer murder, Bowers was acquitted due to a mistrial. But in January 1968, Bowers's luck with the law ran out. He was free but on appeal bond for his conviction for the MIBURN murders. Arrangements were already being made to transfer Grand Wizard power to L.E. Matthews once Bowers went to prison. By early 1968, almost every major player in the White Knights faced or would face some kind of criminal charges. Many, including Bowers, temporarily kept a low profile. Increasingly, they worked through a front organization, Americans for the Preservation of the White Race, to raise money for legal costs. Through that same front, senior WKKKKOM members continued to actively promote Stoner's National States Rights Party in

Meridian and Jackson, mailing out the NSRP's radical newspaper, *The Thunderbolt*.

The lull in Mississippi Klan violence came to an end on February 20, 1968, when the White Knights burned down a grocery store belonging to Wallace Miller, a onetime KKK member who had become an FBI informant and testified in the Neshoba prosecution. Two weeks later, the White Knights bombed the Blackwell Realty Company in Jackson for selling homes to blacks in white neighborhoods. Having endured months of bombings, local and federal law enforcement fought back in unprecedented ways. Unable to secure convictions in local cases, Meridian police formed a special squad under Sergeant Lester Joyner. According to historian Michael Newton, "Joyner's guerillas," as they were known, "fired into Klansmen's homes and detonated explosives on their lawns."[27] As noted earlier, the Jackson field office of the FBI was already experienced with fighting dirty against the local Klan. Clueless as to the perpetrators of the recent bombings, the office doubled down on its efforts to, in the words of Special Agent Jim Ingram, catch the "mad dog" bombing Mississippi's black and Jewish institutions.

No one in federal law enforcement appeared to be paying much attention to the escaped fugitive from Missouri State Penitentiary, James Earl Ray. But Ray began to behave like the notorious figure he would soon become: the most wanted fugitive in the United States. On March 2, 1968, the man known to his classmates as Eric Galt graduated from bartending school in Los Angeles. In the graduation photo, James Earl Ray deliberately closed his eyes to make future identification more difficult. On March 3, 7, and 11, Ray spent a sizable amount of his remaining money on plastic surgery to alter his appearance. Ray later said that the surgery was done to make a future identification more difficult, claiming that he expected his operations with Raul—specifically a gunrunning operation that had started in New Orleans—to become more serious. To believe this, one would have to believe that Ray, a career criminal who had escaped from a federal penitentiary, thought that being an accomplice to a minor gunrunning operation would earn him the same respect from J. Edgar Hoover as John Dillinger had in 1934. Ray was not as foolish as he pretended to be or as others have assumed. If helping a fictional gunrunner wouldn't get Ray on the FBI's Most Wanted list, conspiring to kill Martin Luther King Jr. certainly would.

Ray's recruitment into a King conspiracy was further suggested by Allan O. Thompson, manager of the St. Francis Hotel, where Ray had been staying since late January. Thompson told investigators that he remembered his switchboard operator reporting a series of phone calls to Eric Galt sometime in March, possibly as early as March 1. The calls came from either New Orleans or Atlanta or both, and the caller left the name J.C. Hardin. Sometime in the middle of the month, a stranger who Thompson presumed was Hardin actually visited the St. Francis looking for Galt/Ray.

The likely identity of J.C. Hardin emerged after reexamination of the FBI's investigation into Thompson's claims. Having mined its national files for individuals who used the alias J.C. Hardin, the FBI presented Thompson with a number of pictures. Thompson noted a striking overall similarity between the man who had visited the hotel and a man in one of the FBI photographs. Inexplicably, the FBI dismissed the match because the hair in the photo was different, ignoring the fact that the J.C. Hardin photo had been taken more than a decade before the King murder. Newly released files make clear that Thompson identified James Wilbourne Ashmore from Texas as J.C. Hardin. Ashmore had a steady history of criminal offenses, mostly for theft and forgery, and had served more than one stint in prison. Nothing directly indicated that he was connected to a group like the Dixie Mafia, but such information does not appear in the FBI files of either Donald Sparks or Leroy McManaman, two known Dixie mobsters. Law enforcement only was just beginning to understand the phenomenon that was the Dixie Mafia in the late 1960s.

A truck driver by trade, Ashmore was exactly the kind of individual the Dixie Mafia liked to recruit for its missions: someone who could routinely cross state lines without drawing the attention of law enforcement. More work needs to be done to develop the case that Ashmore, who died in 1973 in California, was possibly an accessory in the King conspiracy.[28] But it seems probable that he was another go-between in the Dixie Mafia/White Knights bounty plot and, quite importantly, the one who finally integrated James Earl Ray into the scheme. Newly discovered information makes this idea even more tantalizing. The FBI originally located the Hardin alias for Ashmore in files that connected him to the 1962 Ole Miss race riots.[29] Those riots not only incited many future members of the WKKKKOM but also drew the attention of radicals from around the nation, notably Identity radical Oren Potito, southeastern leader of the National States Rights Party.

And as of March 17, 1968, James Earl Ray was leaving Los Angeles for good and heading to the Southeast. He promised Marie Martin that he would stop in New Orleans on his way and drop off a package for her family. It was only a detour on his intended destination: Martin Luther King Jr.'s hometown of Atlanta. In a pattern that would repeat itself, King also left Los Angeles on March 17, en route to Memphis.

At approximately the same time Ray was making arrangements to move to Atlanta, Tommy Tarrants took a pilgrimage to the home of his hero, the Reverend Wesley Swift, in Lancaster, California. According to Tarrants's autobiography, he had made contact with Swift some months earlier and, as mentioned previously, had impressed the reverend enough to be invited to become his understudy. Tarrants's interaction with Swift has enormous implications for the King assassination. In writing his excellent 1993 book on anti-Jewish violence in Mississippi, *Terror in the Night*, Pulitzer Prize–winning reporter Jack Nelson used Tarrants as a major source. Nelson quotes a 1991 interview with Tarrants, in which Tarrants admitted buying a rifle from Swift for the purpose of shooting Martin Luther King Jr. "That was my ambition," Nelson quoted Tarrants as saying, "to shoot Dr. King. I hated Dr. King."[30] In a 2007 interview with the Jackson *Clarion-Ledger*, Tarrants seemingly backed off from such comments. By this time he had undergone a dramatic religious conversion to mainstream, evangelical Christianity, a process that he began in the 1970s and that resulted in an early release from prison. (He was convicted in 1969 for his role in the 1967–1968 Mississippi bombing spree and had been sentenced to thirty years behind bars.) To reporter Jerry Mitchell, Tarrants acknowledged that he bought the rifle from Swift in March 1968, but he insisted that he did so to "get acquainted with Swift. I thought a lot of him and listened to his recordings, was under that influence." As to the other quote in Nelson's book about his "ambition" to shoot King, Tarrants acknowledged "having those views," but he said, "A lot of people in the south hated Martin Luther King."[31] Tarrants gave Mitchell's readers the impression that the Swift visit had little to do with a King murder plot.

Newly uncovered information brings this matter into sharper focus. Audio files that Nelson's wife, Barbara Matuszow, donated to Emory University, contain the original Nelson interviews with Tarrants. Nelson first asked Tarrants if the House Un-American Activities Committee (HUAC) had interviewed him. It is likely that Nelson confused HUAC—which did not exist after 1975 but which at one time investigated the KKK—with the HSCA. The HSCA had run concurrent reinvestigations of the John F. Kennedy and Martin Luther King murders from 1976 to 1979. Indeed, Tarrants told Mitchell in 2007 that HSCA investigators did see him in the late 1970s. For reasons that are still unclear, Nelson then turned directly to the issue of the rifle purchase:

NELSON: They must have quoted your testimony at some point in their report or something. Did you say anything about buying a rifle to assassinate King?

TARRANTS: Yeah . . . yeah I told them that.

NELSON: When did you do that?

TARRANTS: I think I bought that from Wesley Swift as a matter of fact.

NELSON: Is he still around?

TARRANTS: No, he died of cancer years ago. [chatter]

TARRANTS: That was my ambition, to shoot Martin Luther King. Oh yeah, I hated him worse than any of the blacks.[32]

Tarrants went on to give vivid detail on the weapon, a .243 Mannlicher (likely a Mannlicher-Schoenauer). His memory was fuzzy, however, as to when exactly he purchased the weapon, although it is fairly clear from the record that it was during his trip to California in March of 1968. Similar to his 2007 interview with Jerry Mitchell, when he denied any involvement in King's murder, Tarrants told Nelson and Matuszow that he never tracked or got close to King. But in the interview with Mitchell, without ever directly commenting on buying the rifle to try to kill King, Tarrants again asserted that he had gotten the weapon simply to impress Swift. Taken in conjunction with the "that was my ambition, to shoot Martin Luther King" statement, the matter at least deserves further clarification from Tarrants. He has chosen not to speak on the matter since his 2007 interview with Mitchell. The immediate temptation is to see the 1991 quote and its timing as evidence that Tarrants was involved in King's murder. But a more likely possibility is that Tarrants's later claim to Mitchell that he had no role in King's murder is likely true. As will become more obvious in the next chapter, what appears to be a suggestive circumstantial case against Tarrants for some kind of involvement in King's murder looks more like the result of a carefully orchestrated effort to frame him for the crime.

The idea of a frame-up is well worn in theories on the King assassination. For decades, the only man convicted in the crime, James Earl Ray, insisted that he was a patsy in the murder. But Ray's actions from the end of March through the beginning of April substantively contradict this assertion. Instead they strongly suggest that he played a conscious role in the crime.

Having dropped off Marie Martin's package in New Orleans on March 21, James Earl Ray ventured to Atlanta, but not before making a highly suspicious stop that took him directly to the vicinity of Dr. King. Almost three years after civil rights marchers in pursuit of voting rights had stood their ground against club-carrying Alabama policemen on horses, King returned to Selma. He was there to give a speech on March 22, one that newspapers had publicized in advance. Any logical route to Atlanta would have taken Ray through Birmingham and not Selma, but Ray found his way to Selma at the same time as King, staying at the Flamingo Hotel. Confronted with this coincidence, Ray claimed that he had made a wrong turn. But Selma is completely out of the way, and maps from the time show that the "wrong turn" described by Ray wasn't even possible given the available exits. As it turned out, at the last minute, weather prevented King from coming to Selma.[33]

King returned to his hometown of Atlanta, and Ray followed, traveling through Montgomery and Birmingham. Ray had never spent any time in Atlanta before. On March 23, he rented a room at a cheap rooming house known to accommodate drunks and vagrants in the Peachtree section of the city. Again, he used the alias Eric Galt. There is little to account for Ray's precise behavior while he was in Atlanta. But evidence suggests that he made contact with someone. Investigators found a receipt for a dinner for two at Mammy's Shanty, a local dive that, according to researcher Lamar Waldron (an Atlanta native and lifelong resident), was frequented by racists.[34] When one of Ray's earliest chroniclers, William Bradford Huie, confronted him about this dinner receipt, Ray was unable to explain it.

Also suspiciously, Ray obtained a commercial map of Atlanta and, as was often his custom, marked areas that were relevant to him. On this map, Ray circled his rooming house but also Martin Luther King Jr.'s home. The FBI claimed that Ray also marked King's church and SCLC headquarters on the map, but this appears to be mistaken or an outright fabrication. Interestingly, diligent efforts by researcher Jerry Shinley offer a different possibility for Ray's markings: They appear very close to a restaurant that served as a front operation for Cliff Fuller, a Dixie Mafia criminal who later turned federal informant. Another mark appears very close to a nightclub frequented by Fuller's partner-in-crime, Harold Pruett. Ray never offered an adequate explanation for why these areas were marked on the map, but the possible connection to Fuller—a man with contacts in the Dixie Mafia in Mississippi, among other places—is tantalizing. Certainly, the double circle around King's home clearly suggests that Ray stalked King not only in Selma but on through Atlanta. For this reason, the offer extended by Leroy McManaman to Donald Nissen takes on new significance. McManaman told Nissen that he could have a stake in the bounty in one of two ways. Nissen could participate in the actual killing or he could case King's movements and report them to the would-be killers. Specifically, McManaman mentioned casing King's movements in Atlanta—Nissen's destination following his immediate release.

It makes sense that any conspiracy involving Ray would use him in the stalker role, as he had no background as a professional killer or sniper. But one could safely assume that as this secondary role was far less risky, it promised much less of the bounty. Whether that would sit well with Ray as he proceeded on through the mission is another matter.

Tarrants says he decided to leave Swift and visit his uncle in San Diego. After that, he and a cousin returned to Mobile. There, Tarrants says, he spotted FBI agents in round-the-clock surveillance of his residence. In going to California, Tarrants had jumped bond for his upcoming trial for the firearms charge. Already upset with the government, Tarrants decided to pursue an even more serious form of resistance against the enemies of white Christians. Robert DePugh, the hard-core leader of the Minutemen group, wanted on firearms and robbery charges, was then singlehandedly leading the FBI on a weeks-long manhunt. Inspired by this example, Tarrants decided that he, too, would become a lone-wolf terrorist. On March 28 he wrote a note that police discovered months later: "Please be advised that since 23, March, 1968, I . . . have been underground and operating guerrilla warfare."[35]

Tarrants's story in March parallels that of another radical whose account only recently became available. Eugene Mansfield at one time was a Grand Dragon in the Texas KKK. For several years, his racist activity was dormant. At least in FBI files, his only recorded offense was an assault charge from 1966. Suddenly, on March 13, 1968, Mansfield left his job on an oil rig in Louisiana, forwarded his last check to L.E. Matthews's residence in Mississippi, and went to stay with Matthews. Documents show that Matthews, who would succeed Bowers as head of the WKKKKOM in 1969, wanted to use Mansfield in a hit or another job. Documents also indicate that in the last two weeks of March, Matthews was in and out of his normal residence, planning some kind of project out of state. Unable to account for his whereabouts in the immediate wake of King's assassination, Mansfield became one of the earliest persons of interest in the crime.[36] Tarrants also spent part of his time living underground with Matthews, but he never gave Nelson specific dates. FBI records indicate that Matthews encouraged Tarrants to visit his next location, a remote site in North Carolina where white supremacists from across the nation perfected their paramilitary skills. According to

Tarrants, he stayed with Swift followers in this area for an unspecified period.

Although Tarrants was a fugitive from a weapons charge, the FBI did not yet know about his months-long bombing campaign in Mississippi, much less his promise to become a one-man guerrilla army waging war against the American government. The agency apparently did not know about his visit to Wesley Swift or the rifle purchase to "shoot King." In short, at the end of March 1968, Tarrants should have raised none of the alarms that Mansfield raised in discussing hits with the soon-to-be Grand Wizard of the most dangerous racist organization in the country. Yet somehow Tarrants garnered just as much immediate interest from law enforcement in connection with the King murder. It seems entirely possible that as the calendar moved closer to April 4, someone was informing on Tarrants. The significance of this will be explored in the next chapter.

As Tarrants wrote his antigovernment screed, Martin Luther King Jr. returned to Memphis. His visit was originally intended for the week before, but scheduling problems forced King to come back on March 28, having promised to lead a nonviolent protest on behalf of the striking sanitation workers. Disappointed with fund-raising and mobilization efforts for the Poor People's Campaign, King saw the Memphis sanitation workers strike, with its national profile, as an opportunity to raise public awareness on issues of economic justice while demonstrating the viability of large-scale nonviolent protest.

The day before King's arrival in Memphis on March 28, James Earl Ray drove his white Mustang from Atlanta to Birmingham and visited a sporting goods store called The Gun Rack, looking for a hunting rifle. He spent considerable time looking at potential weapons but ultimately left without making a purchase. Two days later, on March 29, 1968, Ray visited the Aeromarine Supply Company, a sporting goods retailer that also sold rifles. Dressed in a shirt and tie, Ray looked out of place to a young hunting enthusiast, John DeShazo. The questions Ray asked confirmed DeShazo's impressions; Ray knew nothing about rifles. But Ray purchased a .243-caliber rifle and ammunition using the alias Harvey Lowmeyer. On March 30, Ray reappeared at the Aeromarine to exchange his weapon. FBI experts later concluded that a preservative in the rifle's breech had prevented its proper loading. But Ray made no reference to this problem, even though it would have provided him with a perfectly innocent reason to exchange the weapon. Instead, Ray said that his brother or brother-in-law had examined the .243 and concluded that they needed a better weapon to go "hunting in Wisconsin." Ray said that his brother had told him to get a Remington GameMaster .760. One of the more highly regarded hunting weapons ever produced, it was also more expensive than the .243, meaning the normally frugal Ray was stepping out of character.[37] That Ray had some guidance in choosing a weapon seems likely, not simply because he gratuitously referenced another person but also because he demonstrated little or no understanding of rifles.

Ray, of course, blamed it on Raul, claiming that he told Ray to return to the store and purchase the GameMaster. Under that scenario, Ray referred to Raul as his brother to protect his benefactor's identity. Others who harbor doubts about Raul's existence suggest that it was one of Ray's actual brothers who helped him with the rifle purchase.[38] This cannot be discounted, but direct evidence is lacking.

An interesting possibility for someone who might have advised Ray on the gun purchase emerged from an examination of out-of-state phone calls made from the Sambo Amusement Company, Sam Bowers's business in Laurel, Mississippi. On March 29, 1968, the day of the original rifle purchase, someone at Sambo called a number in Birmingham. It was the only phone call to Birmingham from the fall of 1967 through the summer of 1968. Bowers and his partner, Robert Larson, operated the company with no other employees. The timing is certainly curious, but the phone record has no detail on who was called. Only recently, thanks to research by Charles Faulkner, the number has been traced to the Birmingham Army Reserve, specifically to the senior army advisor for the Army Reserve Advisor Group. Extensive research, including work done by military historians, has yet to generate an actual name for this army advisor, but both the timing and a call by Bowers or Larson to Birmingham are suggestive of a conspiratorial act.[39]

After the purchase of the gun, Ray returned to Atlanta. Ray always denied this, insisting instead that he was told by Raul to go straight to Memphis. The evidence to the contrary—that Ray returned and left his laundry at a dry cleaner in Atlanta—is overwhelming, however. This fact was established not only by the recollection of the manager of the Piedmont Laundry but also by a dated receipt in her files. This is one of Ray's most important and revealing lies. Ray himself acknowledged that if investigations could confirm that he had returned to Atlanta before going to Memphis, the optics would greatly undermine his claims of innocence. This is not simply because King also returned to Atlanta at approximately the same time. Rather, it would be Ray's subsequent trip, from Atlanta to Memphis, that would seriously damage his contention that he was an oblivious dupe for Raul. Martin Luther King Jr. did not specify his date of return to Memphis until April 1, and for Ray to return to Atlanta on March 30 and then follow King to Memphis with a gun was too much for even Ray to pass off as a coincidence. Subsequently, Ray steadfastly insisted that he never took that route. Combining the "accidental" stay in Selma during King's visit and the Atlanta map with marks that "coincidentally" overlap King's home, a rational observer could not escape the conclusion that Ray was stalking King.[40]

Yet it remains unclear exactly what Ray envisioned as his role. To earn the full bounty, Ray would have to directly participate in King's killing. Simply handing a rifle to someone else would not be enough. Analyses of King's murder typically treat Ray as either an unwitting dupe or the driving force behind the crime. A better approach might be to view Ray as an individual with his own agenda, but one who was forced to work within the framework of a larger conspiracy in which he was, at least initially, a peripheral player.

Ray appeared to be performing the role of a stalker, one that presumably carried a lower payday. If Ray wanted a bigger piece of the action, it's possible that he had to create a racist profile that would allow him to directly engage the plot's sponsors. Such a record would have to be sufficiently controversial to earn the respect of the sponsors without looking outwardly radical to law enforcement investigators. But if Ray wanted to expand his role in hopes of making more money, he was running out of time. The purchase of the rifle would be a sure sign to Ray that whatever plan was in motion, King would be killed sooner rather than later.

On April 1, 1968, having delivered his sermon at the National Cathedral in Washington, D.C., King publicly announced his return to Memphis, at the same time Ray was leaving laundry at the Piedmont Laundry under the name Eric Galt. The following day, as Ray drove his Mustang from Atlanta to Memphis, something strange happened at John's Restaurant in Laurel, Mississippi. The restaurant–bar, owned by Deavours Nix, one of Sam Bowers's closest aides in the WKKKKOM, was a place where senior Klan leaders frequently met. According to a report filed by Myrtis Ruth Hendricks, a black waitress at the bar, Nix received an odd phone call that evening. "I got a call on the King," Hendricks recalled Nix saying when she was interviewed by FBI agents on April 22. But she was unable to hear the rest of the conversation. Hendricks recalled additional suspicious activity on April 3, 1968. According to her report, "two men, neatly dressed, with short stocky builds, came to Nix's place where she started to work the evening shift at three P.M. While going to the bathroom, she observed a rifle with a telescopic sight, in a case in Nix's office. Later, the two men took the rifle and a long box, which took three men to carry out, and put them in a sixty four maroon Dodge with a fake 'continental kit' on the back."[41] As we shall see, Hendricks's story did not end there.

Despite a bomb threat delaying his flight, Martin Luther King Jr. returned to Memphis on April 3. With the Poor People's march to Washington, D.C., less than three weeks away, King returned with the goal of proving that nonviolent protest could still work. The bad blood that had developed between civil rights activists and the local police department boiled over as King's entourage, mindful of police informants infiltrating the ranks of the sanitation protesters, refused the security detail usually provided to the minister.

King settled at the Lorraine Motel but not at first in his usual room, 306, where he and his close friend the Reverend Ralph Abernathy often stayed. Someone was temporarily staying in Room 306, so King and Abernathy waited in a second-floor room until they got a call to reclaim 306, which they called the King–Abernathy Suite. At noon that day, King attended a meeting at the Centenary Methodist Church, where he announced a plan for a mass march on April 8. But upon his return to the Lorraine that afternoon, federal marshals served him and his aides with a district court injunction, temporarily preventing them from engaging in future marches.

James Earl Ray also arrived in Memphis on April 3. He checked into the New Rebel Motor Hotel, roughly fifteen minutes from the Lorraine, using the Galt alias. He brought the newly purchased rifle and other gear. In the years that followed, Ray again attributed a number of his actions to the elusive Raul, but he could not keep his stories straight. It is possible that he was in Memphis to meet someone, perhaps to provide the newly purchased rifle to would-be conspirators. More than likely, he was debating his own next move. Would he continue to provide reconnaissance within a prearranged bounty plot against King's life? Or would he try for a greater share of the bounty himself? Anyone wanting to observe Dr. King's movements in Memphis did not have to work very hard—his stay there was widely covered on television and in local newspapers. Ray, who voraciously followed the news while in prison, claims he was all but oblivious to anything having to do with Martin Luther King Jr. while in Memphis.

On the evening of April 3, King delivered his last sermon, at the Mason Temple Church. Referencing both the particulars of the Memphis sanitation workers strike and the general condition of the civil rights movement on the eve of the Poor People's Campaign, King struck an optimistic note, in what history now refers to as "The Mountaintop" speech. He described the wide arc of history from the Exodus of Egypt to the Emancipation Proclamation, marked by the common theme of mankind's saying, "We want to be free." Referring to the challenges to nonviolence, he reminded the crowd of the successes it had brought in places like Birmingham. King ended by extending the theme of the Exodus to its final denouement, when the liberator Moses, having led the Hebrews to the outskirts of Israel, climbed to the peak of Mount Nebo and stood in awe of the Promised Land, which he himself would never visit. King reminded the audience of the bomb threat that had delayed his flight to Memphis and of a 1957 assassination attempt in which a deranged woman had nearly murdered King with a knife. But for a sneeze, King reminded the audience, he would not be alive; but for a sneeze, he would not have seen the triumphs of the civil rights movement. Prophetically, he ended his speech with the following words:

Like anybody, I would like to live a long life. Longevity has its place. But I'm not concerned about that now. I just want to do God's will. And He's allowed me to go up to the mountain. And I've looked over. And I've seen the Promised Land. I may not get there with you. But I want you to know tonight, that we, as a people, will get to the Promised Land! And so I'm happy, tonight. I'm not worried about anything. I'm not fearing any man! Mine eyes have seen the glory of the coming of the Lord![42]

TRIBULATION

OUTRAGE *and the*
INVESTIGATION *into*
WHO REALLY KILLED
KING

On April 4, 1968, just after 6 PM, a message went out from a Memphis police dispatcher: "We have information that King has been shot at the Lorraine. TAC-10, he has been shot." An unidentified officer replied: "OK, TAC-10 advising, King has been shot . . . 6:04." The conversation continued:

"TAC-11, you want us to pull out?"

"TAC-11, you are to pull out."

"OK, TAC-11."

"In the area?"

"A signal Q, A signal Q."

"King has been shot."

"All TAC units on the call, you are to form a ring around the Lorraine Motel. You are to form a ring around the Lorraine Motel. No one is to enter or leave."[1]

The police had more than just "information" that King had been shot. Police surveillance teams had monitored the civil rights leader's every movement since King had arrived in the River City on April 3, 1968. Memphis mayor Henry Loeb feared another riot. Cognizant that it lacked the manpower to respond to further civil unrest, local law enforcement formed special response teams, known as police tactical units (TAC), consisting of, according to historian Michael Honey, "three cars, each of which held four men. A commanding officer could order a unit to a location, where they would quickly form a flying wedge and charge down the street."[2]

Law enforcement also used African American officers to spy on gatherings of striking sanitation workers. One such officer, Ed Redditt, and his partner, Willie Richmond, formed one of the surveillance teams assigned to observe King from Fire Station 2, across the street from the Lorraine Motel, where King was staying. Labor leaders soon uncovered Redditt as a mole, hence his reassignment to surveillance duty. The mutual distrust between the labor strike proponents and their adversaries in the law enforcement community carried an important implication for April 4: King's entourage had refused police protection when King arrived in Memphis the day before.

Fire department officials also worried about a riot and assigned their own men to watch King. But the two fire department officials tasked with watching the Lorraine were active in supporting the sanitation workers strike. They clashed with Redditt, who they saw as a turncoat. Redditt arranged for both firemen to be removed from duty on April 4, as they occupied the same space in Fire Station 2. Then strange events also forced Redditt from his post.

The Memphis police received death threats against Redditt, relayed from an aide to Arkansas senator John L. McClellan. According to an informant, radical black nationalists in Mississippi promised to kill Redditt. Redditt's superior, Lieutenant Eli Arkin, removed Redditt from duty on April 4 as a precaution. The story of the threat, it turned out later, was completely false, leading some to think that the entire affair was part of a wider conspiracy to kill King, to facilitate his murder by stripping the minister of local security. But Redditt did not serve any security function on April 4, and his partner continued to maintain surveillance on King.

A more likely explanation is that McClellan, an ardent segregationist, simply planted a false story as a dirty trick to undermine King, reinforcing an effort by Mayor Loeb to stop King's April 5 demonstration by way of a federal judge's injunction. A threat on a police officer could become a pretext to overcome First Amendment challenges by King's friend and attorney Andrew Young aimed at stopping the injunction. In fact McClellan had pursued similar dirty tricks to undermine the Poor People's Campaign in the preceding months.[3]

Surveillance logs of the Lorraine Motel reveal little in the way of activity on the part of King or his entourage on April 4. King spent most of his time inside the room that he shared with his close friend and fellow activist the Reverend Ralph Abernathy, waiting in room 306 to hear the outcome of Young's legal efforts. The two men formed a formidable duo in their pursuit of civil rights, appealing to different constituencies in the black community through their different preaching styles. King's oratory style resonated more with highly educated and middle-class black elites, while Abernathy's "country" delivery style appealed to working-class and rural audiences.

The night before, Abernathy had sensed that his approach was not working with the congregation at the Mason Temple Church and had coaxed King (exhausted from his travels) to the church to deliver what would become "The Mountaintop" speech. The next day, the mood was lighter in the so-called King–Abernathy Suite. When Young returned with news that the injunction had been overturned, King, Abernathy, and others surprised the young attorney. If those surveilling King could see through walls, they would have witnessed King, Abernathy, and Young engaged in a playful pillow fight.

The men spent the rest of April 4 in meetings and answering phone calls, which delayed a visit to the home of a local minister, the Reverend Billy Kyles, for dinner. In the early evening, with Kyles trying to rush King along and with other civil rights leaders waiting in the parking lot, King exited Room 306 and approached the railing of the second floor balcony of the Lorraine. At 6:01 PM a bullet "fractured Dr. King's jaw, exited the lower part of the face and reentered the body in the neck area. . . . It then severed numerous vital arteries and fractured the spine in several places, causing severe damage to the spinal column and coming to rest on the left side of the back." Rushed to Saint Joseph's Hospital, King was pronounced dead at 7:05 PM.

If Christian Identity radicals had arranged the murder of Martin Luther King Jr. with the goal of igniting a racial holy war, they never came closer to their vision than in the weeks that followed April 4, 1968.

The first signs of the violence that would plague America's cities in the wake of Martin Luther King Jr.'s assassination began in the place where King had delivered his famous "I Have a Dream" speech about the promise of racial harmony five years before: Washington, D.C. Upon hearing of the assassination, "in stunned silence and utter disbelief," a group of young black men, soon joined by Stokely Carmichael, patrolled the Fourteenth and U Street sections of the nation's capital, first asking and then demanding that local businesses close in honor of Dr. King's memory. Carmichael's presence drew a larger crowd, one that grew increasingly angry as the reality of the news settled in. Soon anger turned to violence, but local law enforcement pacified the crowd. Yet this was the calm before the storm in the nation's capital and in the nation as a whole.[4]

The civil disorder that followed has not been matched, in intensity or scope, since 1968. By 8 PM riots had broken out. In the course of two weeks they would spread to more than one hundred American cities, the most widespread outbreak of civil disorder in the nation since the Civil War. *Time* magazine described the situation as a "shock wave of looting and arson" that would, over the next week, lead to thousands of arrests, millions of dollars in damages, and the largest intervention of federal troops on domestic soil since Reconstruction. On April 5, Carmichael called the unrest the "beginning of revolution," and for a while it seemed that way. Even nonviolent stalwarts like former SNCC leader Julian Bond asserted, "Non-violence was murdered in Memphis."[5]

In front of an audience of fifteen hundred people in Cincinnati, an officer for CORE "blamed white Americans for King's death and urged blacks to retaliate." In two days, Cincinnati experienced an estimated $3 million in damages. Similar chaos affected approximately 128 cities in twenty-eight states. Dr. Carol E. Dietrich described the devastation in startling numbers:

In Chicago, federal troops and national guardsmen were called to the city to quell the disorders, in which more than 500 persons sustained injuries and approximately 3,000 persons were arrested. At least 162 buildings were reported entirely destroyed by fire, and total property damaged was estimated at $9 million.

In Baltimore, the National Guard and federal troops were called to curb the violence. More than 700 persons were reported injured from April 6 to 9, more than 5,000 arrests were made, and more than 1,000 fires were reported. Gov. Spiro T. Agnew declared a state of emergency and crisis on April 6, calling in 6,000 national guardsmen and the state police to aid the city's 1,100-man police force.[6]

The hardest-hit city was Washington, D.C., where the rioting had begun. "The District of Columbia government reported on May 1, 1968 that the April rioting had resulted in 9 deaths, 1,202 injuries, and 6,306 arrests," Dietrich noted. Swift and Stoner could not have been more pleased that the heart of the "Jew-controlled" government lay smoldering alongside so much of America.

The jubilant reaction by far-right white supremacists was widespread. Along with members of the White Knights of the Ku Klux Klan of Mississippi, Stoner famously danced in the streets of Meridian, Mississippi, at the news of King's murder. According to the FBI, Stoner predicted "the death of Martin Luther King would bring more Negro demonstrations and violence than anything since the Civil War." Stoner added, "The Black Power niggers will say that non-violence has failed and that violence is the only answer." The Swift follower "welcomed the riots which are expected to follow" and asserted that the NSRP was "glad to see others encouraging Negroes to protest."[7]

Sam Bowers and his colleagues celebrated the onslaught of rioting in America at John's Restaurant in Laurel, Mississippi (where, on April 3, waitress Myrtis Hendricks had observed mysterious men take a rifle from White Knights lieutenant Deavours Nix and leave in a maroon truck). A low-level White Knight—unidentified in tape recordings—told Jack Nelson in 1969 that Bowers and others expected a race war.

Tommy Tarrants told Nelson, years later, that he celebrated the news of King's murder while hiding out at a paramilitary training compound run by Swift followers in North Carolina, waiting to launch his guerrilla campaign against the United States.

In Pennsylvania, the Reverend Roy Frankhouser, leader of the Minutemen, defied a city ordinance and marched with white supremacists through the heart of his town. Stoner promised his own marches in May.

Wesley Swift, on an unexplained sabbatical from his routine sermons, nonetheless led a Bible study on April 24, the first one since King's murder. He commented, "The U.S. News and World Report had pictures of these Negroes looting the stores and coming out laughing. This article said there is no end to the rioting because

Negroes are having a ball. They like this . . . these people shoot one another for excitement. They burn their own houses down just to see the fire. They loot everything. So how can you call them equal to the white man? . . . For the Negro has taken the place of the Indian as your enemy. The African Negroes are coming in, so the white man is going back to carrying a gun again. . . . I think everyone should be armed today. The more of this rioting I see, I think you need . . . weapons."[8]

But a closer analysis of the events in Memphis and the reaction of white supremacists in the wake of the assassination suggests that not everything went according to plan or expectation on April 4.

Without question, there clearly was evidence that white suprema-cists were preparing to kill King in Memphis. Myrtis Hendricks, the waitress at John's Restaurant, overheard Deavours Nix, Bowers's friend, "receive a telephone call on his phone which is close to the kitchen. After this call, Nix said, 'Martin Luther King Jr. is dead.' *This was before the news came over the radio about the murder*" [emphasis added]. Congress found additional information sug-gesting that at John's Restaurant, a frequent hangout for the WKK-KKOM, Sam Bowers in particular shared insider information about a plot in Memphis.[9]

Additionally, J.B. Stoner's very presence in Meridian, Mississippi, raises suspicions of foreknowledge. FBI agents who had the radical white supremacist under constant surveillance witnessed Stoner's celebratory dance. Law enforcement fully expected Stoner to follow his modus operandi—to go to Memphis in a counter-rally against King—and placed him under watch, fearing such rabble-rousing in Memphis. But on April 4, for reasons unknown, Stoner broke type. In fact, the Memphis sanitation workers strike was notable for its utter lack of counter-protests by racist groups.

Unfortunately, rather than consider Stoner's pattern of estab-lishing an out-of-town alibi in his previous racial crimes, in its investigation into the assassination of Dr. Martin Luther King Jr. (code-named MURKIN), the FBI immediately eliminated Stoner as its number-one suspect because he was in Meridian. In a prac-tice condemned by a later congressional inquiry, the FBI assumed that anyone who wasn't in Memphis could not have taken part in a conspiracy against King—the same philosophy that allowed it to eliminate everyone from Sam Bowers to Sidney Barnes from consideration as conspirators.

The Jackson field office spent a considerable amount of time trying to verify the whereabouts of KKK members on April 4, looking to see if their cars were in driveways or if the lights in their homes were on. One member had an easy alibi: On the evening of April 4, 1968, Meridian police ticketed Danny Joe Hawkins, a member with Tommy Tarrants of Bowers's 1968 covert hit squad, for speeding the wrong way down a one-way street.

Yet if Hawkins was attempting to establish some kind of alibi for the murder, assuming he expected it to materialize as it did on April 4, he clearly could have found better ways. For all his jubilation over the riots that followed the King murder, and for all the suspicious activity suggesting that Sam Bowers knew about a Memphis plot in advance, informant reports suggest that the Imperial Wizard did not, at first, like the timing of the death. Something may have been expected in Memphis. But was it the shooting at the Lorraine?

The fact that, according to Donald Nissen, several thousand dollars had exchanged hands between Atlanta and Jackson suggests that something very serious was in play. Such bounties circulated through America's prisons, including the Missouri State Penitentiary, from whence Ray escaped in April 1967. Yes, some evidence suggests that Ray, a native of Jim Crow St. Louis, harbored racial prejudices consistent with his times and upbringing, but little evidence suggests that racism and politics played a major role in his thinking before 1968. Comments made after the assassination by Ray's brother, Jerry, to his girlfriend and her landlady—unaware that the two were informing for the FBI—suggest that Ray was responding to the same incentive that always motivated him: money. Asked by the girlfriend "if his brother shot King," Jerry replied, "I didn't ask him. If I was in his position and had 18 years to serve and someone offered me a lot of money to kill someone I didn't like anyhow and get me out of the country, I'd do it."[10]

But the actual mechanics of the Memphis assassination suggest an ill-conceived plot—perhaps one put together by Ray at the last minute—that preempted a well-planned assassination by actual contract killers at the behest of white supremacists. Those who think Ray was a complete dupe must maintain the most implausible theory of all. Under the far-fetched scenario offered by Ray's last attorney, William Pepper, Ray brought a rifle to Memphis to provide to the mysterious Raul, the actual assassin, completely oblivious to the possibility of an assassination. Raul then completed Ray's setup by having him visit Bessie Brewer's rooming house on the eve of the murder, killing King in Ray's absence, and then framing Ray by planting evidence. But in Pepper's scenario, the puppet master Raul made two huge, critical mistakes in setting up Ray—only to be saved by sheer luck.

First having arranged for Ray to crop off the GameMaster rifle, complete with Ray's fingerprints on them, Raul elected to use an entirely different (and as yet undiscovered) gun for the actual murder, according to Pepper. The Remington GameMaster that Ray took to Memphis was more than capable of firing the assassination round. But according to Pepper, for reasons that are unclear, Raul used a gun that, if not for the vagaries of ballistics, should have clearly pointed to someone other than James Earl Ray.

Much has been made about the inability of forensic experts to match the King murder slug to the GameMaster that Ray purchased in Birmingham and brought to Memphis, the gun found by law enforcement wrapped in a green blanket outside of Canipe's Amusements. But ballistics tests showed that the rifle itself was the problem. Normally, the lands and grooves inside a rifle's barrel etch consistent patterns on a spinning bullet as it is propelled from the gun—patterns that are unique to that rifle. A firearms expert need only fire a test bullet from a suspect's weapon and compare it under a microscope to a crime-scene bullet to see if the slug came from the gun. But with the GameMaster found in Memphis, forensic experts could not get any two test-fired rounds to match each other, meaning that the lands and grooves of the actual murder slug could not be used for a ballistics comparison. The assassination bullet might have come from the same weapon, but there is no way to know. This aspect of the King murder weapon is anomalous; Raul would have had every reason to think that a bullet could and would be matched to the GameMaster. For that reason, Raul's actions, per Ray and his defenders, make no sense. Raul manipulated Ray into buying a rifle in Birmingham, fooled Ray into bringing it to Memphis, and took possession of the GameMaster with Ray's fingerprints on it to frame him. But Raul, under this scenario, decided it would make more sense to use an entirely different gun to assassinate King. Just as he had every reason to (incorrectly) think that the GameMaster would yield a traceable murder bullet, Raul, if he knew anything about rifles, would have known that a different gun would have produced a round that would *not* match the GameMaster. If this is true, Raul went ahead and planted the GameMaster outside Canipe's knowing that, within a matter of days, experts would realize that Ray's weapon was not used in the King murder; ballistics tests, under normal circumstances, would have *cleared* Ray. So why go through the burden of framing James Earl Ray in the first place? More to the point, why wouldn't you simply use the GameMaster to kill King in the first place? Raul thus fails Frame-up 101.

Things get worse for the Pepper scenario, as Raul, having carefully managed Ray's travels with his invisible hand, suddenly decides that it would be wise to let James Earl Ray wander around Memphis on his own accord in the immediate period before and during King's execution. Unfortunately for Ray, and very fortunately for Raul, Ray did not do anything that could establish a firm alibi. For forty years, none of Ray's investigators or lawyers ever found a single reliable witness to place Ray outside the rooming house. Raul must have thanked the conspiracy gods that Ray lacked witnesses or receipts to confirm his alibi.

On the other hand, the events in Memphis do not suggest a well-planned conspiracy either, certainly not if Ray was the designated shooter. For one thing, with professional killers available, it seems unlikely that anyone would call on Ray to murder their "ultimate prize," Martin Luther King Jr. Ray lacked any pedigree as a hit man. A rooming house, furthermore, represents a poor choice for a potential shooting location. No one can guarantee the availability of a room facing the Lorraine, or at least one with a good vantage point. In fact, the room Ray did rent offered a very poor view of Room 306. This likely is what forced Ray (or another assassin) to camp out in the bathroom, per testimony of William Anschutz (a border at the rooming house who testified that the assassin shot from the bathroom window).[11] But a rooming house bathroom is also a less-than-desirable shooting location. At any time—including at the moment a shooter is aiming and ready to pull the trigger—someone can knock on the door looking for access to the community toilet or bath.

And a different problem presents itself with the choice of rifle if, as the evidence seems to suggest, someone told Ray to exchange his original purchase for the GameMaster. If the goal was simply to shoot a relatively stationary target from a short distance, one did not need the more expensive and well-reputed GameMaster. Bessie Brewer's rooming house was just across the street from the Lorraine. If someone told Ray to trade up for the better rifle, the likelihood was that the weapon was meant for a more difficult shot from a longer distance.

The rather haphazard way in which evidence was disposed of at the crime scene also points to a less-than-ideal plan, a last-minute plot formed out of desperation. As a member of the Minutemen confided to the FBI, a professional killer would have used a disassembled rifle, putting the weapon together at the shooting location, firing a shot, and then breaking the gun down so that it could be smuggled out, for instance in a briefcase.[12] Here, not only the rifle but numerous other items, including binoculars and hygiene products, were bundled together in a green blanket and left in the entryway of Canipe's Amusements, not far from Bessie Brewer's rooming house.

Many have pointed to the bundle as convenient—a too-obvious attempt by conspirators to frame James Earl Ray. But anyone shooting from the bathroom in Bessie Brewer's rooming house had few good options available to him if he wanted to escape Memphis that day, short of the breakdown scenario described by the Minuteman. Leaving the material in the rooming house would immediately connect the rifle to any missing boarders inside the building, including any fingerprints or identifying information left behind (something even a cautious assassin could not risk). Carrying the bundle to a vehicle would risk discovery and immediate capture at any kind of roadblock dragnet. In many ways, leaving the bundle on the street was the least bad option.

In fact, whether intended or not, the materials in the bundle confused law enforcement for up to three weeks. Items in the bundle
were initially linked to what appeared to be three or four different
people. The rifle was linked to a Harvey Lowmeyer, who had purchased the weapon in Birmingham. Other items belonged to an Eric
S. Galt, and a prison radio was eventually traced to an escaped fugitive from Missouri State Penitentiary: James Earl Ray. Coupled
with reports of a potential shooter (who had rented a room under
the alias John Willard) fleeing Bessie Brewer's rooming house, it appeared to the FBI as if they were dealing with a conspiracy of at least
three or four people. It took weeks before they connected all the
aliases to Ray, in part because authorities had to "unearth" the serial
number on the prison radio Ray left in the bundle (he scratched out
the numbers and letters to the best of his ability.)

The best explanation for all the facts is a scenario whereby Ray
preempts a legitimate plot against King by choosing to parlay his
limited role as a scout into a more lucrative role as the actual shooter.
He would do this without consulting with the plotters, assuming he
even knew who the major players were, and he would do this at
the last minute, hence the haphazard execution. Several additional
pieces of evidence point in this direction.

First, this explanation helps account for one of the most enduring
and perplexing mysteries of April 4: the CB radio broadcast that
diverted law enforcement away from Ray's escape route. As Ray
fled from Memphis to Atlanta in his white Ford Mustang, someone
led police on a wild goose chase. Some thirty minutes after the
King shooting, a CB radio operator named William Austein heard
a transmission from a fellow CB operator broadcasting a car chase.
Contrary to routine procedure, the broadcaster would not identify
himself, but he reported that he was chasing a white Mustang driven
by King's killer, fleeing east on Summer Avenue from Parkway Street.
The unknown CB operator wanted to make direct contact with the
Memphis police. Austein halted a Memphis police cruiser and relayed periodic reports from the other man's radio broadcasts to a
police officer, who then relayed them to Memphis police headquarters. Lasting for ten minutes, the transmissions reported the chase
of the Mustang through multiple turns and through a red light; the

individual in the white Mustang even fred shots at the heroic citizen. The final broadcast occurred at 6:48 PM, with reports that the vehicle was heading toward a naval base.

It turns out that the broadcast was a hoax. An investigation never established who perpetrated the fraud, but in reaching out to police, refusing to identify his name, and trying to direct police attention to the northern parts of Memphis, the fake CB broadcaster was attempting to pull police resources away from the southern route that Ray likely used to escape the city.[13]

Some claim that the timing of the broadcast, more than thirty minutes after the shooting, speaks against this being a conspiratorial act. But the delay might also suggest that the conspirators themselves were caught off guard. If James Earl Ray short-circuited a more elaborate plot against King (perhaps to obtain a larger share of a bounty), he would have placed any conspirator in Memphis in the uncomfortable position of having to guess what had happened. The delay between the crime and the broadcast may well represent the time it took for conspirators to surmise that someone within their plot had literally jumped the gun. Under this speculative scenario, using the CB stunt to shift police attention away from the likely getaway direction might have been a logical, if delayed, maneuver. Conspirators had good reason to fear what a fleeing shooter might tell law enforcement regarding a wider conspiracy, and if the conspirators realized the unexpected shooter was Ray, they may have surmised that he was heading back to Atlanta. The KKK commonly used CB radios to intercept police broadcasts and stymie police investigations, so much so that Congress cited the practice as widespread in a 1966 report. At one point, in its investigation of the MIBURN murders, the FBI was forced to call in help from the Federal Communications Commission to establish a completely independent communications network—one that was immune to CB radio intercepts by the White Knights.

The possibility that Ray preempted a shooting by professional criminals contracted by the White Knights is further suggested by events that occurred not far from the crime scene. One of the earliest reports from Memphis related to suspicious activity at the William Len Hotel, located just a mile from the Lorraine. As they later described to the FBI, hotel employees observed two men acting suspiciously at 12:05 AM on April 5. The two guests had arrived the previous afternoon and looked nervous while waiting to check out at that odd hour. The suspicious men had registered on the afternoon of April 4 as Vincent Walker and Lawrence Rand and had stayed in two separate but nearby rooms. Both men left in a hurry following King's murder. The FBI was interested in the two men and traced their activities once they left the hotel. One man hailed a cab and asked to go to West Memphis, Arkansas, but some distance into the trip, he insisted that the cab driver turn around and take him to the Memphis airport. The passenger appeared to scout the airport and then told the cabbie to return to the William Len Hotel. Outside, the cabbie met the second man and drove him to the airport. They boarded a flight under the names W. Davis and B. Chidlaw. Their flight departed at 1:50 AM on April 5 and arrived in Houston at 2:50 AM, at which point they took a shuttle and more or less disappeared. The FBI checked the names and addresses on the hotel register, only to find out that they were both aliases. So too were the Davis and Chidlaw names provided at the airport. A fingerprint check revealed no suspects, so the FBI gave up, guessing that these were criminals in town for a separate operation who left because they expected an increased police presence following King's murder. It is worth noting that Cliff Fuller and Hugh Pruett—two Dixie Mafia gangsters who may have been connected to marks on Ray's Atlanta map—were last arrested in connection with burglaries in Houston, the last point of departure for "W. Davis" and "B. Chidlaw." Were Fuller and Pruett—or two other Dixie mobsters—caught off guard by Ray's unilateral decision to kill King himself?[14]

Finally, additional evidence for Ray jumping the gun comes from researcher Lamar Waldron. If Waldron's anonymous source can be trusted, Ray attempted to reach out to conspirators, but again in a haphazard fashion. Having fled Memphis in his white Mustang, Ray phoned Hugh Spake of the Lakeland auto plant. Spake was working on the assembly line, and the call came to a common phone that was available to all workers in the area. The call was likely about money. Calling such a phone at such a time suggests desperation. Coupled with Spake's reaction—he wasn't expecting the call—the call suggests that Ray had a general idea about the bounty sponsors but wasn't in the loop about how to obtain the money. Before long Ray would return to Atlanta, leaving his Mustang at a public-housing parking lot not far from the Lakeland auto plant. Waldron developed further evidence suggesting that Joseph Milteer, the Swift follower who may have syphoned off money for a large King bounty with Spake's help, found his way to Atlanta in the days following King's murder.[15] Ray's subsequent activity indicates that he never received any money from anyone. He ultimately fled to Toronto and then to Europe, but he was forced to rob a bank in England to stay afloat. His actions in the years after his capture and conviction in June of 1968 speak to someone "threading the needle," trying to get out of federal prison while holding out hope of collecting a bounty that he still believed he had earned.

One finds the most convincing evidence tying Ray to a white supremacist plot by examining his associations after the King murder. One must ultimately rely on Ray and his convoluted stories to make sense of his pre-assassination associations, leaving one to speculate as to the truth about his contacts with white supremacists or criminal go-betweens with access to groups like the KKK. But in the immediate aftermath of his capture, and in the decades that followed, Ray insisted on making use of known white supremacists as his legal counsel. That decision makes little or no sense—unless Ray was looking to use these men for some purpose other than simple legal representation.

The use of well-known bigots as attorneys is suspicious for two reasons. First, from 1968 to 1969, when Ray faced trial, it was obvious that to avoid conviction, Ray had to make every effort to distance himself from charges that he had killed King out of racial animus. Yet Ray went out of his way to pursue legal counsel with overt connections to white supremacist groups.

Initially, Ray attempted to elicit the legal services of Percy Quinn of Laurel, Mississippi. Quinn's only clients were members of the White Knights of the Ku Klux Klan of Mississippi, including Sam Bowers himself. Quinn did not even make an effort to secure other clients. Ray's brother had a great deal of difficulty finding Quinn because the lawyer did not have a storefront office or even a listed telephone number. (It is still unclear who referred Quinn to James Earl Ray or how Ray's brother, Jerry, found him.) Why Ray would even consider Quinn is itself a mystery, as Quinn's only recent cases were public failures. Quinn turned Ray down, perhaps for fear of what the link might expose.[16]

But almost on cue, Ray decided to take on another white supremacist attorney with an even higher profile: J.B. Stoner. Ray's other attorneys, including Arthur Hanes (himself a Klan attorney, but one with an excellent legal reputation), warned Ray against using Stoner. But Stoner remained one of Ray's major legal advisors for years and soon employed Ray's brother, Jerry, as a personal assistant at the NSRP. For two decades, Ray made use of an assortment of racist attorneys, including one neo-Confederate lawyer who commissioned a sculpture to honor KKK founder Nathan Bedford Forrest.

These decisions become even less forgivable when one realizes that Ray had an assortment of talented investigators and attorneys already assisting his efforts to get out of prison. This group included noted Freedom of Information Act (FOIA) attorney Jim Lesar, highly regarded New Left attorney Mark Lane, and diligent investigator Harold Weisberg, a legend in the field of JFK assassination research. Ray had no need for racist attorneys—unless perhaps they served another purpose.

When Congress reinvestigated the King murder in the late 1970s, it considered J.B. Stoner a prime suspect, as it should have. But it encountered a serious obstacle in attempting to investigate Stoner: attorney–client privilege. Because he provided legal services to Ray, Stoner could not be compelled to help or assist the congressional investigation. Ray had graciously waived attorney–client privilege for every one of the many attorneys who had helped his case to that point, *except J.B. Stoner*.[17] Ray spun the "Raul set me up" narrative in hopes of securing a new trial and an eventual acquittal. In the event that he succeeded (or escaped prison, as he did again in the early 1970s—only to be recaptured), Ray needed someone with access to the conspirators to get his bounty money. Was Stoner that man?

The congressional committee that looked into issues like this— the HSCA—investigated Stoner, Bowers, Gale, and other white supremacists as suspects in King's murder. It uncovered and analyzed some of the leads and failed plots discussed in the past several chapters but missed others. For instance, the committee did not report or was not told (by the FBI) that the Ben Chester White murder was connected to a 1966 King murder plot conceived by Bowers. Additionally, the HSCA never addressed information, provided by Donald Nissen to the FBI in June 1967, describing the King bounty. Moreover, Congress analyzed each murder attempt as a separate, independent conspiracy. It did not understand that the individuals who tried to kill King shared a common bond of religion. It did not explore Christian Identity theology as the driving force behind many different assassination attempts. Unbeknownst to Congress, several of the main suspects identified in previous plots belonged to a subculture of religious zealots, who by the late 1960s had formed a social network bent on fomenting a race war.

Part of this oversight is forgivable in that it stems from the same limited worldview highlighted in this book and held by many—one that either ignores the anti-Jewish dimension to the violence of the 1960s or sees such violence as secular in nature rather than theological in motivation. Moreover, members of this subculture deliberately obscured their religious motivation to maximize their leverage over rank-and-file segregationists within their respective organizations, people who would never accept a radical view of Christianity but who could be manipulated for a common purpose.

But the HSCA had access to witnesses who could or should have challenged the conventional narrative. In 1976, as the committee was forming, a series of articles published by investigative reporter Dan Christensen highlighted the potential role played by Tommy Tarrants and his associates in the King assassination. We now know that Tarrants, having converted from Christian Identity to mainstream evangelical Christianity, was interviewed by Congress as an anonymous source. But it now appears that Christensen's articles touched off an FBI cover-up that prevented Congress from fully exploring Tarrants's connections to the King murder, a line of inquiry that might have exposed Tarrants—and not Ray—as the original and intended patsy in the King murder. Such an inquiry would have exposed the Bureau to charges that it could have prevented King's assassination.

Christensen's 1976 articles highlighted the importance of information developed by Miami police and FBI informant Willie Somersett in both the Kennedy and King murder investigations.[18] The reader will recall Somersett secretly taped conversations with Sidney Barnes in 1964. In these conversations, Barnes described the September 14, 1963, meeting of Swift followers on the eve of the bombing of the Sixteenth Street Baptist Church. He also taped Swift devotee Joseph Milteer predicting John F. Kennedy's assassination in 1963, two months before the Dallas murder. In the same tape, Milteer described another plot on Martin Luther King Jr.'s life. In fact, Somersett was one of law enforcement's most coveted informants on white supremacist activities for years leading up to 1963. His record of cooperation and his access to key racists prompted the Miami Police Department to use Somersett to explore potential leads in the King assassination. Somersett's tour of the Southeast in the summer of 1968, which brought him into contact with various white supremacists as well as labor leaders (Somersett worked for a labor union), became the focus of Christensen's series. In one article, Christensen focused on a reunion between Somersett and Barnes in Mobile, Alabama.

Somersett did not record the conversation this time, and Christensen protected the still-living Barnes's identity, referring to him simply as X, a house painter. But what Barnes told Somersett in 1968 was no less shocking than what he told the informant in 1964. Barnes referred at first to an incident that earned Tarrants national attention two months after King's murder. In June 1968, Mississippi police ambushed, shot, and wounded Tarrants in a sting operation. Tarrants and his fellow terrorist Kathy Ainsworth were attempting to blow up the home of Rabbi Perry Nussbaum. Neither knew, however, that the men who had encouraged the attack, Alton Wayne and Raymond Roberts, had been turned by the FBI, using private money raised by the Anti-Defamation League. On a cue from an as-yet-unidentified informant in Jackson, Mississippi, law enforcement and the FBI lay in wait for Tarrants. They expected Danny Joe Hawkins to join him, but Hawkins pulled out at the last minute, with Ainsworth taking his place. Research by Jack Nelson makes it clear that the sting had one purpose and one purpose only—to kill

Tarrants. Law enforcement's war against the Klan in Mississippi had reached that point. Instead, Tarrants survived with serious injuries and wound up in prison on a thirty-year sentence for his bombing spree. Ainsworth died in the crossfire, becoming a martyr, which she remains to this day to racists across the country.[19]

Barnes expressed great alarm to Somersett about the potential for Tarrants to expose white supremacists to legal justice. But then he added something else, as Christensen described in his article:

> X says that the car that was used to jam the police cars on relaying messages of the killing of King on Aug. 4 [sic] was a car used by Thomas Tarrants. X says that they have information from the police that Tarrants is talking to the FBI and it looks as if several people may be indicted by the federal government in connection with a bank robbery and murder in the state(s) of Mississippi and Tennessee, including himself, X, who allowed Tarrants to stay at his home a week or ten days after the killing of Martin Luther King.[20]

What Christensen did not know was that this was not the only report placing Tarrants in Memphis on April 4. Independently, Somersett reported to the FBI on a separate visit that he made that summer: to the grieving mother of Kathy Ainsworth, Margaret Capomacchia. Capomacchia also told Somersett that Tarrants—as well as several other White Knights—had participated in a conspiracy on King's life. She reinforced the story that Tarrants had participated in the CB radio diversion and that he had fled to Sidney Barnes's mobile home before escaping to a Christian Identity stronghold in North Carolina.[21] The FBI investigated the whereabouts of several of the people Capomacchia named in connection with the plot and concluded that most or all had alibis for April 4. The Bureau dismissed the story. But just as the Miami Police Department appeared to lack corroboration from Capomacchia, the FBI may never have learned about the information from Barnes.

As it turned out, both Barnes and Capomacchia may have been using Somersett to plant false stories, for whatever reason, to sully Tarrants's reputation. The two were very close. And the record makes it clear that by 1968, those in white supremacist circles had "made" Somersett and were using the informant, unwittingly, to send disinformation to law enforcement. J.B. Stoner circulated such speculation as early as 1962, and records make it clear that when the FBI followed up on Somersett's surreptitious taping of Barnes in 1964, it ruined Somersett's cover. Not surprisingly, by 1965 Somersett had begun to provide increasingly unreliable information to the FBI, to the point where the FBI ceased using him as a source (though the Miami Police Department continued to trust Somersett). That Barnes would call Somersett and invite him to Mobile clearly points to another disinformation campaign; the decision by Capomacchia to invite Somersett to speak with her in Miami soon after his visit to Barnes only reinforces that impression.

The FBI did not buy Capomacchia's story (and never learned about Barnes's similar tale), but it may have had other motives in ignoring the Tarrants lead. For one thing, the FBI does not appear to have even interviewed Tarrants about the allegation. Nor did it make any effort to retrace other leads on Tarrants—equally as tantalizing—in it own files, from earlier in the MURKIN investigation. For example, on April 5, 1968, with the investigation just starting, the FBI did something inexplicable given what we know about the information available to it at the time. Having traced the GameMaster rifle in the green blanket to a gun store in Alabama, the agents showed a handful of pictures—including one of Tommy Tarrants—to staffers at the store.[22] The problem with this, as noted by former Jackson FBI agent Jim Ingram, was that on April 5, 1968, Tommy Tarrants was not on "our radar."[23] The bombings in Mississippi for which Tarrants would soon become famous had not yet been linked to any individual; the perpetrator was simply known as The Man. The FBI connected Tarrants only to the wave of violence against black and Jewish targets at the end of May 1968.

One need only consider the individuals whose pictures were *not* shown at the gun store on April 5 to fully understand the oddness of this investigative effort. It took days before the FBI showed a picture of Byron de la Beckwith, the man it firmly believed had assassinated Medgar Evers in 1963, at the gun store. Agents did not show pictures of Jimmy George Robinson, a Birmingham-based NSRP member who had assaulted King in 1965, for another week.[24]

Indeed, virtually all of the Cahaba Boys, directly responsible for the bombing of the Sixteenth Street Baptist Church in 1963, remained at large in Birmingham—and none of their pictures were shown at the gun store. Yet the FBI showed Tarrants's picture right away, when at that point Tarrants was only a fugitive from Mobile on an illegal firearms charge.

As it turns out, the gun store incident was not even the earliest sign of the FBI's suspicions of Tarrants. The Mobile Field Office removed one of its agents, Gerard Robinson, from his normal assignment routine to visit Tarrants's Alabama home on the evening of April 4. In an interview with the author, the agent remembered the odd nature of the request: He was asked, in violation of strict FBI protocol, to visit Tarrants's residence without his partner. Robinson can't recall another solo visit in his career, and he still does not know why his superiors sent him to Tarrants's residence alone.[25] Furthermore, additional records—in the files of Wesley Swift but not in the FBI's MURKIN files—show that the FBI's Los Angeles field office continued to show pictures of Tarrants in California, again on the possibility that Tarrants was the man who used the alias Eric Galt.[26] The reasons for Robinson's visit, and the reasons for showing Tarrants's picture in the days that followed, are not evident in any available records.

A full search of all MLK records by the National Archives and Research Administration failed to reveal anything justifying the early interest in Tarrants. The author's FOIA request for the Mobile Field Office file from which the Tarrants pictures came revealed that this specific file had been destroyed by the FBI in November 1977,[27] at the height of Congress's renewed inquiry into the case, a year after senior FBI officials had forbidden field offices to destroy any record related to the King crime.[28] Tarrants admits that he became a witness for the new investigation, and the record makes it obvious that he was one of two anonymous sources cited by Congress in its final report on the King murder. To destroy a record of a living individual, much less one who was important to a congressional investigation, defies federal regulations.

The file destruction occurred one year after Christensen published his article linking Tarrants to the King murder, a piece that raised questions about other Floridians—notably former Miami native

Joseph Milteer—and their connections to the crime. As it turns out, the FBI told researcher Ernie Lazar that it had also destroyed its field office file on Joseph Milteer, also in 1977. In fact, the FBI told the author that it had also destroyed the Miami MURKIN file—or at least elements of it—at the same time, in 1977, although this is presently unresolved, as the National Archives claims to have some, and possibly all of the Miami file. In short, it appears that the FBI was removing records that would cast doubt on Tarrants at the very moment that it was vouching for the recently released Tarrants as a source to Congress. What explains the FBI's early interest in Tarrants and its decision to hide that interest from congressional investigators? The answer may have less to do with Tarrants than with a much more valuable secret the FBI was protecting, and continues to protect to this day.

Of course, there was a very good reason for the FBI to hunt for Tommy Tarrants in connection with the King assassination, but it is a reason the FBI should not have been privy to if the available records are complete. Tarrants's own account has him visiting Wesley Swift two weeks before the King murder. There he obtained a rifle with the express purpose of killing Martin Luther King Jr. Tarrants then went underground as part of a guerrilla campaign against the government. Nothing in the records suggests that the FBI knew this information before June of 1968. Yet, if the FBI did *somehow* know about Tarrants's visit with Swift, it would go a long way toward explaining the Bureau's early fascination with Tarrants as a suspect in the King murder. Perhaps the absence of these records is deliberate. For it now appears that the FBI had developed a source who could have informed agents about the Tarrants–Swift episode and warned them about Tarrants's plan to launch a guerrilla campaign. But, as this book alludes to in earlier chapters, the FBI remains reluctant to disclose sources and methods, even decades after an informant was utilized and even after the informant's death. The likely source for the information may well have been one of the FBI's all-time most valuable informants: Sam Bowers's successor, L.E. Matthews.

This book is the first to suggest that Matthews worked as a deep-cover source for the FBI. But the author is not the only person to believe this to be the case. Award-winning investigative reporter

Jerry Mitchell, one of the leading experts on the White Knights of
the Ku Klux Klan of Mississippi, also believes that Matthews was
an informant. Several different pieces of information support this
contention. First, despite his being the head of the WKKKKOM, and
despite the fact that he was the chief bomb maker for the group
in the years before 1968. Matthews was never once charged or indicted for any crime by federal law enforcement after 1968. One
could pass this fact off as simply good luck or skillful evasion on the
part of Matthews, but that explanation does not hold water. When
the FBI finally convicted Byron de la Beckwith, in the early 1970s,
for conspiracy to bomb the New Orleans office of Jewish lawyer Al
Binder, the main evidence against Beckwith was the testimony of law
enforcement agents who saw L.E. Matthews provide Beckwith with
a bomb (uncovered in Beckwith's trunk, according to the state). But
even though the FBI arrested and convicted Beckwith for the crime,
*nothing happened to Matthews, the head of one of the FBI's most
despised racist organizations.*[29] Indeed, Matthews's tenure as head
of the WKKKKOM from the late 1960s through the 1970s was remarkable for the sheer lack of violence perpetrated by his group.
Once considered the most violent white supremacist organization
in the country, the group did almost nothing while Sam Bowers remained behind bars.

But more than anything, it is what we do not have on Matthews
that cinches the case that he was an informant. When Congress reinvestigated the King murder, and included among its host of suspects
J.B. Stoner, Sam Bowers, and Sidney Barnes, the obvious person to
call as a witness was Matthews, who was associated with all of these
individuals. But the available record—the final report from Congress—makes no mention of Matthews. It does, however, refer to
two unnamed informants with intimate connections to all parties
whose identities the FBI wanted to protect. We now know that Tarrants was one of these individuals. It seems likely that Matthews was
the other.

Failed attempts to verify the identity of this second informant
ironically corroborate this hypothesis. The sheer lack of material on
Matthews is too suspicious. When the author requested Matthews's
file by way of FOIA, the FBI provided him with five total pages of

material, two of them duplicates and *all of them from 1983*.[30] It is worth noting that files on individuals of similar significance run into thousands of pages. Deavours Nix, who ranked below Matthews in the WKKKKOM, has an eleven-thousand-page FBI headquarter file. Tarrants's file is of similar length. When he asked if the FBI had destroyed Matthews's records or transferred them to the National Archives, the author was told no. According to leading FOIA attorneys, the FBI often simply pretends that highly confidential and sensitive material does not exist rather than provide it to citizens in a FOIA request. The FBI is under no obligation for full disclosure in response to FOIA requests when national security—or sources and methods—are at stake. Process of elimination shows that either the FBI had an unbelievable lack of interest in a key KKK figure or that it continues to withhold information on Matthews, a practice almost always reserved for its most valued informants.

If Matthews was an FBI informant, it raises an alarming possibility for the King assassination investigation. Circumstantial evidence suggests that Matthews himself could have participated, in some way, in plotting the assassination. Recall that in March of 1968, Matthews offered his home to Eugene Mansfield, the former Grand Dragon who, suddenly and without warning, quit his job in Louisiana and moved in with Matthews. The records show Matthews discussing a hit with Mansfield that month, and law enforcement could not find Mansfield on April 4.

At the same time, FBI records show that Matthews was in and out of his hometown in Mississippi, working on some vague out-of-state project in the month before King's killing. Records also show that Matthews frequented John's Restaurant; he might fit the description of one of the suspicious men that Myrtis Hendricks saw interacting with Nix and Bowers.

The possibility also exists that Matthews engaged in such plotting to curry favor with Bowers, with the knowledge of someone inside the FBI. (Informants, especially at that high level, are often kept secret, even from FBI agents in the same field office.) If so, the FBI and Matthews may have found themselves in a complicated but not unfamiliar position as the plot against King unfolded. Their paradoxical challenge was to figure out how to protect an informant while preventing a major act of domestic terrorism. The temptation is to wait until other witnesses and evidence can be used to stop the crime without compromising new sources and methods. Often, even a low-level criminal can become the basis for implicating higher officials in a plot, until ultimately law enforcement rolls up an entire organization. But then timing becomes key. Act too early and the criminal case may not be solid enough to convict senior members of an organization. Act too late and the crime may well come to pass. The latter leaves the government with the unenviable choice between explaining why it did not prevent a major act of terrorism, and covering up its unintentional complicity and never admitting it to the public.

I already suggested something along those lines when discussing the 1963 bombing of the Sixteenth Street Baptist Church. In Chapter 13 I offer a similar scenario for the 1995 terrorist attack on the Murrah Federal Building in Oklahoma City. If the FBI learned of a potential King plot from L.E. Matthews and failed to act in time to prevent the assassination, this would go a long way in explaining the Bureau's behavior after April 4.

This explanation starts with its handling of Donald Nissen, the fugitive who left his family and a steady job in Atlanta after having been threatened, in December of 1967, for revealing what he knew about a White Knights bounty offer. The FBI's initial investigation into Nissen's claims may well reflect genuine limitations in terms of data-mining capabilities. Larry Hancock and I were able to connect the 1967 bounty offer (from McManaman) on King to the 1964 bounty on King (offered to McManaman's colleague Donald Sparks) only with the help of database technology and the Internet. Similarly, the superficial investigation of Sybil Eure, the woman who appears to have been a cutout for the bounty plot, could easily be attributed to antiquated perceptions about women and violence. But the follow-up investigation into Nissen's claims, after the FBI realized that he had jumped his parole, is harder to understand and more open to less forgiving explanations.

Upon discovering that Nissen had gone AWOL, the FBI reinvestigated his claims about a White Knights bounty. In May 1968, it returned to Jackson, Mississippi, to interview Sybil Eure, the go-between who received the package containing bounty money from Nissen in the summer of 1967. Eure's memory improved upon the second visit. Unlike her August 1967 interview with the FBI, Eure now remembered a story about a $100,000 bounty on Martin Luther King's life. It was all a joke, she claimed. Eure explained that in the spring of 1964, while short on cash and developing a professional relationship with McManaman (whom she identified as a real estate guru), she had seen TV reports linking the Mississippi Burning murders to Neshoba sheriff Lawrence Rainey. She had joked with McManaman that she could get $100,000 from Rainey if they promised to kill Martin Luther King Jr. Perhaps, as it had in 1967, the FBI did not think a woman was capable of participating in a Klan-connected murder conspiracy; the agents once again seemed to take Eure at her word.[31] But in May of 1968, that decision was harder to justify.

For one thing, Leroy McManaman was already back in Leavenworth Penitentiary in the spring of 1964, when the three civil rights workers were killed in Mississippi. Plus, the FBI did not connect Rainey to the Neshoba murders and to the KKK until August of 1964. In other words, Eure could never have been watching TV news reports about the Neshoba murders in April of 1964; she couldn't have made her supposed joke about a King bounty because she wouldn't have been in McManaman's company when the Neshoba murders occurred later that summer. One might be apt to forgive this oversight by the FBI save for one thing: Just a few months before interviewing Eure for a second time, federal prosecutors finally convicted several individuals, including Rainey and Sam Bowers, for plotting the Neshoba murders. The Jackson field office helped lead the effort to ensure the prosecution. It is hard to imagine that the FBI could have failed to see the major problem in the timing of events narrated by Eure.

The FBI missed other problems too. Eure took care to paint her relationship with McManaman as a professional one. But the FBI knew that McManaman identified Eure as the woman he intended to marry when he was released from Leavenworth Penitentiary. Moreover, no one communicated more with McManaman, by way of letters and visits, than Eure. This situation presented the FBI with a logical follow-up question for Eure: Why would McManaman refer Nissen to Eure for something as bold as a bounty offer on Martin Luther King Jr.'s life if it were all a joke? Even if he were simply gullible, McManaman would want to confirm details with Eure, who then would have let him in on the joke. But he instead told another criminal to visit her as part of a plot against King. The FBI never even bothered to find out the details of how and why a career criminal like McManaman was introduced to Eure in the first place. But the FBI did not subject Eure to a thorough interrogation.

Nissen eventually turned himself into the FBI at the end of July 1968. He specifically asked to turn himself into Special Agent Wayne Mack from the FBI field office in Phoenix, Arizona, the state where Nissen spent much of his early adulthood. Mack and Nissen developed a collegial relationship despite being on opposite sides of the law. In St. Louis, where Mack had detoured from a flight for in-service training in Washington, D.C., Nissen reiterated his account of McManaman's bounty offer to Mack. But he also added details of the threat outside the parole office, and in interviews with me, Nissen insisted that he told Mack about the Floyd Ayers money-package to Jackson. No record of that story exists in FBI files detailing Nissen's follow-up interview by Mack. Perhaps Nissen's memory of telling the FBI about Ayers, forty years after the fact, is confused. Perhaps Mack deliberately left those details out of Nissen's story to protect Nissen from potential charges of complicity in the King murder. Or perhaps the files have been sanitized.

Had the FBI looked deep within its files, it would have learned that Floyd Ayers had also been trying to get its attention too. For reasons that are not clear, in the week after Martin Luther King Jr.'s assassination, Floyd Ayers infiltrated King's funeral under false pretenses, attempted an apparent kidnapping of Martin Luther King Sr., and showed up at the White House gates insisting on seeing the president. The Secret Service and the FBI dismissed Ayers as mentally disturbed, and records provide no details of what Ayers told them in interviews.[32]

Without question, Ayers was at best flamboyant and was possibly mentally impaired. But the FBI knew something else about Ayers. Before he infiltrated King's funeral, before the FBI even found James

Earl Ray's Mustang in Atlanta, Georgia, police had suggested Ayers as one of their earliest suspects in the King murder. Not only did Ayers work for KKK leader James Venable, but Georgia law enforcement could not account for his whereabouts on April 4. The FBI dismissed Ayers as a suspect because it could not match his fingerprints to prints recovered at the crime scene. But within two weeks of clearing Ayers in April, the FBI received additional reports casting suspicion on the eccentric salesman.[33] Two witnesses said that Ayers had been referring to King's eventual murder in the months leading up to April 4.

If the FBI eliminated mention of the Ayers story from Nissen's account, this would be consistent with its general apathy toward Nissen's story as of August 1968. Agents did not even interview Leroy McManaman until September of 1968. At that point, McManaman predictably denied any connection to the King murder and denied having any interaction whatsoever with Donald Nissen. The FBI never followed up by confronting McManaman with records showing that the two men had in fact worked together in Leavenworth's shoe factory. More difficult to understand, the FBI did not bother to ask McManaman how, if Nissen had never known him and never spoken with him, Nissen could provide the FBI with the name of the woman McManaman intended to marry and where she lived and worked in Mississippi. The FBI instead closed the book on Nissen's case.

In fact, as of August 1968, the FBI had three separate threads of evidence pointing to a White Knights bounty offer as motivating Dr. King's murder: the Nissen story, which predated the King assassination; the accounts from Capomacchia and Barnes implicating Tarrants; and the reports from Jerry Ray, James's brother, to informants speaking about a bounty offer. Together these pieces of evidence cried out for a renewed interest in the White Knights and white supremacists as conspirators in the King assassination.

But there are no signs of a renewed investigation after the interview with McManaman in September of 1968. James Earl Ray had been captured and by the spring of 1969 had confessed to a judge and been sent to prison on a ninety-nine-year sentence. But the alarming fact is that when Ray's later protests of innocence led to a renewed congressional investigation in 1975 (after Christensen's article raised hackles at the FBI and intrigued investigators for the HSCA), the response by the FBI appears to be a cover-up, including the destruction of files and the use of FBI-legitimated sources to shift blame away from white supremacists. At least one of the sources claimed to Congress that men like Barnes were not dangerous—something contradicted by FBI records—and that the White Knights would never work across state lines—something contradicted by Beckwith's attempt to blow up Al Binder's office in New Orleans. Congress relied so heavily on these sources that it did not even bother to interview Sam Bowers, then in prison. The HSCA forced even hardened Mafia dons to testify on the JFK assassination, but it did not demand that Sidney Barnes testify before investigators when the white supremacist refused to cooperate. The FBI did not emphasize Nissen's story to Congress, and Congress never even approached him.

All of this highlights the alarming possibility that the FBI not only failed to stop King's murder but also failed to fully resolve it after the fact—even though it had the resources to potentially do both. If the FBI was protecting L.E. Matthews, this would not be the first time that sources and methods, and the desire to protect the Bureau's reputation, trumped the imperative for justice.

But an additional and just as disquieting possibility emerges from the events surrounding the King assassination and what they mean to the study of America's domestic, religious terrorism. The uncomfortable reality may be that the very sources (deep-cover informants and constitutionally dubious wiretaps) and methods (including violence) that the FBI used with white supremacists groups, and hid at all costs, prevented a much wider racial conflagration in the months and years following King's murder. Yet even if the ends somehow justified the means in the short term, the failure by law enforcement to more thoroughly investigate the motives of the groups it had infiltrated allowed said groups, during the lull in religiously motivated terrorism in the 1970s, to evolve in ways that would have enormous implications for homegrown terror by the 1980s.

THE END OF AN AGE

the FRAGMENTATION
of the RADICAL RIGHT
in the 1970S

"Now this is a long fight. It is a hard fight," said J.B. Stoner in June of 1969 as he addressed the national convention of the National States Rights Party as its newly elected chairman. Ostensibly, he was referring to the campaign for elected offices in the coming years. But Stoner spoke to a much longer struggle as well. "The Jews have been conspiring and carrying on their campaign on top of the world for centuries . . . and they still don't have it. . . . The Lord Jesus Christ himself called the children of the Jews the children of the devil and that is what they are, the children of the devil. . . . They are Satan's kids. Now they have been fighting for a long time so we have to fight for quite a while. We can't expect to win the fight in a few weeks or few months when the Jews have been after it for centuries."[1]

In many ways, Stoner's speech sounded like a rationale as much as a rallying cry. Despite the riots from the previous year, despite the chaos at the Democratic National Convention the previous summer, the race war so many saw as imminent had yet to materialize.

Yet tensions persisted through 1968 and into 1969. The number of urban riots diminished dramatically, but violence spread into other political arenas. A radical offshoot of Students for a Democratic Society, the Weather Underground became the latest New Left group to embrace violence as a form of political protest. With the ongoing activity of groups like the Minutemen, police estimated that America experienced an average of twenty bombings per week in 1969. So the religious radicals in the NSRP had not yet given up hope.

One speaker at the convention, identified only as Stephens, insisted to the NSRP delegates:

The battle is yet to be won. You and I will wind up being the soldiers that carry the forefront through the line to win the fight. So if

we leave this fight out against the Jewish, nigger revolution that we
are in, and it is a revolution, they sort of proclaim it to be a revolution, you and I are going to end this revolution. When the battle
starts, you and I will be the first ones there. We will be on the front
lines, and when this smoke does clear away from this battle, then
we should see nothing but white faces left in our nation.[2]

Stephens's words echoed the horrific sermon delivered by the Reverend Connie Lynch in Saint Augustine in 1964. "There's gonna be a
bloody race riot all over this country," Lynch insisted. "The stage is
being set for a bloodbath. When the smoke clears, there ain't gonna
be nothing left but white faces."

Lynch escaped incitement charges in 1964 even though a white
mob sent nineteen blacks to local hospitals after his speech. But
Stoner's rabble-rousing friend finally went to prison for instigating
racial violence in Baltimore in 1966; he was not at the 1969 convention. In his stead, at the convention and elsewhere, Neuman Britton
assumed the role of instigator. Like Lynch, Britton was a Christian
Identity minister, and at the convention he echoed the CI preaching
of Wesley Swift: "There is nothing left but blood for America over
the dead cause I know for a sure thing that there will never be any
peace . . . until we removed from these shores the serpent race and
this beastly race that is so prevalent among us." Speaking of the
blood that will flow from the "wine press of wrath," he asserted,
"We have arrived at the apex of this age."[3]

In many ways, 1969 represented the apex for the National States
Rights Party and for *organized* violence by adherents of Christian
Identity. But despite "favorable" conditions, the "Jewish, nigger rev-
olution" never escalated into a race war.

A reasonable question would be: Why not? Certainly, the idea of
a pitched conflict between racial groups, fighting in armies representing their ethnic identities, is hard to fathom, even in an era like
the 1960s. But to many Americans, a civil war based in part on race
and also on class and political ideology seemed more than possible
in 1969. In hindsight, with well-armed elements of the right and
the left openly courting such a war, the violence of the late 1960s,
as unique as it was in its historical intensity, seems somewhat tame

relative to what it could have been. New Left radicals engaged in street battles with law enforcement, and police recovered millions of rounds of ammunition from right-wingers, yet one did not find members of the Minutemen launching mortar shells at machine-gun-wielding members of the Black Panthers. With such willing participants, the lack of open conflict demands an explanation.

A likely answer is one that will unsettle many civil libertarians, who for decades have justifiably highlighted the abuses and dangers associated with programs like COINTELPRO, which surveilled, infiltrated, and provoked dissident groups inside the United States. The American Civil Liberties Union still speaks ominously about how national law enforcement spied on civil rights organizations and antiwar protest groups. The approach undermined legitimate and peaceful dissident groups and put a chill on political free speech. Liberals bemoan the treatment of groups like the Black Panthers and the KKK, even if they dislike what these groups stood for. Recall that to undermine the Klan in Mississippi, the FBI went so far as to use Mafia members to scare or beat confessions out of Klansmen; by all accounts, the sting operation that wounded Tommy Tarrants was ultimately meant to kill him (and did kill Kathy Ainsworth)—with no arrest or trial needed. When it came to the Black Panthers, the record indicates that the FBI either actively facilitated violence or, at best, passively allowed it to take the lives of several leading members, such as Fred Hampton.

But for those who feel that the ends justify the means, there is little doubt that the no-holds-barred approach by federal law enforcement, however distasteful, undermined violent and radical groups. By the early 1970s, many of the top members of these groups were in prison. Robert DePugh, who for years had deferred the most violent Minutemen activity in favor of a massive attack in the future, was in federal prison when the race riots of the late 1960s presented the best opportunity to put his strike teams into coordinated action. Sam Bowers was finally convicted for his role in the Neshoba murders in 1967, and by 1969 he found himself in prison, in part due to testimony from a deep-cover informant. On the other side, H. Rap Brown—who had an anti-riot act named after him in 1968—faced ongoing arrests and trials from 1967 onward. Black Panther leader

Huey Newton served time for manslaughter charges (which were eventually dropped) from 1968 to 1970.

Those known militants not in prisons were under constant surveillance by local police and often by federal law enforcement agencies such as the FBI. For this very reason, Bowers resorted to using Tarrants and Ainsworth in his White Knights campaign against Jewish targets in Mississippi. FBI biannual summary reports from the 1960s include weekly synopses detailing the activities of almost every key white supremacist in every major white supremacist group. Much of this inside information was collected by informants. It now appears very likely that the man who took over as Grand Wizard for the WKKKKOM when Bowers went to prison, L.E. Matthews, worked for the FBI. One of the most visible Klansmen in North Carolina, George Dorsett, was on the FBI payroll.[4] At the peak of the COINTELPRO White program, "the Bureau had over 2,000 Klan members on its payroll, recruiting them at the average rate of two per day."[5] The number of informants turned against the Black Panthers dwarfed even this total: the FBI had more than seven thousand informants inside the Black Panther Party as of 1971.[6] In addition to conventional surveillance and inside informants, wiretaps provided extensive information on white supremacist groups. If the wiretap surveillance on Stoner's law office extended through the 1970s, it would mean that the FBI likely had inside information on a vast array of KKK activities across the nation, as Stoner represented dozens of racists across the country as a legal advisor.

The combination of dirty tricks, electronic and human surveillance, informant activity, and strong-arm tactics debilitated white supremacist groups and greatly limited their freedom of movement until congressional investigations of the COINTELPRO program scandalized the FBI, forcing the operation to close in 1976. Among other things, Congress reported on "black bag jobs"—illegal wiretapping operations as well as warrantless burglaries of offices. The FBI also pursued legal, although questionable, tactics, often deliberately creating schisms within targeted organizations, such as the KKK, using informants to spread rumors of financial mismanagement among rank-and-file members. Under the weight of such government operations, memberships dwindled and the remaining activists shifted allegiance to different leaders or formed separate groups with different agendas.

By the early 1970s, Christian Identity radicals found themselves at a crossroads. Without the large base of influence that came from southern resistance to integration, without the pretext of widespread civil disorder, without friendly treatment from local law enforcement, they lost much of their unity. The 1970 death of Wesley Swift, their charismatic, ideological figurehead, further fractured their movement. In the decade that followed, more than one of Swift's acolytes attempted to heal the divisions within the movement and to foster the kind of solidarity seen in the 1967–1968 lead-up to Martin Luther King Jr.'s murder, but to little or no avail. The aspiration for consolidation could not overcome the reality of fragmentation.

But fragmentation had its benefits. The social turmoil from the previous decade created a residue of conservative, white grievance that manifested itself in many different forms. On the less radical end of the spectrum, it helped fuel the growing neoconservative movement, starting with the campaigns of Richard Nixon, whose "southern strategy" exploited implicit racism under the guise of "law and order" and contributed to two general-election victories.

The latent prejudice also permeated more militant movements, including nativist, patriot, and anti-tax groups. In its decentralized form, Christian Identity theology adjusted itself to the contours of these movements like a medical adhesive and exploited them in much the same way it had coopted southern nationalism and anti-communism in the 1960s. It may have lost its focus, but Christian Identity grew in its raw influence and even shaped offshoot religions and pseudo-religions, some of which attempted (and failed) to distance themselves from two-seedline Christianity. At the same time, with so many different groups and organizations in play, the landscape of religious terrorism in the 1970s became a "laboratory of radicalism." The internecine conflict within groups, and the rivalry between groups, became a proving ground that nurtured and developed some of the most important figures in white supremacist circles, men who would inspire acts of domestic terrorism for three decades.

Nothing illustrated these concurrent developments more than the Posse Comitatus. Named after an 1878 law that forbids federal military intervention in domestic policing, the group did not openly profess any religious imperatives, but it harnessed the resentments of America's farmers in a militant direction with an appeal to extreme federalism. According to the group's charter, no unit of government above the county level was legitimate. The group openly opposed federal income taxes, for instance. But for most of its existence, the group served as a front for Swift's sometime aide and sometime rival, William Potter Gale, who helped found the organization in the 1970s. As described by hate-group expert Daniel Levitas:

> The movement did not gain significant momentum until Gale was able to join his Christian Identity beliefs . . . with the growing anti-tax movement in the United States.
>
> The first phase, when Gale developed all these theories about "citizens' government" and the Posse Comitatus, was in the early to mid-1970s. In reality, Gale's ideas were really nothing more than verbal flourishes used to disguise old-fashioned vigilantism.
>
> The second phase started in the late 1970s, when Gale and his allies were able to take advantage of the agricultural crisis brewing in rural America and use it to disseminate Posse ideology throughout the farm belt.
>
> The third phase was after the Posse really came into public view in 1983, with the killing of two federal marshals by [Posse adherent and tax protester] Gordon Kahl in North Dakota. After that, everybody knew the Posse was trouble with a capital T.[7]

If there was a level of deceit in the message of a group like the Posse Comitatus, it may have been due to the difficulty of developing a large base of members with a radical reinterpretation of Christianity that would strike most Americans as foreign and idiosyncratic. As in the 1960s, plenty of Americans might sympathize with some goals of a Swift or a Bowers—distrust of Jews, a desire for segregation, displeasure with the central government—but to combine all into one package under the umbrella of a new form of Christianity may have been one step too far. Getting someone to hate tax collectors is one thing; getting the same person to reject what she has been taught in Sunday school since early childhood is much more difficult.

It is not surprising that, in the absence of a dominant and far-reaching voice like Swift (who died in 1970), the Church of Jesus Christ–Christian ceased to be the central headquarters for Identity theology and teachings. The movement grew, instead, in small pockets throughout the country under the auspices of several independent ministers. By and large, these men developed Identity theology in a way that mitigated domestic terrorism—to a degree. As individual religious figures took up the mantle of spreading two-seedline ideology, some shifted the theology in a more passive direction. Passive should be carefully defined here; it does not mean that these new leaders became any less anti-Semitic or racist, or any less convinced that a race war was imminent. Rather, passive in this sense means that these leaders became less apt to encourage or engage in violence as a way of provoking that race war. The new Identity churches formed white separatist compounds or communities and stockpiled weapons, but they waited for God to initiate the end-times.

Three people in particular reflect this trend. Starting in the mid-1970s, Dan Gayman of the Church of Israel, situated in southwestern Missouri, became one of the most influential spokespeople for this separatist strain of Identity teaching. In 1972 Nord Davis created a similar Identity community in Topton, North Carolina, eventually calling his group Northpoint Tactical Teams. At present, his compound includes "a farmhouse, numerous outbuildings, an underground bunker and fortifications made of granite, placed as a shield against invading government agents."[8] In 1973 the Reverend Robert G. Millar created an Identity commune with "slightly less than one hundred true believers . . . on a 400-acre tract"[9] in Oklahoma near the border with Arkansas. He called it Elohim City.

But for all their isolation, these men and their groups became indirectly entwined with religious terrorism as the decades proceeded. Gayman's and Davis's teachings helped nurture a young Eric Rudolph, who in the mid- to late 1990s bombed abortion clinics and, most famously, the 1996 Atlanta Olympics. Both Millar and Gayman maintained ongoing associations with militant Identity radicals, and both men's teachings helped inspire at least one separatist hamlet, Zarephath-Horeb in Arkansas, to radicalize into what became an extremist, terrorist camp.

In the mid-1970s, Jim Ellison, a Christian preacher, set up the Zarephath-Horeb Community Church as a refuge for disaffected drug
addicts and individuals who had been victimized by other religious
cults. Described by one observer as a "cross between John the Baptist
and James Dean,"[10] the charismatic Ellison loved to welcome new
members. According to follower Kerry Noble, Ellison would always
cite a favorite passage of scripture: "David therefore departed and
escaped to the cave Adullam. . . . And everyone that was in distress,
and everyone that was in debt, and everyone that was discontented,
gathered themselves unto him; and he became a captain over them,
and there were with him about four hundred men." But Noble, now
a recovering extremist, realizes that this was all a ploy. In his memoir,
Tabernacle of Hate: Seduction into Right-Wing Extremism, Noble
explains, "Although I didn't realize it at the time, here [in the passage
of scripture quoted by Ellison] was the first ingredient necessary for
creating an extremist: a philosophical or theological premise, based
upon discontent, fear, unbelief, hate, despair, or some other negative
emotion. . . . A [potential radical's] view of the present and future had
to be dark and bleak." Noble explains, "Ellison . . . knew that people
who had used drugs and who had previously been in cults were basi-
cally discontented with society and the kind of people he wanted, who
would be easier to mold than regular church people. . . . People often
join groups like this because they are . . . alienated from society . . . to
find a community—sense of belonging."[11]

Too many of Ellison's cult either never came to this realization or,
like Noble, came to it too late. In a four-year span, the church "un-
derwent a frightening metamorphosis from pacifist to survivalist to
paramilitarist to terrorist."[12] Gayman's teachings, reinforced by those
of Millar, who developed a close personal relationship with Ellison
(Ellison later married Millar's daughter), shaped the development of
this radical evolution. Ellison became, in one FBI agent's estimation,
"the General Patton of the Christian Identity Movement." His soldiers
were onetime disaffected souls whom Ellison molded into militant
extremists. While a follower, Noble became the propaganda minister
for what Ellison would relabel the Covenant, the Sword and the Arm
of the Lord (CSA). Members within the CSA became violent terrorists
in the 1980s, as will be described later in the book.

James Warner may have lacked Jim Ellison's public charisma, but he also had deep roots in the Christian Identity movement, becoming an influential figure in white supremacist circles during this transitional period in the 1970s. Warner originally belonged to George Lincoln Rockwell's American Nazi Party. But he famously not only abandoned that group but also stole its membership roster and provided it to his new cause, the National States Rights Party. Nurtured by the likes of Stoner and Fields, and heavily influenced by Swift, Warner may not have had the strong personality of his mentors. But what he lacked in oratory he made up for in his skill at written communication. In 1971 Warner built his own Christian Identity organization, the New Christian Crusade Church, head-quartered in Louisiana. It was there that Warner, an avid writer and pamphleteer, formed a partnership with a highly charismatic radical David Duke. By the 1980s, Duke had parlayed his good looks and down-home charm into a mainstream appeal rarely seen in white supremacist circles. Duke felt comfortable enough to run in the 1988 Democratic presidential primaries, and he won a seat in the Louisiana State Legislature not long after. Distancing himself from his extremist past, he then made a surprisingly, and to many alarmingly, strong bid to become Louisiana's governor in 1991. Republican activist Elizabeth (Beth) Rickey soon put the lie to Duke's public proclamations that he—and his KKK group—were more "pro-white" than anti-black and anti-Jewish by exposing *Did Six Million Really Die?*, a little-known and blatantly anti-Semitic book written by Duke.

But media coverage rarely went far enough to connect this prominent racist with his Identity influences. Rickey described ongoing interactions she had with Duke when he tried to charm her into tempering her coverage of his racist background. But for all his charisma, Duke could not avoid showing his true colors. As Rickey relates,

> From the start . . . it was always Jews. Blacks were not inter-esting to him. He was always upset about something, about a new conspiracy theory: World War I, World War II, the civil rights

movement, bombings—he linked it all to the Jews. . . . [At one point] he propped up Six Million on the table and pointed out passages from the Talmud that he claimed proved the Satanic qualities of Jewish people.[13]

Duke's Knights of the Ku Klux Klan (KKKK) became an important breeding ground for future white supremacists, many of whom cut their teeth in the organization while absorbing Christian Identity ideology. Three notable examples are Tom Metzger, Dennis Mahon, and Louis Beam.

According to the Southern Poverty Law Center, in his late twenties, after serving in the U.S. Army, Metzger became active in anti-communist organizations. He migrated from the John Birch Society to the Minutemen, temporarily formed his own organization in the early 1970s (the White Brotherhood), and eventually joined David Duke's KKK outfit. Metzger worked his way through the ranks of the Klan, and Duke appointed the Los Angeles transplant (Metzger is from Indiana) Grand Dragon of the California chapter of the KKKK.[14] In Duke's organization, Metzger embraced Christian Identity theology, becoming an ordained minister in 1979. At the same time, he began to develop a national platform, spearheading the Mexican Border Watch, an initiative aimed at stemming illegal immigration. According to Michael Zatarain, a Duke biographer,

> The idea was to create a "civilian patrol along the U.S.–Mexican border . . . extending from Brownsville, Texas, to the Pacific Ocean. Klansmen would drive the route in caravans from dusk to dawn. Six Klan "spotters" would work together, with about one-quarter mile between vehicles. Klan members were instructed to report immediately to immigration officials any suspicious-looking people they might find.[15]

As they had with farmers' discontent through the Posse Comitatus, Christian Identity sycophants commandeered nativism to their cause, appealing to a larger audience than they could have acquired if they had made their religious aspirations and ideas more obvious.

But Metzger outgrew Duke's KKKK (and, he says now, Christian Identity), separating to form his own branch of the Klan in California. He eventually left the Klan altogether to start the White Aryan Resistance (WAR) in 1984. As will be detailed later, Metzger, through WAR, became a significant instigator for white supremacist violence. Even today he is regarded as "one of the most notorious living white supremacists in the United States."[16]

If Metzger has a rival for that title, Dennis Mahon is a good candidate. Mahon joined Duke's group with his twin brother, Daniel, in the mid-1970s. Illinois farm boys, they rose through the ranks of the KKK until 1988, when Dennis formed his own group, the Missouri White Knights. He also became an important aide to Metzger with WAR. Mahon did not receive any official ordination in the Christian Identity movement, but his connections to the movement were to remain strong. He maintained a trailer at Millar's Identity compound, Elohim City. That association will become important in the upcoming discussion of the 1995 bombing of the Alfred P. Murrah Federal Building in Oklahoma City. In 2009 federal prosecutors convicted both Mahon brothers for their role in a 2004 mail bombing of a post office in Arizona that injured three people.

Louis Beam, another Christian Identity adherent, left the United Klans of America to join Duke's KKKK in 1976. A Texan and veteran of the Vietnam War, Beam became the group's chief strategist and trainer on issues of guerrilla warfare. Beam's writings on leaderless resistance, in which autonomous, decentralized cells of militants work independently to perform acts of terrorism, became very important as supremacist terrorism evolved in the 1980s and 1990s. But Beam, together with Warner, also influenced Odinism, a new religious movement that combined Norse mythology with Christian symbolism. Based on Viking gods and religious folklore, Odinism found a natural fit with modern white supremacists, just as it had with German Nazis in the 1930s and 1940s. Dennis Mahon, among others, began to shift his religious affiliation to Odinism in the 1980s. Rooted in an ancient European warrior ethic, and embracing the cultural anthropology of Aryanism, radical Odinism honored concepts similar to those of Christian Identity. Social scientist Timothy Miller asserts: "Militant racist Odinists advocate racial cleansing, believing that the manifest destiny of Aryans is to become victorious over the 'lower' races and eradicating them from the face of the Earth." Odinists called their end-times "Ragnarok . . . a final war that will culminate in the restoration of Aryans to power and produce a new Golden Age."[17]

In an odd replay of history, Odinism in the twentieth century seemed to parallel the evolution of its pagan progenitors before the first millennium. When the earliest Christians sought to convert pagans, including Teutonic tribes, to their growing flock, they often found willing proselytes, in part because the converts simply incorporated Christian beliefs, practices, and symbols into their preexisting belief systems. Jesus became simply another major deity, and saints became lesser gods in a process that cultural anthropologists call syncretism. But in the late twentieth century, when it came to militant Odinism, this process seemed to work in reverse. As paganism enjoyed a minor resurgence in the late twentieth century, some white supremacists were attracted to variations of Odinism that were heavily influenced by former Christian Identity sycophants like Louis Beam.

In fact, the ubiquitous presence and influence of radical Christianity within the upper echelons of America's hate groups in the 1960s meant that its theology exercised enormous influence on later belief systems, even when later groups openly ridiculed or distanced themselves from Christian Identity theology. In the early 1970s, two new religious movements, both with origins in the recalibration of right-wing extremism and both with legacies of rationalizing violence for decades thereafter, explicitly condemned Swift's theology but produced alternative belief systems that are indistinguishable from CI. These were Cosmotheism and the Church of the Creator (which came to be called the Creativity movement).

Cosmotheism—the idea that "cosmic order is God"—was the brainchild of one of the most important and influential figures in the history of domestic terrorism in the United States. At the time he founded the church, William Luther Pierce was a middle-aged physicist with an extensive background in white supremacy. Raised in Atlanta on the values of segregation, Pierce's earliest experiences were with groups like the American Nazi Party in the 1960s. Later he joined Willis Carto, a leading public anti-Semite, in presidential politicking. The two converted the Youth for Wallace group—a sort of Young Republicans for racist Alabama governor George Wallace's 1968 third-party presidential campaign—into the National Youth Alliance. But Carto accused Pierce of double-dealing, and the two parted ways in the early 1970s, at which point Pierce, with sole control, converted the National Youth Alliance into the National Alliance. Pierce, who was also associated with the National State Rights Party, rejected the supernatural elements of Christian Identity but created Cosmotheism as a way to provide spiritual direction and solidarity for his membership. Pierce repurposed Cosmotheism in much the same way that Identity theologians coopted Christianity.

The idea that the laws of nature are manifestations of a higher power has a long tradition. Cosmotheism is more or less Deism for racists, and it likely appealed to Pierce in the same way that Deism appealed to Benjamin Franklin, also a scientist. The religion allows for spirituality without the concept of supernatural intervention in the secular world. In Pierce's formulation, a higher power designed the universe, with laws and a purpose, and then got out of the way, letting the laws guide human outcomes. For Pierce, the purpose was a racially pure world. Pierce often ridiculed Identity theology, but he spent his life working with groups and individuals who were influenced by its tenets. As many scholars have observed, Cosmotheism and CI bear a striking resemblance, making it impossible to ignore the influence of Identity ideology on Pierce.[18] For instance, in his essay "What Is the National Alliance," Pierce asserted, "After the sickness of 'multiculturalism,' which is destroying America, Britain, and every other Aryan nation in which it is being promoted, has been swept away, we must again have a racially clean area of the earth for the further development of our people. . . . We will not be deterred by the difficulty or temporary unpleasantness involved, because we realize that it is absolutely necessary for our racial survival."[19] The "temporary unpleasantness" was a euphemism for a race war.

The FBI recognized Pierce's leadership potential before he assumed an influential role within the white supremacist movement. It recognized Pierce's talent for writing political propaganda as early as 1966. As will become clear later, much misery and violence owes itself to Pierce eventually realizing his potential.

Much like Pierce, Ukrainian-born Ben Klassen understood the power of the written word to inspire movements. Having immigrated to North America at a young age, Klassen, like Pierce, eventually became active in the presidential campaign of George Wallace. Like Pierce, he found his voice in the fragmentation and proliferation of white supremacist groups of the 1970s. In 1973 Klassen wrote *The White Man's Bible* and began a movement. The Church of the Creator (COTC), or Creativity movement, continued to influence white supremacist terrorists as late as the 1990s. "Our Avowed Purpose," Klassen asserted in his influential text, is to "again revive the healthy instincts with which Nature endowed even the White Race and to bring it back to sanity so that our people will not only recognize their enemies, but also learn to exercise their instinctive urge to overcome them." Those enemies, Klassen insisted, were "number one, the International Jew, the whole Jewish network, the Jew as an individual. Number two is the mass of colored races, whom we shall designate simply as the mud races."[20] However similar these ideas are to Christian Identity theology, Klassen drew key distinctions. Notably, he called Christianity itself a harmful myth. He not only doubted that Anglo-Saxons had descended from one of the lost ten tribes of Israel but also questioned whether the ten tribes had ever existed. If Pierce's religious ideas represented a new take on Deism, then Klassen's philosophy, observed religious scholar Mattias Gardell, added a quasi-spiritual dimension to social Darwinism. In another book, published the same year as the *White Man's Bible*, Klassen spoke to "Nature's eternal law," whereby the white man has naturally evolved into "a realized Nietzschean superman."[21]

Despite a public fallout between Klassen and the followers of Christian Identity, it is hard to ignore how much CI influenced the COTC, especially when it came to Klassen's vision for the future. Like Swift's followers before him, Klassen set up a military-style training camp. On land in Otto, North Carolina, Klassen's trainees prepared "for total war against the Jews and the rest of the goddamned mud races of the world—politically, militantly, financially, morally and religiously. In fact, we regard it as the heart of our religious creed, and as the most sacred credo of all. We regard it as a holy war to the finish—a racial holy war. Rahowa! is INEVITABLE."[22] Klassen, not a member of Christian Identity, coined the term *racial holy war,* and the abbreviation *rahowa* remains a popular tattoo among white supremacists across the nation.

If the national landscape of white supremacist groups appears to be a panoply of new and idiosyncratic organizations, loosely and independently shaped by the influence of Christian Identity, this was not the objective of all racialist extremists. Some resisted the trend toward fragmentation.

The Reverend Robert E. Miles, a Christian Identity pastor from Michigan, described by scholars as an "elder statesmen" of the movement, attempted to consolidate the trend toward greater cooperation and collaboration among CI-connected hate groups that had begun in the mid-1960s. Calling his movement Unity Now, Miles attempted, in 1970, to unite disparate antigovernment and anti-Jewish groups to attack the establishment. As a gathering of Unity Now in 1973 demonstrated, almost all its key members were racists or Christian Identity zealots. An awards ceremony held at the gathering speaks to the extent to which Identity theology had thoroughly penetrated the ranks of American extremist organizations. Pastor Roy Frankhouser won the Valor Under Fire award; Minister James Freed won the Defense of Christian Law honor; Renato Verani, an American Legion commander, won the Christian Militancy award; CI pastor George Kindred won the Resistance to Taxation prize; and Miles himself took home the honor for White Christian Brotherhood. The groups represented at the conference included the United Klans of America as well as the Western Guard of Canada. The benediction was given by James Forster, a pastor from the Ministry of Christ Church, which was essentially a seminary for Identity preachers. But a heavy concentration of attendees and award winners came from Miles's own state of Michigan, and Unity Now never gained widespread momentum. In 1971 Miles was arrested. He soon went to prison, convicted of firebombing ten empty school buses and of tarring and feathering a school principal in protest of government-imposed integration programs in his home state.[23] Miles aligned himself closely with Frankhouser, but as it turned out, by 1973 the former eastern regional head of the Minutemen was a paid informant for the Bureau of Alcohol, Tobacco and Firearms.

The most enduring effort to unify white supremacist groups relates, not surprisingly, to Wesley Swift. When Swift died in 1972, he left the legacy of the Church of Jesus Christ–Christian to an understudy, Richard Butler, an engineer for Lockheed-Martin. Butler moved the CJCC to Hayden Lake, Idaho, where it became the church for his new group, the Aryan Nations, an organization that welcomed neo-Nazi and KKK factions under one umbrella. In 1979 Butler hosted the Pacific Kingdom Identity Conference, "a springboard for his attempts to align such fairly diverse groups as the Ku Klux Klan, neo-Nazis, Posse Comitatus, and others during the 1980s."[24] By the 1990s, Butler's hate group had become one of the nation's largest and best known, building a base of young, disaffected skinheads using a strategy similar to Jim Ellison's.

But divisions and rivalries continued to make it difficult to unite disparate groups behind some kind of collective action. The Associated Press reported that the Klan in 1979 was a "hodge podge of factions, names and philosophies."[25] In one example, Bill Wilkinson, a key member of David Duke's KKK outfit, split from his mentor's hate group to form his own KKK organization, poaching hundreds of members from Duke's group in the process. Duke ridiculed Wilkinson's group as "illiterate, gun-toting, rednecks." "We're not just a bunch of fools running around in bed sheets," Duke claimed.[26]

As it turned out, Wilkinson had been an FBI informant since 1974. When this fact was exposed in 1981, Wilkinson went into hiding, possibly through the Federal Witness Protection Program. It is difficult to tell if Wilkinson was simply a source of information on the Klan or if he formed his new organization at the government's urging, as yet another attempt to divide and fragment the white supremacist community.[27] For that reason, it is also difficult to say whether the FBI exposed itself to criminal complicity by associating with Wilkinson and his group.

Allegations that the FBI went beyond surveillance and infiltration, graduating to provocation, began to surface in congressional investigations at this time. One of the most controversial charges involved an offshoot of the Minutemen known as the Secret Army

Organization (SAO). With DePugh in federal prison since 1968, the Minutemen splintered and dissolved. But in 1970, a handful of one-time Minutemen decided to reverse course, convinced that government infiltrators, rather than a lack of leadership and organization, lay at fault for the Minutemen's demise. They believed that, if purged of informants, the SAO could continue the fight against "the communists" controlling the American government and against New Left radicals outside of government. With a new and smaller organization, they hoped to avoid infiltration by federal law enforcement. As it turns out, one of SAO's founding members, Howard Godfrey, provided information on the group's activities to the FBI from the start.

Godfrey represented a rare type of informant, someone like the controversial Gary Rowe, who during the 1960s had infiltrated the Ku Klux Klan in Alabama at the FBI's behest. Described by the *Los Angeles Times* as an "unimposing ex-San Diego city fireman," the thirty-two-year-old Godfrey told the press that he had assisted the SAO while it "conducted a reign of terror against the left in a series of attacks including bombings, burglaries and harassment."[28] He confessed that the group had plotted "the assassination of President Nixon and several controversial leftists," stolen "membership files and lists from leftist organizations," and shot "into the home of a Marxist college professor, wounding a woman guest." For five years, using the false identity Captain Mike McGann, Godfrey reported on right-wing activities. He rose from a mere recruit in 1967 to head of the San Diego branch of the Minutemen to co-founder of the SAO.

As noted earlier, infiltrators like Godfrey and Rowe present conflicts of interest to their official handlers in law enforcement because they often must prove their worth to fellow radicals by engaging in criminal activity. Recall that Rowe even became an accessory to a murder in Selma, Alabama, in 1965 while on the federal payroll. The government, to this day, routinely offers waivers to informants who perpetrate crimes in the "call of duty." But with Godfrey, federal law enforcement went way beyond looking the other way while ultra-right-wing militants engaged in violent criminal activity.

When the press uncovered Godfrey's activities, he revealed that he

had told his FBI handler about all SAO criminal operations, sometimes *in advance* of a crime. "We used to meet a couple of times a
week, in parking lots throughout the city, behind stores, anywhere
that happened to be handy. We would grab a few minutes and talk,"
he told the *Los Angeles Times*. What's more, the FBI supplied Godfrey with a substantial amount of money for weapons—$20,000—to
help cover 75 percent of the SAO's operating expenses.[29] It appeared
to some, especially in the New Left, that in supporting Godfrey, the
FBI was more or less subsidizing the group's activities. The ACLU
insisted to Congress that the SAO was set up "on instructions of FBI
officials" to "serve as agents provocateurs, inciting disorders as a
means of exposing 'domestic radicals,' particularly campus leaders
of the New Left protesting the war in Southeast Asia."[30]

The FBI, for its part, maintained that it simply offered Godfrey
passive approval—that it did not encourage any criminal activity.
Yet there is no doubt that after Godfrey and a colleague fired shots
into the home of Professor Peter Bohm, injuring Paula Tharp, Godfrey's FBI handler took the informant's weapon and hid it from the
San Diego police for six months. The extent to which the FBI promoted the activity of the SAO remains a point of contention to the
present day. For instance, in 2013 the Department of Homeland Security updated its database of historic terrorist activity to note that
the SAO "was possibly funded by the FBI."[31]

By 1976 such FBI operations (as well as illegal wiretapping and
"black bag jobs") had been exposed by Congress, leading the FBI
to end COINTELPRO. But as the Wilkinson story shows, the established FBI informant network inside KKK groups had become so
vast that it may have been impossible to reel it back in. The kind of
conflicts described in previous chapters, whereby the FBI was forced
to balance the need to protect sources and methods with the need to
prevent criminal activity, persisted. This dilemma applied not only
to the FBI but also to local law enforcement agencies, which increasingly began to infiltrate white hate groups.

This situation became apparent after an investigation of one
of the most shocking acts of KKK violence in the 1970s. On November 3, 1979, members of the Greensboro, North Carolina, Ku
Klux Klan opened fire on an anti-Klan protest march staged by the

local Communist Workers Party (CWP). Five members of the CWP, which had been trying to organize black factory workers in the area, were killed. Tensions between the two groups had escalated in the previous weeks, with each side openly provoking the other and more than hinting at violence. The name of the CWP rally was Death to the Klan. But film footage of the shooting demonstrates that the KKK, with the help of the American Nazi Party, fired the first salvos on November 3. As many as forty of the sixty to eighty extremists who joined the counter-protest fired on the leftists, some of whom were also armed and returned fire. Police arrested fourteen Klansmen, many associated with Grand Wizard Virgil Lee Griffin's Confederation of Independent Orders of Knights of the Ku Klux Klan, for the murders. But in a decision reminiscent of injustices of the past, an all-white jury acquitted the men.[32]

Years later, new investigations into the crime—including a truth and reconciliation commission modeled on the body that investigated Apartheid-related atrocities in South Africa—uncovered disturbing information. The local police, whose investigative interests extended both to the communists and to the Klan, had employed an informant inside the KKK who, according to several witnesses, encouraged the KKK members to bring weapons to the event. The same man, who worked as a federal informant as well, appears to have warned both the FBI and the local police about the potential for violence, but nothing was done.[33]

One participant in the Greensboro massacre, Frazier Glenn Miller Jr., symbolized many of the developing trends in the white supremacy movement. A Vietnam veteran, Miller was loosely associated with Virgil Lee Griffin's KKK group, which in turn was an offshoot of Bill Wilkinson's KKK group, which in turn was an offshoot of David Duke's KKK group. No one knows if Miller fired a shot on November 3, but he later split with Griffin to form his own KKK chapter, the Carolina Knights of the KKK, and then an antigovernment group, the White Patriots Party. At some point in the early 1980s, he became an Odinist, but he continued to associate with Christian Identity extremists who were swayed to terrorism by the writings of William Pierce. Miller later turned FBI informant and helped law enforcement develop charges against Louis Beam, among others, in a 1987 federal sedition trial. The conviction never materialized, and despite his cooperation with federal authorities, Miller's hatred for Jews and blacks did not abide.[34]

In prison Beam elaborated on his theories on leaderless resistance, adding the idea of "lone wolves" who would "act when they feel the time is ripe, or [would] take their cues from others who precede[d] them." On April 13, 2014, in an ironic and tragic manifestation of Beam's strategy, the seventy-four-year old Miller opened fire at a Jewish community center and a Jewish retirement home in Kansas. When arrested, Miller believed that he had killed three Jews and repeatedly said "Heil Hitler" to police officers. In reality, all three victims were Christians.[35]

Miller had first become attracted to white supremacy when he returned from Vietnam and read a copy of *The Thunderbolt*. He joined the National States Rights Party in 1973. He left the group, he claims, because it was "made up mostly of elderly people who were not that active."[36] For the most part, Miller's observation rings true. By the early 1970s, the NSRP included, according to one estimate, as few as seventy to eighty-five active members. Neuman Britton was literally the only member of the Arkansas NSRP, and despite the best efforts of people like Danny Joe Hawkins, the group could never even establish a chapter in the white supremacist stronghold of Mississippi. What public attention the NSRP could draw had come from J.B. Stoner's campaigns for public office in Georgia—all of which eventually failed, although he did garner seventy-three thousand votes in his 1974 campaign for lieutenant governor.

Increasingly, the NSRP became more open, in its literature, about its religious motivations. Stoner's campaign fliers included biblical citations that would have been very familiar to Identity believers, such as Revelations 2:9 (referring to the "synagogue of Satan"). In the past, one could find evidence of Identity theology in books advertised in *The Thunderbolt*, such as *Still 'Tis Our Ancient Foe*, a 1964 work by Identity minister and Minuteman Kenneth Goff that exposed the phony "Jewish religion."[37] But direct references to religion were rare (although still present) in the text of the periodical itself. In contrast the July 1974 edition of *The Thunderbolt* included an article entitled "The Basic Identity Message." Written by Thomas O'Brien, one-time Kilgrapp (secretary) for James Venable's National Knights of the Ku Klux Klan and former editor of the NKKKK's periodical *The Nighthawk*, the article asserted that "the Jews are not the Hebrews of the Bible, they are not the tribes of Israel and Christ was not a Jew. They are the mongrelized descendants of Satan through Cain."[38] Editions of *The Thunderbolt* in 1974 also included a guest article by one of the founding Identity theologians, Bertrand Comparet, and an advertisement for James Warner's New Christian Crusade Church. But this did nothing to boost core membership.[39]

The NSRP did make strides in other directions. Stoner made visits to European countries as part of an outreach to the growing number of right-wing organizations in places like England and Germany. By 1980 Stoner enjoyed an impressive array of contacts with European white supremacist groups. In fact, on October 13, 1980, Stoner held a multinational conference for racists in Cobb County, Georgia. The following day, in nearby Atlanta, an explosion rocked the Gate-City Bowen Homes Day Care Center. Did J.B. Stoner have one more card to play in his effort to stoke a holy race war?

11

THE TENTH PLAGUE

the ATLANTA
CHILD MURDERS,
1979–1981

"It was so quick," one teacher said, referring to the explosion that demolished the Gate-City Day Care Center in the Bowen Homes housing projects in Atlanta. "All I could think was, 'Get to the door. Get out, children, get out.' I got all 12 of mine out—safe and accounted for."[1]

"It was terrible, really terrible," another teacher observed. "Some of the kids were badly hurt. I saw one little boy whose fingers were missing."[2]

The October 13, 1980, explosion that demolished the day care center killed five African Americans: one teacher and four toddlers. Authorities evacuated some 480 students from nearby schools, in fear of another bombing. The day care center and the schools serviced a local, predominantly African American housing project. Almost immediately, accusations against local hate groups, such as Stoner's NSRP, flowed from Atlanta's black community.

"It was the Ku Klux Klan," one neighborhood resident shouted at Maynard Jackson, Atlanta's first black mayor, when he visited the scene.

The Reverend Joseph Lowery, head of the SCLC, asserted, "There is an organized assault on black people across the country. We are tired of our children being killed."[3]

The Reverend Lowery's reference to an "organized assault" on children came with a context. For the previous two years, a series of killings had ravaged Atlanta's African American community, taking the lives of, among others, at least thirteen victims below the age of thirteen. The name known in history, the Atlanta Child Murders, is something of a misnomer. The victims also included several teenagers between the ages of thirteen and sixteen as well as six victims who were twenty years or older—two as old as twenty-eight.

After a year of killings with no suspects apprehended, Bowen Homes residents booed Mayor Jackson when he came to visit the site of the explosion. Many refused to accept the explanation for the tragedy provided by local authorities and endorsed by Jackson: that the explosion at the day care center had resulted from a faulty boiler. Lee Brown, Atlanta safety commissioner, who led the Atlanta Child Murders investigation, insisted that "absolutely no foul play was involved."[4] The claim seemed too convenient, designed, in the minds of some, to pacify a city described, in several accounts, as on the edge of open racial violence. The explosion at the day care center appeared to be part of a general pattern, an ongoing organized assault on Atlanta's black children. That it came less than twenty-four hours after J.B. Stoner held a conference of international white supremacists in a neighboring county only amplified the suspicions and paranoia of Atlanta's residents. Stoner, after all, had built a reputation for bombing black targets as far back as the late 1950s.

But experts from the FBI; the Bureau of Alcohol, Tobacco and Firearms; and the Atlanta Gas Light Company concluded that Jackson and Brown were right: The explosion was just an accident. Normally, cool water prevents a water-tube boiler from becoming too hot. In this instance the boiler had overheated when a safety device, designed to turn the boiler off if water levels became too low, had malfunctioned. The boiler had reached an untenably high temperature, at which point cool water rushed in, creating a sudden reaction. As the Associated Press reported, "The boiler exploded like a fragmentation grenade, tearing out massive chunks of concrete and steel from the center section of the building."[5]

Yet in casting their suspicions on Stoner, Atlanta's African American community may have, if by accident, identified a key player in the wave of child killings. A group of men who worked for the National States Rights Party likely perpetrated several of the Atlanta Child Murders. These men, members of a notoriously racist family, maintained ongoing contact with NSRP cofounder Ed Fields, and one enjoyed a close working relationship with J.B. Stoner. Due to what appears to be another law enforcement cover-up, this time by the Georgia Bureau of Investigation (GBI), it is impossible to say with certainty that Stoner and Fields instigated or plotted the kidnapping–murder spree in Atlanta from 1979 to 1981. And I have made the case that the NSRP is possibly the closest one can come to an outright religious terrorist organization (one that does not hide its religious agenda from its most active members); it is also impossible to say whether the family in question embraced Christian Identity theology. But a tantalizing, if speculative, case can be made that the Atlanta Child Murders fit the pattern of Christian Identity terrorism since the early 1960s—one in which Stoner and his ilk exploited racial tension in hopes of igniting a race war.

Here, Atlanta's African American community appeared to be right. However accurate Atlanta's political establishment may have been about the accidental explosion at the Gate-City Day Care Center, Atlanta's political elites desperately wanted to temper the very racial antagonisms Stoner may have wanted to inflame. The explosion in the day care center was in many ways a metaphor for a city whose reputation for being "too busy to hate" seemed in jeopardy of collapsing. The October 13 tragedy aroused national and even international attention to the ongoing crisis in Atlanta, with icons such as Sammy Davis Jr. and Muhammad Ali offering huge rewards for anyone who could help stop the killings. Now in the national spotlight, Georgia law enforcement, helped by the FBI, faced additional pressure to solve the crimes. The net result became an investigation that appears to have conflated several unrelated murders into one horrific phenomenon and to have ignored other potential killings, in hopes of finding a tidy and fast resolution to the Atlanta Child Murders. Georgia law enforcement may have identified one likely killer, Wayne Williams, but in so doing, it covered up leads that could have pointed to J.B. Stoner's last act of religious terrorism.

The murder wave had begun in the summer of 1979, but authorities were too slow to link the crimes together or to coordinate a response. Reports of missing children and teenagers found murdered became all too commonplace in the months that followed. The great writer and social critic James Baldwin, in "Evidence of Things Not Seen," his extended essay on the murders, wrote,

> It never sleeps—that terror, which is not the terror of death (which cannot be imagined) but the terror of being destroyed.

Sometimes I think, one child in Atlanta said to me, *that I be coming home* from (baseball or football) *practice and somebody's car will come behind me and I'll be thrown into the trunk of the car and it will be dark and he'll drive the car away and I'll never be found again.*

Never be found again: that terror is far more vivid than the fear of death.[6]

Many of the murder victims obviously were found again. Edward Hope Smith, a fourteen-year-old high school student, last seen leaving a skating rink, vanished on July 21, 1979. An elderly woman collecting cans for deposit money found Smith's corpse alongside another dead body in a wooded area near a dirt road in southwestern Atlanta; Smith had died from a .22-caliber gunshot wound to his upper back. The second body, dressed all in black, was decomposed to the point that authorities took nearly a year to offer a likely identification: Alfred Evans, a thirteen-year-old friend of Smith's, missing since July 25, 1979. Evans's cause of death was "probably asphyxiation by strangulation." On September 14, 1979, fourteen-year-old Milton Harvey disappeared, last seen on his bike delivering a credit-card payment to a bank for his family. His skeletal remains were found on November 16, 1979, a few miles south of the previous two victims; authorities could not determine the cause of death. On October 21, 1979, nine-year-old fifth-grader Yusuf Bell did not return home after going on an errand for his neighbor. He was last seen getting into a blue sedan. A custodian found his body in an abandoned school in downtown Atlanta on November 8, 1979; cause of death: blunt-force trauma to the head followed by asphyxiation. The next victim, found on March 10, 1980, in a wooded area in southwestern Atlanta, was Angel Lenair, last seen watching *Sanford and Son* at her friend's house the week before. Someone had bound and gagged Lenair and strangled her to death. One day later, FBI agents, using trained dogs, found the body of eleven-year-old Jeffrey Mathis in a briar patch; authorities could not determine the cause of death for Mathis, who like Bell had last been seen getting into a blue car, at a service station earlier that month.[7]

By the summer of 1980—what is now commonly called the Summer of Death—fear and frustration had come to a head. The number of missing children approached record levels, but local and state police had yet to publicly link the murders together or to coordinate their approach to the crisis. Whatever person or group was responsible for the crimes, he or they appeared to be getting bolder. In one instance, a witness described seeing an individual break and enter through an apartment window and emerge with seven-year-old Latonya Wilson in his arms. An independent citizen's search found Latonya's skeletal remains weeks later. Soon a group of mothers of missing and deceased children, led by Yusuf Bell's mother, Camille, and calling themselves STOP, the Committee to Stop Children's Murders, insisted on a meeting with local law enforcement. They presented investigators with a list of nine victims of unsolved murders. That summer, law enforcement finally formed a joint task force. Meanwhile, what came to be called the List grew to include as many as twenty-eight names—"all but two of them males; all but five of them children."[8]

But in many ways the List served as much as an albatross as an aid to a legitimate investigation. Chet Dettlinger, an outside investigator who volunteered to analyze the crimes after hearing complaints from victims' relatives, became alarmed at the arbitrary way in which law enforcement decided which names to put on the List. Jeff Prugh, an Atlanta-based journalist who cowrote a book (fittingly called *The List*) with Dettlinger,[9] described the parameters:

> To make The List . . . a victim had to be age 7 to 27, male, female, killed by stabbing, or manual strangulation, or suffocation, or bludgeoning, or "unknown" causes (changed later, in some cases, to "probable asphyxia," which means nothing more than the victim probably stopped breathing). . . . The only constant thread of The List was that all of the victims were black.[10]

If filtered by a different criterion—class, age, or circumstances of death—a list of murder victims who fit some pattern or profile could, in theory, be much more extensive or much more limited at any given moment. For example, a list based on race and age would exclude a twenty-eight-year-old victim who had died under similar circumstances. A list based on another criterion, such as location of bodies, could imply a relationship between two crimes that in fact had nothing to do with each other. Dettlinger, who methodically mapped the crime scenes, including where the victims had last been seen, where they lived, and where their bodies were found, estimated that the List could have grown to include as many as sixty-three additional victims who fit a broader pattern—notably, as Dettlinger established, geographic or social proximity between victims. Police colored their investigation of the crimes with a mono-causal assumption: *one* group (the KKK or a homosexual sex ring) or *one* person (a serial killer) had murdered all the people on the List. To this day, Dettlinger, whose frustrations with the myopic focus of law enforcement became the basis for a 1985 miniseries starring Martin Sheen, questions whether or not multiple patterns of association between the crimes—multiple motives and multiple perpetrators—explain the horrible murder wave of 1979 to 1983.[11]

Dettlinger's investigation uncovered the fact that several of the boys not only knew each other but also appeared to be gay hustlers, who possibly turned tricks for money. The investigator connected at least ten of the victims to a house on 530 Gray Street, believed to be a hot spot for a homosexual sex ring. The house belonged to Thomas "Uncle Tom" Terrell, a sixty-three-year-old who admitted knowing Timothy Hill, a thirteen-year-old whose body was found on March 31, 1981, dressed only in underwear. More than one witness had seen Hill, who knew several of the other victims, at the Gray Street address shortly before he disappeared.[12]

But Dettlinger also noticed that, as the murder spree stretched further into the spring of 1981, the pattern of the crimes began to change: "The victims were getting older and the murders were moving out of the center of the city, they were also moving eastwards."[13] Soon he began to predict where the "the killer would strike next" with such uncanny accuracy that Dettlinger himself became a suspect. Consistent with a pattern identified by Dettlinger, one of the oldest victims, twenty-one-year-old ex-convict Jimmy Ray Payne, was found by fishermen in the Chattahoochee River on April 27, 1981—almost twenty miles northeast of Niskey Lake Cove, where the first two victims (Smith and Evans) had been found in 1979. Law enforcement began to stake out nearby bridges, hoping a killer would once again dump his victims into the waterway.

Soon the strategy bore fruit. In the early morning of May 22, 1981, two police officers staking out the James Jackson Parkway Bridge over the Chattahoochee heard a splash. The same officers heard and then spotted a white 1970 station wagon, which was already being followed by another officer. Officers radioed the FBI, who detained the driver, a twenty-three-year-old African American part-time photographer, part-time radio disc jockey named Wayne Williams.

Williams's explanations for why he was on the bridge at the time did not jibe with investigators, and within several days police found the body of twenty-seven-year-old ex-convict Nathaniel Cater in the Chattahoochee. Circumstantial evidence then began to pile up against Williams, mostly in the form of pattern evidence—fibers and hairs that appeared to connect Williams to multiple crimes. In the end, Atlanta prosecutors charged Williams with only the murders of Cater and Payne, but during the course of the trial they implied that he was responsible for at least ten other crimes. Defense attorneys raised legitimate questions about the validity of the pattern evidence, but Williams ultimately was his own worst enemy. On the witness stand, the seemingly mild-mannered Williams exploded in a fit of temper at prosecuting attorneys, changing from Dr. Jekyll to Mr. Hyde in the eyes of the jurors. Jurors convicted Williams on February 27, 1982, and a judge sentenced him to two life terms for the two murders.

The joint task force ultimately closed its investigation of all twenty-eight murders on the List, on the assumption of a lone murderer and of Williams's sole guilt. Doubts persist over this decision, but prosecutors have always pointed to one trump card: the killings stopped when Williams went to jail.

But whether or not the killings actually stopped depends on how one defines future murders—that is, it depends on the arbitrary nature of the List. In contrast to the prosecutors' opinion, Dettlinger insists that the killings continued after Williams went to prison, citing, among other crimes, the 1984 murder of seventeen-year-old Darrell Davis, a witness whose testimony helped send Wayne Williams to prison. Famed FBI criminal profiler John Douglas, who is certain of Williams's guilt in eleven of the murders, concurred with Dettlinger:

I believe there is no strong evidence linking [Wayne Wiliams] to all or even most of the deaths and disappearances of children in [Atlanta] between 1979 and 1981. Despite what some people would like to believe, young black and white children continue to die mysteriously in Atlanta and other cities. We have an idea who did some of the others. It isn't a single offender and the truth isn't pleasant. So far, though, there's been neither the evidence nor the public will to seek indictments.[14]

Like Douglas and Dettlinger, some victims' families, and even leaders of the original investigation, still wonder whether the increased public and political pressure that followed the day care center explosion led to a rush to judgment once police had arrested Wayne Williams. Even if, as it seems increasingly clear, Williams killed some of the Atlanta victims, the investigation never officially tied him to a large number of the killings on the List, much less to the other victims identified by Dettlinger. Law enforcement agents—both the FBI and the special task force in Atlanta—simply assumed that Williams was a serial killer who had murdered the other victims. Suspicions of a racist conspiracy in the killings, cast on individuals such as Stoner, seemed to subside with the arrest and conviction of Williams—at least among most of those investigating the homicides. But within two years of Williams's conviction, data that pointed to other killers and a cover-up began to leak to reporters.

Aubrey Melton, an Atlanta police detective assigned to investigate the murders, provided *Spin* magazine reporters Barry Michael Cooper and Robert Keating with new evidence related to the murders. Melton's firsthand account, and supporting documents, points to a parallel inquiry into the crime by the Georgia Bureau of Investigation (GBI). With the strong encouragement of their editor, Rudy Langlais, Cooper and Keating published an exposé in a series of articles in 1986 and 1987.[15]

Within months of the first disappearances, both the FBI and the GBI began to receive disturbing reports from their informants. Separate lines of evidence focused attention on a family of racists as potential suspects in the murders. Members of the Sanders family often ran afoul of the law. The family patriarch, Carlton Sanders, boasted a criminal record dating back to 1951 that included "35 arrests for everything from simple assault to wife beating"[16] to child molestation. (That charge was dropped.) Sanders's five sons shared similar histories. Charles Sanders dealt and used narcotics and was active in recruiting for the KKK. Don Sanders was the national secretary for the National States Rights Party; he often dressed in military fatigues when serving as a bodyguard for J.B. Stoner. Three other brothers, Ricky, Terry, and Jerry Lee, also belonged to the NSRP.

Jerry Lee bore a strong resemblance to a police sketch of a potential suspect seen in a green car near one of the child victims. His father, Carlton, closely matched the description, originally given by witness Ruth Warren, of a scar-faced white man connected with the disappearance of fourteen-year-old Lubie Geter. (Warren later changed her identification to say that Wayne Williams was the man she saw with Geter.) The bodies of several victims, including Geter, were found with dog hairs that had come from a Siberian husky. As it turned out, the Sanders family raised Siberian huskies. (Law enforcement later claimed that the hairs could have come from a German shepherd—the kind of dog owned by Wayne Williams.)[17]

The most incriminating evidence against the Sanders family emerged from undercover informants. The GBI first turned its attention to the Sanders clique when a longtime and reliable source for Detective Melton, Billy Joe Whittaker, reported that Geter had once accidentally backed his go-cart into Charles Sanders's car. Whittaker relayed Sanders reaction: "I'm gonna kill that black bastard. I'm gonna strangle him with my dick." Not long after that exchange, police found Geter's body, a victim of strangulation. Geter, in turn, personally knew several of the other child victims, leading the GBI to consider the Sanders family as key suspects in the Atlanta murders. Fearing media leaks if this information were to spread to the much larger joint task force, a small band of GBI investigators began looking into the Sanders angle using Whittaker as well as other informants.[18]

Charles Sanders had once attempted to recruit Whittaker into the NSRP (then directly tied to the New Order of the Ku Klux Klan). At the behest of Melton, Whittaker asked Charles Sanders about Geter. In 1991, when Whittaker testified to an appellate court considering a new trial for Wayne Williams, he recalled Sanders saying, "Yeah I killed the little bastard. We are killing niggers, about 20 of them, and we are going to start killing young black women next."[19] Another informant insisted that "Don Sanders has direct knowledge of who was responsible" for the killings in Atlanta.[20]

Transcripts of wiretaps of Don Sanders's phone went a long way toward supporting that contention. After a brief, mundane conversation in which Don Sanders (identified in the transcripts as DS) asks where his brother Ricky is, Don matter-of-factly tells Terry Sanders (identified in the transcripts as TS) what Don's plans are:

> DS: I'll just give a buzz back, and I might get out and ride around a little bit, and I might come by there.
>
> TS: Go find you another little kid, another little kid?
>
> DS: Yeah, scope out some places. We'll see you later.[21]

Additional tape recordings and transcripts may shed further light on the role of the Sanders family. The GBI claimed to have destroyed the remaining material after clearing the Sanders family of suspicion (and, perhaps not coincidentally, after charging Wayne Williams with the Atlanta crimes). Keating and Cooper imply that the material may be lost forever, but new documents, discovered by the author, suggest that the recordings may have been transferred to the FBI and that the FBI may have done independent electronic surveillance (ELSUR). One document says, "Body recording is being utilized to direct the course of investigation and numerous valuable lead material was obtained from this recording. Elsur cards in this matter were previously submitted to the Bureau."[22] The term *body recordings* likely refers to informants who wear wiretaps, hidden underneath their clothes, to record person-to-person live conversations. In other words, either the GBI or the FBI used wired sources to investigate leads in the Atlanta crimes.

Another document says that the state of Georgia was pursuing Title III authority (that is, wiretapping authority) from the Department of Justice. The Georgians were asking the FBI to process material produced in conjunction with said authority, and the FBI director instructs that "evidence maintained by the FBI, including logs and transcripts, should be filed as though FBI generated."[23] The implication here is that material collected through GBI sources, which could have included the tapes referenced by Keating and Cooper (tapes that the reporters believed were permanently destroyed), may well still exist, perhaps as duplicates, in FBI records. The author is making a Freedom of Information Act request for this material.

What we do know about the recordings comes from disclosures by Detective Melton. Besides the suspicious conversations from Don Sanders, the recordings (and informant reports) show that the Sanders family was trying to procure weapons for the National States Rights Party. The NSRP's gun-trafficking efforts became part of a national trend of white supremacist groups creating paramilitary training camps for a potential racial conflict.

Experts trace the development, in large part, to the Greensboro massacre in 1979 (referenced in the previous chapter), when, after a decade of fragmentation and intergroup rivalry, American Nazis and KKK members joined forces to fire upon a group of protesters at a rally against the Klan in North Carolina organized by the Communist Workers Party. The joint attack in Greensboro failed to yield a single conviction, galvanized white supremacists, and brought a measure of solidarity not seen since the 1960s. Paramilitary camps drew members from a variety of groups: the Aryan Nations, the American Nazi Party, the Posse Comitatus, and various KKK organizations. In Hayden Lake, Idaho, Church of Jesus Christ–Christian and Aryan Nations leader Richard Butler began an annual meeting of leaders of such groups, which became known as the Aryan World Congress. With the newfound esprit de corps among white supremacists came a newfound faith in the prospect of a race war. Stoner and Fields' helped organize camps in the woods and mountains of Georgia, and they turned to the Sanders family for weapons.

Whittaker described a virtual arsenal of material at the Sanders residence, stolen from a National Guard armory. A February 18, 1981, report filed by Melton and provided to the GBI listed: "M 16 rifles; C 3/4 Explosives (plastic in brick form); Electric detonators; handguns; bazookas; machine guns" and "approximately 100 cases of" machetes. Ominously, the men had also obtained police uniforms as well as "other well-known company uniforms" (such as Coca-Cola uniforms).[24]

The same report connected the weapons cache to the Atlanta Child Murders: "Source [Whittaker] advised that [Charles] Sanders told him that the KKK including himself was creating an uprising among the Blacks, that they were killing the children—that they are going to do one each month until things blowup."[25] To the credit of some, including the GBI, the race war angle became a factor in the investigation of the Sanders brothers' involvement in the wave of killings. According to Keating and Cooper, the GBI considered it a distinct possibility that the murders were an attempt to "ignite a race war between blacks and whites in the capital of the south."[26]

The desire to polarize the races and provoke a racial conflagration had rested at the heart of the NSRP's agenda for decades. It was a manifestation of the influence of Christian Identity eschatology among the group's leaders, such as Stoner and Fields. There is no direct evidence that the Sanders family embraced Christian Identity teachings. We must admit that there is also little to suggest that members of Eastview Klavern 13, who bombed the Sixteenth Street Baptist Church in 1963, honored Identity theology either. But, as argued above, men like Stoner and Fields manipulated rank-and-file KKK members like the Sanders family (or, in the case of the Sixteenth Street Baptist Church bombing, conspirators like Robert Chambliss and Tommy Blanton) into taking steps that advanced the Identity agenda. Reports that Ed Fields engaged the Sanders family directly when acquiring weapons for his camps at the very least point to an opportunity for such exploitation to happen vis-à-vis the Atlanta Child Murders.[27]

J.B. Stoner's rhetoric and activity during the crime wave also point to this theologically inspired manipulation. Stoner did not plant a bomb at the Gate-City Day Care Center, but the fact that he would hold an international conference for white supremacists at a time when ten children had been killed and at least four more were missing shows that he wanted to inflame Atlanta's black community. As he had in his campaigns with his late friend Connie Lynch, Stoner used rhetoric to drive apart the races, openly calling for racial violence at rallies in 1980.[28] Stoner chose to do this when Atlanta was becoming a racial powder keg.

The combination of the murders of Atlanta's black children and a major spike in Atlanta's general crime rate had created serious racial tensions in the city by the late 1970s. The separate killings of a white doctor and a white legal secretary in 1979 only worsened this dynamic at a time when the entire nation suffered through ravages brought on by the unusual combination of high prices and high joblessness (stagflation). The city that was supposedly "too busy to hate" may have experienced an easier time of integration than other southern metropolises, such as Birmingham, but Atlanta was still an epicenter for the white supremacist movement, the headquarters for James Venable's National Knights of the Ku Klux Klan and for the NSRP. In a development that must have brought a smile to J.B. Stoner's face, by 1981 radical black nationalist groups had begun to agitate in Atlanta. Armed patrols manned housing projects, and some in the black community spoke about moving in weapons by the truckload. Two leftist groups (the Liberation League and the Movement Against Racism) argued,

> The murders in Atlanta will stop when its residents organize to defend themselves, as the Black veterans and the Techwood [housing project] residents have begun to do. They must seek to shut down white supremacist military camps. They must make Stoner and the NSRP afraid to show their faces in Georgia. . . . The working and oppressed people of Atlanta, when they are organized and prepared to resist the fascists, are the one force that can put a stop to the murders, and to all fascist attacks.[29]

Mayor Maynard Jackson became alarmed at the growing frustration and militancy of the black community, but he also worried about paramilitary groups practicing for a race war in the remote parts of Georgia—and with good reason. Atlanta's first black mayor found himself in much the same situation as America's first black president, Barack Obama: having to walk the fine line between addressing the needs of his base, minority constituency without appearing as too racially partisan to white moderates. In "Evidence of Things Not Seen," James Baldwin observed:

At the very beginning of . . . The Terror . . . it was, instinctively,
assumed that this was but yet another convolution of the Ku Klux
Klan. . . . But the fact, globally resounding, of a Black Administration rendered this assumption not only untenable, but craven.
In the eyes of the world—to say nothing of the eyes of America—
Americans behaved with honor, and altered, upward, the status
of the darker brother. America had, in fact, and with unspeakable
vengeance, done exactly the opposite, but the world had no way
of knowing this and Americans had no reason to face it.[30]

Maynard Jackson kept his deep concerns about possible widespread racial tumult to himself and out of the public view. This re-
luctance to stoke racial tensions filtered down to the GBI. In the
midst of its investigation of the Sanders family, the GBI noted in
an internal memorandum that "the city of Atlanta is faced with an
extremely explosive racial problem." GBI director Phil Peters noted
"how sensitive the investigation would be and how necessary it
would be that the intelligence not be disseminated outside the circle
of investigators who were directly involved." Peters pointed out
that if the intelligence, which the investigation was based on, leaked
out, it would possibly cause "a race riot."[31] Three months after this
warning, the investigation into the Sanders family closed with the
arrest of Wayne Williams.

Those who exposed the possibility of criminal involvement by
the Sanders family in the Atlanta murders, like Keating and Cooper,
believe that with the arrest of Williams, the GBI actively buried the
white supremacist angle for fear of the very race war that someone
like Stoner may have been trying to stoke. Law enforcement cleared
the Sanders family with surprising alacrity and then literally burned
any supporting evidence that could shed light on their guilt. But even
the excellent work done for *Spin* magazine tends to treat the Sanders
family as the sole driving force behind the killings rather than consider the possibility that the family was taking orders from NSRP
higher-ups. Perhaps the Sanders family did originate a murder conspiracy, and perhaps they were motivated by their own independent
Identity convictions. Unfortunately, those with the greatest access to
what sources still existed in the mid-1980s (including informants) all

but ignored the potential influence of Christian Identity on the Atlanta murders, just as historians have failed to recognize its influence in the previous crimes detailed in this book.

At present the evidence is silent on whether the Sanders family embraced radical Identity theology. But the evidence is clear that Stoner and Fields did embrace radical Identity beliefs and that they, like their fellow travelers in other organizations, demonstrated a record of terroristic opportunism, including creating a climate for racial polarization, piggybacking on racial violence to stoke even more chaos, and manipulating people like Carlton Sanders (and his family) into provocative acts of violence.

This pattern would continue, even as Stoner finally faced justice and prison time in 1982 for crimes he had committed during the 1960s. The Atlanta Child Murders may have represented the last dying breath of holy provocation for the likes of Stoner and the NSRP, but a growing number of smaller Identity-influenced groups and individuals continued to terrorize the United States in the name of a holy race war.

12

JEREMIAH'S WARRIORS

the ORDER, *the* CSA,
and the 1984 MURDER *of*
SHOCK JOCK
ALAN BERG

The station promotion assistant at KAO Radio in Denver, Colorado, found something suspicious about the fifty-two-year-old University of Wyoming "writing student" who visited the station, supposedly on a research assignment for an upcoming class. Beyond her age, the "short, chubby" woman asked none of the questions that Patrick O'Connor normally fielded from students. She showed no interest in the "station's ratings, advertising rates or marketing." Instead, the woman focused her inquiry almost entirely on the radio program's personalities—their airtimes, the substance of their shows. O'Connor became even more suspicious when he noticed the woman, later identified as Jean Craig, a Laramie, Wyoming, grandmother, taking photos of the facility, "including an employee-only parking lot behind the building."[1]

The record shows that Craig was on a very different kind of assignment. Her mission at KOA became part of a wider effort by Craig to track the movements of Alan Berg, one of the station's most well-known and outspoken call-in radio personalities. A onetime writer for the brilliant, controversial, and unabashedly foul-mouthed comic Lenny Bruce, Berg had once earned accolades simultaneously as Denver's most-liked and least-liked radio host. By 1984 Berg had made his mark by berating on-air callers, be they liberals or conservatives, men or women. No one escaped Berg's hostile wit, especially not the white supremacists who frequently called in to the Jewish "shock jock." Berg took great pleasure in ridiculing the bigots in his listening audience, specifically challenging members of the Christian Identity movement.

On February 13, 1984, Berg invited two Identity evangelists, Colonel Jack Mohr and Pastor Pete Peters, onto his program for a confrontation. The sixty-eight-year old Mohr belonged to the founding generation of Identity clerics, and while his profile was less national than that of fellow Korean War veteran William Potter Gale, Mohr had self-published a large number of theological tracts while running an informal ministry for forty years. Peters, on the other hand, belonged to a new generation of Identity icons. Born in Nebraska, the "self-styled cowboy preacher" had founded the Laporte Church of Christ in Colorado in 1977. The church included its own outreach arm, Scripture for America.[2] The three-hour program ended in the spirit of outright hostility, but not before a caller phoned into the program, defending the two Identity preachers.

"You ought to have a Nazi on your show,"' the caller said.

"You're sick, perverted," Berg replied. "You are a Nazi."[3]

Berg did not know that the caller, David Lane, belonged to a secret cell of religious terrorists known as the Order, or the Silent Brotherhood. Formed in 1983, the group had developed a six-phase plan to "recruit members, to build a 'war chest' by robbing banks and counterfeiting, and eventually to liberate the Pacific Northwest as a homeland for whites." In January 1984, the group "outlined 'step 5' of the plan, the assassination of prominent Jews."[4] Berg had no way of knowing it, but in antagonizing his white supremacist guests, he had made his way to the top of the Order's hit list. Five months later, Lane drove the getaway car involved in Berg's murder.

On June 18, 1984, with intelligence gathered by Craig's advanced scouting, members of the Order, including founder Robert Mathews, were waiting for Berg when he entered the driveway of his home at 1445 Adams Street in a suburb of Colorado. With thirty-nine-year-old New Yorker Richard Scutari serving as a lookout, Lane, a forty-seven-year-old former KKK member, pulled up behind Berg's VW Beetle in a four-door Plymouth, blocking the radio host's exit from his driveway. Mathews opened the door for another loyal member of the Order, thirty-year-old Christian Identity devotee Bruce Pierce, who opened fire, killing Berg with a .45-caliber MAC-10 submachine gun. As Lane peeled out to escape the scene of the crime, Pierce said to Mathews, "It was like we pulled the goddam rug out from under him the way he went down!"[5]

For some, the killing of Berg marked a radical departure in the tactics of white supremacists. Mark Potok, an expert on extremism from the Southern Poverty Law Center, said, "In a sense, it was one of the opening shots of a truly revolutionary radical right perfectly willing to countenance the mass murder of American civilians for their cause."[6] As has been noted throughout this book, the radical right had been willing to "countenance the mass murder of American civilians" since the late 1950s, especially if those civilians were either black or Jewish. During the 1960s, these plans were limited—first, because radical religious leaders hoped to leverage the large number of rank-and-file racists who were less amenable to wider violence, and second, because law enforcement had fractured the ranks of white supremacist organizations and curtailed their membership at the most opportune time for fomenting racial violence. This pattern persisted through the 1970s, despite the best efforts to unify the ever-shrinking numbers of militant bigots. But in 1979 the Greensboro massacre reignited the white supremacist movement. At the same time, many leading supremacists began to rethink and refine their tactics. In fact, the killing of Berg simply represented the next step in the evolution of domestic religious terrorism, a shift that had been ongoing since the Silent Brotherhood's founder, Robert Mathews, had been a teenager.

Mathews began his journey into radical white supremacy in 1971, as a nineteen-year-old in Arizona, where he and his family had moved from his birthplace in Texas. The Minutemen enjoyed a wide following in the Southwest, and their anti-communist and antigovernment message resonated with the teenager. But with Robert Bolivar DePugh in prison in 1971, the Minutemen were racked by internal rivalries. Failing to graduate from high school, Mathews widened his range of conservative activities to include membership in the Young Republicans, the John Birch Society, and eventually his own radical, paramilitary anti-tax group, the Sons of Liberty. By 1972 he had already drawn the attention of federal law enforcement, but at that point he was more or less living a transient lifestyle and was difficult to trace.

Mathews remained on the periphery of right-wing causes after the Sons of Liberty disbanded in 1975. But he soon joined William Luther Pierce's National Alliance, a white nationalist, anti-Semitic, and white separatist organization. By 1982 he had become active with Richard Butler's Aryan Nations in Idaho and had explored Christian Identity theology via the Church of Jesus Christ–Christian.

Mathews's religious worldview is confusing to some. Some scholars still refer to him as a Mormon, based on his upbringing, but he clearly dabbled with both Christian Identity and Odinism. It is clear that when he formed the Order in 1983, Mathews recruited many members from Christian Identity offshoots, notably from Jim Ellison's Covenant, Sword and Arm of the Lord. As late as 2007, a close associate claimed that much like Louis Beam, Mathews favored a form of Odinism that seemed to incorporate Christian Identity beliefs.

Beam's ideas appear to have influenced Mathews in more than just the religious sense. In 1983 Beam authored his essay, now famous in white supremacist circles, on "leaderless resistance." In this landmark piece, Beam, perhaps with an eye toward groups like the Minutemen and the KKK, insisted that "so-called 'secret army' organizations are sitting ducks for enemy infiltration, entrapment and destruction of the personnel involved," because they relied on top-down, hierarchical, pyramid-style approaches to military organization. Beam argued that white supremacists needed to adopt the cell model of insurgency, whereby smaller militant groups operated "totally independently of the other cells," with information on the government passed from group to group rather than dispersed from some centralized and unifying command.

Beam referred to the cell system used by the Soviets but ultimately rejected the Soviet model because the KGB retained its centralized leadership role in activating cells to achieve a broad objective. Beam instead harkened back to a strategy first articulated by lifelong intelligence agent Colonel Uluis L. Amoss and aptly named the phantom cell. Beam wrote:

The "phantom cell" mode of organization is based upon the cell organization, but does not have any central control or direction. In the Leaderless Resistance concept, all cells operate independently of each other, but they do not report to a central headquarters or top chief, as do the communist cells. . . .

The entire purpose of Leaderless Resistance organization is to defeat the enemy by whatever means possible, all members of phantom cells will tend to react to an objective event in the same way, usually through the tactics of resistance and sabotage.[7]

In many ways, Mathews's new group became the beta test for the phantom cell concept. Without any apparent central direction, the Order engaged in a months-long effort, from 1983 to 1984, to bomb Jewish targets, assassinate political leaders, and undermine the American economic system, all while funding itself through bank robberies and armored-car heists.

But if Beam's ideas informed the strategic framework for Mathews's revolutionary group, then William Luther Pierce provided the playbook for its activities. Writing under the pseudonym Andrew MacDonald, Pierce had authored the 1978 underground best seller *The Turner Diaries*,[8] a how-to guide for would-be terrorist cells. Set in 1991, the futuristic novel assumes the form of a diary written by Earl Turner, a martyr in an insurgent resistance group known as the Organization. The passage of the fictional Cohen Act of 1989, calling for the mass confiscation of guns by the Jewish-controlled government (Turner calls it the System), radicalizes and coheres the Organization, once a ramshackle group of antigovernment conservatives, into a well-heeled militia. The Organization uses bombings, assassinations, and other tactics to fight a guerrilla campaign against the System while constantly facing structural problems, a lack of resources, and a lack of members due to government propaganda. After months of proving his worth "to the Cause," Turner and his girlfriend are summoned for a loyalty test—a foolproof method of weeding out infiltrators. After that they are indoctrinated, through a secret ritual, into a covert subgroup within the Organization: the Order.

When Robert Mathews formed the Order in September 1983, he drew direct inspiration from *The Turner Diaries*. But the "proof" of government tyranny for members of the Silent Brotherhood was not any formal, national effort at gun confiscation. The group radicalized over the "martyrdom" of a handful of extremists who had died resisting the government.

This group included Gordon Kahl, a Christian Identity follower, shot dead in a February 1983 armed standoff with Arkansas law enforcement. Weeks earlier, Kahl, a leader in William Gale's Posse Comitatus anti-tax organization, had killed two U.S. marshals who had sought to arrest the extremist for parole violations. (In 1976 Kahl had served time in federal prison for tax evasion.)[9]

Other martyrs to the antigovernment cause included John Singer, an excommunicated Mormon fundamentalist who had refused to send his children to public schools because they promoted integration. In January 1979, when police attempted to enforce a court order giving custody of Singer's children to his ex-wife, Singer drew a weapon and was shot dead by Utah police officers.[10]

Finally, there was Arthur Kirk, an in-debt Nebraska farmer who, on October 23 1984, wearing a gas mask and armed with an AR-15 submachine gun, exchanged fire with a state law enforcement SWAT team and died in a hail of bullets fleeing his home.[11] Though there is no sign that Kirk was a religious radical, his death became a cause célèbre for Christian Identity zealots, who in their newsletters reported that "Kirk's wounds were not fatal, but the SWAT team then let him bleed to death in a dog pen before they took him to the hospital."[12]

In 1984, when the Order officially declared war on what it called the Zionist Occupied Government (ZOG), it cited all three men as "Aryan yeoman" who "awoke" to fight their government:

> Our heroes and our culture have been insulted and degraded. The mongrel hordes clamor to sever us from our inheritance. Yet our people do not care. . . . Not by accident but by design these terrible things have come to pass. It is self-evident to all who have eyes to see that an evil shadow has fallen across our once fair land. Evidence abounds that a certain vile, alien people have taken control of our country.
>
> All about us the land is dying. Our cities swarm with dusky hordes. The water is rancid and the air is rank. Our farms are being seized by usurious leeches and our people are being forced off the land. The Capitalists and the Communists pick gleefully at our bones while the vile hook-nosed masters of usury orchestrate our destruction. . . .
>
> We now close this Declaration with an open letter to Congress and our signatures confirming our intent to do battle. Let friend

and foe alike be made aware. This is war!—We the following, being of sound mind and under no duress, do hereby sign this document of our own free will, stating forthrightly and without fear that we declare ourselves to be in full and unrelenting state of war with those forces seeking and consciously promoting the destruction of our faith and our race.

Therefore, for Blood, Soil, and Honor, and for the future of our children, and for our King, Jesus Christ we commit ourselves to Battle. Amen.[13]

If the CSA's Jim Ellison consecrated his leadership of malcontents by quoting 1 Samuel 22:2, then members of the Order held Jeremiah 51:20 (God's prophecy for Cyrus of Babylon as a future hero for the Israelites) in highest esteem: "You are My war-club, My weapon of war; And with you I shatter nations, And with you I destroy kingdoms."

To take on the American "kingdom," the Order took its cue from Pierce's fictional Organization and engaged in bombings (of Congregation Ahavath Israel Synagogue in Boise, Idaho) and a murder (of Alan Berg in Denver). Its list of potential assassination and bombing targets was longer and far bolder, but the group initially lacked the resources to pursue its goals. So, in another parallel with William Pierce's fictional universe, Matthew's cadre resorted to robberies to finance its operations, at one point scoring a series of armored-truck heists that netted millions of dollars.

Early on, Mathews assumed what the fictional Earl Turner realized only midway through his insurgency that a movement that hopes to undermine the system can attract adherents only by undermining support for the status quo. As Pierce/MacDonald asserts after Turner enters the Order:

What is really precious to the average American is not his freedom or his honor or the future of his race, but his pay check. He complained when the System began busing his kids to Black schools 20 years ago, but he was allowed to keep his station wagon and his fiberglass speedboat, so he didn't fight.[14]

So, just like the Order in Pierce's fictional account, the Silent Brotherhood begins a major counterfeiting operation to undermine the status quo.

In the make-believe world of *The Turner Diaries*, the counterfeiting operation goes a long way toward bringing down the System. The combination of a militant insurgency and economic sabotage—including destruction of a major power plant in Evanston, New York—creates chaos and brings a growing number of new members to Earl Turner's group. In the novel, the Organization engages in widespread ethnic cleansing and mass murder, including the Day of the Rope, when Jews, "mongrels," and race traitors are summarily executed by hanging in California. The Organization infiltrates and recruits from within the U.S. military and soon gains control over nuclear weapons, engaging in a war of nuclear attrition with the System and with the Soviet Union. Earl Turner, who early in the novel betrays his oath to the Order by failing to kill himself before being temporarily captured, redeems himself through a suicide mission, destroying the Pentagon in a kamikaze attack with a plane full of explosives. In the years that follow, the Organization gains the upper hand, overruns much of the Western world, lays waste to large parts of Asia, and of course exterminates Jews and minority groups by the millions, leaving a world where the fictional Order exercises "its wise and benevolent rule over the earth for all time to come."[15]

In the real world, things did not go as well for Robert Mathews and the Order. The Order's counterfeiting operation produced a number of poorly made bills. The Secret Service traced the fake money to a member of the Silent Brotherhood in Philadelphia. Law enforcement then turned this member, Tom Martinez, into an undercover informant. In his reports, Martinez described to law enforcement the thought process of individuals like Mathews, who hated Jews as much as Stoner or Bowers ever did. Information provided by Martinez had helped bring down the most senior members of the Order by 1985 and ultimately led to a final denouement with Mathews at Whidbey Island in Washington State.[16]

With its rustic cabins, tidal basins, and old-growth forests, bucolic Whidbey Island is now a tourist attraction. But on December 7 and

8, 1984, it was the site of the last standoff between Robert Mathews and federal law enforcement. Weeks earlier, after a shootout in Portland, Oregon, in which an FBI agent was shot, a wounded Mathews escaped to the island. Cornered at a waterfront home on the ironically named Smuggler's Cove Road, Mathews refused to surrender or even negotiate with the "enemy," despite being surrounded by "150 FBI agents from five states . . . plus Island County sheriff's deputies with Coast Guard and Navy support," including "dozens of FBI sharpshooters, explosives specialists, negotiators and antiterrorist experts."[17] On the first day alone, the Odinist unleashed nearly one thousand rounds of ammunition on law enforcement. Knowing that Mathews had a virtual arsenal at the ready to continue his one-man standoff, law enforcement launched illumination flares at the cabin, setting the place ablaze with Mathews in it. "Mathews' blackened bones were found in a bathtub" not long after.[18]

Thus Mathews joined Kahl, Singer, and Kirk—and before them Kathy Ainsworth—as a modern martyr of the white supremacist cause. Perhaps twenty-five years too late, the hunt for the Order, according to Anti-Defamation League expert Marvin Stern, caused "governmental agencies to take a harder look at the (white supremacist) phenomenon. . . . It gave law enforcement the impetus to take a harder look at the threat this posed to them and to all of society."[19]

In pursuing other fugitives connected with the Order, the government turned its attention to a group with close affiliations to Mathews: Jim Ellison's the Covenant, the Sword and Arm of the Lord. Since 1978, due to the influence of Identity pastors Dan Gayman and Robert Millar, the CSA had been moving more and more in a radical direction. In 1982 Ellison had declared himself King of the Ozarks and issued a "Declaration of Non-Surrender":

We, the undersigned, knowing that we stand in the presence of God Almighty and His Son, Jesus Christ, do commit our signature and our willing approval to this document.

In the event of the collapse of this Great Republic or the consideration of surrender of our sovereignty by our duly elected government officials to an internal or external power, we the undersigned, acting in the spirit of our Forefathers and these great documents—the Declaration of Independence and the Constitution of these United States—refuse any and all such treaty, pact or declaration of surrender.

We acknowledge that there can exist no compromise between the principle of Freedom under God and the establishment of a world order based on humanism, materialism, socialism, and communism. We accept the principle that it is better to stand, and if need be fall for the cause of Christ and Country than to submit to the coming attempt of satanic and socialistic world order.

Let it be affirmed in the name of Jesus Christ and in the spirit of our Forefathers.

The people of Zarepath-Horeb and C.S.A.[20]

According to ex-CSA member Kerry Noble, the group imagined an impending end-times scenario whereby the president of the United States surrenders American sovereignty to the "World Socialist Democratic Alliance" without so much as a shot being fired. Under the new system of government, all firearms would be confiscated and "all food, fuel and medical supplies will be impounded for the good of the people" and all "fundamental, independent, Bible-centered congregations will cease operation at once."[21] In this CSA nightmare scenario, publication and distribution of the Bible would be banned.

Returning from Richard Butler's Aryan World Congress in 1983, Ellison spoke about his future plans for the CSA organization, which included "dumping cyanide into the reservoirs of major cities, killing federal agents, blowing up an [Anti-Defamation League] building or overpasses in major cities; maybe even blowing up a federal building." In the case of the latter, a CSA associate, Richard Wayne Snell, approached Ellison and asked "King James" if, "in his opinion . . . it [would] be practical to blow up a federal building in Oklahoma City, or possibly a federal building in Dallas or Fort Worth, Texas."[22] According to criminologist Mark Hamm, Snell joined Ellison and another CSA member, Steve Scott, and

traveled to Oklahoma City where, posing as maintenance workers in brown uniforms, they entered the Murrah Federal Building and

assessed what it would take to destroy it. Ellison carried a notepad
on which he made sketches showing where the building was most
vulnerable to collapse from the explosion of rocket launchers that
were to be placed in a van. Ellison said "[The van] could be driven
up to a given spot, parked there, and a timed detonating device
could be triggered so that the driver could walk away and leave
the vehicle in a position and he would have time to clear the area
before the rockets launched."[23]

Thankfully, Hamm observes, the CSA lacked the criminal skill
and competence to pull off this grand scheme. Instead, it attempted a
number of lower-level crimes as a means to that end: stealing police
uniforms, CB radios, and various merchandise that could be pawned
for cash. In one instance, Snell robbed a pawnshop under the mistaken impression that the owner was Jewish. Snell killed the man
during the robbery. Later, while on the lam, he murdered an African American state trooper who had pulled him over for a traffic
violation.

Neither of Snell's killings was part of any organized CSA terrorism. In terms of directly targeting its enemies, the best the CSA
could muster was two arson attacks: one against the gay-friendly
Metropolitan Community Church in Missouri and the other against
Temple Beth Shalom in Indiana. In both cases, the resulting damage
was minor.

Despite their frustrations, in 1984 Ellison and the CSA issued a
declaration of war, which they called the Aryan Tactical Treaty for
the Advancement of Christ's Kingdom (ATTACK). The document
stated, "It is inevitable that war is coming to the United States of
America. . . . It is predestined. . . . The time has come for the Spirit
of Slumber to be lifted off our people! Arise, O Israel, and Shine, for
thy light is come, and the glory of our Father is risen upon thee. We
shall Attack and Advance into enemy territory within the next two
years. Be Prepared!"[24]

By this time the U.S. government had compromised the CSA, developing seven informants inside Ellison's 224-acre compound in
Arkansas. According to the Department of Justice, these informants
established

that CSA was stockpiling military-type guns, fabricating silencers and grenades, converting semi-automatic weapons to automatic weapons, engaging in paramilitary training, and burying land mines around the compound perimeter. The agents also learned that CSA was involved in such activities as arson . . . attempting to blow-up a natural gas pipeline, and theft. These activities were intended to produce operating funds, to plunder the property of certain "unacceptable" groups, and to hasten the collapse of the government.[25]

With information provided by the moles, the government obtained a warrant to search Zarephath-Horeb in April 1984. Some three hundred federal agents surrounded the estate, fully expecting that the heavily armed CSA members would resist with violence. Despite some initial low-key resistance, no showdown ever materialized. Ellison negotiated a deal whereby he would surrender to law enforcement if federal prosecutors promised that he would be placed in a jail cell by himself. (He feared what would happen if he was placed in a cell with black prisoners.) The FBI convinced Ellison and his CSA compatriots to surrender without ever firing a shot.[26]

The FBI found and arrested two members of the Order, fugitives from the federal manhunt. Inside the compound investigators also found an alarming cache of weapons and military supplies. This included "ninety-four long guns, 30 handguns, approximately 35 machine guns and sawed-off shotguns, one heavy machine gun . . . and several thousand rounds of ammunition," as well as several "improvised . . . land mines . . . and hand grenades."[27] Notably, agents also recovered a thirty-gallon drum of potassium cyanide that Ellison said would be used to poison water supplies in Washington, D.C., and New York City. Hamm, citing terrorism expert Jessica Stern, notes that "potassium cyanide is not a sophisticated weapon of mass destruction."[28] But, as Noble asserted, with additional research the CSA could have learned that the substance can be very lethal if combined with other chemical agents.[29]

A jury convicted Ellison for "racketeering activities . . . interstate travel to promote arson, and . . . firearms-related charges." Sentenced to twenty years in prison, Ellison soon found an opportunity to save his own hide. Together with North Carolina bigot and Order

associate Frazier Glenn Miller, Ellison became part of the government's boldest effort yet to rein in the white supremacist movement:
the Fort Smith, Arkansas, sedition trials. The two radicals became
state witnesses. Claiming to have uncovered an organized plot to
overthrow the U.S. government, federal prosecutors indicted fourteen of the country's leading white supremacists in 1987. They
include Beam, Butler, Pastor Robert Miles of the Unity Now movement, and several members of the Order, including Richard Scutari, David Lane, and Bruce Pierce (all of whom had participated in
the Alan Berg assassination). Almost half of the men were already
serving prison time for previous crimes and convictions. The government argued that on the heels of the "martyrdom" of Gordon Kahl,
the fourteen men had formally conspired to topple the government
while meeting in Butler's Idaho home. A major inspiration for the
plot, according to prosecutors, was *The Turner Diaries*. Prosecutors
introduced over twelve hundred items of evidence, including testimony from Ellison and Miller. On the stand, Miller claimed that the
late Robert Mathews had arranged to deliver substantial amounts
of money, garnered from bank robberies and armored-car heists, to
Butler, Beam, and others (including Miller himself). Ellison claimed
direct knowledge of the antigovernment conspiracy.[30]

Sedition trials are incredibly rare and difficult to prosecute in the
United States for a reason. There is a fine line between the right to free
speech guaranteed by the Constitution and discussing a conspiracy
with credible, subversive intent. To prove the latter, the government
had to rely on witnesses whose radical beliefs compromised their
credibility and who were promised reduced sentences in exchange for
their testimony. Defense attorneys established, among other things,
that Ellison "had two wives, thought he received messages from God
and had himself crowned King James of the Ozarks."[31] Those same
defense attorneys managed to remove all minorities from the jury
during the voir dire process, and two of the remaining white female
jurors fell in love with some of the defendants. One of the jurors
even married one of the defendants when the trial was over. But even
Harvard ethnographer Raphael Ezekiel, who has studied the racist
mind-set and who witnessed the trial, was not convinced by the government's case. On April 8, 1988, the jury acquitted all fourteen

defendants, with Louis Beam gloating, "I think ZOG has suffered a terrible defeat here today. . . . I think everyone saw through the charade and saw that I was simply being punished for being a vociferous and outspoken opponent of ZOG."[32]

Others agreed with Beam, and in what must have made the mastermind behind the concept of leaderless resistance gloat even more, the trial itself became an impetus for the growth of the modern American militia movement. In the decade that followed, thousands of Americans banded together in local groups to practice paramilitary combat, in preparation for a government takeover. But Beam began to reconsider the feasibility of leaderless resistance. In the utopian world of *The Turner Diaries,* experts had foolproof methods for detecting infiltrators. But the actual events of the mid- to late 1980s demonstrated that the "pimps" that J.B. Stoner and Sam Bowers had railed against in the 1960s could penetrate even a small and disciplined group like the Order, which one FBI agent described as "the most organized group of terrorist-type people ever to have operated in the United States." In 1992 Beam made a significant revision to his earlier essay on tactics, introducing the concept of the lone-wolf terrorist alongside the idea of the phantom cell:

> All members of phantom cells or individuals will tend to react to objective events in the same way through usual tactics of resistance. Organs of information distribution such as newspapers, leaflets, computers, etc., which are widely available to all, keep each person informed of events, allowing for a planned response that will take many variations. *No one need issue an order to anyone. Those idealists truly committed to the cause of freedom will act when they feel the time is ripe,* or will take their cue from others who precede them. While it is true that much could be said against this type of structure as a method of resistance, it must be kept in mind that Leaderless Resistance is a child of necessity.[33]

In some ways, events had already illustrated the power of the lone-wolf terrorist. Gordon Kahl, a 1983 martyr for antigovernment extremists, had taken two U.S. marshals and one county sheriff with him before he died in the name of resistance.

At the 1988 Fort Smith sedition trials, one defendant became a living testament to individualized terrorism. Richard Wayne Snell saw the value of acting autonomously as early as 1983, when he and a fellow CSA member plotted to bomb a natural gas pipeline in Arkansas. When acquitted for sedition, Snell had already been sentenced to death for his role in killing the pawnshop owner and the Arkansas state trooper in 1983. Steven Snyder, a federal prosecutor from Fort Smith, says that Snell's eventual arrest and conviction for those crimes likely prevented a much bolder plan: to bomb an IRS building in Oklahoma City in protest for a recent raid on his property.

After years of legal wrangling, the public learned the official date for Snell's execution: April 19, 1995. Logs show that on the day of his execution, Snell requested to watch television and spent the time "smiling and chuckling" at the day's events.[34] The rest of America was stunned.

13

TIM MCVEIGH'S BIBLE

the 1995
OKLAHOMA CITY
BOMBING

At 9:02 AM on April 19, 1995, Robert Dennis, a federal court clerk, waited for an elevator in the Alfred P. Murrah Federal Building in Oklahoma City. He recalls, "I'd just gotten to the elevators when everything went black. There was a crashing, rumbling noise, a terrible sound. My first thought was that a boiler or transformer blew. The dust and smoke were so thick, I couldn't see, I couldn't breathe. I thought I was going to suffocate."[1]

Awaiting execution in Indiana, Richard Wayne Snell "smiled and chuckled" at the most profound act of domestic terrorism in the history of the United States until 2001. The same building that Snell had planned to destroy in 1983 (according to fellow CSA members) now lay in ruins. Inside the ruins were the dead bodies of 168 people, including nineteen children in the building's day care center.

An hour later and eighty miles away, Oklahoma state trooper Charles Hanger, patrolling interstate highway 35, "came upon a vehicle which was a yellow 1977 Mercury Marquis, four-door. It had a primer spot on the left rear quarter panel. And I started around that vehicle in the left lane, it was in the right lane traveling north, I observed that it was not displaying a tag on the rear bumper."[2] Hanger pulled the vehicle over. Receiving unsatisfactory explanations from the driver, twenty-three-year-old army veteran Timothy McVeigh, for the lack of license plates, Hanger took McVeigh into custody. When police searched McVeigh's vehicle, they "found an envelope containing about a dozen documents, among them a copy of the Declaration of Independence and a quotation from John Locke copied in McVeigh's handwriting."[3] "Glued onto one of the pages in the envelope"[4] was a photocopied excerpt from what federal prosecutors would later call Tim McVeigh's Bible, the blueprint and inspiration for his attack on a federal building: *The Turner Diaries*.

Another would-be Earl Turner, McVeigh had highlighted a passage: "The real value of all our attacks today lies in the psychological impact, not in the immediate casualties."[5] The line referred to a series of coordinated Organization attacks in Chapter 9 of Pierce's novel: a mortar attack on Capitol Hill, a massacre of members of the Los Angeles City Council, and the shooting down of a New York-to-Israel passenger plane with a bazooka. But on April 19, McVeigh modeled his bombing of the Murrah Building on an event in Chapter 6 of *The Turner Diaries*, where Turner and his fellow revolutionaries mix ammonium nitrate and fuel oil into what experts call an ANFO bomb. The fictional team places the explosives in a stolen truck, drives it into the garage of another federal building (the FBI building in Washington, D.C.), and detonates the explosives from several blocks away. "A glittering and deadly rain of glass shards continued to fall into the street from the upper stories of nearby buildings for a few seconds, as a jet-black column of smoke shot straight up into the sky ahead of us," Earl Turner wrote in his "diary." "The whole Pennsylvania Avenue wing of the [FBI headquarters] building, as we could then see, had collapsed. . . . Overturned trucks and automobiles, smashed office furniture, and building rubble were strewn wildly about—and so were the bodies of a shockingly large number of victims."[6]

Switch the fictional FBI building with the real Murrah Building on April 19, and McVeigh parroted Earl Turner step for destructive step, including the use of a fertilizer bomb and a truck to deliver and store the explosives. McVeigh and his coconspirator, Kansas farmer and antigovernment radical Terry Nichols, tightly packed several barrels of ammonium nitrate and racing fuel into a yellow Ryder truck, which McVeigh drove from Kansas to Oklahoma City. McVeigh parked the Ryder truck immediately in front of the Murrah Building and walked to his getaway vehicle. On detonation, the explosives destroyed 25 percent of the Murrah Building's structure, obliterating most of the four lower floors, causing damage to buildings nearly a block away.

Tim McVeigh had become enraptured by *The Turner Diaries* in 1988, shortly before joining the army. In some ways, the book reinforced his pre-established views on social decadence. After graduating high school in 1988 and just before entering the military, McVeigh had worked as a driver for an armored-car service that delivered money to banking establishments near welfare agencies.[7] His lawyers' notes, based on discussions with the terrorist, say that when McVeigh

> would drive up, he would see a 3-block line of black welfare re-
> cipients waiting for their welfare checks. Tim would have to push
> his way through the line with his gun drawn to deliver the money.
> During the rest of the months he would drive by their houses and
> he would see them always sitting on their porch waiting for their
> check, hence the name of porch monkey.[8]

Pierce's novel, which described blacks in primal terms as violent hordes leeching off the public dole, resonated with McVeigh. As he read *The Turner Diaries*, McVeigh later recalled, "his views of the world expanded."[9]

McVeigh entered basic training in the spring of 1988. There, at Fort Bravo, Georgia, he met and befriended his future coconspirators, his platoon commander Terry Nichols and fellow enlistee Michael Fortier. The men shared a love of guns and a growing antipathy toward the U.S. government. McVeigh encouraged Fortier's nascent antigovernment feelings, providing the native Arizonan with, among other things, a copy of *The Turner Diaries*. Nichols had grown up in rural Michigan, where banks increasingly foreclosed on family-owned farms, dispossessing their owners. The same process had helped fuel the Posse Comitatus movement across the United States.

Nichols and McVeigh requested and received honorable discharges following their service during Operation Desert Storm, America's first military conflict with Saddam Hussein, in the early 1990s. In the years that followed, their hatred for the federal government only intensified. At one point, Nichols attempted (but failed) to renounce his U.S. citizenship. McVeigh began a somewhat nomadic lifestyle, becoming part of the increasingly popular gun-show circuit, which expanded after federal laws loosened regulations on the private sale of guns. But new laws were already being considered. These same gun shows became an echo chamber for antigovernment paranoia, as the U.S. Congress moved closer and closer to passing the first major pieces of gun-control legislation in more than two decades—the Brady Handgun and Violence Prevention Bill and the Federal Assault Weapons Ban. Gun-rights groups, such as the National Rifle Association, saw the Brady Bill as an entrée to national firearms registration, a Trojan backdoor to the mass confiscation of firearms by a tyrannical government. At gun shows, McVeigh began to sell photocopied versions of *The Turner Diaries,* which begins, recall, with the passage of the fictional Cohen Act of 1989 to strip all Americans of their weapons.

At first McVeigh's concerns about the direction of the social order manifested in a move toward survivalism—a more passive form of antigovernment resistance, whereby one waits and prepares for the collapse of society. But hints that McVeigh was considering bolder action can be seen in letters he wrote to friends and to newspapers. "America is in serious decline," he asserted in an editorial to the *Lockport (New York) Union-Sun* in 1992. "Do we have to shed blood to reform the current system? I hope it doesn't come to that, but it might."[10] McVeigh also joined an Arkansas-based contingent of the Ku Klux Klan, insisting later that he believed that the KKK was simply pro-gun and antigovernment. According to McVeigh, only later did two events push him toward a position of proactive violence.

The first event was in August of 1992, when federal law enforcement raided the remote mountain home of Randy Weaver at Ruby Ridge, Idaho. The Bureau of Alcohol, Tobacco and Firearms (BATF) believed Weaver, a Christian Identity believer, to be the kind of violent, antigovernment firebrand one would find in another part of Idaho—at Richard Butler's Aryan Nations compound. In fact, the government attempted to use a minor firearms charge against Weaver to leverage him into becoming an informant against Butler; Weaver refused. As with the majority of Identity followers, religious ideas about racial purity and the impending end-times manifested in Weaver's desire to separate from society and adopt principles of survivalism, as opposed to engaging in radical terrorism. When, in 1992, BATF agents descended on Weaver's isolated home in the woods of Idaho, under the false assumption that Weaver was stockpiling illegal weapons, they created the conditions for a firefight that never had to happen. A shooting exchange between Weaver's fourteen-year-old son, Sammy; a family friend named Kevin Harris; and federal marshals who had snuck onto the Weaver property quickly resulted in the deaths of a marshal and Sammy. Events escalated from there. By the time the conflict ended, the list of the dead included Weaver's wife, who was shot while carrying her baby. Even though Weaver eventually won a wrongful-death civil suit against the government, his family members' murder infuriated militia groups, Christian Identity believers, survivalists, and antigovernment organizations.[11] Not surprisingly, the raid also incensed McVeigh.

McVeigh's frustration and anger with the government only grew after the federal siege of the Branch Davidian compound at Waco, Texas, in the spring of 1993. David Koresh had created the Branch Davidians as an offshoot of Seventh Day Adventism. Adventists distinguish themselves from other fundamentalist Christian sects by embracing many Jewish traditions, including following Jewish dietary guidelines (that is, keeping kosher) and, most importantly, observing the Sabbath based on a Jewish time from—sundown Friday to sunup Saturday (hence the reference to the "seventh day" in their name). They share the millennial dispensationalist approach of many evangelical Christians described in Chapter 3. Namely, they believe in a rapture that will spare true believers (the elect) from a Great Tribulation that will ultimately see God vanquish the forces of evil, bringing forth the second coming of Jesus. But in his rendition of the book of Revelations, Koresh argued for a mid-tribulation Rapture—that is, one in which the elect must first suffer through part of the Great Tribulation.[12]

For many months, Koresh had been predicting to his followers at the Waco complex that this part of the Revelations prophecy—their tribulation—was imminent and that it could take the form of armed conflict with the government. Koresh believed that he was the Christ who would rise again after he and his followers were martyred. Hence he had been stockpiling the very weapons that caught the attention of the BATF and brought its agents to Waco. As one might expect, the decision to arrest Koresh resulted in a standoff. What the government did not realize was that by its very opposition to Koresh, and by escalating its siege-like preparation for a raid, it was playing right into Koresh's own biblical prophecies: that he was the Messiah and that the end-times were approaching. Koresh hunkered down, and though there would be controversy over who actually started the shooting, the raid resulted in a fire that engulfed the compound, killing Koresh and seventy-five of his followers, including pregnant women and twenty-one children. The date of the siege: April 19, 1993—precisely two years before the Oklahoma City Bombing.[13]

In March 1993, drawn by coverage of the standoff between the government and the Branch Davidians, McVeigh had detoured to Waco from his normal jaunts through the gun-show circuit. He even gave an interview with a reporter at the scene. The ultimate outcomes at Ruby Ridge and at Waco convinced McVeigh of the evil of the federal government. According to McVeigh's own account to reporters Lou Michel and Dan Herbeck in interviews for their book *American Terrorist*,[14] after Waco, he and his former platoon commander, Terry Nichols, resolved to engage in a major act of revolution. In justifying his eventual attack on the government he wrote:

I chose to bomb a federal building because such an action served more purposes than other options. Foremost, the bombing was a retaliatory strike; a counter attack, for the cumulative raids (and subsequent violence and damage) that federal agents had participated in over the preceding years. . . .

Knowledge of these multiple and ever-more aggressive raids across the country constituted an identifiable pattern of conduct within and by the federal government and amongst its various agencies. . . . For all intents and purposes, federal agents had become "soldiers" . . . and they were escalating their behavior. Therefore, this bombing was also meant as a pre-emptive (or pro-active) strike against these forces and their command and control centers within the federal building. When an aggressor force continually launches attacks from a particular base of operation, it is sound military strategy to take the fight to the enemy.[15]

Though he challenged the government's case in court, McVeigh proudly admitted his guilt after his conviction, and juries sentenced two others—Terry Nichols and Michael Fortier—for their role in the Oklahoma City Bombing. Before becoming the first federal prisoner to be executed in fifty years in 2001, McVeigh insisted that he and Nichols had acted without assistance (beyond some early, minimal help from Fortier in Arizona). To Michel and Herbeck, McVeigh more or less conceded the official version of the case: That he had begun planning an antigovernment attack in 1993; that he and Nichols had selected the Murrah Building as the target by December 1994; that they had sold weapons stolen from an associate (Roger Moore, whom McVeigh had met at a gun show in Florida) to finance their operations; that they had obtained the bomb's components and stored them in a warehouse in Kansas, where they ultimately constructed the bomb, obtained the Ryder truck under a false identity, and detonated the bomb on April 19 in Oklahoma City.

McVeigh did not become another Lee Harvey Oswald or James Earl Ray. He never claimed to be anything other than the sole driving force behind the bombing of the Murrah Building. But McVeigh also remained a fan of *The Turner Diaries*. Earl Turner's only regret— one redeemed only through his kamikaze mission at the end of the novel—was in revealing Organization secrets, including names of other members, to the agents of the Jewish-controlled American government while captured and under interrogation. Many experts who took a deeper look at McVeigh's activities leading to the Oklahoma City Bombing believe that McVeigh avoided the fictional Turner's mistake—that he became a martyr for others who had assisted with and possibly planned the Oklahoma City Bombing. One popular theory, favored by several investigative reporters and criminologists, sees McVeigh as a witting member of a Christian Identity conspiracy.

The case is circumstantial and involves five different lines of evidence. The first involves challenging the official account of McVeigh's motivation: the idea, offered by federal prosecutors, that the convicted terrorist was exclusively driven by antigovernment paranoia, untainted by either racism or religion.

Kerry Noble, the former member of the Covenant, the Sword and the Arm of the Lord, is one of many who doubts this limited explanation, affirmed by McVeigh himself. The CSA, recall, was started by Jim Ellison, who fell under the sway of Christian Identity preaching while mentored by the Reverend Robert Millar. By the early 1980s, the CSA had stockpiled weapons and attracted terrorists like Richard Wayne Snell. Many see the obvious connection between the chosen date of the Murrah attack and the anniversary of the Waco siege. But Noble sees much more significance in the chosen date of April 19.

The date of the Oklahoma City Bombing also marked the tenth anniversary of an FBI raid on Jim Ellison's Arkansas compound in 1985. Noble, who was inside the compound, remembered the day as nearly ending in a major gun battle. (But instead it resulted in a "talk-down" by FBI hostage-rescue expert Danny Coulsen.) In fact, Noble, who abandoned the CSA not long after the assault, specifically warned government agencies not to inflame ultra-right groups in mid-April because of its proximity to Easter. According to some, any Identity martyr who died during this time could be resurrected.[16] As others point out, McVeigh obtained a new driver's license under a fake name not long after Snell's execution date had been finally announced; he gave a birth date of April 19 even though his real birthday was April 23.

McVeigh publicly distanced himself from any religious motivation for his crime. He was raised Catholic, but no one described McVeigh as devout in any way. In some public statements, McVeigh asserted something bordering on agnosticism and specifically denounced certain core religious concepts, such as the existence of hell. But in private letters written before the Murrah bombings to childhood friend Steven Hodge, McVeigh asserted, "I know in my heart that I am right in my struggle, Steve. I have come to peace with myself, my God, and my cause. Blood will flow in the Streets, Steve. Good vs. Evil. Free Men vs. Socialist Slave Wannabe Slaves Pray that it is not your blood, my friend."[17] As religious scholar Eugene V. Gallagher noted, "Despite his professed antipathy toward organized religion, with his references to God and prayer and the stark antitheses of good versus evil and freedom versus slavery, McVeigh implied that the events about to take place had ultimate importance and perhaps even divine sanction."[18]

If some sort of religious impulse compelled the otherwise secular McVeigh, it would be one more thing he had in common with the fictional Earl Turner. Once the leadership of the Organization had accepted Turner into the Order, it allowed him to see a sacred manu-script referred to as the Book. In his diary, Turner recorded,

> For the first time I understand the deepest meaning of what we
> are doing. I understand now why we cannot fail, no matter what
> we must do to win and no matter how many of us must perish in
> doing it. Everything that has been and everything that is yet to be
> depends on us. We are truly the instruments of God in the fulfill-
> ment of His Grand Design. These may seem like strange words to
> be coming from me, who has never been religious, but they are
> utterly sincere words.[19]

Of course, that "Grand Design" involved genocidal ethnic cleansing, and McVeigh's other claim, that he lacked any racial prejudice, is simply not believable. As researcher J.M Berger noted, "It is extraordinarily unlikely that *The Turner Diaries* could appeal to anyone who is not a hardened racist. Dripping with racial animus, *The Turner Diaries* does not aim to convince readers of the virtues of white supremacy. Rather, it assumes bigotry on the part of readers and explicitly tries to move them from passive agreement to violent extremism."[20] McVeigh also played down his decision to join a Ku Klux Klan organization in the early 1990s, incredulously claiming that he had entered in ignorance of the group's racist agenda, assuming that the group simply supported gun-owners' rights. Thomas Robb, the leader of the group in ques-tion, the Arkansas Knights of the Ku Klux Klan, had been a major figure in Christian Identity circles since the mid-1980s. In letters to his sister in the months before the Murrah bombing, McVeigh also cast aspersions on Jews and their role in controlling the world financial system. It appears as if McVeigh at least shared many of the sensibilities of Identity followers, a fact that he clearly tried to hide from public scrutiny.

But questions about a Christian Identity conspiracy extend beyond McVeigh's motivations. Many doubt whether McVeigh and Nichols could have executed the plot by themselves, whether the lo-gistics of the actual bombing fit a two-person scenario. Uncertainty extends specifically to the design of the bomb and to the financing of the entire operation, which some see as the second line of evidence pointing to a conspiracy.

There is the curious fact that in a matter of weeks, McVeigh and Nichols graduated from barely being able to compose low-level "backyard" explosive devices to being able to mix together and construct a sophisticated bomb that combined racing fuel and ammonium nitrate fertilizer. At McVeigh's trial, Michael Fortier described how, in the fall of 1994, while planning their attack on the Murrah Building, McVeigh and Nichols had reported the results of an early test of a "milk-jug bomb." "He told me that the blasting cap just sprayed the ammonium nitrate everywhere, it didn't work."[21] Yet just a few months later, McVeigh and Nichols designed a much more sophisticated bomb that nearly demolished a nine-story building.

There is little doubt that McVeigh and Nichols had the know-how to create the weapon by April 19, 1995. In 1999 McVeigh gave very specific details on its construction to Michel and Herbeck from memory, and experts agree that the narrated design could account for the explosion. What is not clear is how McVeigh and Nichols acquired the know-how. Nothing in their backgrounds suggests the required training and level of sophistication in fabricating explosives. Having consulted with demolitions experts, McVeigh's attorney, Stephen Jones, doubted McVeigh's confessions about the bomb and pressed him to divulge the source for the design. McVeigh told Jones that he had studied the bomb-making process from a book at a public library in Arizona, but McVeigh could not remember the title. Jones's investigators could never find any book or resource in that library to account for the ANFO bomb. "There simply is no evidence," Jones insisted to investigative reporter Peter Lance, "that Terry Nichols or Tim McVeigh or anybody known to have been associated with them had the expertise, knowledge, skill [and] patience to construct an improvised device that would bring down a modern nine-story office building."[22]

The implication is that "others unknown," as Jones called them, assisted McVeigh and Nichols in constructing the bomb and that the two men had protected their compatriots. Some researchers believe those same unknown others must have also helped the pair by providing financing. Both men were struggling economically as of

1993, when their plan first took shape. Yes, the pair admitted to robbing Roger Moore, a fellow antigovernment gun-rights enthusiast
whom McVeigh had met on the gun-show circuit, and then selling
weapons from Moore's rare firearms collection to help finance their
operation. But many doubt whether they could have raised the necessary money from that robbery alone. Mark Hamm, an Indiana
State University criminologist whose 2002 book *In Bad Company:
America's Terrorist Underground* outlines a Christian Identity–
backed conspiracy in the Murrah bombing,[23] believes that McVeigh
and Nichols had help in robbing not only Moore but also a series
of banks from 1994 to 1995. Building on research by Oklahoma
reporter J.D. Cash, Hamm even fingers the likely accomplices: a relatively new band of Christian Identity zealots, the Aryan Republican
Army (ARA).

Formed in 1993, in response to the same types of government
raids that dismayed McVeigh, the ARA modeled itself on Robert
Mathews's Silent Brotherhood. An eclectic group of seven core
members based out of Ohio, its numbers included Christian Identity preacher and East Coast Aryan Nations leader Mark Thomas;
transgendered hillbilly Peter Langan, who preferred to be called
Commander Pedro; skinhead musician Scott Stedeford; a would-be
Navy Seal with demolitions training, Richard "Wild Bill" Guthrie;
tenth-grade dropout Kevin McCarthy; and former Eagle Scout Michael Brescia. Committed, like Mathews, to raising money for a revolution, the ARA robbed no fewer than twenty-two banks in the
Midwest and the Great Plains in 1994 and 1995. The robberies were
as idiosyncratic as the group itself, with members disguising themselves as U.S. presidents, Santa Claus, FBI agents, and construction
workers. The robberies followed the same general pattern, as described by terrorism expert Friedrich Seiltgen:

A robbery would begin with Langan running in first, with the
others following behind. Langan would take a running leap and
jump over the counter, brandishing his rifle, and yell, "No alarms,
no hostages" twice. The robbers used two-way radios to communicate with one another and with gang members outside. All
sometimes dressed in camouflage and combat boots. When not

wearing ski masks, they often wore Halloween masks of American presidents.

While Langan cleaned out the teller drawers, a teammate would guard the lobby, yelling foreign-sounding gibberish. They never went to the vault because they believed that would take too much time. When they were finished, they would often toss a smoke grenade behind them, leaving the bank in a cloud. After racing away in a cheap "drop car," they would transfer to another, more reliable car to complete their getaway, monitoring police radio frequencies as they went.[24]

The robberies were always a means to an end: to obtain enough money to help white supremacists finance a holy race war. The ARA eluded federal law enforcement until FBI agents turned Shawn Kenny, an ARA associate, into an informant. Members of the group went to prison in 1997.[25]

Hamm established that McVeigh and Nichols were in the vicinity of several of the ARA robberies at the time of the offenses. "It is highly improbable—if not statistically impossible," Hamm insisted, "for nine men with such violent predispositions and such deep connections within the white power movement, all of whom needed money desperately . . . to randomly come together at the same time in the same geographic location."[26] Based on letters from and interactions with her brother, McVeigh's sister Jennifer provided vague but corroborating evidence in a December 1994 affidavit:

He (Timothy McVeigh) had been involved in a bank robbery but did not provide any further details concerning the robbery. He advised me that he had not actually participated in the robbery itself, but was somehow involved in the planning or setting up of this robbery. Although he did not identify the participants by name, he stated that "they" had committed the robbery. His purpose for relating this information to me was to request that I exchange some of my own money for what I recall to be approximately three $100.00 bills. . . .

It is my belief that this bank robbery had occurred within the recent past. I was not made aware of the details or if there were

any additional robberies involving my brother or any of his associates. I do recall that my brother remarked that the money he
had in his possession represented his share of the bank robbery
proceeds.[27]

Hamm developed additional circumstantial evidence supporting
a far-right conspiracy involving the ARA in the bombing of the
Murrah Building. Hamm established that Guthrie and McVeigh both
belonged to the same KKK group, the Arkansas Knights of the Ku
Klux Klan, run by Christian Identity eminence Thomas Robb. Hamm
also found evidence suggesting that McVeigh and Robb may have
met as early as 1992. In examining early reports about the Roger
Moore robbery, Hamm noticed that descriptions of the assailants,
per Moore, matched members of the ARA, and not McVeigh and
Nichols. (Although Hamm speculates that the two men provided
targeting information to the ARA.) This is odd, since Moore was
well acquainted with McVeigh from the gun-show circuit. Hamm
even managed to get Langan on record confirming that Guthrie
knew McVeigh. He also found records showing that Langan had
told an undercover police officer in 1993 that the ARA intended
to bomb a federal building. This potential connection between
McVeigh, Nichols, and the ARA represents the third line of evidence
pointing to an Identity conspiracy in the Oklahoma City Bombing.
     More than anything, Cash and Hamm developed leads indicating
that one ARA member, Michael Brescia, directly interacted with
McVeigh and aided him in the bombing.[28] This information relates
to the fourth line of evidence suggesting a Christian Identity–backed
conspiracy in the April 19 attack in Oklahoma City: the twenty-four
witness sightings of McVeigh and/or Nichols in the presence of a
stocky, olive-complexioned man commonly referred in official reports as John Doe #2. Witnesses described a man fitting that description in the presence of McVeigh days before, during, and immediately
after the terrorist bombing. The Justice Department concluded that
these witnesses had confused a completely innocent army soldier,
Todd Bunting, for an accomplice to Tim McVeigh. A witness positively identified Bunting as accompanying McVeigh when he rented
the Ryder truck in Kansas, but hard evidence clearly established that

Bunting, who looked like the sketch of John Doe #2, had visited the rental agency the day *before* McVeigh and that he had no connection to McVeigh. In other words, at least one of the witnesses confabulated two different events when implying that McVeigh had an accomplice; skeptics of a conspiracy argue that such mistakes are not uncommon. Other sightings of John Doe #2 may simply be the result of similar confabulations and the cognitive distortions generally associated with eyewitness descriptions and memories of crimes. But this explanation goes only so far. Stress can play games with perceptions, and the brain can force sudden and unexpected events into a false or distorted narrative. But many of the eyewitness accounts occurred days and even weeks before the actual bombing, and others include hallmarks of the ring of truth.

The best compendium of these accounts by witnesses comes from Andrew Gumbel and Roger G. Charles in *Oklahoma City*,[29] their excellent 2012 treatise on the bombing. They identified a number of witnesses whose encounters with McVeigh (or Nichols) and John Doe #2 coincided with unique or memorable events, which, knitted together, form a consistent narrative. This group includes Leonard Long, a black Oklahoma City commuter who nearly collided with a brown van on the morning of April 19; Long positively identified McVeigh (wearing a baseball cap) as the driver but was equally convinced that McVeigh traveled with a "stocky, dark-complexioned" passenger who "spewed racial insults" at Long. Not long after Long's encounter, and not far from the location of his encounter, another witness described two men—a stocky, olive-complexioned man and a tall white man in a baseball cap—walking toward a yellow van. Just twenty minutes before the bombing, Mike Moroz, a mechanic, told investigators about an incident involving occupants of a yellow Ryder truck; the driver, whom Moroz later identified as Tim McVeigh, was wearing a baseball cap and asked for directions to the Murrah Federal Building. Moroz also stated that there was a passenger in the vehicle. Moroz recalled the incident well, because the Ryder truck nearly hit a display when it first peeled into Johnny's Tire Company, where he was an employee, located only blocks from the explosion site.[30]

Similar accounts place McVeigh in the company of an unknown accomplice fitting the John Doe #2 profile days and weeks before

April 19, notably in Kansas when the bomb was allegedly being constructed. But perhaps the most intriguing account of a John Doe #2 comes from a group of go-go dancers at the Lady Godiva Nightclub in Tulsa, Oklahoma. The women recalled seeing McVeigh with two other men, one of whom matched the John Doe #2 description. McVeigh, perhaps drunk, broadcast his upcoming plans, quipping to the dancers, "On April 19, you'll remember me for the rest of my life." Security-camera footage from the nightclub, obtained by investigative journalist J.D. Cash, appears to corroborate the account, but the footage is too grainy for a positive identification of McVeigh or his associates, and the sound is of poor quality. At first blush, the date of the visit, April 8, appears to exclude McVeigh as the boastful customer, because McVeigh is supposed to have been registered then at a motel in Kingman, Arizona, where he had just prepaid for an extra five-day stay. But Hamm established that McVeigh did not receive or make any phone calls from Kingman from April 8 to April 11, and the manager of the motel did not recall seeing McVeigh's car. In fact, the manager said that McVeigh's room looked all but unoccupied during the relevant period.[31]

As for the other two men the dancers saw in McVeigh's company at the Tulsa club, the women managed to identify two individuals from photographs who definitely knew each other and who stayed together during the relevant time: Michael Brescia and Andreas Strassmeir. Brescia, an ARA member, bears a strong resemblance to police sketches of John Doe #2. In April 1995 Brescia roomed with Strassmeir at Elohim City, the Christian Identity compound in Oklahoma City. Strassmeir, a native of Germany, had come to the United States in the mid-1980s in search of government work. Failing to find employment, he found himself ensconced in the world of the American ultra-right. One person he definitely admits having met—only once, at a Texas gun show—is Timothy McVeigh. At the time, Strassmeir belonged to the Texas Light Infantry Brigade, a new militia group formed by Louis Beam. Strassmeir insists that he never met or talked with McVeigh again. But curiously, McVeigh admitted (to Michel and Herbeck) making at least one call to the Elohim City compound in the days leading up to the Oklahoma City attack. He wanted to talk with "Andy the German," McVeigh said. When Joan

Millar, Richard's wife, told McVeigh that Strassmeir was not around, McVeigh responded, "Tell Andy I'll be coming through."[32]

It is the curious circumstances surrounding Elohim City, including suspicions about Strassmeir, that present the fifth line of evidence suggesting a Christian Identity conspiracy in the Oklahoma City bombing. Hamm and Cash have developed a suggestive array of evidence connecting Elohim City to McVeigh and the ARA. It begins with Strassmeir, who admitted meeting McVeigh one time and whom McVeigh called (but never supposedly spoke with) shortly before April 19. Some witnesses contradict Strassmeir. A government informant, John Shults, told the FBI that he had attended a 1994 meeting at Elohim City that had included Christian Identity radical Chevy Kehoe and two Germans. One was named Andy, and Shults was "sure beyond a shadow of a doubt" that the other was Tim McVeigh. Shults remembered the discussion turning toward a bombing and a Ryder truck.[33] Another government informant, Carol Howe, who lived for a time at Elohim City, insisted that McVeigh had visited Elohim City on repeated occasions, using the fake name Tim Tuttle. Howe, a one-time beauty pageant contestant, became close to Dennis Mahon, a major figure in white supremacist circles; she claimed that he had referred to the bombing of the Murrah Building prior to April 19. Mahon and Strassmeir were close associates, and Howe insists that McVeigh stayed in the company of Strassmeir at the compound. Others, including J.D. Cash and Morris Dees, head of the Southern Poverty Law Center, claimed to have informants inside Elohim City who asserted that McVeigh had visited the compound. These informants were never named, and therefore their credibility cannot be adequately evaluated. What is clear is that a speeding ticket places McVeigh in the immediate vicinity of Elohim City in September 1994 and that McVeigh called the compound looking for Strassmeir two weeks before the bombing.[34]

Some argue that Elohim City closes the circle between McVeigh's chosen date of April 19, his ultimate motivation, and the attack on the Murrah Building. Prosecutors from the Fort Smith sedition trial developed evidence that Richard Wayne Snell, executed on April 19, had targeted the Murrah Building for a bombing attack in 1984. There is no evidence that McVeigh ever had anything to do with

Snell, who responded with glee at the reports of the Oklahoma City Bombing on TV while awaiting execution. But Snell did have a very close connection to Elohim City. The Reverend Millar was Snell's personal spiritual advisor, and Snell's body was taken to Elohim City for burial following his execution. Carol Howe also reported that Millar and his Identity followers spoke frequently about an imminent holy race war and about the likelihood that Elohim City would be subject to a similar federal raid. Many former CSA members, including founder Jim Ellison (who was married to Millar's daughter), had moved to Elohim City after the 1985 raid on Ellison's CSA compound in Elijah, Missouri. Howe claimed that residents of Elohim City often spoke about "striking first."

The federal government dismissed the evidence of a conspiracy, and not without cause. The evidence that McVeigh executed the Oklahoma City attack with others as part of a Christian Identity cabal was intriguing but circumstantial. The Waco siege on April 19, 1993, remains the simplest explanation for McVeigh's choice of date for the Murrah bombing. McVeigh definitely visited Waco on the eve of the 1993 raid and definitely became infuriated with the outcome. He never referred to Snell in any letter or correspondence. Howe's account of seeing McVeigh at Elohim City changed more than once, including under oath. Shults's sighting lacks independent corroboration and, coming two years after the Oklahoma City attack, could easily have been colored by revelations in the media. Most importantly, McVeigh himself never conceded to any conspiracy.

That is where the controversy stood at the time of McVeigh's execution, with some suggestions of a conspiracy but with no solid evidence to bring doubt to McVeigh's confession. But soon the government began releasing evidence that raised serious questions about the competence of its investigation. Many see in the subsequent revelations signs that the government hid and possibly even provoked, unwittingly, a conspiracy in the April 19, 1995, bombing. The truth, as it always appears to be in the thorny world of domestic counterterrorism, may be far more nuanced.

The new revelations included a provocative FBI report. "It is suspected that members of Elohim City are involved [in the bombing] either directly or indirectly through conspiracy." So reported an FBI document released in 2003 (that is still heavily redacted) that was written just days after the Oklahoma City bombing. The document came as part of many shocking new files released under the Freedom of Information Act three years after McVeigh's execution. The new information had not been provided to McVeigh's and Nichols's defense attorneys or, for that matter, to the government's own lead investigators in the Oklahoma bombing. The new data lent a measure of additional credibility to Cash and Hamm's theories of a Christian Identity plot involving residents of Elohim City, members of the ARA, and Timothy McVeigh and Terry Nichols. Among other things, the newly released files report that the FBI found blasting caps in the possession of the ARA that closely resembled blasting caps that McVeigh and Nichols stole from a quarry and used for their ANFO bomb; investigators recovered only a portion of the caps that should have been in McVeigh's or Nichol's possession following the attack. Additionally, among materials found in possession of the ARA, federal investigators found a driver's license with the name Robert Miller—an alias used by Roger Moore. Apparently, the FBI agents who had investigated the Midwest bank robberies took seriously allegations (popularized by Cash) that the ARA had helped McVeigh, but they did not provide that information to their counterparts in the Oklahoma bombing investigation. When he learned of this material in 2004, retired agent Dan Defenbaugh, who headed the FBI unit that handled the Oklahoma City bombing investigation, called for a new investigation. (His call was not heeded.) He expressed shock and exasperation when it became clear that the FBI had destroyed the blasting caps and the driver's license without subjecting them to forensic analysis.[35]

The overall performance of the FBI in its investigation of the Oklahoma City Bombing brings to mind the type of behavior seen during its 1963 BAPBOMB and 1968 MURKIN inquiries. Investigators quashed leads too quickly, failed to draw logical connections in developing new leads, left gaps in the basic explanation for the crime, and withheld key pieces of information—even from their own people—at relevant stages of the inquiry. To some, the level of incompetence cannot easily be explained as merely due to chance; to them, the incompetence suggests that the government might be

294 AMERICA'S SECRET JIHAD

hiding some darker secret about the Oklahoma City Bombing. The more radical segments of American society suggest that this secret involves a "false-flag operation," whereby the government actually encouraged the Oklahoma City Bombing to create a pretext for increased government intervention—ironically, the kind of government intervention fictionalized at the beginning of *The Turner Diaries*. Others postulate a more rational alternative explanation for the FBI's incompetence—that the reticence to explore a wider conspiracy and the willingness to stonewall the McVeigh–Nichols defense team paralleled similar cover-ups in the past. Specifically, some say, the incompetence was the result of the FBI's need to hide deep-cover operations from the public (and would-be terrorists) and to avoid revealing embarrassing connections between the government and the very subversives that law enforcement feared. Materials obtained by terrorism scholar J.M. Berger and an investigation by a subcommittee of the U.S. Congress imply that, once again, federal law enforcement agencies would have had to expose their sources and methods—and perhaps their own negligence—had they conducted a comprehensive investigation of the April 1995 attack. Berger in particular exposed a government operation that could have, and perhaps should have, brought McVeigh and any potential accomplices into the crosshairs of federal law enforcement months before the Oklahoma City Bombing.

In 2012, using FOIA, J.M. Berger obtained records describing an undercover operation known as Patriot Conspiracy, or PATCON.[36] As the name implies, the operation targeted the small-scale patriot or militia groups proliferating in the United States in the late 1980s and early 1990s. Given Americans' First Amendment rights to assemble and Second Amendment rights to bear arms, the government could do little to temper the expansion of these openly antigovernment groups. Indeed, most militia groups, then and now, lack any aspiration to terrorism, even if many prepare for a day when they will have to take up arms against a tyrannical U.S. government. But federal law enforcement remained bothered by the prospect of any of these groups becoming radicalized and taking a proactive stance along the lines of the Order. Indeed, law enforcement recovered only a small fraction of the millions of dollars stolen by Mathews's group, and rumors persisted that the Silent Brotherhood remained active and underground, even after law enforcement had imprisoned or killed its core members.

The FBI specifically worried about Louis Beam, one of the men Mathews had provided with booty from the Order's armored-car heists. Beam, an Odinist, assumed the role of Sun-tzu to white supremacists, elaborating on concepts like leaderless resistance, which in a landscape of the growing militia movement presented a nightmare scenario for law enforcement, one where any one of a hundred antigovernment groups could, in response to some signal event, radicalize and morph into a terrorist cell. Faced with this kind of unpredictable, needle-in-the-haystack scenario, the FBI resorted to a practice that would become rampant after 9/11—that is, engaging militia groups in hopes of flushing out would-be terrorists.

To do this, the feds created their own bogus patriot group: the Veterans Aryan Movement (VAM). These undercover agents visited gun shows and antigovernment rallies, posturing as malcontented radicals, offering themselves as bait to individuals and groups that spoke about or hinted at future terrorist activity. According to Berger: "PATCON agents roved the country for more than two years collecting intelligence on . . . patriot organizations and on dozens of individuals, investigating leads on plots from the planned murder of federal agents to armed raids on nuclear power plants to a new American Revolution." In one instance, members of VAM entangled themselves in a proposed plan, by the leader of a right-wing organization, to sell Stinger missiles (surface-to-air projectiles that can be fired with rocket launchers) to antigovernment groups. Such devices could be used to take down a passenger jet near any airport. In another instance, VAM members learned about the potential sale of night-vision goggles to ultra-right radicals and offered themselves as potential buyers.

Those in VAM navigated a narrow space between serving as deep-cover spies and acting as agent provocateurs (those who provoke, rather than monitor, criminal activity). As Berger noted, the VAM only responded to rumors of potential plots; it appears never to have initiated such plots in hopes of luring out reticent terrorists. But Berger documents a number of instances where impatient

PATCON agents pressed their targets for bolder or more aggressive action on such plots. At one point, a PATCON agent hassled a targeted radical for swifter action by accusing the genuine militant of luring the PATCON agent into a government sting. The secret government agent hoped that by falsely accusing a real radical of working for federal law enforcement, he would scare the real radical into accelerating and actualizing the missile sale.[37]

This practice created the same problems as similar sting operations in the past: the specter of unconstitutional entrapment. If a defense attorney can show that the government instigated criminal activity—that agents did not simply respond to or prevent a dangerous plot but actually encouraged or initiated said plot—a judge can toss out the entire case. Law enforcement is not supposed to create criminal activity to provoke would-be felons, and prosecution cases built on such tactics are effectively poisonous once they reach a courtroom.

This issue becomes even more problematic for an ongoing undercover operation, as a criminal prosecution invariably would require that an informant present himself or herself at a trial as a witness, ending his or her tenure as a potential source on future criminal activity and probably terminating the overall surveillance project. A prosecutor faces the possible embarrassment of an acquittal, one that literally and figuratively would endanger government operatives and operations. Such a calculus allowed J.B. Stoner to escape a trial for a conspiracy that ultimately led to the attempted bombing of civil rights activist Fred Shuttlesworth's church in 1958. In initiating the 1958 bombing conspiracy by offering Stoner money for attacks on civil rights targets, the undercover Alabama law enforcement operatives ruined their own hopes for a prosecution. Stoner may have elaborated on the proposal, but because he did not originate the bombing plan, Alabama prosecutors would not risk a trial. Similar thinking stopped the FBI from helping Alabama prosecutors subdue the Cahaba River Group for plotting the bombing of the Sixteenth Street Baptist Church in 1963. Not surprisingly, despite two years of ongoing operations, PATCON yielded only one prosecution. Law enforcement was nonetheless happy with the results, as the operation created the type of dissension and paranoia amid the ranks of militia groups that COINTELPRO had helped encourage within KKK groups in the 1960s.

Berger's revelations regarding the PATCON operation present students of the Oklahoma City Bombing with an alarming possibility: the chance that the government could have (or should have) known about McVeigh prior to the bombing. As Berger notes, from 1991 to 1993, "Timothy McVeigh literally drove through the middle of PATCON's investigative landscape. . . . McVeigh interacted with members and associates of the targeted groups."[38] Berger specifically documents McVeigh's interactions with members or close associates of two patriot groups: the Civilian Military Assistance (CMA) and the Texas Light Infantry Brigade (TLIB). The former group, run by Tom Posey, "started out as an anti-communist group supporting the Contras in Nicaragua, but . . . turned into a racist right-wing white supremacist group," according to government reports.[39] Posey's group lay behind the missile plot described above. The TLIB was formed and run by Louis Beam, one of PATCON's chief targets.

As McVeigh submerged himself more and more into the mind-set and lifestyle of the antigovernment racist right, he traveled the nation's gun-show circuit and met the likes of Roger Moore and Andreas Streissmeir. Moore enjoyed a close relationship with Tom Posey; Streissmeir consulted with Beam's TLIB. McVeigh made no effort to hide his radicalism, selling *The Turner Diaries* at gun shows and openly speaking about his antigovernment philosophy. It stands to reason that such activity could have attracted the interest of PATCON agents, but no evidence suggests that PATCON identified McVeigh or, for that matter, individuals like Moore and Streissmeir.

The FBI ended its PATCON operations by 1993 at approximately the same time McVeigh shifted from a revolutionary mind-set to a revolutionary plan of action. What remains unknown is how federal law enforcement evolved at this time, what operations and countermeasures followed PATCON. Clearly, militia groups and leaders such as Beam remained targets of interest to law enforcement. The use of Carol Howe as an informant suggests that federal agencies continued to monitor groups and individuals who came into contact with McVeigh.

Related and more disturbing revelations come from a little-known government investigation of the Oklahoma City Bombing by a congressional subcommittee led by Representative Dana Rohrabacher of California. Following the 2004 document dump by the FBI, Rohrabacher, already suspicious of a potential conspiracy in the attack, pursued various leads in the case, among them the possible involvement of the ARA in the Oklahoma City Bombing. Every one of the living ARA members denied a connection to either McVeigh or the bombing, although the report characterized their stories as "murky, if not contradictory." But more alarmingly, the committee could not even find one of the bombers, despite its best efforts. The committee's final report noted that Kevin McCarthy, one of the ARA members who had stayed with Strassmeir (and Michael Brescia) at Elohim City, for reasons unknown had entered the Federal Witness Protection Program. The report noted,

> Continuing the attempt to locate McCarthy, the subcommittee chairman contacted the head of the Department of Justice's federal witness protection program. The official confirmed that in the past McCarthy had been in the program but had no information on his current status. Similarly, the subcommittee also discovered, through a private source, that McCarthy is no longer attached to the Social Security Number he had at the time of entry into the federal prison system. These facts raise questions about whether McCarthy is, in fact, still under some sort of federal protection as well as why the Department of Justice was unable or unwilling to help find him. It is astonishing that officials from the Department of Justice and other law enforcement agencies were unwilling to permit congressional investigators to question a former bank robber with a possible connection to a large-scale terrorist attack.[40]

A better question would be: What would prompt the Justice Department to offer federal protection to someone *immediately after* he served his prison sentence for bank robbery? The other ARA members were already serving their prison sentences, and none of the others was subject to additional prosecution. Perhaps McCarthy provided information on other white supremacists, but that possibility is tempered by the fact that McCarthy had been "out of the game" and in prison for several years before becoming a source. A more disturbing possibility is that the government never wanted others to interview McCarthy, especially after the 2004 revelations further tying the ARA to McVeigh and Nichols. There is no obvious reason to cover for the ARA if it did in fact have nothing to do with the Oklahoma City Bombing—that is, unless the ARA–McVeigh–Elohim City angle could expose an even darker secret about the April 19, 1995, bombing.

Here one gets into highly speculative territory, in part because the government continues to withhold information about the case. But more than one student of the Oklahoma City Bombing has questioned whether the government had advanced warning of the bombing from informants in places like Elohim City. Oklahoma state representative Charles Key, who launched his own pseudo-investigation of the crime in 1997, reported in a March 12, 1997, letter to concerned citizens that "the Oklahoma City Fire Department received a call from the FBI the Friday before the bombing and was told to be on alert for a terrorist attack on a government building."[41] Gumbel and Charles tell of several witnesses reporting men who appeared to be bomb-squad experts, replete with bomb-sniffing dogs, searching the area of the Murrah Building on the morning of April 19, *before* the explosion. Gumbel and Charles add,

> On the morning of April 19, the head of the Oklahoma Highway Patrol's tactical team, John Haynie, was in Oklahoma City with a bomb truck, even though he was stationed in Ardmore, near the Texas border. Ostensibly, he was in town to run another training session—quite a coincidence. In 1998, Haynie told a grand jury that his session was called to hone his team's surveillance skills. OHP time records, however, show that at least three of the team members who might have been expected to attend were off work or on vacation.[42]

When confronted with this anomaly, Haynie said, "There's no benefit that I can see to talking about anything to do with anything I've ever done." On a related front, Gumbel and Charles note,

A question hangs over the Oklahoma State Bureau of Investigation, which brought three out-of-town agents into Oklahoma City on the evening before the bombing, for reasons it has never adequately explained. Rick Stephens, who came in from the Tulsa area, would not say if he or other OSBI agents had been forewarned of a bomb attack. "That's been rumored for years," he said. Invited to issue a categorical denial that the OSBI was responding to a threat, he said "I won't confirm or deny anything."

If federal and local authorities were warned about a potential attack, the record offers some possibilities as to the motive. Carol Howe insists that she told her BATF case officer, *prior* to April 19, "of the activities of Mr. Mahon and Mr. Strassmeir and Elohim City residents in (1) believing a Holy War was imminent, (2) that Elohim City should strike first, (3) that Elohim City was the next Waco, (4) that Strassmeir and Mahon wanted to bomb and blow up buildings, including federal buildings and installations, and (5) among these buildings was the Federal Building in Oklahoma City."[43] Howe changed her story on more than one occasion. No documents directly support her account, and the BATF denied the essence of her story. But the BATF also refuses to release the raw tapes and transcripts of thirty-eight conversations that Howe recorded for her handlers during the time she spied inside Elohim City.

Others speculate that Andreas Strassmeir tipped the government off to a pending attack, indicating that he served as an informant for U.S. law enforcement, German intelligence, or both. The son of a top aide to former German chancellor Helmut Kohl, Strassmeir served for seven years in the German military. He told reporter Ambrose Evans-Pritchard that he "received military intelligence training. Part of his work was to detect infiltration by Warsaw Pact agents, he explained, and then feed them disinformation."[44] He came to the United States, by his own admission, "hoping to work for the operations section of the DEA [Drug Enforcement Agency]." He claimed to Evans-Pritchard that this "never worked out" and that he soon became drawn into the right-wing subculture, first joining Beam's TLIB. But when Evans-Pritchard dug more deeply, he found reason to doubt Strassmeir. Among other things, the reporter discovered that when Strassmeier's car had been impounded in 1992 for a simple traffic violation, a host of federal and international public officials had brought considerable pressure on the Oklahoma Highway Patrol to release the vehicle. Evans-Pritchard also found that Strassmeir's behavior raised alarms with members of the ultra-right. Members of the TLIF became so suspicious that they "placed a 'tail' on Strassmeir and followed him one night. Strassmeir went into a federal building in which was housed a local ATF office. On the doors of this particular federal building, there were combination locks and in order to gain entrance, the person had to punch in the correct combination. . . . The members of the Texas Light Infantry reported that they watched while Strassmeir punched in the proper code, unlocked the door and went into the building."[45]

The government's actions—or lack thereof—toward Strassmeir only reinforce the perception that he may have been an informant. There is no doubt that Howe informed the FBI about Strassmeir no later than April 21, 1995. Yet, as Representative Rohrabacher's investigation observed, "For nearly a year after the bombing, the FBI did not interview Strassmeir. Only when he had fled the country was he queried briefly on the phone by the FBI." The Justice Department also misled McVeigh's defense attorneys, as well as the federal judge presiding over the terrorist's trial, by telling them that law enforcement had never seriously considered Strassmeir for any possible role in the crime. Judge Richard Matsch forbade the defense from pursuing the Elohim City angle, largely based on federal prosecutor Beth Wilkinson's assurances that Strassmeir was a "mere wisp of the wind." But in a 1997 special report on ABC News's *20/20*, reporters revealed that in private conversations, a law enforcement official had admitted that Strassmeir was a significant person of interest. The family of one of the Oklahoma City Bombing victims even attempted to include Strassmeir in a wrongful-death lawsuit, naming the German as a "US federal informant with material knowledge of the bombing."

Strassmeir, for his part, denies that he was an informant, just as he denies that he had any involvement in the Oklahoma City Bombing.

But in a revealing exchange with Evans-Pritchard for the *London Sunday Telegraph* in 1996, Strassmeir claimed to have a "very reliable source" on the Oklahoma City Bombing operation. The reporter recounted:

"The different agencies weren't cooperating," [Strassmeir] said. "In fact, they were working against each other. You even had a situation where one branch of the FBI was investigating and not sharing anything with another branch of the FBI." . . .

"It's obvious that it was a government 'op' that went wrong, isn't it? The ATF had something going with McVeigh. They were watching him—of course they were," he asserted, without qualification. "What they should have done is make an arrest while the bomb was still being made instead of waiting till the last moment for a publicity stunt. They had everything they needed to make a bust, and they screwed it up."

He said that the sting operation acquired a momentum of its own as the ATF tried to "ice the cake" for more dramatic effect. "Whoever thought this thing up is an idiot, in my opinion. I am told they thought it would be better to put a bigger bomb in there. The bigger the better. It would make them more guilty. . . . McVeigh knew he was delivering a bomb, but he had no idea what was in that truck. He just wanted to shake things up a little; you know, make a gesture."

"According to your source?"

"That's correct. The bomb was never meant to explode. They were going to arrest McVeigh at the site with the bomb in hand, but he didn't come at the right time. . . . Maybe he changed the time, you never know with people who are so unreliable."[46]

Evans-Pritchard became increasingly suspicious that Strassmeir was himself the source, despite the German's repeated denials. Eventually he confronted his subject with his doubts:

"Either you are a mass murderer, or you are an undercover agent," I said. "Either you killed all those people, or you risked your life to penetrate a group of vile, dangerous people. Take your pick,

Andreas, but don't think you can stick your head in the sand and hope that it will all go away. It won't go away."

"You don't understand," [Strassmeir] said.

"You know what I think already," I persisted. "I think you're a very courageous man. I think you did everything you could to stop that bombing. You did your part; you got inside the most deadly terrorist conspiracy in the history of the United States; you got these maniacs to believe in you; your cover was brilliant; and somebody let you down, didn't they, Andreas?"

"You don't understand," he repeated almost plaintively.

"I do understand, Andreas. I understand that it wasn't your fault. Are you listening to me? It wasn't your fault. So why not just come out and tell the whole rotten truth, and get it over and done with? You don't have to cover for the ATF."

"You think it's as simple as that?" he stammered.

"I don't know, Andreas. You tell me. Who were you working for anyway? Did the Germans send you over?"

"No! No, they would never do that."

"So who was it then? The ATF? The Bureau? Who were you working for?"

"Look, I can't talk any longer."

"Just listen to me, Andreas. They're going to hang you out to dry. When this thing comes down they're going to leave you holding that bomb, or—and you know this as well as I do—you'll fall under a train one day on the U Bahn, when nobody's looking."

"I've got to go to work."

"There comes a time in every botched operation when the informant has to speak out to save his own skin, and that's now, Andreas."

"How can he?" he shouted into the telephone. "What happens if it was a sting operation from the very beginning? What happens if it comes out that the plant was a provocateur?"

"A provocateur?"

"What if he talked and manipulated the others into it? What then? The country couldn't handle it. The relatives of the victims are going to go crazy. He's going to be held responsible for the murder of 168 people."

"That is true."

"Of course the informant can't come forward. He's scared shit-less right now."[47]

In some ways, Strassmeir spoke to a problem we've seen repeated over and over throughout this book. Investigations of domestic terrorism often place law enforcement in a quandary. Faced with a potential terrorist plot, the government must debate whether or not to expose the crime and consequently risk the safety of important and ongoing sources and methods, specifically human informants, who could potentially uncover even more nefarious plots in the future or develop evidence against more senior members of a domestic terrorist group. The government must often look the other way as said informants continue to commit crimes. The infiltrators often find themselves in the ambiguous space between monitoring a plot and provoking it. If the decision is made to expose the informant in some sort of a sting operation, timing becomes key, as the government seeks to maximize its chances of developing the best possible case against the greatest number of the most senior terrorists. If Strassmeir is right, the Oklahoma City Bombing may represent a tragic example of what happens when such a sting is poorly timed, and possibly provoked.

It might also be the case that the government was legitimately trying to stop an attack, but one for which it had only vague outlines. Even if one believes that Howe warned the BATF of a plot, she gave three different potential targets and no date. Predicting and preventing such an attack would be even more problematic for the government if it was largely a bottom-up plan driven by one or two lower-level men rather than a top-down plot hatched by radicals like Dennis Mahon at Elohim City. A top-down plot is less adaptable because all the players in the conspiracy must be coordinated and kept informed, and the conspiracy is even more open to infiltration by government sources. Grassroots terrorism, on the other hand, allows individuals to adjust their plans as needed and to more easily elude serious penetration by law enforcement agencies. This was Louis Beam's insight in applying the concept of leaderless resistance to domestic terrorism.

McVeigh and Nichol's actions still point to the two men as the driving force behind the attack, but as the phantom cell in Beam's schema. McVeigh's private writings and letters, and the testimony of people like Michael Fortier, clearly reveal a man who became radicalized in reaction to government raids and who was more than willing to engage in domestic terrorism, even before he met anyone in the ARA or at Elohim City. Both men, regardless of how they did it, acquired extensive knowledge of demolitions design and clearly stole the materials necessary to make the weapon. A top-down conspiracy that included those with extensive knowledge of demolitions, like ARA members Langan and Guthrie, would not have needed to outsource something as vital as building the bomb to two men like McVeigh and Nichols. A more likely bet is that McVeigh and Nichols reached out to others (including possibly John Doe #2) to help them with their plan as needed. Perhaps they received financial support from people in the ARA, but even Hamm's research suggests that the two men crossed paths with an ARA bank robbery in only one place—Fayetteville, Arkansas—for a limited time. If McVeigh and Nichols had ongoing connections to the ARA, they clearly didn't need to risk robbing someone they knew, such as Roger Moore. McVeigh's strange pattern of phone calls also indicates someone who is looking for coconspirators rather than someone who is a participant in an ongoing conspiracy. In other words, McVeigh appears to have been in the driver's seat rather than as someone who was being manipulated as a pawn or as a bit player in a larger plan. The calls, for one, all seem to come at the last minute, in April 1995. In addition to the call to Elohim City, McVeigh made repeated phone calls to William Luther Pierce's National Alliance, but the records show that he never got anything other than an answering machine. The calls suggest a hint of desperation on the part of McVeigh, like someone looking for last-minute help on a job that may be over his head.

Perhaps the most persuasive evidence that McVeigh and Nichols pursued the bombing plot with limited outside assistance comes from an ironic and unlikely source. In 2007 Nichols revealed to private and government investigators a wider conspiracy in the Murrah bombing. Already serving several years of a life sentence at a super-maximum-security prison, Nichols offered a number of shocking claims in an affidavit. Among other things, Nichols insisted that McVeigh and Roger Moore were agent provocateurs who, at the behest of FBI agent Larry Potts (who had managed the raid at Ruby Ridge), had used the bomb plot to lure "others unknown" into some kind of sting operation. Nichols said that McVeigh eventually made contact with the intended targets but that Nichols never met and could not identify any of them, although Nichols implied that these others were connected to Andreas Strassmeir, a friend of McVeigh's per Nichols's affidavit. Nichols insisted that McVeigh and Moore had staged the robbery of Moore's rare gun collection to provide Moore with plausible cover in the event that McVeigh's crimes in "the line of duty" could be connected back to Moore. Nichols said that McVeigh admitted all of this to him not long before the bombing. Nichols's affidavit fundamentally limits his own role. He claimed that the bomb that eventually detonated in Oklahoma City was different from the one that he and McVeigh had designed together in Kansas, and he insisted that he had gone to the Philippines to avoid any connection to McVeigh's deeds. In its essence, Nichols implied something along the lines of what Strassmeir told Evans-Pritchard: that the bombing was a government operation gone awry.[48]

On the face of it, the Nichols story is absurd, and the timing of its release is highly suspicious. For one thing, if McVeigh had detonated the bomb as some sort of bungled government operation, he has to go down as the most dutiful FBI undercover agent in history, because McVeigh not only carried out the operation but he steadfastly allowed himself to be executed without so much as hinting at his service to the FBI. He also put on an Oscar-caliber performance for more than a decade, convincing everyone from associates to family members, friends, investigative reporters, and defense lawyers that he hated the federal government. None questioned his sincerity. More to the point, Nichols's decision to keep this information from the public for more than a decade is completely counterintuitive. If the account is true, Nichols denied himself an incredibly powerful defense that could have minimized his role in one of the most gruesome attacks in American history. He had no reason to protect McVeigh, who, if Nichols's account is correct, allowed his onetime army buddy to spend the rest of his life in a federal prison for unwittingly helping a government operation.

But if one discounts Nichols's story, which conveniently melds together elements from various well-publicized conspiracy theories, the question persists: Why didn't Nichols tell a pro-conspiracy story back in 1995? Why doesn't he have a more plausible story to tell now? Nichols could have minimized his involvement and possibly reduced his own sentence by implicating coconspirators. Fortier received a reduced sentence for doing just that (testifying against McVeigh and Nichols). It stands to reason that if the Oklahoma City Bombing was a top-down plot originating from Elohim City and sponsored by the ARA, Nichols would have been privy to some or most of the particulars. Yet Nichols seems content to spend the rest of his life in prison hiding this fact. A more logical suggestion is that if some individuals aided and abetted Nichols and McVeigh, their roles were either too minor or too indirect to warrant Nichols's attention. Or, said individuals found their way into the conspiracy at the last minute, as McVeigh literally moved closer to Oklahoma City while Nichols became less important to the execution of the attack.

The reports of early warnings and roving bomb-squad units at the Murrah Federal Building, if accurate, suggest that the government was responding in an ad hoc fashion to prevent an attack because it had limited information. Rumors of a McVeigh–Nichols plot may have spread from places like Elohim City throughout the wider extremist community and even dovetailed with parallel plots being proposed by other radicals. Perhaps these rumors reached the ears of federal agents through undercover informants. Strassmeir painted a picture to Evans-Pritchard of bureaucratic compartmentalization, with one agency trying to prevent an attack while another agency was simultaneously trying to harness the plot in some sort of major sting operation. That too remains a disturbing possibility.

The most likely scenario, which helps explain the most data, suggests that McVeigh reached out for assistance at various times when the circumstances demanded it or when the opportunity presented itself—for instance, when he needed money to finance the bombing operation or when he needed expertise to help design the ANFO bomb. In obtaining or pursuing that assistance, McVeigh may well have exposed the broad outlines of his intended operation to govern-ment informants, whose handlers either failed to take the McVeigh plot seriously or saw an opportunity to mount a sting operation. In either of those two scenarios, federal agencies, in their incom-petence, failed to prevent the actual attack and would have ample reason to cover up any connection between McVeigh and their un-dercover operatives. But until additional materials are released by the government, all of this remains speculative.

Less speculative are the leading roles played by Nichols and espe-cially McVeigh in planning the bombing. McVeigh's claims that anti-government hostility motivated his activity to the exclusion of all other impulses seems to be a case of the subject gilding his own biography. As noted earlier, it is very likely that anti-Jewish and racist sentiments, maybe even a sense of a divine calling, combined with McVeigh's rad-ical patriotism to produce the Oklahoma City bombing. In that sense, McVeigh, at the very least, represents some sort of unwitting soldier in the Christian Identity army. To the extent that he had help, McVeigh also represents a transitional figure between the type of organized vi-olence sponsored by the Order and the ARA and the grassroots, lone-wolf violence anticipated by Louis Beam. By the mid-1990s, Beam's vision was increasingly becoming a reality for domestic religious ter-rorism. It remains a reality to this day.

14

ZEALOUS FOR HONOR

LONE-WOLF
TERRORISM *through*
the NEW MILLENNIUM

America in the 1990s saw an alarming amount of racist and anti-Jewish violence, rivaling the horrors of the 1960s. The year 1999 stood out for the number of high-profile attacks. The Associated Press reported on June 19, 1999: "Arsonists Set Three Synagogues on Fire in Sacramento Area."

The fires, that the Associated Press said were set by arsonists within minutes of each other, "caused moderate damage to two synagogues and gutted a third temple's library." Months later, two brothers, twenty-nine-year-old James Tyler Williams and thirty-one-year old Benjamin Williams, pled guilty to charges of "conspiracy, arson and destruction of religious property."[1]

They were also charged with firebombing of an abortion clinic. In a separate trial, a jury found the two brothers guilty of murdering a gay couple, Winfield Mowder and Gary Matson, in northern California on July 1, 1999. Both brothers, raised in a devout, fundamentalist Christian household, had become enamored with Christian Identity theology as teenagers. Of the arson, which caused $3 million in damages, Ben Williams said, "I kind of regretted they didn't burn to the ground." Of the murder, he asserted, "I am not guilty of murder. I'm guilty of obeying the laws of the Creator." Hoping for a death sentence that he ultimately did not receive, he hoped he would become a "Christian martyr," according to the AP, and "encourage others to kill homosexuals, Jews and other minorities."[2]

Days after the Matson and Mowder murder, white supremacist violence struck America's heartland. The AP reported, "Gunman on Spree Kills 2nd Victim: White Supremacist Terrorizes Midwest."

During that Independence Day weekend, Benjamin Smith, a twenty-one-year-old "ex-member of a white supremacist church" traveled through Chicago and Indiana, engaging in a series of "drive-by shootings, targeting his .380 semiautomatic and .22 caliber handgun at Asians, Orthodox Jews, and blacks. A dozen people were injured and three killed—including Smith, who pointed a gun under his chin during a chase by police."[3] Smith left no note or explanation for his actions. But he belonged to the World Church of the Creator (WCOTC), the social-Darwinian, pantheistic theology started by Ben Klassen in the 1970s, which argued that a race war—and the triumph of the white race—was the preordained and inevitable destiny of mankind.

"In Wake of Shooting, a Frantic Search Ensues," wrote the Associated Press on August 11, 1999. One day before, Buford Oneal Furrow had "strode into" the North Valley Jewish Community Center in Los Angeles "and wordlessly started pulling the trigger," firing "more than 70 bullets from an assault-style gun before slipping away and vanishing in metropolitan Los Angeles." Isabelle Shalometh, a receptionist, "dove behind the counter as bullets shredded a stack of papers on a desk, grazed her back and arm and hammered into the walls. . . . In seconds, a setting of swimming lessons, art classes and summer fun turned into a scene filled with random horror."[4] Furrow wounded five people at the center, including a five-year-old boy, who sustained bullet wounds to his abdomen and leg and required six hours of surgery. An hour later, on the lam, Furrow killed a postal worker, Joseph Ileto. Furrow later said that he saw Ileto, whom he shot nine times, as "a target of opportunity," in part because Ileto worked for the federal government but also because Furrow thought the Filipino mail carrier was Hispanic.

When he turned himself in to authorities on August 12, Furrow, who had once worked at the Aryan Nations compound in Idaho, assumed that he had killed far more people. "You are looking for me" he matter-of-factly told police in Las Vegas. "I killed the kids in Los Angeles." Like Ben Williams, he wanted his attack on the Jewish community center "to be a wake-up call to America to kill Jews" according to an FBI source who spoke anonymously to the AP.[5]

The series of attacks in the summer of 1999 worried Jews and minority groups across the nation. On September 6, 1999, the *New York Times* printed the headline, "Synagogues, Responding to Violence, Add Security as High Holy Days Near." The article began,

"After a year of high-profile anti-Semitic violence . . . Jewish groups in the New York metropolitan region are planning increased security for services during the approaching High Holy Days."

The groups, which the *Times* described as paying for "extra police patrols, private security guards and new alarms and surveillance cameras," were prescient. Within just a few days of the *Times* article, "the tires of three cars parked at the South Huntington (L.I.) Jewish Center were slashed while their owners attended pre-High Holy Day services Saturday night, and a few hours later in Centereach, L.I., other vandals scrawled swastikas and anti-Semitic and anti-black epithets on a public school." Given the concentration of these transgressions in Suffolk County, New York, many questioned whether the vandalism was connected to an August 15, 1999, arson fire at the business office of Temple Beth Chai in Hauppauge, New York. That crime has never been solved.

The anti-Jewish and racist attacks did not abate as the new millennium approached.

On November 30, 1999, an eight-liter bottle filled with concrete smashed against a window of Temple Emanu-El in Reno, Nevada's oldest Jewish house of worship. Carl DeAmicis, an "unemployed drifter from the Sacramento area," then threw a Molotov cocktail at the front of the window, thinking it would breach damaged glass and ignite inside the synagogue. But the first projectile had only damaged, not shattered, the window; the firebomb "only scorched the sidewalk." Despite his failed effort, DeAmicis, who joined three other men in the attack, still received his mark of honor from his fellow supremacists: a "4-inch-high swastika just above the right ear on DeAmicis' shaved head. It was outlined in black and red in the middle."[6]

Law enforcement investigators at first thought the Reno attack might be connected to the attacks in Sacramento. But the fact was that nothing connected the multiple racist and anti-Semitic attacks across the United States that started during the summer of 1999. In 1999 no group assumed the role the Confederate Underground had played in 1957–1958, linking synagogue fire bombings from region to region. There were no obvious puppet masters, no J.B. Stoners or Sam Bowers masterminding events. By 1999 Louis Beam's vision of leaderless resistance seemed prophetic; it appeared as if individuals and very small groups were spontaneously engaging in violence, in aggregate sparking fear in the supposed "Zionist Occupied Government."

In that sense, and in many other ways, the events of 1999 represented a culmination of the domestic, religious-based terrorism during the fifteen years that preceded the millennium and foreshadowed the fifteen years of domestic, religious-based terrorism that followed it. The developments followed federal raids against the Covenant, the Sword and the Arm of the Lord and its close cousin, the Order, in the early to mid-1980s, and their effects could be seen as late as December 2014 in a Christian Identity shooting spree in Austin, Texas. From 1985 to 2014, with the far right more decentralized than ever, religious terrorism evolved in a number of significant ways: to target a wider range of "infidels," as was the case with the Williams brothers' offenses; to involve a more diverse set of racist theologies, as was the case with Ben Smith's attack; to embrace lone-wolf terrorism not simply as a tactic but as religious imperative, as was the case with Buford Furrow; and to exploit an increasingly younger, more suburban, and more urban caste of radicals, as was the case with the arson attempt in Nevada. At the same time, federal and local law enforcement finally started to appreciate the nuances and challenges of dealing with religiously motivated terrorists. That they have yet to fully internalize those insights is reflected in their myopic approach to the events in Hauppauge.

The Williams brothers were true lone wolves—self-radicalized into Christian Identity without the mentorship of someone like CSA founder Jim Ellison. They lacked any of the connections to white supremacist leaders and organizations enjoyed by Robert Mathews and his close aides in the Order. Nor did the Williams brothers embrace the kind of paramilitary, survivalist lifestyle favored by these groups. They lived in and operated out of suburban areas, not in some isolated rural or mountain compound. But in other key ways, the groups led by Mathews and Ellison anticipated the activities of the Williams brothers. Like the Williams brothers, the Order had composed a hit list for assassinations. Significantly, Robert Mathews's list included not only Jews like Alan Berg but also prominent homosexuals, a target largely ignored by hate groups in the 1960s and 1970s. But as homosexuals became increasingly open and accepted in American society, they became targets for white supremacists, especially Christian Identity adherents. As early as 1983, individuals from the Covenant, the Sword and the Arm of the Lord had set fire to a gay-friendly church in Missouri. Christian Identity–influenced skinhead groups, of which much more will be said shortly, increasingly engaged in gay bashing throughout the 1990s. In murdering a gay couple in 1999, the Williams brothers took this trend even further.

Similarly, in targeting an abortion clinic, the brothers assailed another class of enemy increasingly popular among religious terrorists. For obvious reasons, attacks against abortion clinics were all but unknown prior 1973. Then the U.S. Supreme Court, in *Roe v. Wade*, forbade state legislatures from criminalizing the medical procedure. The first reports of anti-abortion arson date to 1976. Attacks inspired by religion tended to increase and track with the general increase in anti-abortion activism that grew to a crescendo in the early 1980s, fueled by the rise of the Moral Majority and the Christian right. The number of attacks reached its apex in 1984 with "eighteen bombings, six cases of arson, six cases of attempted bombing or arson, twenty-three death threats, and nearly seventy clinic invasions with acts of vandalism."[7] The group most associated with anti-abortion violence was the Army of God, led by minister Michael Bray. In his ethical defense of anti-abortion violence, called *A Time to Kill,* Bray argued, "We do not know the best strategy to resist the evil of 'abortion.' But we cannot condemn that forceful, even lethal, action which is applied for the purpose of saving innocent children."[8] Many mistake the Army of God for a Christian Identity group or offshoot—partly because both groups share an orthodox view of the Bible, honoring Old Testament practices that have been abandoned by even most fundamentalist Christians. But whereas both groups believe that human beings must help bring the secular world in line with God's teachings to facilitate the end-times, the Army of God does not share the radical reinterpretation of the book of Genesis that is unique to Christian Identity and that shapes the character of its eschatology. In short, the Army of God does not share Christian Identity's anti-Semitism and racism.

Part of the confusion over the connection between Christian Identity and the Army of God may stem from the actions of Eric Rudolph, infamous for bombing abortion clinics throughout the Southeast and for detonating explosives at the 1996 Olympic Games in Atlanta. Rudolph grew up in Topton, North Carolina. His mother exposed him to Identity teachings from minister Nord Davis, who operated a nearby compound. He also spent part of his teenage years in Schell City, Missouri, where he was influenced by the teachings of Identity preacher Dan Gayman. As noted in Chapter 9, Davis and Gayman both became influential figures in contemporary Christian Identity circles. But while both advocated two-seedline theology, they did not push for the same kind of proactive violence advocated by predecessors like William Gale and Wesley Swift. Davis's followers still stockpile weapons in preparation for Armageddon, but they are separatists who divorce themselves from America's mixed-race society. Moreover, it is not clear that Christian Identity ideas even resonated with Rudolph in adulthood, and he specifically denied any affinity for them. Nor did Rudolph have any direct connection to the Army of God, although some suspect that the group provided Rudolph with aid and comfort for the five-year period (1998 to 2003) when he evaded law enforcement while ensconcing himself in the dense forests of Appalachia. Rudolph appears to be another lone wolf, but one who opposed abortion for different reasons than the Williams brothers. For Christian Identity zealots like the two brothers, opposition to abortion, and violence against abortion clinics, was rooted in the threat that widespread abortion supposedly posed to the future of the white race. For Aryan Nations leader Richard Butler, legal abortion was part of the "Jewish anti-Christ strategy" for "TOTAL ELIMINATION OF THE WHITE ARYAN NATIONS FROM THE FACE OF THE EARTH."[9]

In the 1990s, anti-abortion and anti-gay violence became part of the Phineas Priesthood, an offshoot of Christian Identity radicalism that many believe influenced Buford Furrow when he opened fire at the Jewish community center in Los Angeles. When police found Furrow's abandoned van, it contained "ammunition, bulletproof vests, explosives and freeze-dried food" and two books: an Army Ranger handbook and *War Cycles, Peace Cycles* by Richard Kelly

Hoskins. The latter work, by "unlocking the mysteries and hidden
secrets of the Bible," predicts an apocalyptic economic catastrophe
inspired by Jewish usury and "explains the necessity for the assassination of national leaders."[10] Hoskins, a reclusive Virginia-born
Korean War veteran, has authored a number of tracts that combine
fundamentalist theology, anti-Semitism and racism, and economic
history. His most famous work, *Vigilantes of Christendom*, published in 1990, has to rank alongside *The Turner Diaries* as one of
the most influential books for white supremacist, religious terrorism.
In it, Hoskins recounts the biblical story of Phineas, the nephew
of Moses, as a model for the kind of God-sanctioned activity that
Hoskins felt was necessary to combat the growing satanic Jewish
conspiracy. The Bible describes an episode in the ongoing rivalry
between Israel and the neighboring tribe of Moab in which Hebrew
men "indulge in sexual immorality with Moabite women" and begin
to worship Moab's pagan idols. The Hebrew God, infuriated with
this behavior, punishes the Jewish people with a plague that ceases
only when Phineas drives a spear through a Hebrew man and a
Moabite woman.

Several aspects of this account are important to Hoskins. First,
God's anger is driven, according to Hoskins, not simply because
the Hebrews strayed from God's commandments but by the act
of miscegenation between the chosen people and a heathen tribe.
Phineas shares in that anger and acts on his own accord, according
to Hoskins. Moreover, Phineas does not ask permission of Moses,
his father (the priest Eleazar), or even God. Yet God celebrates the
deed in Chapter 25 of the book of Numbers: "Phineas . . . has turned
my anger away from the Israelites. Since he was as zealous for my
honor among them as I am, I did not put an end to them in my
zeal." Finally, Hoskins finds it relevant that God ended the plague
against the Jews but then immediately ordered Moses to war against
the Moabites. Taking this material together and filtering it through
the prism of Christian Identity theology, Hoskins argues that the
modern, true Christian, as part of an ongoing holy war, must take
it upon himself or herself to punish those who violate God's law
and who mix with other races. God honored Phineas "and his descendants" with a "covenant of a lasting priesthood," and so some

Christian Identity radicals, taking their cue from Hoskins, refer to themselves as members of the Phineas Priesthood. Hoskins wrote, "There are those who obey God's Law and those who don't. Those who obey are Lawful. Those who disobey are outlawed by God. God has specified the outlaw's punishment. The Phineas Priests administer the judgment, and God rewards them with covenant of an everlasting priesthood."[11] Jim Nesbitt of the Religious News Service wrote in 1999 that the Phineas Priesthood is "less an organization than a call to action and a badge of honor, followers of this blood-stained faith strive to live up to the example of Phineas."[12]

The *Vigilantes of Christendom* became a clarion call for a generation of self-directed domestic terrorists, acting alone or in very small groups to victimize interracial and homosexual couples, abortion providers, and secular-liberal institutions as well as Jews and minorities. Hoskins, while celebrating the intentions and activities of those in the Order, warned against any set of Phineas priests becoming as relatively large and interconnected as Mathews's group. He said that groups should avoid having more than six members. Would-be Phineas priests took heed.

In a case reminiscent of the Order, in one of the first known acts with Phineas dimensions, Walter Eliyah Thody joined others, whom he refused to identify, in a string of bank robberies in hopes of financing "an assassination squad dedicated to killing advocates of one-world government." Described as "gangly [and] bespectacled . . . with the long, ragged beard of a prophet," Thody explicitly claimed to be a Phineas priest. In a 1996 prison interview, Thody asserted, "We're having to fight to keep our country. Killing is normally murder. . . . Theft is theft. But if you're in warfare, then those same acts are acts of war. I'm at warfare against the enemies of my country."[13]

Another major act of apparent Phineas terrorism occurred in 1996. Three men engaged in a months-long spree of violence in Spokane, Washington, detonating pipe bombs at an abortion clinic (which failed to kill the employees only because they were attending a conference in another building), a newspaper office, and a handful of banks, which the men had robbed beforehand. At each scene, the men left behind biblical literature signed with a symbol: "a black cross superimposed with the letter P . . . a symbol of members of the Phineas Priesthood."[14] Law enforcement arrested three men, Charles Barbee, Robert Berry, and Jay Merrell, all with connections to Christian Identity–based groups. The men never openly proclaimed their membership in the Phineas Priesthood, but that may have been for legal purposes, to deny the state motive-based evidence in their trial. Federal prosecutors could not prove, to the satisfaction of a jury (that deadlocked), that the men had *directly* participated in the robberies and bombings, so the government settled for convictions for conspiracy to commit such crimes, as well as "interstate transportation of stolen vehicles and possession of hand grenades."

The *Vigilantes of Christendom* also heavily influenced the Aryan Republican Army, whose members held a copy of the book up for cameras in their videos, calling it a "handbook for revolution." When a jury finally convicted Byron de la Beckwith for murdering Medgar Evers in 1994, Beckwith publicly claimed to have recently become a Phineas priest. Violent acts attributable to Phineas priests have occurred as recently as late November 2014, when Larry Steve McQuilliams, a forty-nine-year-old unemployed Texan with a criminal history, opened fire with "two long rifle guns" on the Mexican Consulate in Austin, Texas. Over one hundred rounds pierced the walls of the building, although no one was hurt. Police found the *Vigilantes of Christendom* in McQuilliams's rented van, "along with a note and Bible verses indicating he planned on fighting 'anti-God people.'" The Austin police chief observed of McQuilliams, a self-described "high priest" of Phineas, "Hate was in his heart. He is a homegrown American terrorist trying to terrorize our people."[15]

Although high profile in nature, Phineas attacks remain relatively small in number. But that may be a function of the problems faced by students of terrorism in disentangling the multilayered influences that various hate groups and ideologies have on perpetrators. Beyond his connections to the Phineas Priesthood, Buford Furrow also once worked at the Aryan Nations compound in Idaho; he had married Debbie Mathews, widow of the founder of the Order, and thus may have been influenced by Odinism. McQuilliams harbored general anti-immigrant feelings associated with his lack of employment. Criminology professor Brian Levin of California State

University–San Bernardino told the Religious News Service, "You can really craft your own philosophy from this extremist buffet. You don't have to stay married to one philosophy or another—you can pick and choose. You see a lot of morphing out there."[16] The legal implications of admitting a connection to a well-known, violent philosophy (as seen in the Spokane case) encourage less-zealous terrorists to obscure or hide their agendas from the public (and prosecutors). Hence the actual examples of Phineas Priesthood terrorism could be more numerous than reported.

Other legal developments make it even harder to qualify and quantify acts of domestic, religious terrorism. These developments create incentives for leaders of Christian Identity (and similar) groups to obscure their connections to supposed lone-wolf terrorists. The connection between Furrow and Butler provides a suggestive case study. Butler definitely knew about Furrow, who once served as a security lieutenant at Butler's Idaho compound. Butler, in turn, served as the master of ceremonies when Furrow married Debbie Mathews. He described Furrow to the *New York Post* as "a good learner, he was passionate about the cause. . . . He was very intelligent, very sincere and quiet." In the same interview, Butler said Furrow was a "good soldier" and someone who "was very well-respected among" the denizens of Hayden Lake. Butler became coy, however, when pontificating on Furrow's violent actions. "Sometimes you have to do these kinds of things for the cause," he asserted at one point. "He is a frustrated male like all us members of the Aryan Nation—with the Jews and nonwhites." But then the Swift mentee calibrated his comments: "I don't know why he did what he did, but I cannot condemn what he did—nor do I condone it."[17]

In the 1970s, Butler may not have been so circumspect in his support for an act of terrorism, but financial more than criminal concerns likely gave him pause in 1999. Starting in 1981, the Southern Poverty Law Center (SPLC), under the leadership of civil rights activist attorney Morris Dees, began to pursue civil actions against leaders of white supremacist groups who incited others to violence. The SPLC (and later the Anti-Defamation League) used this approach to great success against groups such as the New Order Knights, Ed Fields's successor organization to the National States Rights Party, and Tom Metzger's White Aryan Resistance, of which more will be said later. These efforts virtually bankrupted both groups. In fact, in 1999 Butler faced an SPLC lawsuit stemming from an incident involving a mother and son, Victoria and Jason Keenan, who had driven through the Aryan Nations property in Hayden Lake, Idaho, on their way home from a wedding. As the SPLC describes it:

> After Jason retrieved a wallet he had accidentally dropped out the car window, the two started toward home again. But something—a car backfire or fireworks—led the untrained, paranoid guards on the compound to think that they were under attack by their enemies. Within seconds, at least three neo-Nazi Aryans had leaped into a pickup truck and sped out after the Keenans, firing at them as they went and, after about two miles, shooting out a tire and forcing them into a ditch.[18]

One reading of Butler's comments about Buford in his 1999 interview could be that the pastor was fearful that his words would become grist for the upcoming SPLC lawsuit. (The SPLC eventually won the Keenan lawsuit and forced Butler to relinquish the Aryan Nations compound and land to the Keenan family in September 2000.)

Another interpretation of Butler's reticence could be that the Aryan Nations leader feared that any recent contact between him and Furrow could trigger an entirely new civil lawsuit. Butler may have feared that he would be accused of inciting Furrow to the 1999 community center shooting. In 1987 Butler and others had escaped criminal liability for sedition, in part because, even if they had discussed a government takeover in the presence of violent followers, it is difficult to separate political speech, however inflammatory, from an actual criminal conspiracy. But Morris Dees created a legal foundation, in *civil* court, to argue that white supremacist leaders bore monetary responsibility for instigating criminal activity. (No direct evidence shows Butler in contact with Furrow after Furrow left the Aryan Nations facility in the mid-1990s.)

A similar fear of a civil lawsuit almost certainly impacted Ben Smith's preparations for his 1999 killing spree in the Midwest over Independence Day Weekend. For the months prior to his murder-suicide, Smith had belonged to the World Church of the Creator (WCOTC; at first called simply the Church of the Creator or the Creativity movement), the 1970s brainchild of Ben Klassen, author of *The White Man's Bible*. Klassen had expressly rejected any kind of supernatural foundation for white supremacy while simultaneously predicting a holy race war, which he abbreviated as rahowa. Klassen continued to write racist and anti-Semitic treatises from his compound in the hills of North Carolina. But he committed suicide in 1993 after an SPLC lawsuit nearly bankrupted both him and his group. Another individual, a law student from Illinois named Matthew Hale, reinvigorated the World Church of the Creator in 1995. Hale, as the so-called Pontifex Maximus, or supreme leader, of the church, continued to distance the group from Christian Identity while offering a near-duplicate proscription for America's supposed satanic Jewish problem.

Ben Smith not only joined the group; he became a devout member, distributing thousands of flyers on behalf of the WCOTC. Hale even named Smith "creator of the month" in August 1998. According to the SPLC, records show that Hale engaged in nearly thirteen hours of phone conversations with Smith in the three weeks leading up to the multistate murderous rampage, with twenty-eight minutes of conversation two days before the crime began. Yet for reasons he failed to explain or justify, Smith left a letter announcing that he had officially abandoned the church on the eve of the July killings. Many believe that Hale, privy to the upcoming violence but fearing another SPLC lawsuit, encouraged Smith to write the official letter, thereby releasing Hale and the WCOTC from civil liability for Smith's crime spree. For his part, Hale offered a mixed review of Smith's activities:

> He was a selfless man who gave his life in the resistance to Jewish/ mud tyranny—a man who for whatever reason ultimately decided that violence was the way to strike back against the enemies of our people—enemies who had used violence against our people for centuries. He was loyal to the core and who always put the interests of his Race before his own. . . . That the Church does not condone his acts does not affect the reality that when a people is kicked around like a dog, someone might indeed be bitten. . . .

Our Brother August Smith will continue to live on in all of us. His actions resulted in Creativity being brought to the attention of the world. Now it is up to us to utilize the attention Creativity has received and ride the wave of publicity which his actions either intentionally or unintentionally created for us. This is what he would have wanted, and what we must indeed do. RAHOWA![19]

Throughout the 1990s, the WCOTC became, along with forms of neopagan Odinism, a popular choice in the ideological "buffet" for white supremacists. Smith, for instance, started his religious journey as a racist Odinist in 1997 and converted to Creativity months later. From 1995 to 2002, according to the SPLC, Hale increased the number of chapters from fourteen to eighty-eight, "making it the neo-Nazi group with the largest number of chapters in America" during its peak.[20]

For a white supremacist, Hale became something of a media darling. He "appeared repeatedly on NBC's 'Today' show and other national TV news programs." He also built his organization by staying on the vanguard of another media trend that became key in sustaining white supremacist terrorist groups, the World Wide Web. As early as 1995, the Anti-Defamation League (ADL) reported,

Many extremist groups are on the web; the neo-Nazi National Alliance, and a covey of supporters, racist skinhead purveyors of "Aryan" music, some rabidly anti-Semitic "Identity" churches, groups sympathetic to the Ku Klux Klan and several Holocaust deniers have sites. These efforts represent a well-thought out campaign to reach more people than these groups ever could have contacted through traditional mailings, handouts and demonstrations. The World Wide Web, the newest Internet technology, is an effective merchandising tool.[21]

By 1997 the SPLC had identified 163 hate group sites on the World Wide Web; by 1999 that number had grown by 60 percent to 254. By the spring of 2001 almost four hundred hate group sites carried racist and anti-Semitic messages to anyone who could find them in a search engine. At last count, in 2014, the SPLC had identified 926 hate sites. This figure includes only group-based sites. The Simon Wiesenthal Center, which uses a special algorithm to count both group-based and individual hate sites, puts that total number at more than ten thousand. As to specific Christian Identity websites, the number is hard to tally, but an anonymous CI adherent with the screen name of Obadiah listed fifty-nine Identity sites in 2012. More telling statistics come from an analysis of two of the most well-known Identity websites, Christogenea.org and Kingdom Identity Ministries. Analytics data on the former, which prominently features transcribed sermons by the Reverend Wesley Swift, show that from 2010 to 2014, the site welcomed 417,111 unique visitors. Kingdom Identity Ministries, one of the oldest Identity websites, receives an average of 2,487 visits per month. To be fair, neither site directly advocates terrorism.

But many hate sites indirectly promote such violence, according to technology experts Beverly Ray and George Marsh II. These sites include links to guerrilla warfare manuals and to how-to books like *The Anarchist Cookbook*. Several sites offer guidance to potential lone-wolf terrorists. For instance, the Aryan Underground and sites like it link directly to Louis Beam's essay on leaderless resistance. Other sites, hoping their viewers will self-radicalize, speak directly to would-be isolated terrorists. Per Ray and Marsh, the Christian Identity hate site run by the Aryan Nations links to a page run by the Ayran Underground, which includes the following advice:

Always start off small. Many small victories are better than one huge blunder (which may be the end of your career as a Lone Wolf). Every little bit counts in a resistance. . . . The less any outsider knows, the safer and more successful you will be. . . . Communication is a good thing, but keep your covert activities a secret. This will protect you as well as others like you. . . . Never keep any records of your activities that can connect you to the activity. . . . The more you change your tactics, the more effective you will become. Random chaos is never predictable. . . . Have a "rainy day" fund set aside in a safety deposit box (out of your local area and not in a high activity area), complete with new ID just in the event that something unexpected goes wrong.[22]

Much of the hate group activity online focuses on recruitment. A former skinhead, T.J. Leyden, described the process and the appeal: "We have a generation of MTV kids, and for them, visuals are just as important as audio, and these websites have dripping blood, they have things that come popping out at you."[23] Once someone is hooked, Leyden observed, the recruiting process becomes self-perpetuating, as the new recruits constantly reinforce each other's views in the online echo chamber: "When you had a kid in Sioux City, Iowa, a kid in Lincoln, Nebraska, a kid in Billings, Montana, these kids if they were lucky got together once a year at an Aryan festival or got together once in a great while at a concert. These kids now get together constantly, every night on the Internet."[24]

The rapid expansion in the number of hate groups that create websites suggests that the approach has increased either membership or sources of revenue. The sites themselves have expanded into fields like e-commerce, notably selling the types of digital music that have become the soundtrack for white supremacy since the mid-1980s. White power music, often punk or heavy metal in style, is sold on many websites. William Pierce, author of *The Turner Diaries* and leader of the National Alliance, went so far as to develop his own music studio and production company, Resistance Records.

Matthew Hale helped turn the WCOTC into a national brand using the Internet. The WCOTC even produced a "creativity for kids" website "that offers downloadable coloring book pages and crossword puzzles about 'white pride' in a subtle 'kid-friendly' format." Hale became particularly effective at marketing the WCOTC to women through the Web. Leadership positions in the WCOTC were fully open to women, and the organization developed the Women's Frontier, a website just for women, run by information coordinator Lisa Turner.

As it turned out, its marketing focus ultimately undid the World Church of the Creator. In changing the name of Klassen's Church of the Creator to *World* Church of the Creator, Matthew Hale unwittingly encroached on the naming rights that belonged to the Te-Ta-Ma Truth Foundation, a New Age spiritual organization. In the ultimate of ironies, a group that favored the "family unification of mankind" successfully sued Hale and the racist World Church of the Creator for copyright infringement. Hale then became his own worst enemy. He openly ridiculed judge Joan Lefkow's ruling (it did not help that she was Jewish) and then quietly arranged to have her killed. But Hale's choice of contract killer turned out to be an FBI informant. A jury convicted Hale for conspiracy to commit murder in 2004, and he is presently serving a forty-year sentence in federal prison. Some suspected that Hale, in failing to kill Lefkow, ultimately arranged for the murder of her husband and mother in Lefkow's Chicago home. But investigators later identified the killer as Bart Ross, who resented Judge Lefkow for a ruling in a medical malpractice case and confessed to the crime in a suicide note. With Hale in prison, the World Church of the Creator withered into irrelevance.

One might get the sense, from stories like Hale's, that the government and anti-racist organizations have become incredibly effective at combatting religious terrorism. The Williams brothers and Buford Furrow went to prison; so did Walter Thody, Charles Barbee, Robert Berry, and Jay Merrell. When hate groups were not being undone in criminal court, the SPLC and the ADL were bankrupting them in civil court.

There is no doubt that by 1999, local and especially national law enforcement were becoming increasingly more sophisticated in recognizing and understanding the nuances of domestic terrorism, with an increased focus on the religious component that motivates at least some of the violence. With the new millennium approaching, the FBI became noticeably concerned about apocalyptic terrorism. Director Louis Freeh commissioned one of the first major analyses of religious terrorism that focused on something other than Islamic jihadism. The FBI named its study Project Megiddo, after a hill in Jerusalem, the site of many Old Testament battles and the place that many fundamentalist Christians believe will host the final battle of Armageddon. "The Hebrew word 'Armageddon,'" the FBI prefaced its strategic assessment, "means the hills of Megiddo. . . . The name 'Megiddo' is an apt title for a project that analyzes those who believe the year 2000 will usher in the end of the world and who are willing to perpetrate acts of violence to bring that end about."[25]

The FBI report explained,

Adherents of racist belief systems such as Christian Identity and
Odinism, and other radical domestic extremists are clearly fo-
cusing on the millennium as a time of action. Certain individuals
from these various perspectives are acquiring weapons, storing
food and clothing, raising funds through fraudulent means, pro-
curing safe houses, preparing compounds, surveying potential targets, and recruiting new converts. . . .

Christian Identity . . . believes in the inevitability of the end of
the world and the Second Coming of Christ. It is believed that
these events are part of a cleansing process that is needed before
Christ's kingdom can be established on earth. During this time,
Jews and their allies will attempt to destroy the white race using
any means available. The result will be a violent and bloody struggle—a war, in effect—between God's forces, the white race, and
the forces of evil, the Jews and nonwhites. Significantly, many adherents believe that this will be tied into the coming of the new
millennium. . . .

After the final battle is ended and God's kingdom is established
on earth, only then will the Aryan people be recognized as the one
and true Israel.

Christian Identity adherents believe that God will use his chosen
race as his weapons to battle the forces of evil. Christian Identity
followers believe they are among those chosen by God to wage
this battle during Armageddon and they will be the last line of
defense for the white race and Christian America. To prepare for
these events, they engage in survivalist and paramilitary training,
storing foodstuffs and supplies, and caching weapons and ammunition. They often reside on compounds located in remote areas.[26]

The report added that only a small fraction of Identity believers
favored a proactive effort to instigate a race war. It noted that
Identity radicals were part of a movement more than a centralized organization and that the movement's decentralized character
could lead to lone-wolf terrorism. But it also noted that the galvanizing nature of the approaching millennium was engendering a
greater level of cooperation among groups. It astutely observed that
while "the radical right encompasses a vast number and variety of

groups," these "groups are not mutually exclusive and within the subculture individuals easily migrate from one group to another." Yet "Christian Identity is the most unifying theology for a number of these diverse groups and one widely adhered to by white suprem- acists. It is a belief system that provides its members with a religious basis for racism and an ideology that condones violence against non-Aryans."[27]

The assessment may just as well have been describing the white supremacist milieu from 1957 to 1968—and that is the problem. While it acknowledged the Reverend Wesley Swift as the seminal figure in the development of radical Christian Identity, the Megiddo report failed to consider the full and accurate context for domestic, religious terrorism. It begins its discussion of actual Identity ter- rorism with the Order, not with the Confederate Underground, the National States Rights Party, or the White Knights of the Ku Klux Klan of Mississippi. A longer-term perspective on Christian Identity terrorism would yield a greater appreciation for the determination of these zealots and also for their adaptability. Their optimism at the prospect of a race war may ebb and flow according to external events, but the goal of waging war against "the Synagogue of Satan" and "the mud people" never changes for Identity radicals. Sam Bowers and J.B. Stoner were as determined to provoke an ethnic Armageddon as any Identity terrorist eyeing the coming millennium. A smarter approach to combatting Identity terrorism, one informed by history, would consider how Identity terrorists adapt and operate when they do not have the benefit of a galvanizing event to spur recruitment and incite their members to violence.

In that sense, studying Stoner's or Bowers's modus operandi would be just as valuable as studying contemporary Identity terrorists such as Robert Mathews. Indeed, in missing the earlier antecedents for the situation in 1999, the report looked past a key element of how the early Identity terrorists worked: by ascending to positions of leader- ship in secular racist or antigovernment groups, manipulating rank- and-file members, and coopting said groups' agendas. The report acknowledged the danger of the Identity movement but downplayed the threat posed by the KKK, failing to see how one movement can influence another. Men like Thomas Robb and Dennis Mahon, who

share strong Christian Identity influences, ran major KKK organizations into the 1990s. Thankfully, the report's oversight did not have an
immediate impact on domestic security, and the country avoided any
major attacks when the ball fell in Times Square on January 1, 2000.

But the report may well have undermined an investigation into
a wave of firebombing and arson attacks that plagued the United
States from 1995 to 1999. Segments of the public, especially those
in the African American religious community, became alarmed at
a sudden spike in arson activity in 1995, when fifty-two houses of
worship, including several black churches (as well as synagogues
and Hindu temples) suffered damage. The entire nation became concerned when that number grew to 297 in 1996 and began to include
an increasing number of synagogues, Sikh temples, and even white
churches. On the surface, the crimes seemed to be concentrated in
regional clusters, raising the specter of a wider conspiracy.

The media picked up on that angle, and soon President Bill
Clinton organized the National Church Arson Task Force, unifying
what had been separate investigations by the BATF, the FBI, the
Department of Treasury, and the Department of Justice. The first
series of reports, published in 1997, raised major questions about
a conspiratorial explanation for the attacks. As more and more arrests began to be made in these crimes, no evidence of an interstate
or even an intrastate criminal conspiracy materialized. Even when
investigators could link two or three fire bombings in the same community to one source, the perpetrator was almost always one person
or a very small group. In more than one instance, the arsonist turned
out to be a disgruntled ex-congregant rather than an outsider. Some
criminologists suggested that the extensive media coverage of the
church fires actually inspired other alienated loners to target religious institutions. Seeing this, the media began to question its own
initial reporting, which had raised the specter of a wider conspiracy.
More and more, reporters and pundits pushed the opposite narrative: that the spike in attacks resulted from self-perpetuating mass
hysteria that encouraged copycats.

There may be a great deal of truth in that assessment, but in re-
versing the course of its coverage, the media may well have made a
premature assessment. Given the decentralized nature of the far right

in the 1990s and the ubiquitous presence of government-paid informants, the idea of a regional or even statewide white supremacist conspiracy seems farfetched. Such coordination is not unheard of—Stoner
managed a multistate bombing campaign, using the Confederate Underground, in 1958. But almost every white supremacist group, during
the time of Stoner's campaign and immediately after, already operated
as a multistate organization, with a central headquarters and many
state chapters. In the 1990s, few groups, and few leaders, enjoyed
much influence outside of their narrow regional bases.

That being said, law enforcement was solving far too few of the
cases to commit to either a pro-conspiracy or no-conspiracy narrative. By 1999, of the 827 arson and firebombing attacks reported
since 1995, more than 60 percent remained unsolved. (Most still
remain unresolved as of 2015.) That hate groups did not contribute
to any of these attacks is hard to believe as a blanket assertion. Consider that from 1995 to 1999, investigators solved only two of eleven
firebomb or arson attacks on black churches in Chicago, headquarters for the World Church of the Creator; only seven of twenty-two
firebomb or arson attacks on black churches in Georgia, the home
state of Ed Fields and J.B. Stoner (released from prison in 1986); and
only seven of nineteen firebomb or arson attacks in North Carolina,
where Creativity's original founder, Ben Klassen, sold his compound
to National Alliance leader William Pierce.[28]

The leaders of these organizations need not have plotted the details of the crimes or even recruited the foot soldiers. Through appeals to emotion and the power of their charisma, they fostered a
mind-set that made such attacks more likely. Pierce's Cosmotheist
National Alliance, Butler's Christian Identity–based Aryan Nations,
Hale's Creativity-based World Church of the Creator—all of these
groups included impressionable members whose mind-sets could be
geared toward violence. For his study *The Racist Mind*, Harvard
ethnographer Raphael Ezekiel spent considerable time with white
supremacists and observed and interviewed several hate group
leaders. He described the archetypical hate group leader as

a man who is clever, who is shallow, and who does not respect
people. He thinks almost all people are dumb and easily misled.

He thinks almost all people will act for cold self-interest and will cheat others whenever they think they will not be caught. His disrespect includes his followers. He respects only those, friend or foe, who have power. His followers are people to be manipulated, not to be led to better self-knowledge.[29]

One finds in Ezekiel's observation echoes of college-educated Sam Bowers and his contempt for Mississippi "rednecks." Such sentiments can also be found in statements by Pierce, the former college professor, who referred to others as lemmings. One is also reminded of Matt Hale's suspicious relationship to Ben Smith in the lead-up to the latter's shooting spree on Independence Day Weekend.

With people like Smith and Furrow in mind, former FBI agent Mike German, who infiltrated supremacist groups for the Bureau from the 1990s through the turn of the millennium, argued in a *Washington Post* column that "'Lone extremism' is not a phenomenon; it's a technique, a ruse designed to subvert the criminal justice system."[30] He added,

Imagine a very smart leader of an extremist movement, one who understands the First Amendment and criminal conspiracy laws, telling his followers not to depend on specific instructions.

He might tell them to divorce themselves from the group before they commit a violent act; to act individually or in small groups so that others in the movement could avoid criminal liability. This methodology creates a win-win situation for the extremist leader—the violent goals of the group are met without the legal consequences.[31]

German insists that "these aren't the type of conspiracies cooked up by a few guys in a back room. But they are conspiracies nonetheless because they involve conscious discussions, decisions and encouragement for others to break the law by destroying property or taking lives. By providing both the motive and method for violence, these leaders become part of the conspiracy."[32] Recognizing the legal hurdles involved in prosecuting these cases, German argued that the Justice Department, like the SPLC, should pursue civil litigation against hate groups, in much the same way the Justice Department uses the courts to get financial restitution from white-collar criminals.

The SPLC demonstrated that this was possible, yet again, in the church arson cases. It won the largest lawsuit ever against the KKK, suing the South Carolina Christian Knights of the Ku Klux Klan for its role in instigating arson fires at the Mount Zion AME Church and the Macedonia Baptist Church on June 20 and June 21, 1996. Horace King, the SCCKKKK leader, did not initiate, directly order, or plot the attacks, but the two men who burned the churches down said that they had discussed their general plans with the Grand Wizard weeks before the event. In the interim period, King made frequent references, in general rallies, to burning black churches. "If we had this garbage in South Carolina, we would burn the bastards out," he said at one. He told a KKK member who turned out to be an undercover reporter for the *South Carolina Star Reporter*, "The only good nigger church is a burned nigger church."[33]

King predicted to the reporter that a race war would come in 2000. In his trial testimony, King claimed, "I never told no one to go out there and fight blacks or do any harm to blacks. But I have said this in the past: Be prepared. If a race war ever did come, then you should be ready."[34] Lest there be any doubt that the race war reference emerged from Christian Identity theology, Tim Welch, one of the men who set the fires, testified, "They use the Bible to say that blacks aren't human, Jews aren't human . . . whites, whites, that's it. So . . . if you allow blacks, you can't be Christian. The only Christian thing to do was to get rid of them."[35]

Despite the involvement of Justice Department and FBI officials in the Church Arson Task Force investigation, the insights from the Megiddo analysis never found their way into task force reports. When the task force published its fourth report in 2000, it only hinted at the Klan affiliations of the arsonists in the South Carolina affair, never even mentioning the lawsuit.

It is thus no surprise that the task force also failed to consider an even less direct kind of conspiracy, one in which a hate group creates a social climate that maximizes the chances that disparate and unconnected individuals and small groups will, independently of one another, throw firebombs at churches. Here again, the failure of law enforcement to fully consider the historical roots of domestic, religious terrorism impoverishes the current approach to similar crimes. The Megiddo report deserves credit for recognizing Wesley Swift as the pivotal figure in popularizing radical Christian Identity theology. But the FBI diminished his influence by failing to understand how Swift encouraged the violence of his era. Swift certainly did not coordinate or directly manage Identity-based violence in the 1960s, but by force of personality he created a subculture and offered a compelling message that perpetuated and inspired such violence during his lifetime and even afterward.

No singular figure occupied the same prominent space as Swift in Identity theology after he died, but the Internet, as a communications platform, has served the same function as Swift's sermon-tape distribution network in the 1960s. Hate group websites not only provide an ideological foundation for new recruits—including tape recordings of Swift's sermons in some cases—they also help promote the subculture that makes violence possible, notably by promoting and selling white power music. The Anti-Defamation League notes:

Hate music not only tries to stir up anger and resentment, but also acts as a call to action. Confrontation and war are frequent themes in hate music, ranging from crude calls to strike at one's "enemies" to visions of future race wars or apocalyptic battles. H8 Machine's (New Jersey) song "Wrecking Ball" is typical. "Wrecking, destroy all of your enemies/Fight back, hit back, hit back takeout another victim/Break down, the walls of opposition." The song "Thirst for Conquest" by Rebel Hell evokes a grander image: "To war the call we hear, the world trembling in fear/Storming to power, hail to the call/Marching in as one, the blitzkrieg rolling on/As über alles meaning over all." So too does Before God's (Minnesota) "Under the Blood Banner": "Legions attack, shoulder to shoulder/Striking the alien hordes/In battle formation, defending thy nation/With fury we wage, lighting wars!" Sometimes the message is simply one of crude violence, as in the Bound for Glory (Minnesota) song, "Onward to Victory." "Onward to Victory, the blood is gonna flow/Onward to Victory, we're gonna overthrow/Onward to Victory, in our battle stride/ Onward to Victory, with our racial pride."[36]

What hateful and violent messages they do not take in through their ears, white supremacists often brandish on their skin—with common symbols and messages popularized on the Internet. Nazi swastikas and icons from Norse (Odinist) mythology cover many a contemporary supremacist, sometimes literally from head to toe. One of the most common tattoos lists a motto, the so-called fourteen words. Penned by Alan Berg's murder conspirator, David Lane, whose tenure with the Order turned him into a celebrity among white supremacists and who became a leading advocate for Wotanism (a form of radical Odinism), the motto reads: "We must secure the existence of our people and a future for White children." Another favorite tattoo is "Rahowa," which stands for racial holy war.

Forty-year-old Wade Michael Page is a perfect example of the mind-set this subculture can foster. He not only listened to white power music, but he played guitar in two white power bands, one under contract with William Pierce's Resistance Records. Harboring no strong religious convictions, he nonetheless sported the "rahowa" and fourteen-word tattoos. With no history of violence, and with no public explanation, Page opened fire on congregants exiting a Sikh temple in Wisconsin in 2012, killing six and wounding four others; he then committed suicide. Page himself may not have been motivated by Christian Identity imperatives or by radical Odinism, but his action fits into a broad pattern described by former undercover agent Mike German. Wade was a byproduct of a "pack mentality"; "a follower of these movements bursts violently into our world, with deadly consequences."[37] Only it is the pack mentality, not the follower, that is informed by radical religion. Hence someone like Page becomes a servant to a militant religious agenda without recognizing its influence.

It is hard to imagine that some fanatic, connected to a white supremacist group and awash in messages, music, and imagery promoting a holy race war, would *not* be inspired to act amid the widespread media coverage of church and synagogue bombings from 1995 to 1999. Indeed, three of the synagogue attacks that frightened Jewish leaders in the summer of 1999 became part of the Church

Arson Task Force's database of potential hate crimes. The attack by the Williams brothers on two synagogues in Sacramento, California, is one example. But the report never mentioned or discussed the role that Christian Identity religion played in inspiring those attacks, or any other arson attack in the database for that matter.

This would include the attempted firebombing of Temple Emanu-El in Reno by Carl DeAmicis and four others, also in 1999 (described earlier). Prosecutors in that case were surprised to find that the five young men, ranging in ages from nineteen to twenty-six, were motivated by religious ideology. But in the supremacists' "clubhouse," with its walls adorned with Nazi flags, a "Whites Only" sign, and a poster of men in KKK robes, investigators found Christian Identity literature. One of the five perpetrators, twenty-year-old Daniel McIntosh, said he was "doing something for his race" in targeting Jews, because "they are evil, they control the media and they put racial mixing on TV and that is wrong."[38] If their Identity connections came as a surprise to investigators, one thing was obvious about the young terrorists from their appearance. They bore shaved heads and skinhead tattoos.

An investigator who studies trends in white supremacist violence would be forgiven if he or she suspected that skinheads perpetrated at least some of the unsolved attacks on America's houses of worship from 1995 to 1999. Importing their aesthetic of shaved heads and punk fashion from the United Kingdom, skinheads became part of the white supremacist scene in the early 1980s. They became a national force within white supremacist circles over the next two decades, with their numbers growing by tenfold from 1986 to 1991. They developed their own culture, defined, according to the SPLC "by loud hate-rock, cases of cheap beer, bloody 'boot parties' directed against immigrants and others, and the flagrant display of neo-Nazi iconography and paraphernalia."[39] Older and senior members over time formed regional networks, such as the Hammerskins, but for the most part, skinheads roved urban and suburban areas as small bands or gangs. They became known for harassment, vandalism, and at times violent vigilante attacks on gays and minorities. These small-scale attacks, when aggregated, nonetheless represented one of the most common sources of white supremacist violence in the 1990s. Jack B. Moore, an American studies professor at the University of South Florida and author of *Skinheads: Shaved for Battle*, observed, "In less than a decade violence committed by skinheads catapulted them to perhaps the leading position among hate groups practicing violence in America."[40]

Harvard ethnographer Raphael Ezekiel, who interviewed and observed dozens of skinheads for several years, described a group of "male, young dropouts without work skills, with a deep fear of personal annihilation—social isolates."[41] According to criminologist Mark Hamm, "The social and political contentions of the Reagan era seemed to have produced conditions conducive to extreme alienation among white, working-class youths in the United States. In turn, this extreme alienation caused certain white kids to shave their heads, tattoo themselves with swastikas, espouse racist beliefs, and commit hate crimes; usually with baseball bats, work boots, guns or knives."[42] Moore quotes the 1989 edition of the SPLC's periodical *Klanwatch*: "The emergence of skinhead gangs represents a unique and frightening phenomenon in the history of white supremacy in America: for the first time, a nationwide racist movement is being initiated by teenagers who are not confined to any single geographic region or connected by any national network, but whose gangs sprang up spontaneously in cities throughout the country."[43]

The picture painted by the SPLC is something akin to a zombie apocalypse, with random hordes of testosterone-filled vigilantes defying age-old, predictable patterns of racial violence. Offered when the skinheads were just becoming a force in American society, the description became less and less accurate as the group evolved. As noted earlier, the skinheads did eventually network into organizations; the largest, the Hammerskin Nation, boasts nineteen chapters across the United States (as well as ten international franchises). The SPLC did highlight the salient feature of the group, its members' ages, but it failed to accurately gauge the full implications of that demography. Yes, their ages may have made skinheads more open to violence. But far from being uncontrollable and unpredictable hordes, the young and socially alienated skinheads were perfect candidates for the kind of manipulation and exploitation that has been the hallmark of religious terrorist leaders for decades.

Leaders of America's most dangerous hate groups, who had previously manipulated southern nationalists, farmers, and nativists, never had a more malleable group of foot soldiers to exploit than the skinheads. Men like Fields, Butler, Pierce, and Metzger openly hailed the young men, dressed in Dr. Martens boots and military-style fatigues, as the vanguard of white supremacy. It is worth noting that Ezekiel's observations about white supremacist leaders who privately harbor contempt for their ignorant and gullible rank-and-file followers derived almost entirely from interviews with skinhead leaders. In her study *Skinheads in America: A Movement toward Violence*, researcher Regina Raab comments that the "movement seems to be fueled mostly by sustained hatred toward several targeted groups that is manipulated by relatively few leaders to achieve direct action by individual Skinheads." SPLC leader Morris Dees has asserted that the skinheads are "easy prey for older white supremacist leaders, who cynically offer a sense of family and purpose—along with a hate-filled ideology."

Scott Shepherd, a onetime KKK Grand Dragon who now crusades against racism, saw this exploitation from the inside. "[The leaders] prey on the short comings of rank and file," he insisted.[44] Christian Identity theology, which Shepherd says is now "embedded in the [white supremacist] movement and continues to grow," is an important part of that dynamic. "Racial war and racial holy war is their [the leaders'] main goal they want this to happen . . . and try and provoke it." The idea of a racial holy war is "not discussed or used as recruitment subject but after members had joined it was part of the indoctrination and pushed widely." He lamented, "You had a lot of troubled kids that fell into that trap."[45]

No white supremacist leader exploited skinheads more than Tom Metzger. The onetime Christian Identity minister formed the White Aryan Resistance (WAR) at approximately the same time the skinhead movement began to take hold in the United States. Michael Waltman and John Haas, in their book *The Communication of Hate*, report that "Metzger set out to create, through WAR, an organizational structure that would permit him to distribute his ideas to skinheads, providing them with more ideological grounding than they possessed in the past. By mentoring skinhead groups across

California, he hoped to create a cadre of young racist warriors who would take the racial holy war to individual Jews and minorities across California."[46] Metzger's influence became public knowledge when the SPLC sued him for inciting skinhead Dave Mazzella to violently assault an Ethiopian immigrant (who later died) in Portland, Oregon. A onetime organizer for Metzger, Mazzella claimed to have been brainwashed by the WAR leader, and he detailed Metzger's Machiavellian relationship with Portland's skinhead community. The SPLC won a multimillion-dollar judgment for the victim's family. According to Waltman and Haas, Metzger's subsequent "bankruptcy and the belief among many skinheads that they were being 'used' and exploited by Metzger contributed to his diminishing influence on racist skinheads."[47]

Yet the authors note that the skinheads increasingly came under the sway of Matthew Hale and the WCOTC, with many identifying themselves as Creativity ministers. Others flocked to the welcoming arms of Richard Butler and the Aryan Nations. Michigan skinheads interviewed by Ezekiel were heavily influenced by Christian Identity ideology, much like the five young men who tried to set Temple Emanuel-El on fire in December 1999.

In missing or ignoring the relevance of Christian Identity (or Odinism or Creativity) theology and its influence on one of the fastest-growing supremacist groups in the country, the Church Arson Task Force may have missed an opportunity to solve at least some of the arsons and firebombings in its database. The task force did take great care to analyze firebombings and arson attacks on black churches as a separate category of crimes, in hopes of identifying patterns that suggested a racist conspiracy. History, of course, is full of examples of KKK chapters sponsoring waves of church bombings, and that is the prism through which investigators looked when considering the possibility of a wider plot against religious institutions. But the history covered in this book shows that Christian Identity radicals were often more than happy to launch waves of violence that targeted both black and Jewish religious institutions. Stoner did this in 1957–1958; Bowers did this in 1967–1968.

When viewed through that prism, subsets of the hundreds of arson and firebombing attacks that were never solved offer a new avenue of investigation: Look for an attack on a synagogue that occurred relatively close in time and distance to an attack on a black church and then explore possible connections between local supremacist groups with religious affiliations and either crime. The Church Arson Task Force posted lists of solved and unsolved crimes, and at least a handful of unsolved cases fit the profile of Identity-influenced crimes. One is the Temple Beth Chai arson in Hauppauge, New York, on August 15, 1999, described earlier. On the same day someone set fire to the temple's business office, an arsonist struck the black First Presbyterian Church in Staten Island, one hour away by car. Neither case has been solved, and there is no evidence that the task force considered the possibility that the two crimes were connected, despite the propinquity.

Attacks on Jewish houses of worship represent a small fraction of the database's cases. But the database does not include vandalism of Jewish houses of worship (or Jewish cemeteries) or attacks on broadly defined Jewish institutions. For instance, Furrow's attack on the Jewish community center would not have made the database. If Christian Identity ideas motivated such ancillary attacks, expanding the types of criminality under consideration and then correlating them with attacks on black targets could conceivably yield additional leads and suspects in the 1995–1999 arson wave. As the South Carolina case illustrated and as the history of Christian Identity violence suggests, Identity zealots, or those under their influence, often find black targets more readily available. Identity ideas about Jews became more widespread and accepted in the 1980s, but it was still the case, per Ezekiel, that recruits entered hate organizations with antagonism toward blacks and Hispanics and then were inculcated with hatred toward Jews. Thus it was likely easier to sway members to go after black targets than after Jewish targets, much as it was during Sam Bowers's tenure as Grand Wizard in Mississippi. The only difference in the current environment is that Bowers directly ordered his attacks, while Identity terrorists, since 1985, had been inspired by or socially conditioned by men like Bowers but have operated as individuals or through small groups.

Law enforcement scrutiny forced domestic terrorists into ever-more-decentralized units of activity; the result was atomized, individual fanatics—Louis Beam's lone wolves—who are limited in their capacity for mass casualty or debilitating attacks but who can only be managed and contained. Identifying a lone wolf or preventing his actions is, as former FBI man Mike German concedes, daunting: "like finding a needle in a haystack." But German argues that law enforcement must therefore start looking at the "needle factory"—the leaders, groups, and subculture that make the terrorism possible. That effort must include recognition of a religious impulse that motivates some terrorists directly and that indirectly shapes the contours of the terrorist mind-set of many others. For all its flaws, the Megiddo report represented an important first step in that regard, but the timing of its release, in 2000, could not have been more inopportune.

Within a year, Al Qaeda launched the most deadly terrorist attack on American soil in the nation's history. If failing to appreciate the full history of religious terrorism in America, from Martin Luther King Jr.'s assassination to the arson wave of 1995–1999, has obscured law enforcement's understanding of crimes, then this same ignorance, in regard to both domestic and foreign extremists, continues to jeopardize American security.

15

REVELATIONS

APOCALYPTIC
RELIGIOUS TERRORISM
POST-9/11

On September 11, 2001, Al Qaeda launched the most deadly terrorist attack on American soil in the nation's history. The tragedy fundamentally reoriented law enforcement's approach to terrorism. Understandably, the government focused its resources on identifying and disrupting Al Qaeda cells inside America's borders to prevent another mass casualty attack. Domestic terrorist groups became a secondary concern, so much so that FBI agent Mike German, who infiltrated white supremacist groups for the agency, resigned in 2005 and became a whistleblower. He gave interviews and wrote columns that attempted to put the terrorism problem in perspective, specifically highlighting the danger still posed by domestic terrorism. An examination of acts of terrorism (and attempted terrorism) on U.S. soil shows that in terms of the number of acts, as opposed to the number of people killed or injured, incidents of American right-wing terrorism far outnumber instances of foreign jihadi terrorism.

More and more terrorism experts have been arguing this point. Among them is journalist Peter Bergen, author of several books on terrorism and one of the only people to interview Osama Bin Laden. In a 2014 article for CNN's website, cowritten with terrorism expert David Sterman and titled "U.S. Right Wing Extremists More Deadly Than Jihadists," Bergen wrote,

Since 9/11 extremists affiliated with a variety of far-right wing ideologies, including white supremacists, anti-abortion extremists and anti-government militants, have killed more people in the United States than have extremists motivated by al Qaeda's ideology. According to a count by the New America Foundation,

right wing extremists have killed 34 people in the United States for
political reasons since 9/11. . . .

By contrast, terrorists motivated by al Qaeda's ideology have
killed 21 people in the United States since 9/11. . . .

Moreover, since 9/11 none of the more than 200 individuals
indicted or convicted in the United States of some act of jihadist
terrorism have acquired or used chemical or biological weapons
or their precursor materials, while 13 individuals motivated by
right wing extremist ideology, one individual motivated by left-
wing extremist ideology, and two with idiosyncratic beliefs, used
or acquired such weapons or their precursors.[1]

The article was responding to Frazier Glenn Miller's April 13,
2014, assault on a Kansas City, Missouri, Jewish community center
and retirement home. Bergen and Sterman, who research terrorism
for the nonpartisan New America Foundation, highlight the fact
that Miller shouted "Heil Hitler" after being arrested for his crimes.
They then pose an interesting thought experiment in which "instead of shouting 'Heil Hitler' after he was arrested, the suspect had
shouted 'Allahu Akbar.' Only two days before the first anniversary of
the Boston Marathon bombings, this simple switch of words would
surely have greatly increased the extent and type of coverage the
incident received."

The double standard highlighted by Bergen and Sterman extends
not just to the media but to law enforcement. Consider two recent
prosecutions of two different groups of people, one right wing and
one (supposedly) jihadist. The first group is the Hutaree Militia,
concentrated in southeastern Michigan but with affiliated members
throughout the Rust Belt. At the end of March 2010, law enforcement authorities arrested nine of its members on federal "charges of
seditious conspiracy, attempted use of weapons of mass destruction,
teaching the use of explosive materials, and possessing a firearm
during a crime of violence." Based on information obtained from
two undercover informants, the FBI concluded that the Hutarees
intended "to ambush and kill a local police officer and then use his
or her funeral as a stage for further killings using explosive devices."

One FBI informant, fifty-seven-year-old Dan Murray, infiltrated the Hutarees by attending meetings and earning their trust over time. He, in turn, introduced the next undercover informant, Steven Haug, as his best friend. Haug so convincingly endeared himself to the group's leader, David Stone, that he served as the best man at Stone's wedding. Both Murray and Haug surreptitiously recorded Stone making comments like the following: "We need to quit playing this game with these elitist terrorists and get serious because this war will come whether we are ready or not." Of the scenario targeting police officers Haug recorded Stone as saying, "And if I kill their wives and their children inside, then so be it, because I'm sending a message to the rest of them."

The government presented evidence that the Hutarees had trained (with Haug) to develop explosives, that they had a "kill list" for potential assassinations, and that they had cached as much as 148,000 rounds of ammunition. The Hutarees' defense team did an excellent job of challenging much of the government's case. It pointed out that Hutaree members had never actually detonated an explosive device—only Haug had done so—that the kill list included names of people who were already dead; that the government had selectively excerpted parts of the tape recording to highlight its case; that Murray often tried to bait Stone into making incriminating statements; and that the plans for the attack were defensive in nature, not offensive. This last point is particularly important, as the Hutaree Militia followed the teachings of Christian Identity. The war they referenced in the recordings was a holy race war. Their defense attorneys, as assistant religious studies professor Susan Palmer noted in her study of the case, emphasized the religious dimensions of their militia at trial:

> Swor described his client as a firm believer in the *Book of Revelation* and the rise of the Antichrist. "The anti-Christ as David Stone understands it will come from overseas, and the troops of the anti-Christ will take over America. That is the resistance that David Stone was preparing for." Swor emphasized the religious purpose of Hutaree training, as "contingency training for the Day of Apocalypse, when the forces of the Antichrist *literally*—not

figuratively, not symbolically, not allegorically—but *literally* invaded the U.S. and took over the U.S. government and proceeded to impose the will of the Antichrist on the people." The Hutaree saw themselves as training for that day, Swor noted—but they would never give a date.[2]

William Swor's point was twofold: first, to argue that the supposed plotting on the tape was too vague to constitute an actual conspiracy plot (as opposed to "just talk"), and second, to show that the plot was too fantastic to be taken seriously by the government in the first place. U.S. district court judge Victoria Roberts agreed with the defense; she "gutted the government's case against seven members of a Michigan militia, dismissing the most serious charges in an extraordinary defeat for federal authorities."[3] In her ruling, Roberts asserted that this was a case of free speech: "The court is aware that protected speech and mere words can be sufficient to show a conspiracy. In this case, however, they do not rise to that level."[4] The prosecution had presented evidence that the Hutarees had engaged in dangerous activities and were hostile to the U.S. government, but it had never presented any concrete plan, developed by the Hutarees, for an actual conspiracy, she argued. The government's case fell apart, and all that remained were convictions for illegal firearms possession against two members; the perpetrators got time served. To add insult to injury, members of the Hutaree Militia subsequently sued the government for damages and won.

Contrast the outcome of the Hutaree Militia case with that of the so-called Newburgh Four, four Muslim men from the working-class Riverdale community in the Bronx, associated with the Masjid al-Ikhlas Mosque in Newburgh, New York. In 2009 the federal government charged them with conspiring to blow up Jewish institutions and to shoot down military aircraft. Taped conversations from an undercover government informant played a key role in the Newburgh trial, much as they had in the Hutaree prosecution. With the blessing of the FBI, Shaheed Hussain, a hotel operator, had built a rapport with one of the four men, forty-two-year-old James Cromite, inside and outside the mosque. After four months, Hussain (falsely) claimed to be a member of a Pakistani terrorist group and made a proposal to Cromite: the group would give Cromite $250,000 if he helped plot a terrorist attack against U.S. interests. Cromite actually ceased contact with Hussain until weeks later, when the former lost his job. At that point, Cromite recruited three other alleged conspirators: David Williams, Onta Williams (no relation), and Laguerre Payen. Veteran journalist and fellow at the Center on National Security Phil Hirschkorn reported that authorities arrested the four men "on May 20, 2009, moments after placing three 'bombs' each equipped with 30 pounds of C-4 plastic explosives inside cars parked outside two synagogues in the Riverdale section of the Bronx."[5] The explosives, and Stinger missiles also found in the possession of the men, "were duds created by the FBI and made available to the men through Hussain."

The fact that the men were caught with the materials represented a clear advantage to federal prosecutors, one not enjoyed by the government lawyers in the Hutaree case. But in many other ways, the Newburgh case was far weaker. None of the men involved in the Newburgh conspiracy had any military background or training with explosives, and one clearly suffered from cognitive impairment. Despite the connection to the mosque, none of the men were particularly devout or pious. Hussain failed to record a number of key exchanges with the men, notably his first encounters with Cromite. In one of the recordings, the men actually expressed concern to Hussain about the loss of human life. More than anything, as Hirschkorn points out, Hussain seems to have served more as an agent provocateur than an informant. "Hussain did all the driving on 'surveillance' trips. Hussain suggested the targets and the means of attacking them, and then provided the fake weapons to do so. Even when the temple 'bombings' went down, it was Hussain, not the Newburgh Four, who turned on the fake detonators." But an entrapment defense did not work, and the men received mandatory minimum twenty-five-year sentences. Even the district court judge, Colleen McMahon, asserted during sentencing that "The government did not act to infiltrate and foil some nefarious plot; there was no plot to foil. . . . I doubt James Cromite had any idea what a Stinger missile was."

More than one observer has pointed to the surprising discrepancies between the outcomes in the two cases. Judges in both cases voiced serious reservations about the government's case, but one did it while throwing out the basis for the government's charges while the other did it following a jury conviction. But the government's failure to secure a conviction in the Hutaree case may have as much to do with preconceived notions and ignorance about the history of religious terrorism as it does with free speech. In the Hutaree case, the government presented the religious motivation of the Hutarees but then let defense attorneys dismiss the end-times beliefs of Stone and his followers. Palmer notes how Stone's lawyer, Swor, "emphasized the ludic, speculative quality of Hutaree battle plans." She quotes his closing argument:

> They liked to sit around and fantasize about their battles in the End Time. Someone suggested that they hire strippers to act as decoys in the future battle with the Devil (that shows you how realistic they were). Mr. Stone was constantly talking about the End Time. All you have to do with Mr. Stone is say 'Hello'—and he's off![6]

The defense lawyers refer to Stone's eschatological beliefs as "fantasy." Here again, a full understanding of radical Christian Identity and its connection to domestic terrorism would have led to the realization that the apocalyptic claims of the Hutarees, far from being fantasies, had factored into countless terrorist attacks and attempted attacks by a variety of American far-right paramilitary groups dating back to the 1960s. The individuals who plotted or carried out these attacks often imagined the same exact scenario offered by David Stone on tape: a small-scale attack followed by provocative acts of violence that would metastasize into something much greater—a holy race war. Ignorance of the past here led to a gross underestimation of the danger.

The double standard regarding prosecuting terrorism in the United States reveals prejudices about which religious faiths are more prone to violence and terrorism. Few experts doubt that the Newburgh conspirators' Islamic background played a role in their conviction. That is why the defense attorneys in that case did everything to minimize their clients' piety.

In contrast, the Hutaree Militia attorneys embraced their clients' Christian devotion (while dismissing concerns about their unusual eschatological beliefs) and won a startling victory. A thought experiment, similar to the one proposed by Bergen, puts an accent on the contradiction. Imagine if the Hutaree group had been a terrorist cell of the Islamic State of Iraq and Syria (ISIS) instead of being Christian Identity militants. In an excellent study of the group for a recent article in *The Atlantic*,[7] Graeme Wood outlines the key features of ISIS's ideology. Its members believe that their legitimacy comes from occupying land governed by strict Sharia law; they believe that the end-times is soon approaching and that the final battle will take place in Syria; and they believe that their soldiers will play an active role in fighting the forces of the Antichrist until Jesus (who is the second-most-important prophet in Islam) vanquishes the enemy and ushers in a paradise. Many experts believe that by publicizing its shocking acts of violence, ISIS hopes to bait the West into invading the Middle East. The group's interpretation of the end-times in Islam requires an invasion from "Rome," which could mean the United States. It is not hard to see the parallels to Christian Identity militants, but it is almost impossible to imagine a defense attorney owning up to this comparison, ridiculing it as a fantasy, and leveraging that to convince a federal judge that members of ISIS are not a threat.

Wood's article enters into dangerous territory when it asserts that a group like ISIS (or Al Qaeda) is "Islamic. *Very* Islamic" and that it *"derives from coherent and even learned interpretations of Islam."*[8] It is true that some leaders of ISIS are devout Muslims whose hyperliteral and orthodox application of Islam and Sharia date back to the late eighteenth century, to an Islamic offshoot known as Salafism. Attempts to minimize this connection by pointing to the large number of young, disaffected rank-and-file members who form the bulk of ISIS's constituency and appear to be recent converts with little or no familiarity with Islam, misses the point. The degree to which the young foot soldiers are motivated by genuine religious fervor rather than socio-ethnic grievances is irrelevant. If they advance the goals of devout leaders, even obliquely, the result still serves an apocalyptic and religious agenda. This is no different from what happened with skinheads in the 1990s.

It is also true that most Salafis represent a small subset of the Islamic community and that most Salafis are apolitical and nonviolent. But that, by itself, also does not mean that those who do embrace violence are perverting the religion; Islam is not an inherently pacifistic faith. But those in ISIS and Al Qaeda break from long-standing traditions and norms within their faith in a key way: their willingness to excommunicate supposed infidels and apostates in their own community. The concept, known as *takfir,* involves the expulsion and treatment of those within the Islamic faith who betray its core values; such individuals could be subject to harsh punishments if one takes a literal reading of the Quran and the Hadith. But in the fourteen-hundred-year history of Islam, this kind of excommunication is very rare and is applied only after consensus of a host of scholars and clerics.

In contrast, Al Qaeda and ISIS excommunicate fellow Muslims en masse and seemingly allow just about any ISIS (or Al Qaeda) operative to judge and execute apostates. The process effectively creates thousands of enemies whose presence in the Middle East demands immediate attention and action. Couple that with another relatively new innovation in militant Islamic theology—the idea, spread by Ayman Al-Zawahiri's mentor, Egyptian theologian Sayyid Qutb , that the West, by promoting materialism and promiscuity, is engaged in a cultural assault on the Muslim community—and one has the core and idiosyncratic basis for militant Salafi jihadism. For the vast majority of Muslims, *jihad* refers to an internal struggle to become a better believer, not a holy war against external enemies. Muhammad's words and teachings hold that "Muslims constitute one brotherhood"; that Muslims should not "do injustice" to any fellow Muslim; that they should allow nonbelievers to live in peace if they pay a tax. One seeing a Middle Eastern world where Muslims are the most victimized group by ISIS and Al Qaeda, and where non-Muslims are beheaded or crucified, is wrong to blame Islam for this calamity. It is not by applying Islam that terrorists justify their behavior but by widening the scope of those to whom *they do not have to apply Islam*—and then creating something like a siege mentality (fears of cultural imperialism) among alienated foot soldiers. Here too one finds echoes of a Wesley Swift, who fundamentally reinterpreted the book of Genesis to move Jews and minorities outside the orbit of Christian concern, who constantly warned of an impending Armageddon to encourage and justify violence against Jews and blacks.

This gets to the heart of the current debate between the Obama administration and its detractors in the military, in the Republican Party, and in conservative media outlets over how to define one's enemy. Obama has argued that extremists of all religions have perverted their faiths to engage in terrorism; his supporters offer the Ku Klux Klan as an example. The war on terrorism is really a war on extremism, the president has argued. He refuses to say that radical Islam is the root cause of terrorism because that would legitimize extremists. Obama's critics (even including a few liberals like Bill Maher) imply that there is some fundamental aspect of Islam that accommodates violence in ways that Christianity does not and that defining the "enemy" with the broad term *extremist* distorts the anti-terrorism campaign in practical ways. They argue that one should not spend resources to combat or undermine extremists of all stripes when the obvious source of terrorism is Islamic radicalism. If the president just says that this is a war on Islamic radicalism, they argue, he will crystalize the objective and focus the nation's resources accordingly.

In ignoring the legacy of Christian Identity terrorism, both sides risk putting the nation's security in danger, however. But in pointing out the influence of Christian Identity theology on the history of U.S. terrorism, we do not want to fall into the trap of overgeneralizing. Defining an enemy too broadly is problematic, and the generic example of the Ku Klux Klan illustrates the point. Factions of the KKK undoubtedly were terrorists, but for much of the Klan's history, Christianity was an ad hoc cover for neo-Confederate, secular terrorism. The Klan used religious imagery—the fiery cross—and quoted scripture, but its members could never fully reconcile their religious veneer with their actual conduct. At the peak of the Klan's influence, in the revival of the 1920s, it featured Romans 12 as its key passage of scripture, a facade so incongruous with its record of violence that even the FBI ridiculed it in reports.

The very fact that the influence of the KKK ebbed and flowed over its 150-year history shows its secular core. The widely recognized four waves—during Reconstruction, during the 1920s, during the civil rights era, and during the Reagan and first Bush administrations—were all obvious reactions to secular political developments: the expansion of political rights to freed slaves, the influx of foreign immigrants and the migration of blacks to the North, the movement toward racial integration in the South, and the economic dislocation of working-class whites throughout the country, respectively. In contrast, Christian Identity terrorists legitimately saw themselves as warriors in God's army. From the 1950s on, Christian Identity radicals infiltrated several KKK groups and exploited them for their religious agenda. But that did not happen in all KKK organizations. For example, there is little evidence that the United Klans of America, the largest KKK group in the United States during the civil rights era, was hijacked by Identity radicals; Robert Shelton, the longtime Grand Wizard of the UKA, does not appear to be a Swift follower in any way.

The danger in broadly characterizing all KKK activity as extremist and hence lumping a secular KKK group together with a group like the NSRP is that the two operate differently and require different responses from the government. Most experts on terrorism are careful to distinguish between religious and ethnonationalist terrorists for that very reason. Religious terrorists are more willing to engage in provocative acts of violence, to accept "collateral damage" to civilians, to use "propaganda of the deed," and to persist in the face of adversity.[9] As the waves of KKK history show, secular-nationalist groups tend to die out depending on whether or not they succeed through their reactionary violence (as the KKK did following Reconstruction) or fail with those same reactionary tactics (as the KKK did following the Voting Rights Act of 1965). In contrast, even during the period of fragmentation following the death of Wesley Swift in the 1970s, the number of Christian Identity believers grew. The reason offered by scholars of terrorism is easy for a layman to grasp: religious terrorists desire and expect a massive and profound change in the world order whereas secular terrorists pursue some limited political aim.

But if the Obama administration is making a mistake in conceiving of the problem too broadly, the president's critics are failing to apprehend the dangers that come with lack of precision in defining one's enemy. Here too the history of Christian Identity terrorism would benefit those sincerely concerned with domestic security. As noted many times, not all Christian Identity believers favor proactive violence. The failure to make that distinction may well have inspired almost a decade's worth of terrorism in the 1990s. No event did more to radicalize domestic terrorists than the raid on Randy Weaver's Idaho estate in 1992, when Weaver's wife and son were killed by federal agents. As noted in Chapter 13, Weaver believed in a passive form of Christian Identity. He was a survivalist and a white separatist, not a Robert Mathews type convinced that violence would bring about a white utopia and ready to die in a blaze of glory. But in conflating Weaver with the latter type of Identity militant, the government grossly mistook him as a threat and responded in a disproportionate manner.

A similar lack of nuance applied to the raid on Waco in 1993. David Koresh may have deserved some level of scrutiny from law enforcement, but the Branch Davidians were not the Covenant, the Sword and the Arm of the Lord. The irony is that in the latter raid, the government did a better job of negotiating a surrender. The unintended consequences of this lack of precision also include the Oklahoma City Bombing, as well as many lone-wolf attacks.

Even a label as exacting as "militant Salafi jihadist" could be problematic in the so-called War on Terror, as Al Qaeda and ISIS are actually rivals that compete for the same pool of potential recruits. Al Qaeda favors the teachings of Sayyid Qutb, an Egyptian religious scholar whose time spent in the United States in the 1940s convinced him that the "far enemy"—the United States and the West—represented the greatest threat to the Muslim community by way of cultural imperialism and moral corruption. His student Ayman Al-Zawarhiri became Osama Bin Laden's chief advisor and has run the group since Bin Laden's death. On the other hand, the leader of ISIS, Abu Bakr al-Baghdadi, in placing an emphasis on a caliphate in the Middle East, is more concerned with the "near enemy"—nations like Jordan and Saudi Arabia that do not apply an orthodox-enough version of Sharia law. This distinction is a matter of priorities more than anything else; Al-Zawarhiri despises the "infidels" in the West, and al-Baghdadi despises what he sees as Western puppet governments in the Arab world. Differences between the two groups suggest different responses and courses of action—possibly attempting to pit one group against the other.

Fomenting factionalism, not just between but within groups, became an important part of law enforcement's efforts to subvert white supremacist organizations in the United States, whether the group was secular or influenced by Christian Identity. Anyone who shares a religious worldview like Christian Identity—who imagines that the forces of the devil are constantly conspiring against him—is inherently prone to paranoia. So infiltrating, surveilling, coopting, and subverting such people are all highly effective strategies. Such human intelligence is as important as electronic intelligence in fighting terrorist organizations. But targeting nonviolent groups such as the SCLC with the same tactics one would apply to the Black Panthers has not only undermined legitimate forms of dissent that are valuable within a democracy but also wasted valuable resources.

Conserving resources also means taking stock of the government's failures when employing human sources rather than burying and concealing these failures. One can only imagine the time and money wasted infiltrating subversive groups that cannot be punished because the government operation veered into any number of improprieties, from informants running amuck to informants provoking actual violence. This is to say nothing about the cost in human lives and property when terrorists start operating with some sense of immunity. Ignoring the mistakes of the past or hiding them from future law enforcement agents and task forces contributes to a lack of institutional memory, which makes the same failures much more likely in the future. (Federal law enforcement agencies can start to rectify this deficit by releasing files and materials related to the crimes discussed in this book, many of which are more than thirty years old.)

The type of pseudo-entrapment seen in the Newburgh case was not new in domestic counterterrorism, and the practice has continued after 2011. This has helped contribute to the impression that the government is profiling or out to get Muslims—an impression that is likely to persist if politicians continue speaking broadly about "Islamic radicalism" without being more precise. In so doing, the United States is making itself less, not more, safe, because the

government is increasingly alienating one of the most important resources America has in preventing a domestic attack: the Muslim
American community. America's frontline defense against any effort
by an Al Qaeda phantom cell to launch a mass-casualty attack would
be Muslim Americans who could work in conjunction with the FBI
and local police to identify suspicious characters in their own communities. As terrorism expert Tony Gaskew has argued, "Muslim
Americans are the resident experts on Islam in the United States and
the only reliable eyes and ears for law enforcement in their often
'exclusive' communities."[10]

Pundits ranging in ideological orientation from Sean Hannity to
Bill Maher have shown a disrespect, bordering on contempt, toward
Muslims in general, American Muslims included. If the goal is to protect American security rather than score points in some sort of culture
war, to officially label the current conflict the "war on radical Islam"
suggests bad faith. The spirit behind President Obama's refusal to use
the term *radical Islam* is important; the country does not benefit from
alienating its law-abiding Muslim community. If Muslim Americans
distrust the government and law enforcement, if they fear they could
be targets rather than allies in the fight against terrorists, it could undermine the very security Obama's critics claim to hold dear.

If those same pundits argue that a more precise definition of the
enemy, "militant Salafi jihadism," is too complicated for Americans
to understand, they miss the point of naming one's enemy in the first
place. The goal is to understand the threat and to direct limited resources against those most likely to do the country harm. American
law enforcement would be making a huge mistake if it treated members of the Westboro Baptist Church, however abhorrent one may
find their views and practices, with the same scrutiny and tactics that
it directs at the Aryan Nations. The latter is violent; the former is a
nuisance.

In his article for *The Atlantic,* Graeme Wood highlights a similar
distinction between militant Salafis and what he calls Salafi quietists.
The latter are reminiscent of Randy Weaver in that they embrace the
hard-core belief system of their fellow militants, but they do not favor
violence. In Wood's estimation, the kind of propaganda war implied in
President Obama's approach of combatting "extremism" can go only

so far. It might prevent someone from becoming radicalized, but it is unlikely to "reform" someone who has already become radical. Defining one's enemy precisely, in this case, means accepting the reality of "extremist" *thought*, perhaps by funneling budding extremists into the quietest camp, to minimize the potential for extremist violence.

A similarly pragmatic, if risky, approach has never been tried with homegrown religious terrorism in part because it has yet to be taken as seriously as it should be. Many of the very same people who demand that the Obama administration make "radical Islam" the centerpiece of America's antiterrorism campaign have openly worked against acknowledging almost any kind of homegrown terrorism. A 2009 report by the Department of Homeland Security (DHS) that pointed out the sharp rise in hate groups since President Obama's election and argued that economic and political conditions (as they always have) could push right-wing groups to violence was lambasted by conservative media icons. Conservative blogger and Fox News contributor Michelle Malkin called it a "piece of crap report" and a "hit job on conservatives," and her views were hardly exceptional. In fairness to Malkin, the term *right-wing*, and even *far right*, is in many ways too imprecise, and the DHS report should have been more nuanced.

But a 2013 report that did attempt to draw those kinds of distinctions, written by Professor Arie Perliger, a scholar at West Point Military Academy's Combating Terrorism Center, drew a similar, if more muted, reaction.[11] Although Perliger continued with the broad label "far-right terrorists," he divided terrorist groups into three main subgroups: racist/white supremacy groups (like the KKK, the Hammerskins, and the National Alliance), anti-federalist groups (like militias), and religious fundamentalist groups (like antiabortion and Christian Identity organizations). The conservative overreaction was almost breathtakingly defensive: the head of the American Life League, Julie Brown, called the report a smear tactic against pro-life activists. A constitutional law professor, Herb Titus, called Perliger a "propagandist" for the Obama administration who "disagrees with those who favor small government, cutting back of federal government encroachments upon the powers of the state, and to discredit this movement [he] focuses on a few gun-toting militia."[12]

Politicizing Perliger's report meant ignoring very important data.
He had tabulated twenty years' worth of incidents of domestic terrorism and violence and offered some important insights. The KKK
had perpetrated the largest number of attacks (264) in that span, but
it was much less likely than other groups to engage in mass-casualty
attacks that targeted human beings (as opposed to property). Skinheads had engaged in 205 violent acts, numerous enough to secure
second place among radical groups, but these young militants were
much more likely to target human beings (96 percent of the time)
than the KKK (28 percent of the time.) Christian Identity groups,
to whom Perliger attributed only sixty-six attacks since 1991, had
targeted human beings nearly as often as skinheads (94 percent of
the time) but did so through mass-casualty attacks far more often
than skinheads (13.6 percent versus 2.4 percent). The only groups
to "outperform" Christian Identity terrorists were militias, but the
numbers were highly skewed by Timothy McVeigh's and Terry Nichols's 1995 Oklahoma City attack.

That the bombing of the Murrah Building qualifies as a militia
attack illustrates one of the weaknesses of Perliger's report. Without
question, McVeigh and Nichols both actively associated with militia
groups, but they never were officially tied to any group. On the other
hand, McVeigh may have been influenced by Christian Identity ideas
and likely looked for help and assistance from Christian Identity
radicals. Skinheads, as noted in Chapter 14, were highly influenced
by Christian Identity teachings as well as Odinist and Creativity theologies, neither of which are counted in Perliger's statistics. To his
credit, Perliger recognized the influences of Identity on other groups,
writing that the theology:

Functioned as a source of intellectual inspiration and moral justification for the violent activities and operations of ideologically related
movements. Hence, it is not surprising that many of the prominent
ideologues of the white supremacist and anti-federalist movements
intensively cooperated with—and at times saw themselves as part
of—the fundamentalist movement. This dynamic allowed the penetration of non-identity ideas into the movement, and in many ways

facilitated the narrowing of the gaps between the fundamentalist movement and other streams of the American far right.[13]

But his quantitative analysis does not consider the degree to which these movements cross-affiliated and shared ideological influences. As noted time and time again, Identity leaders control and Identity theology permeates many KKK groups and skinhead organizations, even patriot militias. Part of Perliger's problem is his misreading of history. In echoes of the Megiddo report, he asserts that "the fundamentalist movement's militant and violent nature was relatively late to develop. For many years . . . the fundamentalist movement did not produce violent sub-groups."[14] Had he understood the dynamics of groups such as the Christian Defense League, the National States Rights Party, the White Knights of the Ku Klux Klan of Mississippi (under Sam Bowers), or the Minutemen, perhaps he would have been more open to the idea that Identity leaders spent their "early development" appropriating the agenda of groups like the KKK. They did the same over the next four decades with farmers' protest movements, anti-immigration groups, anti-federalist groups, and skinheads, becoming more open about their goals for a race war while the white supremacist movement became more and more decentralized in the face of law enforcement scrutiny.

But for a fortunate stroke of fate, Perliger and others may have become much more aware of this history in the early 1990s. Scott Shepherd, the onetime Grand Dragon for the Tennessee KKK, recently discussed a journey he once took with Byron de la Beckwith, Medgar Evers's convicted assassin. In the late 1980s, Shepherd developed a close relationship with the onetime White Knight; Beckwith even attempted to convince Shepherd to become a Phineas priest. Beckwith rarely asked Shepherd to go on long car rides, but, as Shepherd would learn, this was a special occasion. The trip occurred sometime near the turn of the decade (1980s to 1990s). The destination was Meridian, Mississippi, and a meeting with Sam Bowers. Joining Bowers and Beckwith was J.B. Stoner.

Both Bowers and Stoner had been more or less inactive in recent years—Stoner for the obvious reason that he had only just been released from prison, and Bowers because the WKKKKOM had vanished over time under the management of L.E. Matthews in the 1970s (while Bowers was in prison). They did not discuss the Order at that meeting, but on later occasions Beckwith made it clear to Shepherd that the Silent Brotherhood helped inspire the old hands to return to terrorism. Bowers and Stoner made it clear at the meeting that they wanted back in, and in a major way.

According to Shepherd, the men began outlining the contours of a major terrorist operation. The idea would be to harness the growing skinhead movement, by way of the Hammerskins. Records show that both Stoner and his friend Ed Fields had developed ties to skinheads in Georgia. The plan would involve decentralizing the Hammerskins into strike teams, similar in structure and function to the phantom cells described by Louis Beam. Some signal would trigger the strike teams to begin their operation: blowing up federal buildings and assassinating prominent African Americans. But the 1990s marked renewed interest by law enforcement in solving decades-old civil rights cold cases, such as the 1963 Sixteenth Street Baptist Church bombing (likely masterminded by Stoner) and the murder of voting rights activist Vernon Dahmer (ordered by Bowers). The three old hands at that meeting in Meridian faced law enforcement scrutiny at a level they had not experienced since the 1960s and were forced to abandon their plans. The prosecution of Beckwith in 1994 jump-started a wave of new prosecutions. In 1998 justice also found Sam Bowers, who was convicted of ordering the Dahmer slaying. Both men died in prison, Beckwith in 2001 and Bowers in 2006. Stoner escaped further justice for his past crimes but suffered from ill health, according to Shepherd. He died in 2005 in his home state of Georgia.

If the foiled plot outlined by Stoner, Bowers, and Beckwith at that Meridian meeting bore striking similarities to Identity conspiracies of the past, it was no accident. Bowers, who in 1964 had talked about strike teams and assassination plots to an audience of White Knights days before the Neshoba murders, said that he wanted to revive the old playbook. The three zealots discussed their objective openly in front of Shepherd: "It was a race war plan," they argued, "that was the plan from the start."[15]

APPENDIX: *List of Key People and Groups*

PHOTOGRAPHS

The Reverend Wesley Albert Swift, from California. Once an active leader in a KKK group, Swift formed the Church of Jesus Christ—Christian in 1946. Under his interpretation of the Christian scripture, Armageddon would come from a race war that would "cleanse" the world of Jews and other minorities. Tapes of Swift's sermons were sent across North America through a mailing list and his message was amplified through a network of traveling ministers. Source: FBI Field Office.

Samuel Holloway Bowers, Jr. The Imperial Wizard of the White Knights of the Ku Klux Klan of Mississippi. Bowers was heavily influenced by the racist message of Wesley Swift. Under his leadership, the White Knights were the most violent Klan group in America in the 1960s according to the FBI. Source: The Mississippi Department of Archives and History.

Sidney Crockett Barnes. An extremist who left Florida for Alabama in the 1960s, Barnes was one of Wesley Swift's most devoted followers. He helped spread the Christian Identity message and the vision of an end-times race war to a number of individuals in the southeast, including to a young Tommy Tarrants, who become a terrorist for Sam Bowers. Files show that Barnes plotted to kill Martin Luther King in 1963 and 1964. Source: Jackson Field Office.

J.B. Stoner, a leader and co-founder for the racist National States Rights Party. Stoner would run on the NSRP ticket as their Vice Presidential candidate in 1964. Alongside Connie Lynch, a minister for Wesley Swift, Stoner inflamed audiences across the country with his message of white supremacy. He was one of James Earl Ray's attorneys.

Thomas Albert Tarrants III, aka Tommy Tarrants, in a mug shot taken after his arrest, in 1967, for possession of an illegal firearm. Tarrants was arrested with Sam Bowers after their vehicle was pulled over for reckless driving in Mississippi. Responsible for several acts of violence in Mississippi, Tarrants was not connected to these crimes until May of 1968. Yet he was inexplicably investigated in connection with the King murder within days of the act. Tarrants rejected the Swift message in favor of traditional Christianity in the 1970s and is now an evangelical minister. Source: Jackson Field Office.

Donald Sparks's 1967 FBI Most Wanted Photo. Sparks was a home burglar and a contract killer in a criminal network that would later be popularized as "The Dixie Mafia." FBI records indicate that Sparks was approached with a bounty contract on Martin Luther King, Jr.'s life in 1964 by the White Knights of the Ku Klux Klan of Mississippi. A member of Sparks's criminal gang would later be connected with a bounty offer, from the same Klan, in 1967. Source: FBI.

Above: Bessie Brewer's rooming house the day after King's murder. It shows extensive brush still present, contradicting the claims by some that the area was cleared immediately after King's murder. Some argue that an assassin may have fired from within the brush rather than from the building itself; others assert that the brush was too thick and thus not an ideal shooting location. Source: Shelby County Registry of Deeds.

Above: The picture shows the rear side of Bessie Brewer's rooming house and, specially, Canipe's Amusement Company. The accused assassin, James Earl Ray, allegedly dropped a bundle of incriminating items, including the murder weapon, in the alcove outside Canipe's. Some argue he was afraid he would confront police officers with the material in hand. Source: Shelby County Registry of Deeds.

Above: The rear of Bessie Brewer's rooming House, the side facing the Lorraine Motel, where Martin Luther King, Jr. was staying. Accused assassin James Earl Ray allegedly fired the shot that killed King from the second floor. Source: Shelby County Registry of Deeds.

Above: The bathroom on the second floor of Bessie Brewer's rooming house. This is where law enforcement and prosecutors believe accused assassin James Earl Ray fired the shot that killed King. Source: Shelby County Registry of Deeds.

Above: The view of the Lorraine Motel from the opening in the second floor bathroom window at the rear of Bessie Brewer's rooming house. A shooter would have had a clear view of King from this vantage point. The markings, indicate the location of King's body (C) and his room (B). Source: Shelby County Registry of Deeds.

Above: View of the rear of Bessie Brewer's rooming house from the second floor of the Lorraine Motel across the street. Source: Shelby County Registry of Deeds.

Above: The green blanket that contained several key pieces of allegedly incriminating evidence, including a rifle and binoculars, found at the alcove in front of Canipe's Amusement Company. The material in this bundle would, over time, lead the FBI to James Earl Ray. Ray would claim that someone else planted the material to frame him. Source: Shelby County Registry of Deeds.

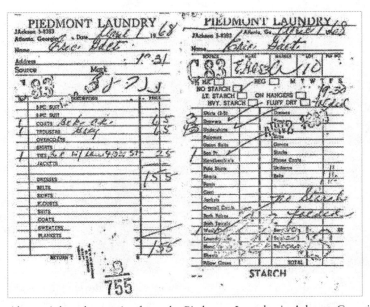

Above: A laundry receipt from the Piedmont Laundry in Atlanta, Georgia, for Eric Galt, James Earl Ray's alias, dated April 1, 1968. This receipt, as well the confirmation from the laundry's owner, presented a dilemma for James Earl Ray and his attorneys. Hoping to avoid the incrimination charge that Ray was stalking King prior to the Memphis murder, Ray asserted that he went to Memphis before King even decided on a return date to lead another sanitation workers' strike. This receipt was strong evidence that Ray first went to Atlanta, King's hometown, and only went to Memphis after King announced his plans. Source: House Select Commitee.

Above: The contents, sans rifle, found wrapped in a green bundle outside of Canipe's Amusement Company. Through diligent work, the FBI was able to trace several of these items to accused assassin James Earl Ray. Source: National Archives.

The Remington Gamemaster 30.06 rifle found in the bundle outside Canipe's restaurant. Authorities claim this was the murder weapon, but ballistics tests were inclusive. The rifle was traced to a gun shop in Birmingham, Alabama, and eventually to James Earl Ray. Ray bought a different weapon the day before but returned that gun for the Gamemaster. The store owner remembered Ray as claiming that he exchanged weapons on the advice of his brother-in-law. Ray claims this was a false reference to Raoul. Source: National Archives.

James Earl Ray's wanted photo, issued by the FBI in their massive manhunt for the alleged King assassin. It was only by the third week of April 1968 that the FBI finally connected Ray to the numerous aliases he used in Memphis and elsewhere. Source: Shelby County of Deeds.

Both of these pictures were separately identified by James Earl Ray as being (or bearing a striking resemblance to) the mysterious figure Raul, the man who Ray claims manipulated his movements and eventually helped frame him for killing King. The photo on the left is of an individual photographed in Dealey Plaza after President John F. Kennedy's assassination; Ray said this person bore a "striking resemblance" to Raul. The photo on the right is a passport picture of an individual identified by Ray's last attorney, William Pepper, as being Raul; Ray positively identified this person as Raul. The Justice Department, in their 2000 investigation, checked this individual's whereabouts on the day of the King murder and determined he had a firm alibi. In either event, the reader is left to judge for himself if Ray's near-definitive identifications of both pictures as Raul are mutually exclusive; e.g. if the two pictures could possibly be identified as the same person by Ray. Source: Justice Department.

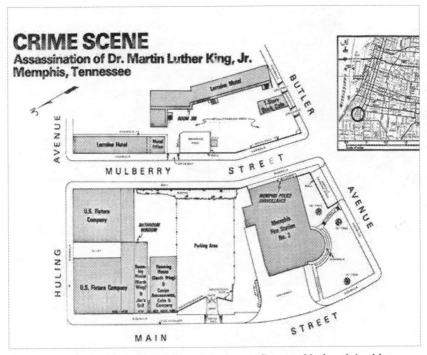

Above: A schematic layout of the crime scene. Source: National Archives.

PEOPLE

Dr. Wesley Swift: A militant extremist and Klan organizer who formed the Church of Jesus Christ Christian in 1946 in Lancaster, California, where he lived, Swift advocated a variation on Christianity that held that Jews were really the offspring of Satan, and that they manipulated other, non-white minorities, into a conspiracy against white Christians. Swift believed the world would be purified of Jews and minorities through a race war. His sermons on these matters, distributed through a network of newsletters and tape recordings, inspired militant white supremacists across the country, including Sam Bowers, J. B Stoner, Sidney Barnes, Colonel William Potter Gale, and others.

Samuel Holloway Bowers: Bowers was the Imperial Wizard, or leader, of the White Knights of the Ku Klux Klan of Mississippi (WKKKK) in the 1960s. Under Bowers's leadership, the WKKKK became, according to the FBI, the most violent Klan group in America. A devoted follower of Wesley Swift, Bowers was personally responsible for plotting the murders of the three civil rights workers in the Mississippi Burning case, and for ordering the firebombing of the home of voting rights activist Vernon Dahmer in 1966, that resulted in Dahmer's death. He also plotted the murder of farmer Ben Chester White in hopes of luring Martin Luther King Jr. into an ambush if King came to protest the White killing. He was investigated by Congress as a potential suspect in King's murder, but investigators never interviewed him. Bowers was convicted for his role in the Mississippi Burning murders in 1967 and sentenced to ten years in prison; he was not convicted for the Dahmer murder until 1998, when he was sentenced to life in prison. He died in prison in 2006.

Jesse Benjamin "J. B." Stoner: A Nazi aficionado, J. B. Stoner was one of the most active and outspoken white supremacists in America from the 1950s on through the 1970s. Stoner was the legal counsel for the supremacist group the National States' Rights Party and one of its leading voices, running for office under its banner on a number of occasions. With his close associate Conrad "Connie" Lynch, a minister in Wesley Swift's church, Stoner led counter-rallies against King's marches and other similar protests. He was suspected of plotting numerous bombings across the Southeast against black and Jewish targets. He offered a contract on Martin Luther King Jr.'s life in 1958, and was investigated by Congress in the 1970s as a possible suspect in King's murder. He was protected by attorney-client privilege, however, as he was one of convicted assassin James Earl Ray's attorneys in 1968–69. Stoner also had connections to James Venable and Joseph Milteer; some of the leading members of the White Knights of the Ku Klux Klan of Mississippi actively supported Stoner. Stoner was speaking to a several White Knights on the evening of April 4, 1968, when MLK was killed.

James Venable: The longtime leader of the National Knights of the Ku Klux Klan (NKKKK), the second-largest KKK group in America in the 1960s, headquartered in Stone Mountain, Georgia, with subordinate groups across the country as far as California. Venable shared a law office with J. B. Stoner in Atlanta, Georgia. Venable was suspected of plotting to kill Martin Luther King Jr., with Stoner, in 1965. Venable also knew Joseph Milteer and employed Floyd "Buddy" Ayers.

Floyd "Buddy" Ayers: An associate of James Venable, Ayers was, according to one witness, the "bagman" for the King murder, supplying money from Atlanta to Mississippi in connection with a bounty offer on Dr. King. Ayers gained national attention when he infiltrated MLK's funeral in 1968, and then later allegedly tried to kidnap MLK's father.

Joseph Milteer: A rabid white supremacist, Joseph Milteer was an active supporter of the National States' Rights Party, a devoted follower of Wesley Swift, and the founder of his own, independent (racist) political group, the Constitution Party. Independently wealthy, Milteer traveled the country as a salesman, often meeting with other white supremacists, such as James Venable. Milteer is famous for having been secretly caught on tape, two weeks before the assassination of President John F. Kennedy, predicting JFK's assassination with a high-powered rifle from a high-story building. On that same tape, he said that others were plotting to kill MLK. Milteer was in Atlanta, Georgia, when James Earl Ray fled to that city after the murder of Martin Luther King Jr. A confidential source of researcher Lamar Waldron says that Milteer secretly raised the money to kill King in 1968.

Colonel William Potter Gale: Gale was a chief aide to General Douglas MacArthur before returning to the United States and becoming one of the leading white supremacists in the country. He was a minister in the Church of Jesus Christ Christian and formed his own paramilitary group, the California Rangers. In the 1970s, Gale was investigated by Congress as a suspect in the King murder. Congress specifically connected Gale to a King murder plot involving Admiral John Crommelin, Noah Jefferson Carden, and Sidney Crockett Barnes.

Admiral John Crommelin: A WWII naval hero before entering civilian life and becoming one of the major voices of white supremacy in the nation, he was a leading member of the National States' Rights Party and ran on the party's ticket for vice president of the United States of America in 1960. He was also a devoted follower of Wesley Swift. He helped indoctrinate Thomas Tarrants into Swift's worldview. He was also investigated by Congress as a suspect in the King assassination in the late 1970s; he cooperated but denied he had any involvement.

Noah Jefferson Carden: A member of the White Citizens' Council of Mobile, Alabama, a group that led "formal" opposition to the civil rights movement in that city. He was close to Sidney Barnes and also knew Thomas Tarrants. He was investigated by Congress as a suspect in the King assassination.

Sidney Crockett Barnes: A white supremacist from Florida who was forced to flee to Mobile, Alabama, in the early 1960s because he was "too hot" for authorities. Barnes would later become a minister in Wesley Swift's church. He played tapes of Swift for anyone who would listen, and helped indoctrinate many into Swift's cause, including a young Thomas Albert Tarrants III and Kathy Ainsworth. Swift was investigated by Congress as a suspect in the King assassination in the late 1970s (see above). He openly refused to cooperate with the investigation. In 1968, he moved to Jackson, Mississippi, where he was closely associated with a number of men in the White Knights of the Ku Klux Klan of Mississippi, including Danny Joe Hawkins.

Danny Joe Hawkins: A militant member of the White Knights of Mississippi, Hawkins's entire family, especially his father, Joe Denver Hawkins, were known for their extreme hatred of blacks and Jews. Hawkins, along with Tommy Tarrants and Kathy Ainsworth, participated in a series of bombings from 1967 to 1968. On April 4, 1968, the day MLK died, Hawkins was arrested going the wrong way on a one-way street after attending J. B. Stoner's rally in the WKKKK stronghold of Meridian, Mississippi.

Kathy Ainsworth: A young Mississippi schoolteacher who led a double life as one of the chief terrorists of the WKKKK in 1967–68, Ainsworth was raised by her white supremacist mother, Margaret Capomacchia, to hate Jews and blacks, She was very close to Sidney Crockett Barnes, who gave her away at her wedding. Ainsworth joined Danny Joe Hawkins and Tommy Tarrants in a string of attacks against black and Jewish targets in 1967–1968. In one of those attacks, in Meridian, Mississippi, in June 1968, she replaced Danny Joe Hawkins as Tarrants's partner-in-crime, only to be shot and killed in a sting operation. Her mother would later relay supposed inside information to FBI informant Willie Somersett, information related to the King murder that implicated Tommy Tarrants.

Thomas Albert Tarrants III, a.k.a. "Tommy" or "The Man": Tarrants was the self-described chief terrorist for the White Knights of the Ku Klux Klan of Mississippi in 1967–1968. Only in his twenties at the time, Tarrants was already closely affiliated with a number of white supremacist leaders, notably John Crommelin and Sidney Barnes. Having engaged in "petty" acts of racism from his high school days in 1963–66, Tarrants moved to Laurel, Mississippi, in 1967 and convinced Sam Bowers to use him in violent bombing operations directed at black and Jewish targets. He joined forces with Kathy Ainsworth and Danny Joe Hawkins. His participation was unknown to the FBI until late May 1968. In the week prior to King's murder, Tarrants went "underground" to launch a guerilla campaign against the U.S. government. The reporter Jack Nelson includes references that suggest Tarrants may have been considering assassinating MLK, and he was a person-of-interest to the FBI in the immediate wake of King's murder. Tarrants was wounded in the June 1968 sting operation that killed Ainsworth. He was sentenced to thirty years in prison, but was released early after he made a conversion to mainstream Christianity. He is now an active evangelical minister who has renounced his past views and ways. He denies any involvement in the King murder, and the authors believe efforts were made to frame him for the crime.

Donald Eugene Sparks: A major criminal in the 1960s, he was known for burglaries but was also a contract killer. His exploits eventually earned him a place on the FBI's Ten Most Wanted List. He was part of a gang of traveling criminals known as the new James gang, after its informal leader, Jerry Ray James. The group was concentrated in Oklahoma and included his close associate Rubie Charles Jenkins, among others. Law enforcement would later consider the Jerry Ray James gang, and many others like it, as a major criminal threat, and label it the "Dixie Mafia," even though these groups lacked the organization of the Sicilian Mafia and were not all concentrated in the Southeast. The so-called "Dixie Mafia" may have, however, been responsible for more killings than other organized crime groups in the 1970s. Separate reports say that Sparks was approached with an offer to kill Martin Luther King Jr. by the WKKKK in 1964.

LeRoy McManaman: Described by the FBI as a "big time criminal operator," McManaman was a career miscreant who was known for organizing a string of home burglaries in Kansas and for running an interstate car-theft ring with Rubie Charles Jenkins. Jenkins said that McManaman, who spent considerable time in Oklahoma, was a part of a gang with Jenkins and Sparks. McManaman is alleged to have approached a fellow, soon-to-be-released inmate, Donald Nissen, with a $100,000 bounty offer on MLK's life in 1967. Nissen reported that plot to the FBI, who superficially dismissed it.

GROUPS

The Church of Jesus Christ Christian (CJCC): This is the ministry formed by Wesley Swift in 1946 that preached an extreme and violent form of Christian Identity beliefs. These included the ideas that Jews were the offspring of Satan and that other minorities were subhuman. A major tenet for the church was the idea that a race war would purify the world, especially of Jews. This ideology continues to have a powerful influence over white supremacists and racist groups to this day.

The White Knights of the Ku Klux Klan of Mississippi (WKKKK): The most violent Klan group in America, led by Samuel H. Bowers, its Imperial Wizard, the WKKKK was formed in December 1963 with members from the Original Knights of the Ku Klux Klan (out of Louisiana) and others in Mississippi. These men were disaffected with the lackluster response to integration in the South, and pushed for greater and bolder acts of violence. At its peak from 1964 to 1965, the White Knights membership may have had reached ten thousand, though by 1968 membership was less than a few hundred. The FBI credits the group with over three hundred separate acts of violence; most notably, the White Knights are credited with killing three civil rights workers in Neshoba County, Mississippi (the Mississippi Burning murders); killing voting rights activist Vernon Dahmer in 1966; and a wave of bombings against black and Jewish targets from the fall of 1967 on through the summer of 1968. Its most notable members, beyond Bowers, included Danny Joe and Joe Denver Hawkins, Burris Dunn, Julius Harper, Alton Wayne and Raymond Roberts, Byron de la Beckwith, Deavours Nix, and L. E. Matthews. Kathy Ainsworth and Thomas Tarrants may have been "informal" members of the group, as some documents describe them as members of the "Swift Underground" who performed terrorist acts on behalf of the WKKKK.

The National States' Rights Party (NSRP): The NSPR was the overt, political face of white supremacy in the 1960s, even as it covertly recruited and inspired groups and individuals to perform acts of extreme violence. Formed by J. B. Stoner and Edward Fields in 1958, the group ran candidates for office, including vicepresident of the United States, although they never received even a small fraction of the national vote. On the other hand, the NSRP was actively involved in some of the most violent acts of resistance to integration in America, acts so extreme that they even offended local Klan groups, such as the United Klans of America in Alabama. The NSRP had its headquarters in Atlanta, Georgia, and then in Birmingham, Alabama, and it focused its activities in the Southeast. Its major publication, *The Thunderbolt*, was a major source of information for racists across the nation.

The National Knights of the Ku Klux Klan (NKKKK): This was, in the 1960s, the second-largest Klan organization in the United States, after the United Klans of America (UKA), in terms of membership. Headquartered in Stone Mountain, Georgia, the NKKKKwas led by Imperial Wizard James Venable. The NKKKK had affiliated groups and Klaverns across the country, including in Ohio and California. Notably, the California Knights of the Ku Klux Klan (CKKKK), formed in 1966 and led by Wesley Swift minister William V. Fowler, were an offshoot of the NKKKK. James Venable spoke to the CKKKK on several occasions in 1967.

The "traveling criminals" or "Crossroaders" or "Dixie Mafia": These were loosely knit groups of outlaws willing to commit crimes, especially robbery and theft, across long distances. More of a phenomenon than an official organization, career criminals would join forces in decentralized gangs and work across state lines for major "jobs." Primarily engaged in bootlegging across state lines as some states remained "dry" after Prohibition was repealed in 1934, these criminals expanded their activities in the late 1950s and through the 1960s. This became more and more common as increasingly available phone communication and interstate travel, by plane or over the new interstate highway system, made cross-state activity more possible. The "traveling criminals" were especially active in two regions: the Southeast (stretching from the Mississippi Delta to Florida) and the Great Plains. Not to be confused with the Sicilian Mafia, these criminals lacked a hierarchy and were far less structured than conventional, organized crime syndicates. They were often, at the same time, more bold than the Sicilian Mafia, targeting even law enforcement officials (famously Sheriff Buford Pusser in Tennessee) and federal judges. By the 1970s, this loose-knit coalition was one of the major forces for criminal activity in the United States, with some crediting its members as having committed more actual killings than the Sicilian Mafia. In the late '60s and early '70s, in response to this growing criminal gang, law enforcement began using the shorthand "Dixie Mafia," even though both terms are misnomers.

White Citizens Councils: These groups were formed, major city by major city, in the 1950s after the *Brown v. Board of Education* decision by the U.S. Supreme Court set the stage for ending segregation; their goal was to "formally" undermine integration. Often comprised of prominent business and civic leaders, they used their influence and resources to outwardly oppose the civil rights movement in a more "respectable" and legal way than that of the Ku Klux Klan. However, many White Citizens' Council members were directly and indirectly tied to more violent groups, such as the NSRP and the KKK, even if those connections were often informal and covert. Joseph Milteer claimed to be an "informal" member of the Atlanta White Citizens' Council, and Noah Jefferson Carden was a member of the Mobile White Citizens' Council. Both men were connected with purported plots to kill Martin Luther King Jr.

Americans for the Preservation of the White Race (APWR): Formed in the mid-1960s in Mississippi, this group was similar to the White Citizens Councils, in providing an outwardly "civil" response when undermining integration efforts. The group would, for instance, raise money for the defense funds for racists accused of hate crimes or publish newsletters opposing the integration of schools. However, the FBI recognized the APWR as a front for the WKKKK, and its most prominent members and leaders were almost all, to a person, followers of Sam Bowers.

ACKNOWLEDGMENTS

If this book forces a new dialogue about terrorism and fosters a deeper understanding of the nature of religious violence in American history, as I hope it will, it does so only because of the help of many people. The first iteration of my thesis was explored in a cowritten book, *The Awful Grace of God: Religious Terrorism, White Supremacy, and the Unsolved Murder of Martin Luther King Jr.*, in 2012. The more developed argument in *America's Secret Jihad* would not have been possible without the insights of my *Awful Grace of God* coauthor, Larry Hancock. Publisher Charlie Winton and the staff at Counterpoint have shown great patience and enthusiasm for my research, despite the controversial nature of the thesis. A very special thanks must go to developmental editor Eric Brandt for his input and care in preparing the manuscript. I am grateful to my students,—April Nicklaus, Swetha Subramaniam, Rithesh Neelamagam and Niranjan Shankar—for helping with the editing process. Jerry Mitchell, an award-winning investigative reporter for the Jackson (Mississippi) *Clarion-Ledger*, has been an inspiration and a resource for my investigation of civil rights cold cases. Charles Faulkner provided important information for my work on the King assassination. Researcher Ernie Lazar donated a treasure trove of FBI and other material—a lifetime of work—which is now available to researchers and historians for free in a fully text-searchable format online; the late Harold Weisberg did the same through the archives at Hood College; programmer and historian Rex Bradford did the same (albeit through a paid service) for The Mary Ferrell Foundation. This material, coupled with documents available at the National Archives and Research Administration in Maryland, whose staff is always helpful, was fundamental to my research. The FBI's Freedom of Information Act staff was likewise very helpful and responsive to my requests for new documents. Several witnesses, among them Donald Nissen, Scott Shepherd, Bob Eddy, and former Alabama Attorney General Bill Baxley, also provided key insights for a number of chapters. Finally, my family and friends—my parents especially—have done nothing but encourage my efforts, on this and everything else I do. This book is dedicated to them.

NOTES

CHAPTER 1

1. Jewish Telegraphic Agency, "Attempt to Dynamite Charlotte Synagogue Fails; Police Investigate," JTA, November 27, 1957, http://www.jta.org/1957/11/27/archive/attempt-to-dynamite-charlotte-synagogue-fails-police-investigate#ixzz3GpJQ8aRo.

2. Jewish Telegraphic Agency, "FBI Investigates Bombing of Jewish Centers in Miami and Nashville," JTA, March 18, 1958, http://www.jta.org/1958/03/18/archive/f-b-i-investigates-bombing-of-jewish-centers-in-miami-and-nashville#ixzz3GpLZfNLU.

3. Clive Webb, "Counterblast: How the Atlanta Temple Bombing Strengthened the Civil Rights Cause," Southern Spaces, June 22, 2009, www.southernspaces.org/2009/counterblast-how-atlanta-temple-bombing-strengthened-civil-rights-cause.

4. JTA, "FBI Investigates."

5. Jewish Telegraphic Agency, "Jews in Jacksonville Map Plans for Checking Anti-Jewish Terror," JTA, April 30, 1958, http://www.jta.org/1958/04/30/archive/jews-in-jacksonville-map-plans-for-checking-anti-jewish-terror.

6. John McKay, *It Happened in Atlanta: Remarkable Events That Shaped History* (Guilford, CT: Morris Book Publishing, 2011), 110.

7. Jewish Telegraphic Agency, "Eisenhower Condemns Bombers of Synagogues as 'Gangsters,'" JTA, October 16, 1958, http://www.jta.org/1958/10/16/archive/eisenhower-condemns-bombers-of-synagogues-as-gangsters#ixzz3P6Gla3xr.

8. JTA, "FBI Investigates."

9. Webb, "Counterblast."

10. Jewish Telegraphic Agency, "People in South Not Influenced by Ku Klux Klan Anti-Jewish Propaganda," JTA, June 16, 1958, http://www.jta.org/1958/06/16/archive/people-in-south-not-influenced-by-ku-klux-klan-anti-jewish-propaganda#ixzz3P6L6wqsv.

11. Melissa Fay Greene, *The Temple Bombing* (New York: Da Capo Press, 1996), 179.

12. Stuart Wexler and Larry Hancock, *The Awful Grace of God: Religious Terrorism, White Supremacy, and the Unsolved Murder of Martin Luther King Jr.* (Berkeley, CA: Counterpoint Press, 2012), 51.

13. "Speech to the Aryan Nations Congress in Hayden Lake, Idaho, in 1994," YouTube, uploaded by priapus2222 on August 15, 2010, http://www.youtube.com/watch?v=nUsHMymEJag.

14. Anti-Defamation League of B'nai B'rith, "Anti-Semitism in the United States in 1947," Documenting Maine Jews, accessed April 17, 2015, http://mainejews.org/docs/Colby/ADLReportAntiSemitism1947.pdf.

15. Clive Webb, *Fight against Fear: Southern Jews and Black Civil Rights* (Athens: University of Georgia Press, 2011), 52.

CHAPTER 2

1. Webb, "Counterblast."

2. Federal Bureau of Investigation, "National States Rights Party, Part 1 of 1," FBI, accessed April 16, 2015, http://vault.fbi.gov/National%20States%20Rights%20Party/National%20States%20Rights%20Party%20Part%201%20of%201%20/view.

3. Raymond Arsenault, *Freedom Riders: 1961 and the Struggle for Racial Justice* (Oxford: Oxford University Press, 2006), 92.

4. Wexler and Hancock, *Awful Grace of God,* 55.

5. Patsy Sims, *The Klan,* 2nd ed. (Lexington: University Press of Kentucky, 1996), 135.

6. Ibid.

7. Wexler and Hancock, *Awful Grace of God,* 66.

8. Clive Webb, *Rabble Rousers: The American Far Right in the Civil Rights Era* (Athens: University of Georgia Press, 2011), 106.

9. Our Campaigns, "Faubus, Orval E.," Our Campaigns, accessed March 3, 2015, http://www.ourcampaigns.com/CandidateDetail.html ?CandidateID=4200.

10. Our Campaigns, "Crommelin, John G.," Our Campaigns, accessed March 3, 2015, http://www.ourcampaigns.com/CandidateDetail.html ?CandidateID=19159.

11. Our Campaigns, "Kasper, John," Our Campaigns, accessed March 3, 2015, http://www.ourcampaigns.com/CandidateDetail.html?Candidate ID=4498.

12. National States Rights Party, "They Called It the Speech of the Century," *Thunderbolt,* April 1962, https://archive.org/stream/foia_NSRP -Chicago-2A/NSRP-Chicago-2A#page/n41/mode/2up/search/scheme.

13. *Daytona Beach Morning Journal,* "How about These 'Outsiders'?" *Daytona Beach Morning Journal*, August 5, 1964, http://news.google

.com/newspapers?nid=1873&dat=19640805&id=dpooAAAAIBA
-J&sjid=k8wEAAAAIBAJ&pg=716,781543.

14. Stephen E. Atkins, *Encyclopedia of Right-Wing Extremism in Modern American History* (Santa Barbara, CA: ABC-CLIO, 2011), 137.

15. Edwin Black, "Eugenics and the Nazis: The California Connection," SFGate, November 9, 2003, http://www.sfgate.com/opinion/article /Eugenics-and-the-Nazis-the-California-2549771.php.

16. Nicholas Goodrick-Clarke, *Black Sun: Aryan Cults, Esoteric Nazism, and the Politics of Identity* (New York: NYU Press, 2003), 237.

17. Lothrop Stoddard, *The Rising Tide of Color against White World Supremacy* (New York: Scribner, 1921), 90–91.

18. Goodrick-Clarke, *Black Sun*, 237.

19. Hiram Wesley Evans, "The Klan's Fight for Americanism," North American Review, 1926, http://faculty.atu.edu/cbrucker/Engl5383/Evans.htm.

20. Committee on Un-American Activities, "Activities of the Ku Klux Klan Organizations in the United States," Internet Archive, accessed April 16, 2015, https://archive.org/stream/activitiesofkukl03unit#page/2486 /mode/2up/search/romans.

21. Ibid.

22. Michael Barkun, *Religion and the Racist Right: The Origins of the Christian Identity Movement* (Chapel Hill: UNC Press Books, 1997), 30–32.

23. Ibid.

24. Clarence Taylor, *Reds at the Blackboard: Communism, Civil Rights, and the New York City Teachers Union* (New York: Columbia University Press, 2013), 197.

25. Alan Brinkley, *Voices of Protest: Huey Long, Father Coughlin, and the Great Depression* (New York: Knopf Doubleday, 2011), 212.

26. Ibid., 171.

27. S.T. Joshi, *Documents of American Prejudice: An Anthology of Writings on Race from Thomas Jefferson to David Duke* (New York: Basic Books, 1999), 413.

28. Robert Singerman, "Contemporary Racist and Judeophobic Ideology Discovers the Khazars, or, Who Really Are the Jews?" (lecture, Thirty-ninth Annual Convention, Association of Jewish Libraries, Brooklyn, 2004).

29. Barkun, *Religion and the Racist Right*, 177.

30. Stephen R. Haynes, *Noah's Curse: The Biblical Justification of American Slavery* (Oxford: Oxford University Press, 2002), 73–75, 133, 203–205.

31. Wexler and Hancock, *Awful Grace of God*, 93.

32. Ibid., 24.

33. Michael Newton, *The Ku Klux Klan: History, Organization, Language, Influence, and Activities of America's Most Notorious Secret Society* (Jefferson, NC: McFarland and Company, 2007), 170.

34. Wexler and Hancock, *Awful Grace of God*, 40.

35. Ibid., 37.

36. D. Boylan, "A League of Their Own: A Look inside the Christian Defense League," Cuban Information Archives, 2004, http://cuban-exile .com/doc_026-050/doc0tml.

37. Office of the Attorney General, "Para-Military Organizations in California," Harold Weisberg Archive, Hood College, accessed April 17, 2015, http://jfk.hood.edu/Collection/Weisberg%20Subject%20 Index%20Files/L%20Disk/Lynch%20Report/Item%2001.pdf.

38. Federal Bureau of Investigation, "Wallace, Hugh Allen, Et al, Bombing of the Temple, Atlanta Georgia, October Twelve Last, Information Concerning," Internet Archive, accessed April 17, 2015, https://archive.org /stream/foia_Allen_Wallace_H.-HQ-9/Allen_Wallace_H.-HQ-9#page /n27/mode/2up/search/destroy.

CHAPTER 3

1. Wesley Swift, "As in the Days of Noah, 9-30-62" Wesley Swift Library, accessed April 16, 2015, http://swift.christogenea.org/book/export /html/528.

2. Wright Thompson, "The Ghosts of Mississippi," ESPN: Outside the Lines, accessed April 16, 2015, http://sports.espn.go.com/espn/eticket /story?page=mississippi62.

3. Ibid.

4. Ibid.

5. Ibid.

6. Millard J. Erickson, *A Basic Guide to Eschatology: Making Sense of the Millennium* (Grand Rapids, MI: Baker Books, 1998).

7. Conrad Gaard, "Spotlight on the Great Conspiracy," Israel Elect of Zion, accessed April 17, 2015, http://israelect.com/reference/Conrad Gaard/Spotlight%20on%20the%20Great%20Conspiracy.htm.

8. Barkun, *Religion and the Racist Right,* 240.

9. Ibid., 258.

10. Swift, "As in the Days of Noah."

11. Chester Quarles, *Christian Identity: The Aryan American Bloodline Religion,* (Jefferson, NC: McFarland and Company, 2004), 180.

12. Thomas A. Tarrants, *The Conversion of a Klansman: The Story of a Former Ku Klux Klan Terrorist* (Garden City, NY: Doubleday, 1979).

13. Ibid., 50.

14. Wesley Swift, "Armageddon—Local and Worldwide (5-5-63)," Wesley Swift Library, accessed April 16, 2015, http://swift.christogenea.org /content/armageddon-local-and-worldwide-5-5-63.

15. Martin Luther King Jr., "Letter from a Birmingham Jail," African Studies Center, University of Pennsylvania, accessed April 16, 2015, http://www.africa.upenn.edu/Articles_Gen/Letter_Birmingham.html.

16. Associated Press, "Federal Troops Poised to Move into Birmingham,"

Quebec Chronicle-Telegraph, May 13, 1963, https://news.google.com /newspapers?nid=957&dat=19630513&id=eoRhAAAAIBAJ&sjid =OswFAAAAIBAJ&pg=2700,2625710&hl=en.

17. Wesley Swift, "Evidence of Divine Assistance (5-13-63)," Wesley Swift Library, accessed April 16, 2015, http://swift.christogenea.org /content/evidence-divine-assistance-5-13-63.

18. John C. Henegan, "Medgar W. Evers—'Turn Me Loose,'" Capital Area Bar Association, May 2013, http://www.caba.ms/articles/features /medgar-evers-turn-me-loose.html.

19. Wesley Swift, "Strategy of the False Prophet (6-23-63)," Wesley Swift Library, accessed April 16, 2015, http://swift.christogenea.org /content/strategy-false-prophet-6-23-63.

CHAPTER 4

1. Federal Bureau of Investigation. "Airtel from SAC Miami to FBI Director re: BAPBOB, Sidney Crockette Barnes a.k.a. Racial Matters," FBI, March 12, 1964. http://mlkkpp01.stanford.edu/index.php/ encyclopedia/documentsentry/doc_eulogy_for_the_martyred_children

2. United Press International, "Bomb Hurled into Church from Auto," *St. Petersburg Times,* September 16, 1963, https://news.google.com /newspapers?nid=888&dat=19630916&id=xp5PAAAAIBAJ&sjid=NFIDA AAAIBAJ&pg=5701,2906766&hl=en.

3. Ibid.

4. Martin Luther King Jr., "Eulogy for the Martyred Children," Martin Luther King Jr. Research and Education Institute, accessed April 16, 2015, http://mlk-kpp01.stanford.edu/index.php/kingpapers/article /eulogy_for_the_martyred_children/.

5. Mike Clary, "Birmingham's Painful Past Reopened," *Los Angeles Times,* April 14, 2001, http://articles.latimes.com/2001/apr/14/news/mn-50901.

6. Diane McWhorter, *Carry Me Home: Birmingham, Alabama, the Climactic Battle of the Civil Rights Revolution* (New York: Simon & Schuster, 2001), 114–15.

7. McWhorter, *Carry Me Home*; Petric J. Smith, *Long Time Coming: An Insider's Story into the Birmingham Church Bombing That Rocked the World* (Birmingham, AL: Crane Hill, 1994); T.K. Thorne, *Last Chance for Justice: How Relentless Investigators Uncovered New Evidence Convicting the Birmingham Church Bombers* (Chicago: Chicago Review Press, 2013). All of these books were valuable in reconstructing basic events.

8. His name is being withheld because he is still alive.

9. Pamela Colloff, "The Sins of the Father," *Texas Monthly,* April 2000.

10. David Mark Chalmers, *Backfire: How the Ku Klux Klan Helped the Civil Rights Movement* (Lanham, MD: Rowman & Littlefield, 2005), 19.

11. Susan Willoughby Anderson, "The Past on Trial: The Sixteenth Street

Church Bombing and Civil Rights History," American Bar Foundation, accessed April 16, 2015, http://www.americanbarfoundation.org
/uploads/cms/documents/anderson_abf_talk_nov_2010.pdf; see foot
note on page 17.

12. Gary May, *The Informant: The FBI, The Ku Klux Klan, and the Murder
of Viola Liuzzo* (New Haven, CT: Yale University Press, 2008), 102.

13. McWhorter, *Carry Me Home,* 540.

14. Gary May, "Forty Years for Justice: Did the FBI Cover for the Birmingham Bombers?" *Newsweek/Daily Beast,* September 15, 2013,
http://www.thedailybeast.com/articles/2013/09/15/40-years-for-
justice-did-the-fbi-cover-for-the-birmingham-bombers.html.

15. Birmingham Police Department, "Interview with Phillip Maybry," File
1125.3.3, Alabama Police Department Surveillance Files 1947–1980,
Birmingham Public Library Archives. This document appears to be an
FBI file saved by the Birmingham Police Department, but the cover
page that might provide FBI information is missing.

16. Dan Carter, *The Politics of Rage: George Wallace and the Origins of
the New Conservativism* (Baton Rouge: LSU Press, 2000); see endnote
25 on page 490.

17. Thorne, *Last Chance,* unpaginated.

18. Bob Eddy, interview with the author, September 6, 2013.

19. Federal Bureau of Investigation, "Memorandum for the Attorney General," FBI, accessed April 16, 2015, http://vault.fbi.gov/16th%20Street
%20Church%20Bombing%20/16th%20Street%20Church%20
Bombing%20Part%2047%20of%2050/view.

20. Ibid.

21. Bill Fleming, interview with the author, September 9, 2013.

22. William Baxley, interview with the author, August 21, 2013.

23. Stephen E. Atkins, *The Encyclopedia of Right-Wing Extremism in
Modern American History* (Santa Barbara, CA: ABC-CLIO, 2011), 42.

24. Ibid.

25. Carter, *Politics of Rage,* 189.

26. Swift, "Armageddon."

27. Ed King, interview with the author, September 25, 2014.

28. Ibid.

CHAPTER 5

1. Douglas O. Linder, "The Mississippi Burning Trial (U.S. v. Price, et
al.)," Famous Trials, accessed April 16, 2015, http://law2.umkc.edu
/faculty/projects/ftrials/price&bowers/Account.html. The preceding account draws heavily from Professor Linder's excellent Web source.
Subsequent endnotes reference subdivisions within Linder's website.

2. Ibid.

3. Federal Bureau of Investigation, "Confession of Horace Doyle

Barnette," FBI, accessed April 16. 2015, http://law2.umkc.edu/faculty /projects/ftrials/price&bowers/barneteconfession.html.

4. Ibid.

5. Robert Cohen, *Freedom's Orator: Mario Savio and the Radical Legacy of the 1960s* (London: Oxford University Press, 2009), 52.

6. Sims, *Klan*, 241.

7. Charles Marsh, *God's Long Hot Summer: Stories of Faith and Civil Rights* (Princeton, NJ: Princeton University Press, 1999), 63.

8. Ibid., 60.

9. Ibid., 54.

10. William H. McIlhany, *Klandestine: The Untold Story of Delmar Dennis and His Role in the FBI's War against the Ku Klux Klan* (New York: Arlington House, 1975), 38–47.

11. Douglas O. Linder, "Sam Bowers," Famous Trials, accessed April 16, 2015, http://law2.umkc.edu/faculty/projects/ftrials/price&bowers /Bowers.htm.

12. "The Klan Ledger," Candy Brown Papers, Wisconsin Historical Society: Freedom Summer Digital Collection, accessed April 16, 2015, http://cdm15932.contentdm.oclc.org/cdm/ref/collection/p15932col2 /id/34854.

13. Ibid.

14. Marsh, *God's Long Hot Summer,* 64–66.

15. Rebecca N. Ferguson, *The Handy History Answer Book* (Canton, MI: Visible Ink Press, 2005), 201.

16. Federal Bureau of Investigation, "FROM: SAC Jackson to Director; Reference Bureau airtel set out instances of threats from the main file on King," Mary Ferrell Foundation, accessed April 16, 2015, http:// www.maryferrell.org/mffweb/archive/viewer/showDoc.do?doc Id=145174&relPageId=33. The document has Bowers warning two men who approached him with an offer to kill King to be cautious. On the other hand, he appears to have assigned two other men to kill King with "high powered rifles" that same summer (1964). That fact becomes interesting in our discussion of the alpha plot.

CHAPTER 6

1. Malcolm X, "To Mississippi Youth," *Malcolm X Speaks: Selected Speeches and Statements* (New York: Grove Press, 1965), 139.

2. Ibid., 143.

3. Ibid., 145.

4. Rufus Burrow Jr., *A Child Shall Lead Them: Martin Luther King Jr., Young People, and the Movement* (Minneapolis: Augsburg Fortress Publishers, 2014), 195–96.

5. Akinyele Omowale Umoja, *We Will Shoot Back: Armed Resistance in the Mississippi Freedom Movement* (New York: NYU Press, 2013), 120.

6. Associated Press, "Harlem Rioting Leaves One Dead," *Tuscaloosa News*, July 20, 1964, https://news.google.com/newspapers?nid=1817 &dat=19640720&id=FxAdAAAAIBAJ&sjid=-poEAAAAIBAJ&pg =5339,2725361&hl=en.

7. United Press International, "Curfew Extended for Third Day in Riot-Torn Rochester," Bulletin, July 27, 1964, https://news.google.com /newspapers?nid=1243&dat=19640727&id=J_hYAAAAIBAJ& sjid=TvcDAAAAIBAJ&pg=4880,4815124&hl=en.

8. Ellesia Ann Blaque, "Philadelphia (Pennsylvania) Riot of 1964," in *The Encyclopedia of American Race Riots,* vol. 2, eds. Walter C. Rucker and James N. Upton (Westport, CT: Greenwood Publishing Group, 2007), 507.

9. William J. Collins and Robert A. Margo, "The Economic Aftermath of the 1960s Riots in American Cities: Evidence from Property Values," National Bureau of Economic Research 10493 (May 2004): 22, Table 1.

10. Eric Avila, "Social Flashpoints," in *A Companion to Los Angeles,* eds. William Deverell and Greg Hise (Hoboken, NJ: John Wiley & Sons, 2010), 96.

11. Martin Luther King Jr., "MLK Speaks to the People of Watts," King Center, accessed April 16, 2015, http://www.thekingcenter.org/archive /document/mlk-speaks-people-watts.

12. Ibid. The speaker who responds to King is not identified.

13. Jim Vertuno, "LBJ Library Releases Tapes Showing King Feared Race War," *Times Daily,* April 13, 2002, https://news.google.com /newspapers?nid=1842&dat=20020413&id=E2weAAAAIBAJ& sjid=VskEAAAAIBA*AwfulGraceofGod*J&pg=2671,1610048&hl=en.

14. Wexler and Hancock, 73–74.

15. Ibid.

16. Ibid.

17. Collins and Margo, *Economic Aftermath.*

18. Donald Jason, "Guards Bayonet Hecklers in Cicero's Rights March," *New York Times,* September 5, 1966, 1.

19. Stokely Carmichael, "Black Power," *American Rhetoric,* accessed April 16, 2015, http://www.americanrhetoric.com/speeches/stokely carmichaelblackpower.html.

20. James T. Patterson, *Grand Expectations: The United States: 1945–1974* (London: Oxford University Press, 1996), 658.

21. United Press International, "Baltimore Ripped by Violence," *Bulletin,* July 29, 1966, https://news.google.com/newspapers?nid =1243&dat=19660729&id=-_5XAAAAIBAJ&sjid=JPcDAAAAIBAJ&pg =6427,457917&hl=en.

22. Wesley Swift, "The Coming Liberation of America (1-30-66)," Wesley Swift Library, accessed April 16, 2015, http://swift.christogenea.org /content/coming-liberation-america-1-30-66.

23. Boylan, "A League of Their Own."

24. City of Miami Police Department, "Report of Detective Lochart F. Gracey, Jr.," Harold Weisberg Archive, Hood College, accessed April 16, 2015, http://jfk.hood.edu/Collection/Weisberg%20Subject%20 Index%20Files/M%20Disk/Milteer%20J%20A/Item%2009.pdf.

25. Minutemen, "A Short History of the Minutemen," Harold Weisberg Archive, Hood College, accessed April 16, 2015, http://jfk.hood.edu /Collection/Weisberg%20Subject%20Index%20Files/M%20Disk /Minutemen/Item%2001.pdf.

26. Eric Norden, "The Paramilitary Right," *Playboy 16,* no. 6 (1969), Harold Weisberg Archive, Hood College, accessed April 16, 2015, http://jfk.hood.edu/Collection/Weisberg%20Subject%20Index%20 Files/M%20Disk/Minutemen/Item%2006.pdf.

27. Ibid.

28. William Turner, "The Minutemen (The Spirit of '66)," *Ramparts,* January 1967, Harold Weisberg Archive, Hood College, accessed April 16, 2015, http://jfk.hood.edu/Collection/Weisberg%20Subject%20 Index%20Files/F%20Disk/FBI/FBI%20to%201967/Item%2037.pdf.

29. Ibid.

30. Norden, "Paramilitary Right."

31. Ibid.

32. Gerald McKnight, *The Last Crusade. Martin Luther King Jr., the FBI, and the Poor People's Campaign* (Boulder, CO: Westview Press, 1998), 93.

33. Ibid., 124.

34. Jim Ingram, interview with the author, March 2, 2008.

35. Wesley Swift, "Zero Hour (2-4-62)," Wesley Swift Library, accessed April 16, 2015, http://swift.christogenea.org/content/zero-hour-2-4-62.

36. Wesley Swift, "2-12-67 Bible Study Q&A," Wesley Swift Library, accessed April 16, 2015, http://swift.christogenea.org/content/ 02-12-67-bible-study-qa.

37. Ibid.

38. Don Koenig, "Revelation Commentary: Chapter 14—The Grapes of Wrath Are Crushed," *Prophetic Years,* accessed April 16, 2015, http:// www.thepropheticyears.com/The%20book%20of%20Revelation Revelation%20Chapter%2014.htm.

CHAPTER 7

1. Martin Luther King Jr., "Remaining Awake through a Great Revolution" (Oberlin), Electronic Oberlin Group, accessed April 16, 2015, http://www.oberlin.edu/external/EOG/BlackHistoryMonth/MLK /CommAddress.html.

2. Martin Luther King Jr., "Remaining Awake through a Great Revolution" (National Cathedral), Martin Luther King Jr. Research and Education

Institute, accessed April 16, 2015, http://mlk-kpp01.stanford.edu/index. php/kingpapers/article/remaining_awake_through_a_great_revolution/.

3. Ibid.

4. Max Herman, "Newark (New Jersey) Riot of 1967," in *The Encyclopedia of American Race Riots,* vol. 2, eds. Walter C. Rucker and James N. Upton (Westport, CT: Greenwood Publishing Group, 2007), 452.

5. Sandra West, "Negro Reporter Tells Detroit Riot Story," *Times-News,* July 24, 1967, https://news.google.com/newspapers?nid =1665 &dat=19670724&id=T59PAAAAIBAJ&sjid=ayQEAAAAIBAJ&p g=6942,1623294&hl=en.

6. Collins and Margo, "Economic Aftermath."

7. Marquis Childs, "Guns Sales Mount as Tension Grows in This Strange Moment in History," *Morning Record,* August 15, 1967, https:// news.google.com/newspapers?nid=2512&dat=19670815&id=Wi VIAAAAIBAJ&sjid=XgANAAAAIBAJ&pg=775,5019331&hl=en.

8. Martin Luther King Jr., "The Other America," Gross Pointe Historical Society, accessed April 16, 2015, http://www.gphistorical.org/mlk /mlkspeech/mlk-gp-speech.pdf.

9. Tavis Smiley, with David Ritz. *Death of a King: The Real Story of Dr. Martin Luther King Jr.'s Final Year* (New York: Little, Brown and Company, 2014), 243.

10. Federal Bureau of Investigation, "FBI Director to All Offices; Counterintelligence Program, Black Nationalist—Hate Groups, Internal Security," March 4, 1968. http://whatreallyhappened.com/RANCHO /POLITICS/COINTELPRO/COINTELPRO-FBI.docs.html

11. King, "Remaining Awake" (National Cathedral).

12. Wexler and Hancock, *Awful Grace of God.*

13. Wesley Swift, "Power in the Word (3-31-68)," Wesley Swift Library, accessed April 16, 2015, http://swift.christogenea.org/content/power -word-3-31-68.

14. Ibid.

15. Wexler and Hancock, *Awful Grace of God,* 21–31. Our original work goes into each plot in greater depth than in the synopsis that follows. We discuss at least one additional plot—in 1964 in St. Augustine— that was never solved and thus cannot be firmly tied to Christian Identity. That plot has been excluded from this synopsis.

16. Bernie Ward, *Kansas Intelligence Report: The Dixie Mafia* (Topeka, KS: Office of Attorney General Vern Miller, 1974).

17. Michael Newton, *The Encyclopedia of Unsolved Crimes* (New York: Infobase Publishing, 2009), 199.

18. Federal Bureau of Investigation, "Airtel from SAC Oklahoma City to Director re: Donald Eugene Sparks," Mary Ferrell Foundation, accessed April 16, 2015, http://www.maryferrell.org/mffweb/archive /viewer/showDoc.do?docId=145174&relPageId=9.

19. Jerry Mitchell, "KKK Killed Ben Chester White, Hoping to Lure and Kill MLK," *Mississippi Clarion-Ledger,* June 10, 2014, http://www.clarionledger.com/story/journeytojustice/2014/06/10/ben -chester-white-kkk-mlk/10277517/.

20. Ibid.

21. Wexler and Hancock, *Awful Grace of God,* 211.

22. Federal Bureau of Investigation, "From SAC, Atlanta to Director; re: National Knights of the Ku Klux Klan," Internet Archive, accessed April 16, 2015, https://archive.org/stream/foia_National_Knights _KKK-19/National_Knights_KKK-19#page/n37/mode/2up/search /nighthawk, see 38-40.

23. Interview with the author, November 2009. The source does not wish to be named.

CHAPTER 8

1. While earlier chapters draw heavily from *The Awful Grace of God,* my previous book (coauthored with Larry Hancock), this chapter draws heavily from the e-book update, *Killing King,* released by Counterpoint Press in April 2015.

2. Donald Nissen, interview with the author, November 9, 2009. This interview is one of dozens, formal and informal, conducted with Nissen from 2009 to 2014. His story has never waivered, and he has never sought to profit from it. He kept quiet about his account, provided to the FBI in June 1967 and August 1968, until 2009, when I was able to track him down. A career criminal, Nissen experienced a religious conversion in prison and presently works for church groups that help young ex-prisoners transition from their criminal pasts to productive lives.

3. Federal Bureau of Investigation, "Airmail from Tampa to Director," July 4, 1974, MURKIN 44-38861; Janet Upshaw, interview with the author, December 15, 2010.

4. House Select Committee on Assassinations, "Evidence of a Conspiracy in St. Louis," Mary Ferrell Foundation, accessed April 16, 2015, http://www.maryferrell.org/mffweb/archive/viewer/showDoc .do?docId=800&relPageId=389.

5. "The Assassination of Martin Luther King Jr.," Mysterious Deaths and Disappearances, accessed April 16, 2015, http://cuchculan.hpage .co.in/martin-luther-king_49125488.html.

6. Jerry Mitchell, "Did the Mafia Help Solve the Mississippi Burning Case?" *Mississippi Clarion-Ledger,* June 22, 2014. Few reporters are more respected on the issue of civil rights violence and law enforcement's response than Mitchell, who confirmed the use of Mafia don Gregory Scarpa to help solve the Dahmer case. Per Mitchell, "Scarpa

and an FBI agent bought a television from Klansman Lawrence Byrd just as he was closing his business, Byrd's Radio & TV Service in Laurel. Byrd helped carry the TV to the car, and Scarpa shoved him into the back seat, where Byrd was pistol-whipped." Federal judge Chet Dillard, referenced in Mitchell's article, also firmly believes, based on FBI documents, that the FBI used Scarpa.

7.   Jack Nelson, *Terror in the Night* (Jackson: University of Mississippi Press, 1993), 139. No book does a better job of covering the rivalry between law enforcement and the KKK in Mississippi.

8.   Ibid.

9.   Nissen, interview with the author, November 9, 2009.

10. Federal Bureau of Investigation, "Re: Alleged Offer of $100,000 by the WKKKKOM to Anyone Who Kills Martin Luther King, Jr.," July 24, 1967, File 157-7990, Jackson Field Office.

11. "Atlanta Mayor: 'Get King Away from Him Right Now," *Jet*, May 2, 1968, https://books.google.com/books?id=UTgDAAAAMBAJ &pg=PA17&dq=ayers+AND+bond+AND+jet&hl=en&sa=X&e i=Hm4nVa4495qxBNbOgPAF&ved=0CC4Q6AEwAA#v=onepage &q=ayers%20AND%20bond%20AND%20jet&f=false.

12. The Reverend John Ayers, interview with the author, November 16, 2010.

13. Lamar Waldron, with Thom Hartmann, *Legacy of Secrecy: The Long Shadow of the JFK Assassination* (Berkeley, CA: Counterpoint, 2008), 339–40, 500–501.

14. Thorne, *Last Chance for Justice*. Thorne does not have page numbers in her book. The relevant passage says that Bob Eddy was told by Bill Holt that a "Brown" from Tennessee had helped train the Cahaba Boys to make an acid detonator. Other sources say that a "Brown" from the Constitutional Party participated in the Birmingham bombing. Together, these clues strongly point to Jack Brown, a known associate of Stoner and Milteer. Thorne notes that the police later cleared Jack Brown because they could verify his whereabouts in Tennessee on the day of the attack. But none of the material presented to law enforcement suggests that Brown participated in the actual September 15, 1963, attack; he may have simply been an accessory.

15. FBI, "Re: Alleged Offer of $100,000."

16. "Fourth Suspected Robbery Gang Member Held," *Gadsden Times*, July 6, 1966, 16, http://news.google.com/newspapers?id=z2ofAAAAIBAJ& sjid=MdUEAAAAIBAJ&pg=1586,811537&dq=sparks+and+payne +and+mayor+and+robbery&hl=en.

17. "James Earl Ray: Selected Chronology," Harold Weisberg Archive, Hood College, accessed March 30, 2013, http://jfk.hood.edu /Collection/White%20Materials/White%20Assassination%20 Clippings%20Folders/Miscellaneous%20Folders/Miscellaneous%20 Study%20Groups/Misc-SG-109.pdf.

18. Philip Melanson, *The Martin Luther King Assassination: New Revela-tions on the Conspiracy and Cover-Up* (New York: SPI Books, 1994), 42.

19. James Earl Ray, *Who Killed Martin Luther King, Jr.? The True Story of the Alleged Assassin* (New York: Marlowe, 1997), 125.

20. William Pepper, *Act of State: The Execution of Martin Luther King* (London: Verso, 2003), 248.

21. Harold Weisberg, letter to Mark Lynch, August 26, 1985, Harold Weis-berg Archive, Hood College, accessed April 16, 2015, http://jfk.hood.edu/Collection/Weisberg%20Subject%20Index%20Files/A%20Disk/ACLU/ACLU%2008.pdf.

22. Philip Melanson, *The Murkin Conspiracy* (New York: Praeger, 1989), 44–50.

23. John Nicol, "Was the King Assassination 'Triggered' in Canada?" CBC News, accessed December 15, 2010, www.cbc.ca/world/story/2008/04/28/fray-hearings.html. I am not revealing their identities because both men are still alive.

24. Charles Faulkner, "Murdering Civil Rights: Martin Luther King, Jr., White Supremacy, and New Facts Supporting the Guilt of James Earl Ray," Mary Ferrell Foundation, accessed April 16, 2015, www.maryferrell.org/wiki/index.php/Essay_-_Murdering_Civil_Rights.

25. Gerald Posner, *Killing the Dream: James Earl Ray and the Assassina-tion of Martin Luther King Jr.* (New York: Harcourt Brace and Co., 1998), 170–71.

26. Nissen, interview with the author, November 9, 2009.

27. Michael Newton, *The Ku Klux Klan in Mississippi: A History* (Jef-ferson, NC: McFarland, 2007), 179–180. Newton is one of the most informed and most prolific authors on the KKK in general.

28. Wexler and Hancock, *Awful Grace of God,* 213–15.

29. "Notes on FBI Hardin Documents," Harold Weisberg Archive, Hood College, accessed March 30, 2013, http://jfk.hood.edu/Collection/Weisberg%20Subject%20Index%20Files/H%20Disk/Hardin%20James%20C/Item%2030.pdf.

30. Nelson, *Terror in the Night,* 140.

31. Jerry Mitchell, "Book Probes MLK Killing," *Mississippi Clarion-Ledger,* January 3, 2008, www3.nd.edu/~newsinfo/pdf/2008_01_03_pdf/Book%20probes%20MLK%20killing.pdf.

32. Jack Nelson, "Transcript of Interview with Thomas Albert Tarrants, III, June 20, 1991," MSS 1237, Box 3, Jack Nelson Collection, Man-uscript Archive and Rare Book Library, Emory University. With the help of researcher Charles Faulkner I obtained the audio of the tape, which, with a few very minor discrepancies, confirms the substance of the transcript.

33. Select Committee on Assassinations of the U.S. House of Represen-tatives, "Findings on MLK Assassination," National Archives,

accessed April 16, 2015, www.archives.gov/research/jfk/select-committee-report/part-2a.html#.

34. Waldron, *Legacy of Secrecy,* 510–11, 545.
35. Tarrants, *Conversion,* 59–60.
36. FBI, "Teletype from Jackson To New Orleans" (April 10, 1968), Jackson Field Office MURKIN file 157-9586, CD-ROM 59161160, 147–149.
37. "James Earl Ray: Selected Chronology."
38. Jeffrey Cohen and David Lifton, "A Man He Calls Raoul," *New Times,* April 1, 1977, Harold Weisberg Archive, Hood College, accessed April 16, 2015, http://jfk.hood.edu/Collection/Weisberg%20Subject%20 Index% 20Files/C%20Disk/Cohen%20Jeff/Item%2006.pdf.
39. Faulkner, "Murdering Civil Rights." Larson, who was Bowers's business partner at Sambo, was a senior officer in the military reserve. But we do not know if he made the call or if he had a connection to Alabama. The timing of the call still cries out for an explanation.
40. House Select Committee on Assassinations, "Final Report," Mary Ferrell Foundation, accessed April 16, 2015, www.maryferrell.org/mffweb/ archive/viewer/showDoc.do?mode=searchResult&absPageId=69366.
41. Federal Bureau of Investigation, "Urgent Teletype from Dallas Field Office to Director, Memphis and Jackson," April 23, 1968, MURKIN 44-38861-1836.
42. Martin Luther King Jr., "I've Been to the Mountaintop," Martin Luther King Jr. Research and Education Institute, accessed April 16, 2015, http:// mlk-kpp01.stanford.edu/index.php/encyclopedia/documentsentry /ive_been_to_the_mountaintop/.

CHAPTER 9

1. *MLK: The Assassination Tapes,* television documentary (Washington, DC: Smithsonian Channel, 2012).
2. Michael Honey, "King's Last Crusade," History News Network, George Mason University, accessed April 16, 2015, http://history newsnetwork.org/article/37087.
3. Wexler and Hancock, *Awful Grace of God,* 307–309.
4. Betty Nyagoni, "Washington (D.C) Riot of 1968," in *The Encyclopedia of American Race Riots*, vol. 2, ed. Walter C. Rucker and James N. Upton (Westport, CT: Greenwood Publishing Group, 2007), 683–85.
5. Michael Honey, *Going Down Jericho Road: The Memphis Strike, Martin Luther King, Jr.'s Last Campaign* (New York: W.W. Norton & Company, 2007), 445–46.
6. Carol Dietrich, "King, Martin Luther Jr., Assassination of (1968)," in *The Encyclopedia of American Race Riots,* vol. 2, eds. Walter C. Rucker and James N. Upton (Westport, CT: Greenwood Publishing Group, 2007), 341.

7. Federal Bureau of Investigation, "Jesse B. Stoner," April–May 1968, 157-3082, Jackson Field Office.

8. Wesley Swift, "4-24-68 Bible Study Q&A," Wesley Swift Library, accessed April 16, 2015, http://swift.christogenea.org/content/04-24-68 -bible-study-qa.

9. Federal Bureau of Investigation, "Urgent Teletype from Dallas Field Office to Director, Memphis and Jackson," April 23, 1968, MURKIN 44-38861-1836.

10. Federal Bureau of Investigation, "Airtel from SAC, Newark to Director (Attn: FBI Identification Division), 11 Jun 1968," Harold Weisberg Archive, Hood College, accessed March 29, 2013, http://jfk.hood.edu/Collection/Weisberg%20Subject%20Index%20 Files/F%20Disk/Fetters%20Marjorie%20Possible%20PCI /Item%2002.pdf.

11. Melanson, *Martin Luther King Assassination,* 137.

12. Federal Bureau of Investigation, "Teletype from Charlotte to Director, Memphis, New Haven and Jackson," April 7, 1968, MURKIN. Interestingly, the Minuteman in question, a former White Knight (name redacted), suggested the White Knights as strong suspects in the MLK assassination.

13. House Select Committee on Assassinations, "Final Report."

14. Wexler and Hancock, *Awful Grace of God,* 283–85.

15. Waldron, *Legacy of Secrecy,* 604.

16. Federal Bureau of Investigation, "King Assassination Documents—FBI Central Headquarters File, Section 72," Mary Ferrell Foundation, accessed September 15, 2010, www.maryferrell.org/mffweb/archive /viewer/showDoc.do?mode=searchResult&absPageId=1132538.

17. House Select Committee on Assassinations, "Final Report."

18. Dan Christensen, "FBI Ignored Its Miami Informer," *Miami Magazine,* October 17, 1976, 37–38, Cuban Information Archives, http://cuban-exile.com/doc_101-1225/doc0114.html.

19. Ibid.

20. Ibid.

21. Federal Bureau of Investigation, "King Assassination Documents—FBI Central Headquarters File, Section 68," accessed April 17, 2015, Mary Ferrell Foundation, www.maryferrell.org/mffweb/archive/viewer /showDoc.do?mode=searchResult&absPageId=1131536.

22. Federal Bureau of Investigation, "BH 44-1740, Airtel: SAC Birmingham to Director," report by Special Agents Robert Barrett and William Saucier, April 8, 1968.

23. Jim Ingram, interview with the author, June 20, 2009.

24. Federal Bureau of Investigation, "BH 44-1740, Airtel: SAC Birmingham to Director," report by Special Agents Patrick J. Moynihan and Neil P. Shanahan, April 16, 1968.

25. Gerard Robinson, interview with the author, October 2, 2011.

26. Federal Bureau of Investigation, "Memorandum from SA Richard F. Kilcourse to SAC Los Angeles," April 23, 1968, 62-5101.

27. Justice Department correspondence with the author, November 9, 2009.

28. Federal Bureau of Investigation, "Admin Folder J1: HSCA Administrative Folder, HSC-A Tickler Volume I," accessed April 17, 2015, Mary Ferrell Foundation, www.maryferrell.org/mffweb/archive/viewer/showDoc.do?docId=9975&relPageId=49. This fourth page references a bureau teletype from November 1976 saying that no King-related records should be destroyed.

29. Jerry Mitchell, interview with the author, September 25, 2014.

30. Justice Department correspondence with the author November 9, 2009.

31. FBI, "Re: Alleged Offer of $100,000."

32. Chester Higgens, "Hair-Raising Experience: 'Kidnap' Try of King, Sr. Foiled; Add More Police Protection," *Jet,* May 2, 1968, http://books.google.com/books?id=UTgDAAAAMBAJ&pg=PA14&d-q=hair-raising+experience+kidnap+king&hl=en&sa=X&ei=9BpjUb_NDJC30QHYtYCQDw&ved=0CDEQ6AEwAA#v=onepage&q=hair-raising%20experience%20kidnap%20king&f=false.

33. Federal Bureau of Investigation, "Latent Fingerprint Section Work Sheet, Answer to SAC, Atlanta, Named Suspect: Floyd Eugene Ayers," April 7, 1968. The request was made at 10:17 PM.

CHAPTER 10

1. National States Rights Party, "FOIA: NSRP—Chicago 16," Internet Archive, 155, accessed April 17, 2015, https://archive.org/stream/foia_NSRP-Chicago-16/NSRP-Chicago-16#page/n153/mode/2up/search/kids.

2. National States Rights Party, "FOIA: NSRP—Chicago 16," Internet Archive, 127, accessed April 17, 2015, https://archive.org/stream/foia_NSRP-Chicago-16/NSRP-Chicago-16#page/n127/mode/2up/search/smoke.

3. National States Rights Party, "FOIA: NSRP—Chicago 16," Internet Archive, 114, accessed April 17, 2015, https://archive.org/stream/foia_NSRP-Chicago-16/NSRP-Chicago-16#page/n115/mode/2up/search/apex.

4. David Cunningham, *Klansville, USA: The Rise and Fall of the Civil Rights-era Ku Klux Klan* (London: Oxford University Press, 2013), 199.

5. Greensboro Truth and Reconciliation Commission, "Federal Investigations of White Supremacists and the WVO," Greensboro Truth and Reconciliation Commission, accessed April 16, 2015, http://www.greensborotrc.org/1979_feds.pdf.

6. Kathleen Cleaver and George Katsiaficas, *Liberation, Imagination*

and the Black Panther Party: A New Look at the Panthers and Their Legacy (New York: Routledge, 2014), 95.

7. Southern Poverty Law Center, "Hate Group Expert Daniel Levitas Discusses Posse Comitatus, Christian Identity Movement and More," *Intelligence Report* 90 (Spring 1998).

8. Carol Mason, *Killing for Life: The Apocalyptic Narrative of Pro-life Politics* (New York: Cornell University Press, 2002), 31.

9. Atkins, *Encyclopedia of Right-Wing Extremism*, 152.

10. Danny O. Coulson, *No Heroes: Inside the FBI's Secret Counter-terror Force* (New York: Simon & Schuster, 201), 204.

11. Kerry Noble, *Tabernacle of Hate: Seduction into Right-Wing Extremism* (New York: Syracuse Press, 2010), 24, Freedom of the Mind Resource Center; "About Kerry Noble," Freedom of the Mind Resource Center, accessed April 16, 2015, https://freedomofmind.com /Info/articles/KerryNoble.php.

12. Freedom of Mind, "About Kerry Noble," Freedom of Mind Resource Center, accessed April 16, 2015, https://freedomofmind.com/Info/articles/KerryNoble.php.

13. John Maginnis, *Cross to Bear* (Gretna, LA: Pelican Publishing Company, 2011), 60.

14. Southern Poverty Law Center, "Tom Metzger," SPLC, accessed April 16, 2015, http://www.splcenter.org/get-informed/intelligence-files /profiles/tom-metzger.

15. Michael Zatarain, *David Duke: Evolution of a Klansman* (Gretna, LA: Pelican Publishing Company, 1990), 243.

16. SPLC, "Tom Metzger."

17. Timothy Miller, *Spiritual and Visionary Communities: Out to Save the World* (Farnham, UK: Ashgate Publishing, 2013), not paginated.

18. Barkun, *Religion and the Racist Right*, 225–29.

19. Southern Poverty Law Center, "William Pierce," SPLC, accessed April 16, 2015, http://www.splcenter.org/get-informed/intelligence-files /profiles/william-pierce.

20. Ben Klassen, *The White Man's Bible*, Ben Klassen, 1981, https://archive.org/stream/WhiteMansBible/WhiteMansBibleOrig#page/n1/ mode/2up.

21. Mattias Gardell, "Black and White Unite in Fight?" in *The Cultic Milieu: Oppositional Subcultures in an Age of Globalization*, eds. Jeffrey Kaplan and Heléne Lööw (New York: Altamira Press), 167.

22. Southern Poverty Law Center, "Creativity Movement," SPLC, accessed April 16, 2015, http://www.splcenter.org/get-informed/intelligence-files /groups/creativity-movement.

23. Anti-Defamation League of B'nai B'rth, *Extremism on the Right: A Handbook* (Bloomington: Indiana University, 1983), 113–14.

24. Charles Fruehling, *Springwood, Open Fire: Understanding Global Gun Cultures* (Oxford: Berg Publishers, 2007), 171.

25.   Monte Plott, "Ideological Differences Divide America's Klansmen," *Star-News,* November 8, 1979, https://news.google.com/newspapers? nid=1454&dat=19791108&id=qdZQAAAAIBAJ&sjid= ORMEAAAAIBAJ&pg=6253,1551484&hl=en.

26.   Chalmers, *Backfire,* 125.

27.   Associated Press, "Klan Leader Admits Providing Information," *Star-News,* August 31, 1981, https://news.google.com/newspapers?nid =1454 &dat=19810831&id=yx1OAAAAIBAJ&sjid=UBMEAAAA IBAJ&pg=6997,6453630&hl=en.

28.   Narda Zacchino, "Man Tells Story of Right-Wing 'Terror,'" *Los Angeles Times,* January 26, 1976, https://news.google.com/newspapers ?nid=861&dat=19760126&id=UxRZAAAAIBAJ&sjid=YEYNAAA AIBAJ&pg=2382,4186112&hl=en.

29.   John M. Crewdson, "Kelley Discounts FBI's Link to a Terrorist Group," *New York Times,* January 12, 1976.

30.   Everett R. Holles, "ACLU Says FBI Funded 'Army' to Terrorize Anti-War Protestors," *New York Times,* June 27, 1975, http://jfk.hood.edu /Collection/White%20Materials/White%20Assassination%20 Clippings%20Folders/Security%20Folders/Security-FBI/Item%20 0848.pdf.

31.   National Consortium for the Study of Terrorism and Responses to Terrorism, "Secret Army Organization," University of Maryland, accessed April 16, 2015, http://www.start.umd.edu/tops/terrorist _organization_profile.asp?id=4258.

32.   Civil Rights Greensboro, "The Greensboro Massacre," University of North Carolina, accessed April 16, 2015, http://libcdm1.uncg.edu /cdm/essay1979/collection/CivilRights.

33.   Ibid. His name was Eddie Dawson.

34.   Ed Payne, "Suspect in Jewish Center Shootings 'Entrenched in the Hate Movement,'" CNN Online, April 14, 2014, http://www.cnn.com /2014/04/14/us/kansas-shooting-suspect-profile.

35.   Abby Ohlheiser, "Kansas City Shooter Was Well-Known to Hate Group Watchers," *Atlantic,* April 14, 2014, http://news.yahoo.com/kansas -city-shooter-well-known-hate-group-watchers-135126451.html.

36.   Ibid.

37.   National States Rights Party, "Book and Literature List," *Thunderbolt,* March 1964, https://archive.org/stream/foia_NSRP-Chicago-3A /NSRP-Chicago-3A#page/n23/mode/2up/search/goff.

38.   National States Rights Party, "The Basic Identity Message," *Thunderbolt,* July 1974, https://archive.org/stream/foia_NSRP-Chicago-6A /NSRP-Chicago-6A#page/n23/mode/2up/.

39.   National States Rights Party, "A Kingdom of Priests," *Thunderbolt,* March–April 1974, https://archive.org/stream/foia_NSRP-Chicago -6A/NSRP-Chicago-6A#page/n23/mode/2up/.

CHAPTER II

1. Associated Press, "Explosion Rips Daycare Center," *Star-News,* October 13, 1980, https://news.google.com/newspapers? nid=1454&dat=19801013&id=ocksAAAAIBAJ&sjid=QxMEAAAAIBAJ&pg=5443,2918309&hl=en.

2. Ibid.

3. Associated Press, "Blast Called Accidental," *Star-News,* October 13, 1980, https://news.google.com/newspapers?nid=1979&dat=198010 13&id=ZQiAAAAIBAJ&sjid=u6kFAAAAIBAJ&pg=1030,7358 255&hl=en.

4. Associated Press, "Human Error Is Blamed for Fatal Atlanta Blast," *Sarasota-Herald Tribune,* October 30, 1980, https://news.google.com /newspapers?nid=1755&dat=19801030&id=mZwcAAAAIBAJ&sjid =2mc EAA AAIBAJ&pg=6600,7184342&hl=en.

5. Ibid.

6. James Baldwin, *Evidence of Things Not Seen* (New York: MacMillan Publishing, 1985), xiii.

7. "Atlanta's Missing and Murdered," Atkid, accessed April 16, 2015, http://atkid.weebly.com. This site does an excellent job of compiling information on the murder victims from various sources.

8. Jeff Prugh, "Wayne Williams and 'The List,'" *Atlanta Magazine,* February 1985, http://jfk.hood.edu/Collection/Weisberg%20Subject%20 Index%20Files/P%20Disk/Prugh%20Jeff/Item%2010.pdf.

9. Chet Dettlinger and Jeff Prugh, *The List* (Atlanta: Philmay Enterprises, 1983).

10. Prugh, "Wayne Williams."

11. Dettlinger and Prugh, *The List,* 389–92.

12. Ibid., 264.

13. Nigel Cawthorne, *The Mammoth Book of Killers at Large* (London: Little, Brown Group, 2011), 198.

14. John Douglas and Mark Olshaker, *Mindhunter: Inside the FBI's Serial Killer Crime Unit* (New York: Pocket, 1995), 223.

15. Barry Michael Cooper and Robert Keating, "A Question of Justice," *Spin,* September 1986; Robert Keating, "Atlanta: Who Killed Your Children?" *Spin,* October 1986.

16. Cooper and Keating, "Question of Justice," 59.

17. Ibid.

18. Ibid.

19. Associated Press, "Informant Says Klan Involved in Killings," *Observer-Reporter,* October 9, 1991, https://news.google.com/newspapers?nid =2519&dat=19911009&id=IBeAAAAIBAJ&sjid=7mENAAAAIBA-J&pg=3479,2469801&hl=en.

20. Cooper and Keating, "Question of Justice," 59.

21. Ibid., 60.

22. Federal Bureau of Investigation, "Atlanta Child Murders Part 2 of 24," FBI, 30, accessed April 17, 2015, http://vault.fbi.gov/Atlanta%20 Child%20Murders/Atlanta%20Child%20Murders%20Part%20 2%20of%2024.

23. Ibid., 96.

24. Special Agent J.B. Jackson, "Serial: 30-0092-25-81," Georgia Bureau of Investigation, accessed April 16, 2015, http://www.mltranslations .org/us/Rpo/kkk/kkkdoc1.htm.

25. Ibid.

26. Cooper and Keating, "Question of Justice," 57.

27. Keating, "Atlanta: Who Killed Your Children?" 73.

28. Associated Press, "Rights Leader Questions Town OK for Klan Rally," *Ocala Star-Banner,* January 13, 1983, https://news.google.com /newspapers?nid=1356&dat=19830113&id=bGRIAAAAIBAJ&s-jid=1AUE AAAAIBAJ&pg=6931,6382573&hl=en. Note that although the article was written in 1983, the Reverend Joseph Lowery of the SCLC is recalling Stoner's antagonistic behavior in 1980—during the height of the tension.

29. Revolutionary Political Organization, "The Klan Killed the Children in Atlanta: The Cover-up," Marxist-Leninist Translations and Reprints, accessed April 16, 2015, http://www.mltranslations.org/us /Rpo/kkk/kkk2.htm.

30. Baldwin, *Things Not Seen,* 27.

31. Georgia Bureau of Investigation, "Document No. 3," Marxist-Leninist Translations and Reprints, accessed April 16, 2015, http://www. mltranslations.org/us/Rpo/kkk/kkkdoc3.htm. The website has a definite ideological slant, but it posts original documents and images obtained through legal requests.

CHAPTER 12

1. Rory Marshall, "Woman's Visit to Station Aroused Suspicion," *Spokesman-Review,* October 29, 1985, https://news.google.com /newspapers?nid=1314&dat=19851029&id=X1lWAAAAIBA J&sjid =MO8DAAAAIBAJ&pg =7015,8075864&hl=en.

2. Jeffrey Kaplan, *Encyclopedia of White Power: A Sourcebook on the Radical Racist Right* (Lanham, MD: Rowman & Littlefield, 2000), 239.

3. "Jury Told of Plan to Kill Radio Host," *New York Times,* November 8, 1987, http://www.nytimes.com/1987/11/08/us/jury-told-of-plan-to-kill-radio-host.html.

4. Ibid.

5. Kevin Flynn and Gary Gerhardt, *The Silent Brotherhood: The Chilling Inside Story of America's Violent, Anti-Government Militia Movement* (New York: Penguin, 1995), 244–50.

6. "The Murder of Alan Berg in Denver: 25 Years Later," *Denver Post,* June 18, 2009, http://www.denverpost.com/recommended/ci _12615628.

7. Louis R. Beam, "Leaderless Resistance," *Inter-Klan Newsletter and Survival Alert,* 1983, 12. This is the original 1983 version.

8. Andrew MacDonald, *The Turner Diaries* (Hillsboro, WV: National Vanguard Books, 1978). There is a consensus among serious scholars that Pierce uses "Andrew MacDonald" as an alias. He used the same alias with the novel *Hunter* in 1989. The two books reinforce the same basic message (white power and supremacy). From this point forward, I list Pierce as the author of *The Turner Diaries.* The full text of *The Turner Diaries* can be found online at https://archive.org/stream/TheTurnerDiariesByAndrewMacdonald /turner-diaries-william-luther-pierce#page/n1/mode/2up.

9. Flynn and Gerhardt, *Silent Brotherhood,* 112–14, 423.

10. Ibid., 423.

11. Ibid., 383–84, 423.

12. Christian Identity, "More on Dead Nebraska Farmer," *Covenant Messenger,* January 1985, http://christianidentityministries.com/messenger /1985-Jan.pdf.

13. Goodrick-Clarke, *Black Sun, 246.*

14. William Luther Pierce, *The Turner Diaries,* Internet Archive, accessed April 16, 2015, https://archive.org/stream/TheTurnerDiaries ByAndrewMacdonald/turner-diaries-william-luther-pierce#page/n57/ mode/2up/search/speedboat.

15. Ibid.

16. Thomas Martinez and John Guinther, *Brotherhood of Murder: How One Man's Journey through Fear Brought the Order—the Most Dangerous Racist Gang in America—to Justice* (New York: McGraw-Hill, 1988).

17. Tim Klass, "Death of the Order: A Look Back at Whidbey Island Siege—Raid 10 Years Ago Led to the Splintering of White Supremacists," *Seattle Times,* September 11, 1994, http://community.seattle times.nwsource.com/archive/?date=19941211&slug=1946516.

18. Ibid.

19. Ibid.

20. Noble, *Tabernacle of Hate,* 124.

21. Ibid., 125.

22. Mark S. Hamm, *Terrorism as Crime: From Oklahoma City to Al-Qaeda and Beyond* (New York: NYU Press), 103.

23. Ibid.

24. Noble, *Tabernacle of Hate,* 156.

25. United States v. Ellison, 793 F.2d 942 (8th Cir. 1986).

26. Ibid.

27. Ibid.

28. Hamm, *Terrorism as Crime,* 105.
29. Noble, *Tabernacle of Hate,* 310.
30. Atkins, *Encyclopedia of Right-Wing Extremism,* 215–16.
31. Ibid., 215.
32. Associated Press, "Thirteen Supremacists Are Not Guilty of Conspiracies," *New York Times,* April 8, 1988, http://www.nytimes.com/1988/04/08/us/13-supremacists-are-not-guilty-of-conspiracies.html.
33. Louis Beam, "Leaderless Resistance," *Seditionist* 12 (February 1992), http://www.louisbeam.com/leaderless.htm.
34. Jonathan Franklin, "God City," *Vibe,* November 1997, 101–104.

CHAPTER 13

1. "Judicial Family Responds to Crisis in Oklahoma City," *Third Branch,* May 1995, http://www.uscourts.gov/News/TheThirdBranch/95-05-01/Judicial_Family_Responds_to_Crisis_in_Oklahoma_City.aspx.
2. Douglas O. Linder, "Timothy McVeigh Trial: Documents Relating to McVeigh's Arrest and the Search of His Vehicle," Famous Trials, accessed April 16, 2015, http://law2.umkc.edu/faculty/projects/ftrials/mcveigh/mcveigharrest.html.
3. Patrick E. Cole, "McVeigh: Diaries Dearist," *Time,* March 31, 1997, 1.
4. Ibid.
5. Linder, "Timothy McVeigh Trial."
6. Pierce, *Turner Diaries,* 24–25.
7. Public Broadcasting Service, "McVeigh Chronology," PBS Frontline, accessed April 16, 2015, http://www.pbs.org/wgbh/pages/frontline/documents/mcveigh/. The website posts the chronology and notes developed by Timothy McVeigh's defense team.
8. Ibid. See "06.86-05.88."
9. Ibid.
10. Court TV, "Terror on Trial: Who Was Timothy McVeigh?" CNN, December 31, 2007, http://edition.cnn.com/2007/US/law/12/17/court.archive.mcveigh2/.
11. Richard Cockle, "Twenty Years after Ruby Ridge Siege, Extremists Are Fewer in Northern Idaho but Still Remain," Oregonlive.com, August 27, 2012, http://www.oregonlive.com/pacific-northwest-news/index.ssf/2012/08/20_years_after_ruby_ridge_sieg.html.
12. 367 Paul A. Djupe and Laura R. Olson, *Encyclopedia of American Religion and Politics* (New York: Infobase Publishing, 2014), 351–52.
13. Ibid.
14. Dan Herbeck and Lou Michel, *American Terrorist: Timothy McVeigh and the Tragedy at Oklahoma City* (New York: HarperCollins, 2002).
15. Timothy McVeigh, "McVeigh's Apr. 26 Letter to Fox News," FoxNews

.com, April 26, 2001, http://www.foxnews.com/story/2001/04/26/mcveigh-apr-26-letter-to-fox-news/.

16. Mark Juergensmeyer, *Terror in the Mind of God: The Global Rise of Religious Violence* (Oakland: University of California Press, 2003), 136.

17. Herbeck and Michel, *American Terrorist,* 154.

18. Eugene Gallagher, "Catastrophic Millennialism," in *The Oxford Handbook of Millennialism,* ed. Catherine Wessinger (London: Oxford University Press, 2011), 27. Gallagher proposes that Timothy McVeigh believed in "catastrophic millennialism." Paraphrasing Wessinger, he explains that this "pessimistic view of society, history, and human beings anticipates the imminent, violent destruction of the world as we know it; but it also envisages that God will then act, with or without human assistance, to accomplish a total renovation of the world." It is hard to imagine a more apt description of Christian Identity eschatology.

19. Pierce, *Turner Diaries,* 42.

20. J.M. Berger, "PATCON: The FBI's Secret War against the 'Patriot' Movement, and How Infiltration Tactics Relate to Radicalizing Influences," New America Foundation, May 2012, http://newamerica.net/sites/newamerica.net/files/policydocs/Berger_NSSP_PATCON.pdf.

21. Douglas O. Linder, "Testimony of Michael Fortier in the Timothy McVeigh Trial," Famous Trials, accessed April 16, 2015, http://law2.umkc.edu/faculty/projects/ftrials/mcveigh/mfortiertestimony.html.

22. Peter Lance, "1,000 Years for Revenge: Chapter 30 John Doe No. 2," Peterlance.com, accessed April 16, 2015, http://peterlance.com/wordpress/?p=218.

23. Mark S. Hamm, *In Bad Company: America's Terrorist Underground* (Lebanon, NH: University Press of New England, 2002). Hamm's book does an excellent job of synthesizing his work with that of J.D. Cash. To a large extent, when I reference Cash, the direct source is Hamm.

24. Friedrich Seiltgen, "Aryan Republican Army Hits 22 U.S. Banks," *Counter Terrorist,* December 2011–January 2012, http://onlinedigital publishing.com/article/ARYAN_REPUBLICAN_ARMY_HITS_22 _U.S._BANKS/883803/87543/article.html.

25. Hamm, *In Bad Company,* 142.

26. Ibid., 145.

27. J.D. Cash, "McVeigh's Sister Laundered Bank Robbery Proceeds," *McCurtain Daily Gazette,* January 28, 1997, http://www.constitution .org/okc/jdt03-05.htm.

28. Hamm, *In Bad Company,* 295–98.

29. Andrew Gumbel and Roger Charles, *Oklahoma City: What the Investigation Missed—and Why It Still Matters* (New York: HarperCollins, 2012), 10–43.

30. Ibid.

31. Hamm, *In Bad Company,* 214–15.

32. Ibid., 213.

33. Associated Press, "FBI Linked McVeigh to Group after Bombing," *USA Today,* February 12, 2003, http://usatoday30.usatoday.com/news /nation/2003-02-12-fbi-linked-mcveigh_x.htm.

34. Mark S. Hamm, *Terrorism as a Crime: From Oklahoma City to Al-Qaeda and Beyond* (New York: New York University Press, 2007), 179.

35. AP, "FBI Linked McVeigh."

36. Berger, "PATCON," 1–31.

37. Ibid.

38. Ibid., 4.

39. J.M. Berger, "PATCON Revealed: An Exclusive Look inside the FBI's Secret War with the Militia Movement," Interlwire.com, October 8, 2007,http://news.intelwire.com/2007/10/patcon-revealed-exclusive -look-inside.html.

40. Oversight and Investigations Subcommittee of the House International Relations Committee, "The Oklahoma City Bombing: Was There a Foreign Connection?" House of Representatives, accessed April 16, 2015, https://rohrabacher.house.gov/sites/rohrabacher.house.gov/files /documents/report%20from%20the%20chairman.pdf.

41. Charles Key, "Letter to Concerned Citizen on the Facts of the Oklahoma Bombing," American Patriot Friends Network, March 12, 1997, http://www.apfn.org/apfn/OKC_key.htm.

42. Gumbel and Charles, *Oklahoma City,* 23.

43. Stephen Jones, "Petition for Writ of Mandamus of Petitioner-Defendant, Timothy James McVeigh and Brief in Support," FAS Intelligence Resource Program, March 25, 1997, http://fas.org/irp/threat/mcveigh /part06.htm.

44. Ambrose Evans-Pritchard and Andrew Gimson,"Did Agents Bungle US Terror Bomb?" *London Sunday Telegraph,* May 20, 1996, http:// whatreallyhappened.com/RANCHO/POLITICS/OK/ok2.html.

45. Ibid.

46. Ibid.

47. Ibid.

48. Geoffrey Fattah, "Nichols Says Bombing Was FBI Op," *Deseret News,* February 22, 2007, http://www.deseretnews.com/article/660197443 /Nichols-says-bombing-was-FBI-op.html?pg=all.

CHAPTER 14

1. Associated Press, "Two Brothers Are Indicted in Three Synagogue Fires," *Victoria Advocate,* March 18, 2000, https://news.google.com

/newspapers?nid=861&dat=20000318&id=y71HAAAAIBAJ&
sjid=W4AMAAAAIBAJ&pg=3491,3908199&hl=en.

2. Associated Press, "Brothers May Be Looking at Death Penalty," *Lodi News-Sentinel,* November 24, 1999, https://news.google.com/newspapers?
nid=2245&dat=19991124&id=Wuk0AAAAIBAJ&sjid=MSE-GAAAAIBAJ&pg=6809,3036356&hl=en.

3. Jeff Elliott, "Benjamin 'August' Smith: Poised to Kill," *Albion Monitor,* July 26, 1999, http://www.albionmonitor.com/9907a/wcotc.html.

4. Associated Press, "Nightmare Scene Now All Too Familiar," *Hour,* August 11, 1999, https://news.google.com/newspapers?nid=1916&
dat=19990811&id=tB9JAAAAIBAJ&sjid=SgYNAAAAIBAJ&p-g=1416,1332495&hl=en.

5. Associated Press, "Neo-Nazi Surrenders, Confesses to Jewish Center Shootings," *Gettysburg Times,* August 12, 1999, https://news.google
.com/newspapers?nid=2202&dat=19990812&id=XBEmAAAAIBAJ
&sjid=vf0FAAAAIBAJ&pg=3316,967052&hl=en.

6. Associated Press, "Skinheads Sentenced for Attempted Fire," *Los Angeles Times,* December 2, 2000, http://articles.latimes.com/2000
/dec/02/news/mn-60126.

7. Sandra Morgen, *Into Our Own Hands: The Women's Health Movement in the United States, 1969–1990* (New Brunswick, NJ: Rutgers University Press, 2002), 190.

8. Michael Bray, *A Time to Kill: A Study Concerning the Use of Force and Abortion* (Portland, OR: Advocates for Life Publications, 1994), 18.

9. Richard G. Butler, "A Call to Arms," Aryan Nations, accessed April 17, 2015, http://www.aryan-nation.org/RGB/CalltoArms.html.

10. Jim Camden, "Book Familiar to Extremists," *Spokesman-Review,* August 12, 1999, https://news.google.com/newspapers?nid=1314&
dat=19990812&id=Mo9XAAAAIBAJ&sjid=HPIDAAAAI
BAJ&pg=6731,667190&hl=en.

11. Shane Hensinger, "Beware the Lone Wolf—the Phineas Priesthood," *Daily Kos,* October 13, 2009, http://www.dailykos.com/story/2009
/10/13/792922/-Beware-The-Lone-Wolf-The-Phineas-Priesthood#.

12. Jim Nesbitt, "White Supremacist Groups Inspiring Individual Acts," *Religion News Service,* October 20, 1999, http://assets.baptiststan
dard.com/archived/1999/10_20/pages/supremacist.html.

13. Ibid.

14. Daryl Johnson, *Right Wing Resurgence: How a Domestic Terrorist Threat Is Being Ignored* (Lanham, MD: Rowman & Littlefield, 2012), 83.

15. Abby Ohlheiser and Elahe Izadi, "Police: Austin Shooter Was a 'Home-grown American Extremist,'" *Washington Post,* December 1, 2014, http://www.washingtonpost.com/news/post-nation/wp/2014/12/01
/police-austin-shooter-belonged-to-an-ultra-conservative-christian
-hate-group/.

16. Nesbitt, "White Supremacist Groups."
17. Adam Miller, "Neo-Nazi Guru Stands by His Disciple," *New York Post,* August 14, 1999, http://nypost.com/1999/08/14/neo-nazi-guru -stands-by-his-disciple-refuses-to-condemn-good-soldier-furrow/.
18. Southern Poverty Law Center, "Victoria Keenan Discusses Run-in with Aryan Nations," *Intelligence Report* 100, Fall 2000, http://www .splcenter.org/get-informed/intelligence-report/browse-all-issues/2000 /fall/he-looked-like-the-devil.
19. Matt Hale, "Our Fallen Brother: Ben 'August' Smith," Internet Archive, accessed April 17, 2015, https://archive.org/details/OurFallen BrotherBenaugustSmithByMattHale.
20. Southern Poverty Law Center, "Creativity Movement," SPLC, http://www.splcenter.org/get-informed/intelligence-files/groups /creativity-movement.
21. Anti-Defamation League, "Hate on the Internet—New ADL Report Reveals Neo-Nazis and Others Exploiting Technology," ADL, November 17, 1995, http://archive.adl.org/presrele/asus_12/2609_12.html.
22. Beverly Ray and George E. Marsh II, "Recruitment by Extremist Groups on the Internet," *First Monday* 6, no. 2 (February 2001), http://ojphi.org/ojs/index.php/fm/article/view/834/743.
23. Barbara Perry, *Hate Crimes* (Westport, CT: Greenwood Publishing Group, 2009), 234–35.
24. Ibid.
25. Federal Bureau of Investigation, Project Megiddo (1999), Center for Studies on New Religions, accessed April 17, 2015, http://www .cesnur.org/testi/FBI_004.htm.
26. Ibid.
27. Ibid.
28. National Church Arson Task Force, "Fourth Year Report for the President," NCATF, September 2000, https://www.hsdl.org/?view &did=1402. The analysis in this chapter is based on statistics and charts provided in this report.
29. Raphael S. Ezekiel, "An Ethnographer Looks at Neo-Nazi and Klan Groups," *American Behavioral Scientist* (2002), 51–71, http://www .sagepub.com/martinessstudy/articles/Ezekiel.pdf.
30. Mike German, "Behind the Lone Wolf, A Pack Mentality," *Washington Post,* June 5, 2005, http://www.washingtonpost.com/wp-dyn /content/article/2005/06/04/AR2005060400147.html.
31. Ibid.
32. Ibid.
33. Independent Television Service, "Civil Trial: Jury Hits Klan with $37 Million Verdict," ITVS, accessed April 17, 2015, http://archive.itvs .org/forgottenfires/story_b.html.
34. "Clarendon Klan Trial Deals Another Blow to Area Image," Item, July

26, 1998, https://news.google.com/newspapers?nid=1980&dat=1998
0726&id=fJkoAAAAIBAJ&sjid=LwYGAAAAIBAJ&pg=2162
, 4817433&hl=en.

35. Seeking Solutions with Hedrick Smith, "Hate Crime," PBS online, ac-
     cessed April 17, 2015, http://www.hedricksmith.com/site_solutions
     /hate/chcTranscripts.htm.

36. Anti-Defamation League, "Neo-Nazi Hate Music: A Guide: Themes,"
     ADL, November 4, 2004, http://archive.adl.org/main_extremism/hate
     _music_in_the_21st_century250d.html#.VShZcZOgVfY.

37. German, "Behind the Lone Wolf."

38. Associated Press, "Skinheads Sentenced."

39. Southern Poverty Law Center, "Skinheads in America," SPLC, accessed
     April 17, 2015, http://www.splcenter.org/get-informed/publications
     /skinheads-in-america-essay.

40. Jack B. Moore, *Skinheads Shaved for Battle: A Cultural History of
     American Skinheads* (Madison, WI: Popular Press, 1993), 5.

41. Ezekiel, "Ethnographer."

42. Mark S. Hamm, *American Skinheads: The Criminology and Control
     of Hate Crime* (Westport, CT: ABC-CLIO, 1994), 6.

43. Moore, *Skinheads,* 5.

44. Scott Shepherd, interview with the author, March 1, 2015.

45. Ibid.

46. Michael Waltman and John Haas, *The Communication of Hate* (New
     York: Peter Lang Press, 2011), 21.

47. Ibid., 22.

CHAPTER 15

1. Peter Bergen and David Sterman, "U.S. Right Wing Extremists More
    Deadly Than Jihadists," CNN.com, April 15, 2014, http://www.cnn
    .com/2014/04/14/opinion/bergen-sterman-kansas-shooting/.

2. Susan J. Palmer, "Religion or Sedition? The Domestic Terrorism Trial
    of the Hutaree, a Michigan-based Christian Militia," in *Legal Cases,
    New Religious Movements, and Minority Faiths,* eds. James T. Rich-
    ardson and François Bellanger (Burlington, VT: Ashgate Publishing,
    2014), 89–118.

3. Associated Press, "Michigan Militia Sue Authorities over Home
    Raids," *Huffington Post,* April 9, 2013, http://www.huffingtonpost
    .com/news/hutaree-militia/.

4. Palmer, "Religion or Sedition?" 109.

5. Phil Hirschkorn, "The Newburgh Sting," *Huffington Post,* April 29,
    2014, http://www.huffingtonpost.com/phil-hirschkorn/the-newburgh-
    sting_b_5234822.html.

6. Ibid.

7. Graeme Wood, "What ISIS Really Wants?" *Atlantic*, March 2015, http://www.theatlantic.com/features/archive/2015/02/what-isis-really -wants/384980/.

8. Ibid.

9. Bruce Hoffman, "'*Holy Terror*': The Implications of Terrorism Motivated by a Religious Imperative," Rand Corporation, 1993, http:// www.rand.org/content/dam/rand/pubs/papers/2007/P7834.pdf.

10. Tony Gaskew, "Peacemaking Criminology and Counterterrorism: Muslim Americans and the War on Terror," *Contemporary Justice Review* 12, no. 3 (September 2009): 345–66.

11. Arie Perliger, "Challengers from the Sidelines: Understanding America's Violent Far-Right," Combatting Terrorism Center at West Point, January 15, 2013, https://www.ctc.usma.edu/posts/challengers-from-the-side lines-understanding-americas-violent-far-right.

12. Michael Carl, "West Point: 'Far Right' Dangerous to U.S." *World News Daily*, January 18, 2013, http://www.wnd.com/2013/01/west -point-far-right-dangerous-to-u-s/.

13. Perliger, "Challenges from the Sidelines," 72.

14. Ibid.

15. Scott Shepherd, interview with the author, March 1, 2015.

INDEX

Page locators for cities are not repeated under states, nor are organizations listed by city.